CW01594058

Sciencecheck

ASSESSMENT PAPERS FOR NATIONAL CURRICULUM SCIENCE

Working towards Level Description 3

Graham Peacock, Jill Jesson and Heather Ridgeway

Collins Educational
An imprint of HarperCollins*Publishers*

Published by Collins Educational
An imprint of HarperCollins*Publishers* Ltd
77-85 Fulham Palace Road
London
W6 8JB

www.**Collins**Education.com
On-line support for schools and colleges

© HarperCollins*Publishers* Ltd

First published 1998

Reprinted 1998, 2001

ISBN 0 00 317 235 X

Graham Peacock, Jill Jesson and Heather Ridgeway assert the moral right to be identified as the authors of this work.

Any educational institution that has purchased one copy of this publication may make duplicate copies for use exclusively within that institution. Permission does not extend to reproduction, storage in a retrieval system, or transmittal, in any form or means, electronic, mechanical, photocopying, recording or otherwise, of duplicate copies for loaning, renting or selling to any other institution without either the prior consent in writing of the Publisher or a licence permitting restricted copying in the United Kingdom issued by the Copyright Licensing Agency Ltd, 90 Tottenham Court Road, London W1P 0LP.

British Library Cataloguing in Publication Data
A catalogue record for this book is available from the British Library.

Cover and series design by XAB
Text page design by Neil Adams
Illustrations by John Booth, Bethan Matthews and Rhiannon Powell
Printed by Martins the Printers, Berwick

Sciencecheck

Contents

Introduction

These tests do not try to imitate SATs in their layout since teachers have ready access to old papers. Instead, the tests are densely packed to provide teachers with a wide range of accurately levelled assessment material. The material is very flexible and can be used to:

- check the level of children's understanding before beginning a new area of science;
- provide extension pen and pencil activities for more able children;
- provide reinforcement pen and pencil activities for children who need it;
- assess the understanding of children midway or at the end of teaching on a topic;
- set homework at an appropriate level;
- check that the work being undertaken in the class is at an appropriate and demanding level for the children;
- provide information for teacher assessment.

All the tests use pencil and paper only and no science equipment is needed. However, many teachers will see opportunities to use the activities suggested here in a variety of ways. The material can be:

- photocopied and handed out to individuals to do at school or as homework;
- selectively used on the board as assessment;
- read aloud to small groups/the whole class as appropriate;
- the starting point for practical science.

The pages at the back of the book provide short authoritative answers which are aimed at teachers.

What is Level 3 in science?

To match Level Description 3 for science, pupils should be able to:

AT1 Experimental and Investigative Science

- put forward their own ideas
- make simple predictions
- make measurements and observations using simple equipment
- explain why a test is fair
- provide explanations for patterns

AT2 Life Processes and Living Things

- describe some differences between living and non-living things
- explain how changes in diet, food or water affect living things
- identify some ways in which animals are suited to their environment

AT3 Materials and their Properties

- describe ways to sort materials
- explain why some materials are suitable for a purpose
- recognise that some changes can be reversed and that others cannot

AT4 Physical Processes

- link cause and effect
- make simple generalisations about physical phenomena

Key words and their meaning at Level 3

fair test
At Level 3 children should be able to carry out a test with help and be able to explain why the test is fair.

prediction
At this level only simple predictions are expected and these may or may not be based in scientific knowledge. A child at this level may predict, for instance, that grass covered for a week with carpet will go brown. The prediction is incorrect (it will go yellow) and even though the child has not explained why, it may still be possible that the child matches the level description for Level 3.

patterns
The ability to detect a pattern in results is an important feature of this level. At Level 3 a child should be able interpret a simple table of results and be able to spot, for instance, that tights stretch further when more weight is placed in the foot.

explanations
At Level 3 children should be able to offer simple explanations about events such as a plant dying because it lacked water.

classify
The ability to classify changes and materials is a feature of this level.

generalise
This is the skill of being able to move from the particular to the general. So, if a child notices that in the playground sounds are fainter the further away you are, then they will be able to apply this insight into a range of other observations about the volume of sound.

cause and effect
The linking of an event with the thing which caused it is important. A child looking at a dim light bulb, who suggests that the battery is flat, is linking cause and effect.

Sciencecheck	**NAME**	**DATE**
Sc1, Level 3 **Test 1, Series A**	**EXPERIMENTAL AND INVESTIGATIVE SCIENCE** **Planning investigations** Pupils should be taught to plan experimental work.	

1 **Ellie is right handed.**

She wants to find out if she can write more quickly with her right hand or her left hand.

a. What test could she do?

____

____

b. How she could make her test fair?

____

____

2 **Toni wants to find out if plants will grow well in a dark place.**

a. Where could she put two different pots of cress to test this idea?

____

b. Which pot of cress do you think will grow best?

____

3 **Class 3 want to see if white sugar or brown sugar dissolves the fastest.**

a. What could do they do to find out?

____

____

____

b. Write down two things they should keep the same in each test.

1) ______________________________

____

2) ______________________________

____

4 **Jim is testing which type of sweet people most like to taste.**

He thinks that they should wear a blindfold.

Why is this a good idea?

____

____

Sciencecheck	NAME	DATE
Sc1, Level 3 Test 2, Series A	**EXPERIMENTAL AND INVESTIGATIVE SCIENCE** **Obtaining evidence** Pupils should be taught to obtain evidence from measurements and observations.	

1 **Match the apparatus on the left to the activity on the right.**

stopclock	measuring temperature
spring balance	measuring length
thermometer	measuring weight
ruler	measuring time

2 **Ravi is measuring the temperature of cups of water.**

He writes down three readings.

5°C   20°C   60°C

Fill in the table by putting the temperatures in the correct place.

Cup	Temperature
warm water	
hot water	
cold water	

3 **Class 3 put the same amount of water in three containers.**

They wanted to see from which container the water evaporated first.

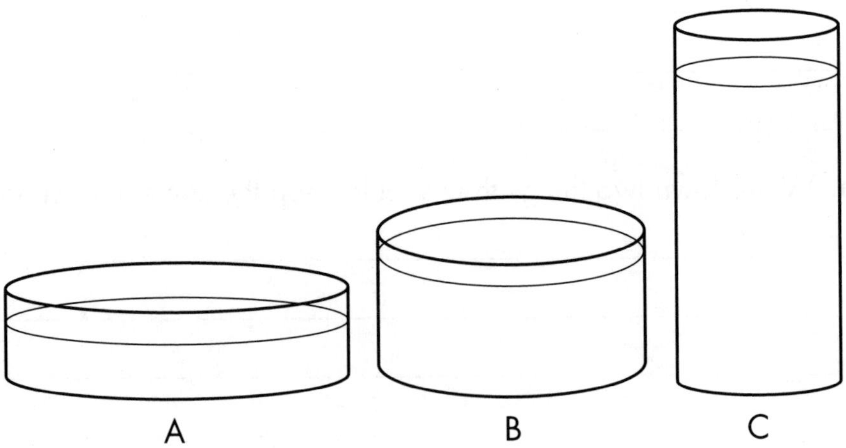

a. How long should they leave the experiment? Tick one box.

one hour ☐

one day ☐

one week ☐

one year ☐

b. Which container do you think will dry first?

____

c. Give one reason for your idea.

____

Sciencecheck © HarperCollins*Publishers* Ltd 1998

Sciencecheck	NAME	DATE
Sc1, Level 3	**EXPERIMENTAL AND INVESTIGATIVE SCIENCE**	
Test 3, Series A	**Considering evidence** Pupils should be taught to consider evidence from experimental work.	

1 **One plant was put in a box for a week.**
Another plant was put in a clear tank.

Place	Colour of leaves
box	yellow
tank	green

Why was the plant in the box yellow?

___

2 **Jon bounced a ball on different surfaces.**

It bounced 2 times on the carpet.
It bounced 4 times on the playground.
It bounced 5 times on the wooden floor.

a. On which surface did the ball bounce best?

___

b. On which surface did the ball bounce least well?

___

c. Do you think the ball would bounce well on sand?

___

3 **This pie-chart shows the food eaten by an owl.**

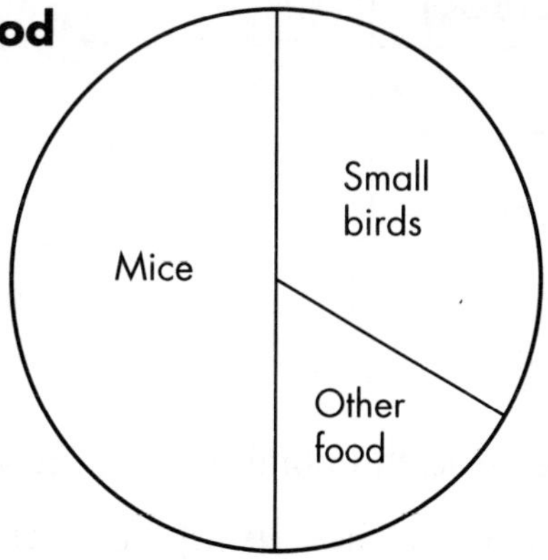

a. What was the main food eaten by this owl?

___

b. Is the owl a meat-eater or a vegetarian?

___

Sciencecheck	**NAME**	**DATE**
Sc1, Level 3 **Test 3, Series A**	**EXPERIMENTAL AND INVESTIGATIVE SCIENCE** **Considering evidence** Pupils should be taught to consider evidence from experimental work.	

4 **Aisha rolls a toy car down a ramp.**

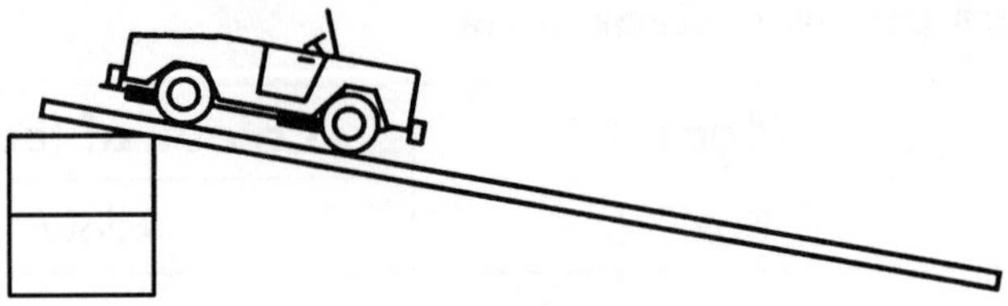

Here are the results.

Number of bricks under the ramp	Distance travelled by the car
1	20 cm
2	25 cm
3	30 cm

Write about the pattern you can see in these results.

____

____

____

5 **Helen made some spinners.**

She made the wings different lengths.
She dropped each one and timed
how long it took to fall by clapping.

Length of wing	Time to fall (number of claps)
10 cm	12
8 cm	11
6 cm	10
4 cm	

a. Look at the last line of the table. Add the number of claps you would expect.

b. On the back of this sheet, draw a bar chart using the information from the table.

c. Give the bar chart a title.

d. Read the sentence and write the correct word in the space. **shorter** **longer**

If you make the wings of a spinner _______________ it falls faster.

e. Read the sentence and write the correct word in the space. **slowly** **quickly**

A spinner with long wings falls _______________.

Sciencecheck © HarperCollins*Publishers* Ltd 1998

Sciencecheck	**NAME**	**DATE**
Sc2, Level 3 **Test 4, Series A**	**LIFE PROCESSES AND LIVING THINGS** **Life processes** Pupils should be taught that there are life processes common to plants and animals.	

1

Aziz went for a walk on the beach.
He made a list of all the things he could see.

a. Look at the picture and write down 4 things which are alive and 4 things which are not alive.

Alive	Not alive
1	1
2	2
3	3
4	4

2 **How do you know these animals are alive?**

Write two things which tell you.

1)

2)

3 **Put ticks in the table to show what these things can do.**

	Breathe	Feed	Grow
dog			
doll			
tree			
aeroplane			

Sciencecheck	**NAME**	**DATE**
Sc2, Level 3	**LIFE PROCESSES AND LIVING THINGS**	
Test 4, Series A	**Life processes** Pupils should be taught that there are life processes common to plants and animals.	

4 **This diagram shows the stages in the life cycle of a human being.**

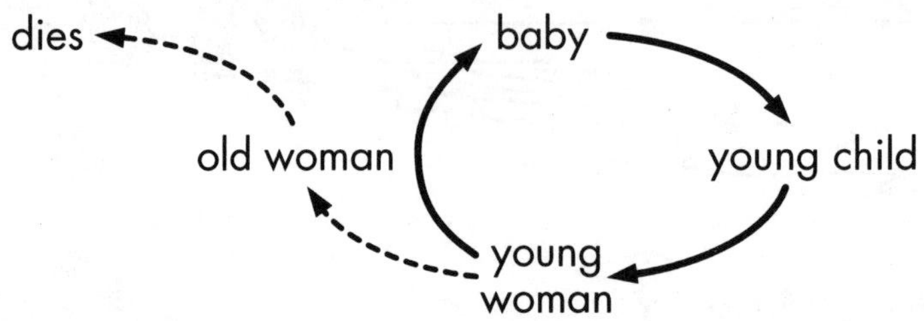

a. Look at the diagram and write about the life cycle of a human being.

____

____

____

____

This diagram shows the stages in the life cycle of a frog.

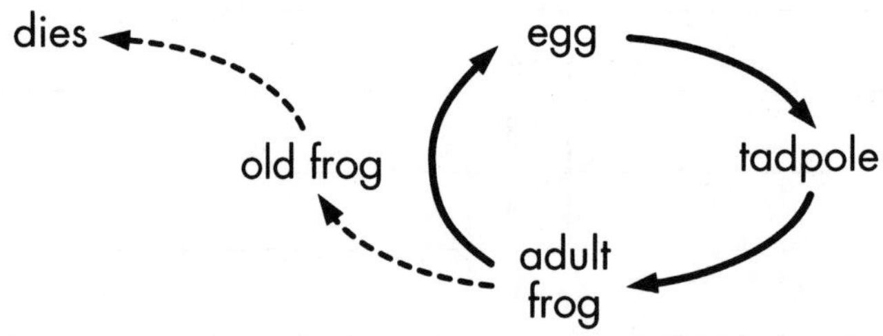

b. Look at the diagram and write about the life cycle of a frog.

____

____

____

____

c. Write about one difference between the life cycle of a frog and a person.

____

____

5 **Draw a line from the animal to the way it begins life.**

Animal		Way it begins life
human		tadpole
bird		caterpillar/pupa
frog		egg with a hard shell
butterfly/moth		born live from its mother

 © HarperCollins*Publishers* Ltd 1998

Sciencecheck	**NAME**	**DATE**
Sc2, Level 3 / **Test 5, Series A**	**LIFE PROCESSES AND LIVING THINGS** **Humans as organisms** Pupils should be taught about humans as organisms.	

1 **Jim's second teeth have just come through.**

Write two ways that he can help to keep them healthy.

1) ______________________________

2) ______________________________

2 **Jennifer eats an apple.**

Which teeth does she use to:

a. bite off chunks of her apple? ______________

b. grind it into pulp? ______________

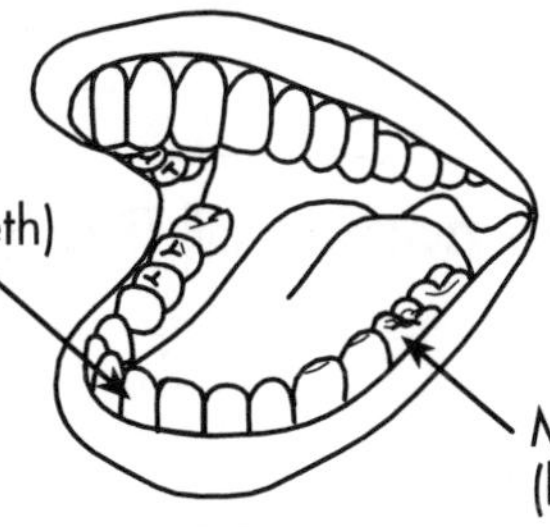

3 **Underline all the senses Michael will use to cross the road safely.**

hearing smell sight feel taste

4 **Draw a line to link the organ to the job it does.**

brain	breathe
lungs	digests food
stomach	thinks

5 **Name these bones.**

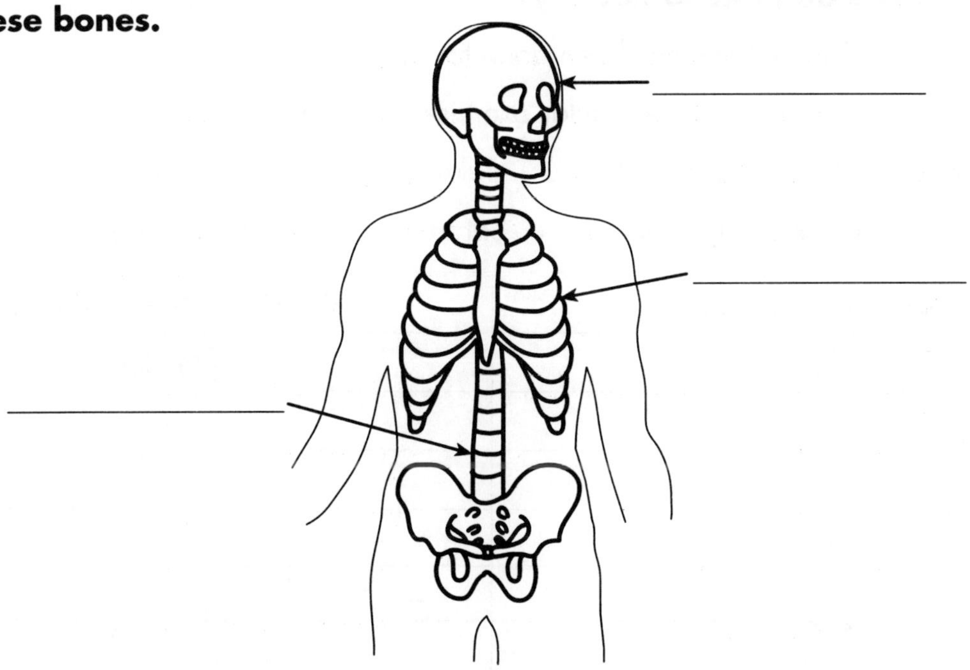

Sciencecheck	NAME	DATE
Sc2, Level 3	**LIFE PROCESSES AND LIVING THINGS**	
Test 6, Series A	**Healthy living** Pupils should be taught about nutrition, circulation and health.	

1 **Jack likes to keep fit.**

Join his pulse rate to the type of activity he does.

Activity		**Pulse rate**
sleeping		fast
skipping		slow
walking		very fast

2 **Tick the names of five sorts of food which will make a healthy lunch.**

- fizzy pop ☐
- fruit juice ☐
- crisps ☐
- chocolate bar ☐
- sweets ☐
- apple ☐
- cheese sandwich ☐
- low fat yoghurt ☐
- carrot sticks ☐
- toffee ☐

3 **What should you do to keep healthy?**

Complete the table. The first one has been done for you.

Smoke Take regular exercise Get enough sleep

Eat good meals Eat lots of fat Take drugs Use protection in the sun

Drink plenty of water Eat fruit Eat lots of toffee

Do these things	Don't do these things
	Smoke

 Sciencecheck © HarperCollinsPublishers Ltd 1998

Sciencecheck	**NAME**	**DATE**
Sc2, Level 3	**LIFE PROCESSES AND LIVING THINGS**	
Test 7, Series A	**Green plants** Pupils should be taught about the growth and nutrition of plants.	

1 **What is the job of each of these parts of a plant?**

Roots ____________________

Leaves ____________________

Flowers ____________________

Seeds ____________________

Flower stem ____________________

2 **Robert bought three plants. He kept them for two weeks.**

Write what you think happened to each of the plants.

He watered one and kept it in a bright place.

____

He forgot to water one.

____

He watered one but kept it in a dark cupboard.

____

3 **Jenny grows cress seed in different boxes.**

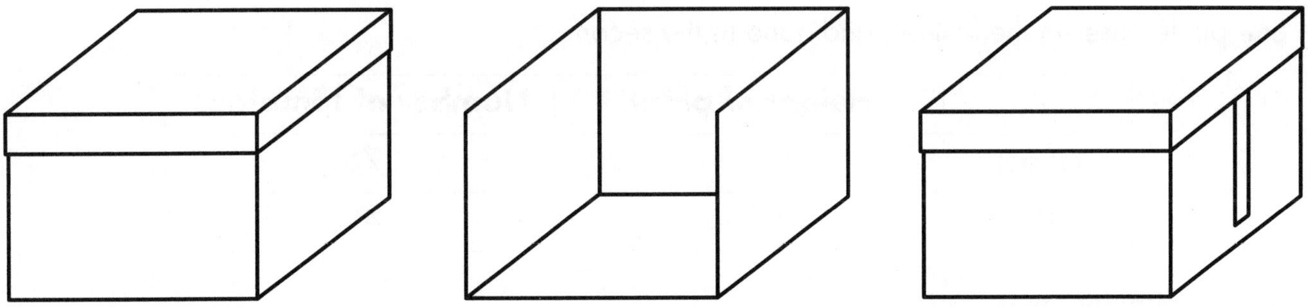

Box A　　Box B　　Box C

Write A, B and C in the correct place to complete the table.

Box	Growth of cress
	tall and strong
	tall and spindly
	growing to one side

Sciencecheck	**NAME**	**DATE**
Sc2, Level 3	**LIFE PROCESSES AND LIVING THINGS**	
Test 7, Series A	**Green plants** Pupils should be taught about the growth and nutrition of plants.	

4 **Kate keeps her rabbit hutch on the grass.**

a. What colour do you think the grass will be under the hutch after two weeks?

____

____

b. Why do you think the grass changes colour?

____

____

c. How do you think Kate could stop the grass from changing colour?

____

____

5 **Circle two things that all plants need to stay alive and healthy.**

fields water sunlight

soil walls people

6 **Tim's grandma grew two pots of tomatoes in the same greenhouse.**

She put fertiliser in the first pot and none in the second.

	Height of plant	**Number of tomatoes**
1st pot	2 m	75
2nd pot	1.5 m	40

a. Which plant grew best?

____

b. Explain how you know.

____

c. What do you think caused the difference in the two plants?

____

 Sciencecheck © HarperCollins*Publishers* Ltd 1998

Sciencecheck	NAME	DATE
Sc2, Level 3 Test 8, Series A	**LIFE PROCESSES AND LIVING THINGS** **Variation and classification** Pupils should be taught how animals and plants can be assigned to groups.	

1 **Some of these animals eat plants and some eat meat. Write them under the correct heading.**

cow rabbit owl cat sheep snail dog

Eats meat	Eats plants

2 **a.** Write the name of the minibeast in the correct column.

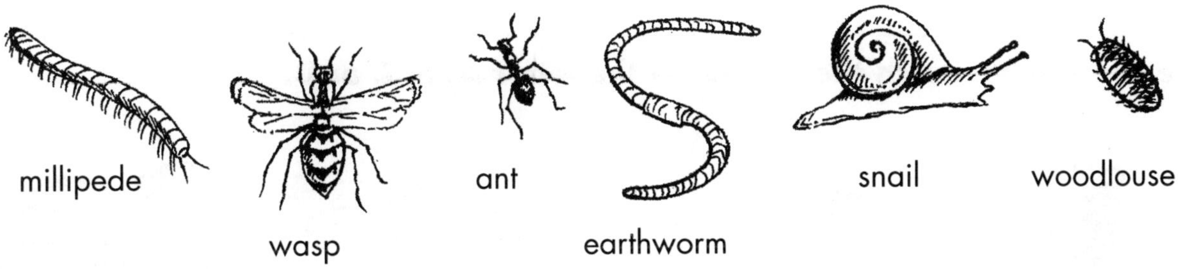

No legs	Six legs	More than six legs

b. Write the names of 3 other minibeasts you know, putting one in each column.

c. Write the names of these animals:

It has six legs and a stripy body. ____________________

It is long and thin and does not have legs. ____________________

It is long and thin and has many legs. ____________________

Sciencecheck	NAME	DATE
Sc2, Level 3 Test 8, Series A	**LIFE PROCESSES AND LIVING THINGS** **Variation and classification** Pupils should be taught how animals and plants can be assigned to groups.	

3 **Conifers have narrow leaves which look like needles. Most deciduous trees have broad leaves.**

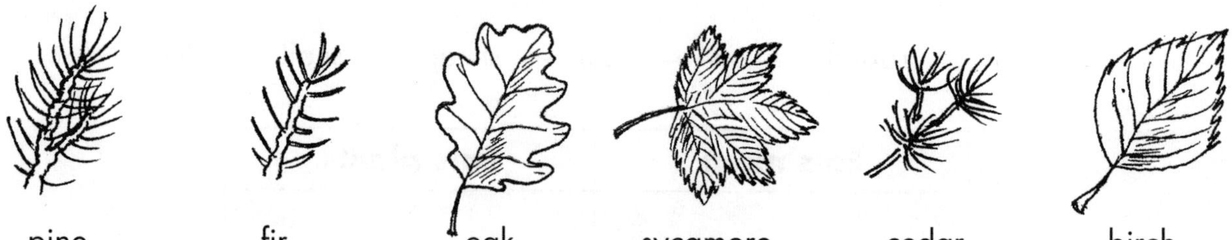

pine fir oak sycamore cedar birch

Write the name of the tree in the correct box.

Conifer
Deciduous

4 **Use the key to match the animal to the letter A, B, C or D.**

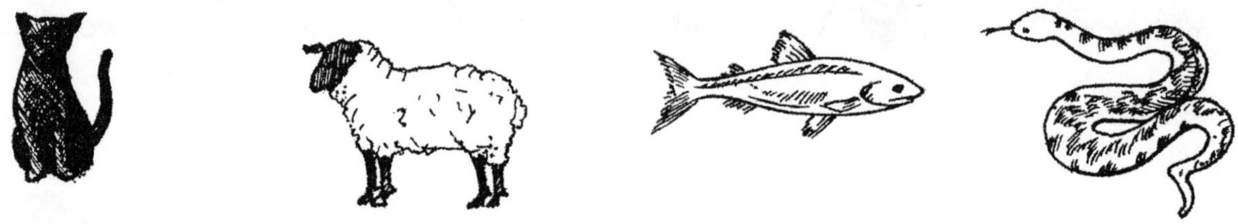

Does it have legs?

- YES → Does it have a woolly coat?
  - YES → Animal A
  - NO → Animal B
- NO → Does it have fins?
  - YES → Animal C
  - NO → Animal D

Animal A is a ______________

Animal B is a ______________

Animal C is a ______________

Animal D is a ______________

 Sciencecheck © HarperCollins*Publishers* Ltd 1998

Sciencecheck	**NAME**	**DATE**
Sc2, Level 3 / **Test 9, Series A**	**LIFE PROCESSES AND LIVING THINGS** **Living things in their environment (adaptation)** Pupils should be taught how animals and plants are suited to their environment.	

1 **Write two ways in which a fish is suited to living in water.**

1) ______________________________

2) ______________________________

2 Camels can drink lots of water and store it in their body. They have wide feet to help them walk on soft sand. They have long, thick eyelashes to stop sand getting into their eyes.

Give two reasons why camels can live easily in the desert.

1) ______________________________

2) ______________________________

3 **a.** Write one thing about a Polar bear which helps it to live in snowy places.

____

b. Write one thing about an otter which helps it to live in rivers.

____

c. Write two things about a lion which help it to catch zebras.

1) ______________________________

2) ______________________________

4 **Match the start and finish of each sentence.**

Polar bears have thick coats...	...to stop animals eating them.
Eagles have sharp claws...	...to keep them warm.
Blackberries have thorns...	...to catch earthworms.
Moles dig through the earth...	...to hold on to their prey.

5 **Write about how each of these animals catches its food.**

Spider ______________________________

Wildcat ______________________________

Hawk ______________________________

Sciencecheck	**NAME**	**DATE**
Sc3, Level 3	**MATERIALS AND THEIR PROPERTIES**	
Test 10, Series A	**Grouping and classifying** Pupils should be taught to group and classify materials.	

1 **Sort these materials.**

Write the name of each material on to the correct bin.

wood wool cotton tin can stone metal scissors fur gold ring

Does conduct electricity

Does not conduct electricity

2 **a.** Tick the materials which are flexible.

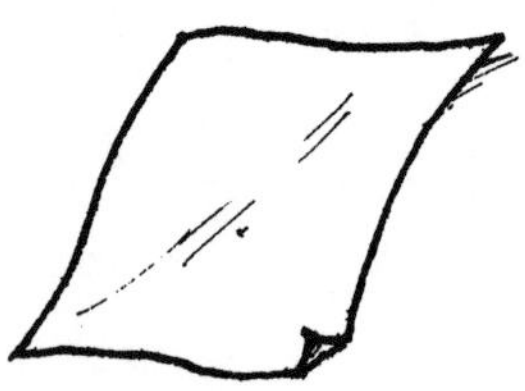

paper

thin card

wooden twig

wooden spoon

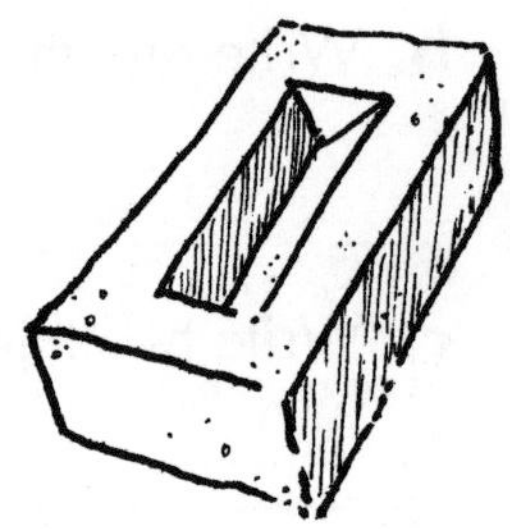

brick

b. Is your desk stiff or flexible? How do you know?

____

3 **a.** Name a plastic object which is very flexible.

____

b. Name a plastic object which is very stiff.

____

c. Name a plastic object you can see through.

____

d. Name a strong plastic object.

____

Sciencecheck © HarperCollins*Publishers* Ltd 1998

Sciencecheck	NAME	DATE
Sc3, Level 3	MATERIALS AND THEIR PROPERTIES	
Test 10, Series A	Grouping and classifying Pupils should be taught to group and classify materials.	

4 **a.** Tick the things which will be attracted to a magnet.

b. What are the things you have ticked made from?

____

____

5 **Why are Lizzy's toys made from these materials?**

Her car is made of metal because ______________________

Her teddy is made of fabric because ______________________

Her boat is made of wood because ______________________

6 **Tim has one spoonful of each food.**

List them in order from the lightest to the heaviest.

popcorn butter flour

7 **Tick the sentences which are correct.**

Flour is a powder.

Oil is solid.

Metal things soak up water.

Some glass is transparent.

Plastic is magnetic.

Woollen clothes come from animals.

Sciencecheck	**NAME**	**DATE**
Sc3, Level 3	**MATERIALS AND THEIR PROPERTIES**	
Test 11, Series A	**Changing materials** Pupils should be taught that materials can be changed.	

1 **Zoe puts a mug of water in the freezer.**
Ann puts a mug of water in the fridge.

What happens to:

a. Zoe's water? ______________________

b. Ann's water? ______________________

2 **Tick two materials which will dissolve in water.**

wax salt sugar cornflakes earth sand

3 **Water can turn to ice.**

a. Circle the word which describes water turning to ice.

melt dissolve freeze evaporate

b. Tick the reason for water turning to ice.

Water temperature is below 0°C.

It is winter.

It is not sunny.

c. What happens to ice cubes left in a bowl in a room?

____

4 **Heather is making a clay model.**

a. What does the clay she is using feel like?

____

b. How does it feel when it has dried?

____

c. Could she make it go soft again?

____

d. How does wet clay look different from dry clay?

____

e. How could she stop her wet clay drying out?

____

Sciencecheck © HarperCollins*Publishers* Ltd 1998

Sciencecheck	**NAME**	**DATE**
Sc3, Level 3	**MATERIALS AND THEIR PROPERTIES**	
Test 11, Series A	**Changing materials** Pupils should be taught that materials can be changed.	

5 **a.** What happens to ice-cream on a very warm day?

____

b. How can you stop this from happening?

____

6 **a.** Why is wool not a good fabric for a swimsuit?

____

b. Why is nylon a good fabric for making tights?

____

7 **Tick the foods which melt when heated.**

bread

jam

chocolate

carrots

butter

jelly

8 **How does an egg change when you fry it?**

____

9 **How does a potato change when you fry it?**

____

10 **Circle the materials which will burn.**

iron paper clay bread wax water plastic cloth

Sciencecheck	**NAME**	**DATE**
Sc3, Level 3 / **Test 12, Series A**	**MATERIALS AND THEIR PROPERTIES** **Separating mixtures** Pupils should be taught about separating mixtures of materials.	

1 **Zak has a pan of peas and water.**

How can he separate the peas from the water?

____

2 **Jake has some paperclips.**

Some are plastic and some are steel.

What can he use to separate them?

____

3 **Jade drops a mixture of wood shavings and steel screws into water.**

a. How does this help to separate them?

____

b. What will happen to the screws if they stay in the water?

____

4 **Tick the sentences which are true.**

Wood shavings are attracted to a magnet.

Magnets attract steel pins.

Plastic is sometimes attracted to a magnet.

All metals are attracted to a magnet.

Iron filings are attracted to a magnet.

5 **Jane has some mixtures.**

Tick the mixtures she can separate with a sieve.

sweets and sugar

sugar and salt

potatoes and water

milk and water

6 **Which would be the best way to separate a mixture of raisins from flour?**

____

Sciencecheck © HarperCollins*Publishers* Ltd 1998

Sciencecheck	**NAME**	**DATE**
Sc3, Level 3 **Test 13, Series A**	**MATERIALS AND THEIR PROPERTIES** **Using materials** Pupils should be taught to relate the properties to the everyday uses of materials.	

1 **Match each material to a use.**

Material	**Use**
glass	shoes
gold	windows
wool	bracelets
leather	plates
pottery	jumpers

2 **List two of the materials you are wearing or holding now.**

Write what they are used for.

1) ____________________

2) ____________________

3 **a.** What are coins made from?

____

b. Why are coins not made from card?

____

4 **Alex is looking at a bike.**

a. Draw a line from the material to its use on the bike.

Material	**Use**
plastic	tyres
rubber	bike frame
steel	seat cover

b. Explain why steel is used to make the bike chain.

____

5 **Why is glass used to make windows?**

____

6 **Circle the materials which could be used to make a candleholder.**

glass paper wax iron jelly

Sciencecheck	**NAME**	**DATE**
Sc4, Level 3	**PHYSICAL PROCESSES**	
Test 14, Series A	**Electricity** Pupils should be taught about simple electric circuits.	

1 **The bulb won't light in each of these circuits.**

Write the reason why next to each circuit.

a.

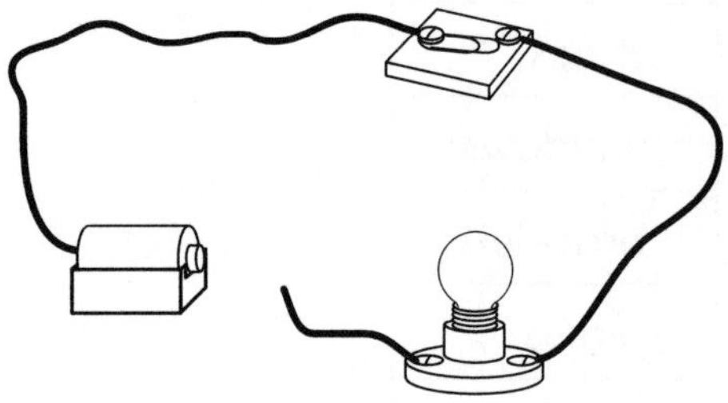

____

____

____

b.

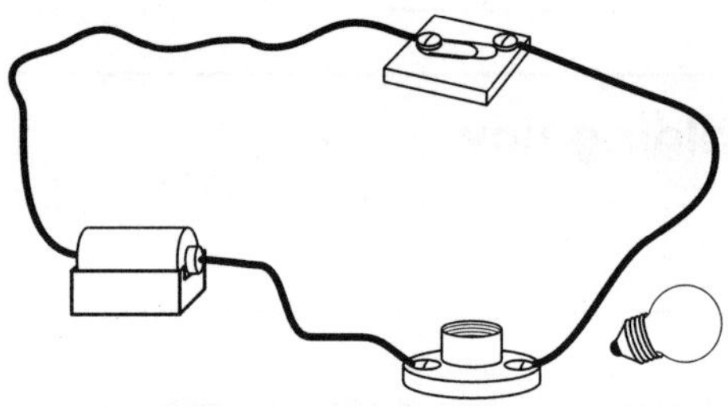

____

____

____

c.

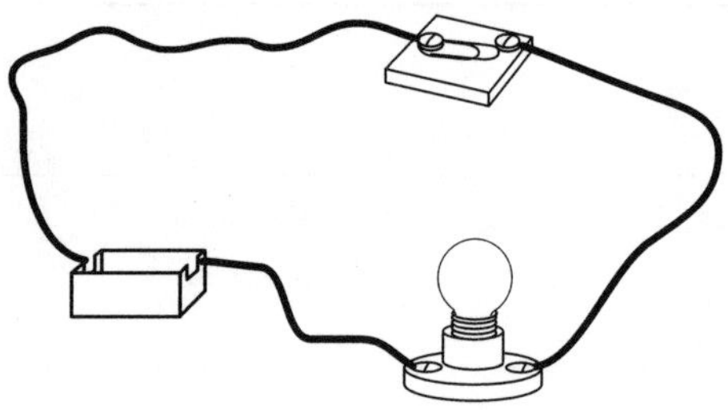

____

____

____

d.

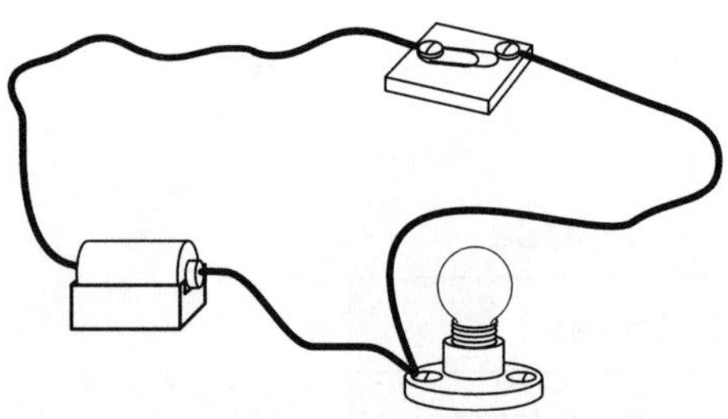

____

____

____

2 **Jon has tried this battery with all four bulbs. None of them will light.**

What do you think might be wrong?

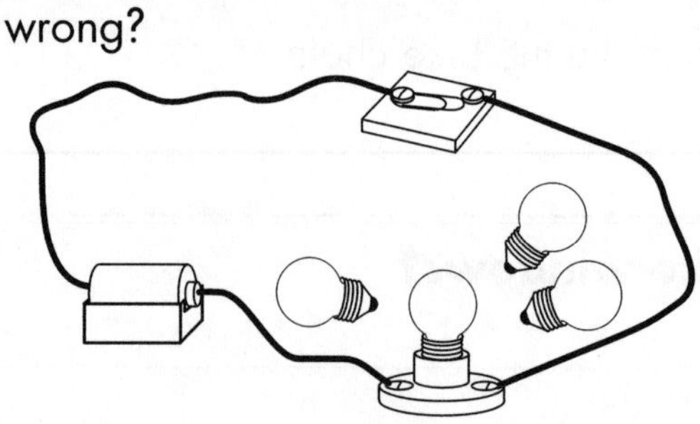

____

____

Sciencecheck © HarperCollins*Publishers* Ltd 1998

Sciencecheck	**NAME**	**DATE**
Sc4, Level 3 **Test 14, Series A**	**PHYSICAL PROCESSES** **Electricity** Pupils should be taught about simple electric circuits.	

3 **What happens when each of these switches is turned on?**

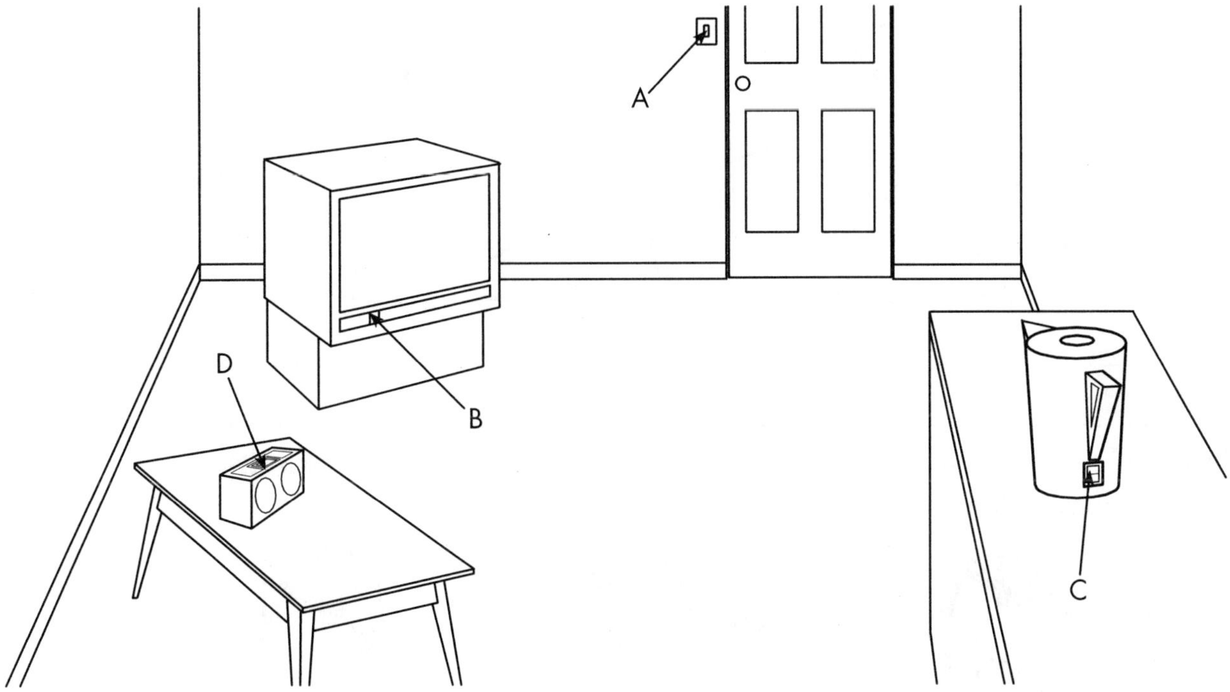

Switch A ______________________________

Switch B ______________________________

Switch C ______________________________

Switch D ______________________________

4 **Jan plays with her electric car for an hour. Then it begins to slow down.**

What do you think has happened?

____

____

Sciencecheck	**NAME**	**DATE**
Sc4, Level 3	**PHYSICAL PROCESSES**	
Test 15, Series A	**Gravity and magnetism** Pupils should be taught about gravity and magnetism as forces.	

1 **Which one of these bags would be hardest to pick up?**

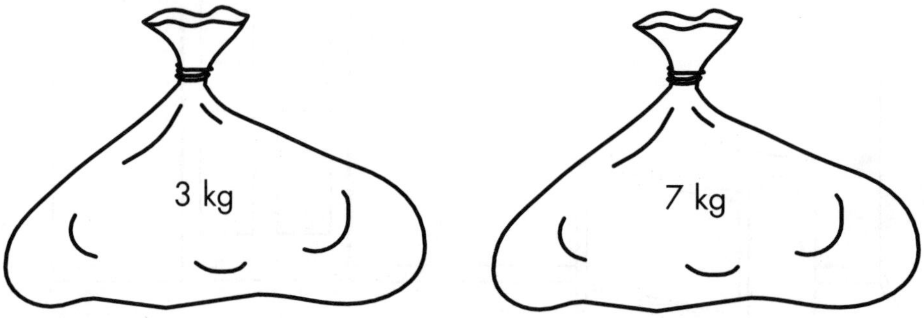

2 **Which of these arrows shows the direction of the pull of gravity?**

Circle the correct drawing.

3 **a.** Draw arrows to show how each ball will fall.

b. Why will each ball fall in the way you have drawn?

 Sciencecheck © HarperCollins*Publishers* Ltd 1998

Sciencecheck	**NAME**	**DATE**
Sc4, Level 3 / **Test 15, Series A**	**PHYSICAL PROCESSES** / **Gravity and magnetism** / Pupils should be taught about gravity and magnetism as forces.	

4 **Jim is playing with magnets.**

Tick the sentence which is true.

North poles attract north poles. ☐

North poles repel south poles. ☐

South poles repel south poles. ☐

5 **Helen held a magnet against a thick piece of wood.**

She noticed that a paperclip was attracted to the wood opposite the magnet.

What did this experiment show?

____

6 **Helen plays a trick.**

She picks up a matchbox with a magnet.

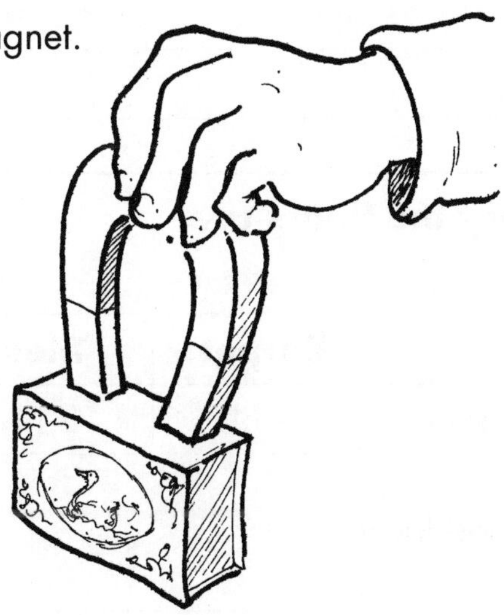

Explain how she does it.

____

____

Sciencecheck	**NAME**	**DATE**
Sc4, Level 3	**PHYSICAL PROCESSES**	
Test 16, Series A	**Friction and air resistance** Pupils should be taught about friction and air resistance as forces which slow moving objects.	

1 **Jon put the same weight on a large parachute and a small parachute.**
He noticed that the large one dropped more slowly.

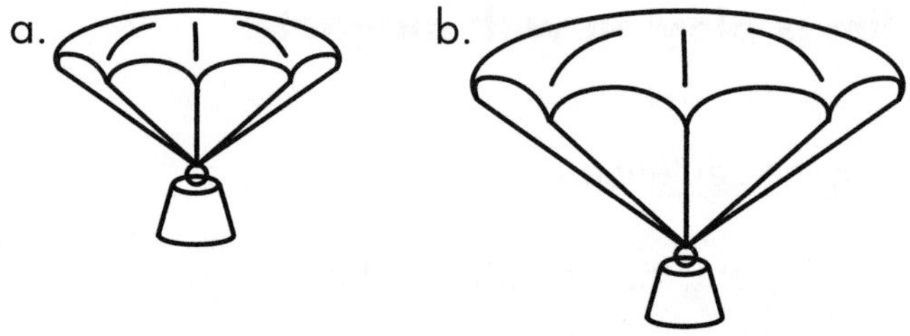

Why do you think this happened?

____

2 **Julie has made a rope slide for her toy.**

a. What will happen if she makes the slope steeper?

____

b. She put a cloak on her toy. The cloak slowed it down.

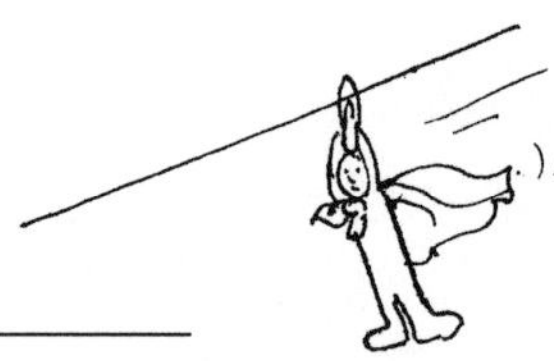

Why did this happen?

____

3 **Samina is running in the playground. She thinks that she can run faster without her baggy jacket on.**

How can she find out if she is right?

____

____

4 **Julie tested how slippery the floors are.**
Here are her results.

	Carpet	**Tiles**
Force needed to pull the shoe	4 N	2 N

a. Which surface has the most friction?

____

b. Which surface is the most slippery?

____

Sciencecheck © HarperCollins*Publishers* Ltd 1998

Sciencecheck	**NAME**	**DATE**
Sc4, Level 3 **Test 17, Series A**	**PHYSICAL PROCESSES** **Springs and elastic bands** Pupils should be taught about the forces on springs and elastic bands.	

1 **Becky is hanging weights from elastic bands.**

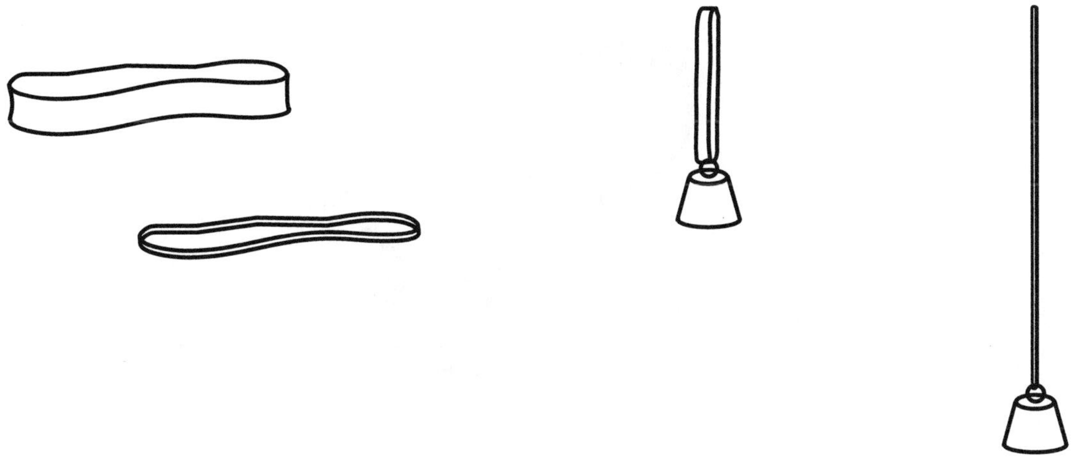

Here are her results.

	Thick band	Thin band
Length of unstretched band	10 cm	10 cm
Length of band with weight attached	12 cm	15 cm

a. Which band stretched the most?

____

b. What will happen to the length of the bands when Becky removes the weights?

____

2 **Becky put some weights into the legs of a pair of tights.**

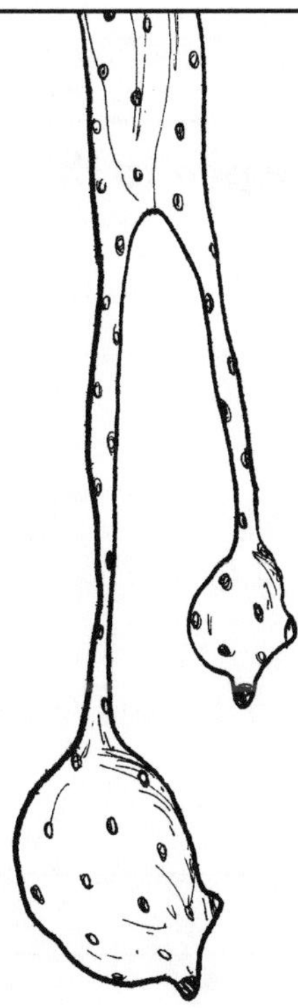

Why do you think one leg stretched more than the other?

____

____

____

Sciencecheck	**NAME**	**DATE**
Sc4, Level 3 / **Test 17, Series A**	**PHYSICAL PROCESSES** **Springs and elastic bands** Pupils should be taught about the forces on springs and elastic bands.	

3 **What will happen to this spring when Tim lets go?**

4 **What will happen to this spring when Ben lets go?**

5 **What will happen to this spring if more water is added to the tank?**

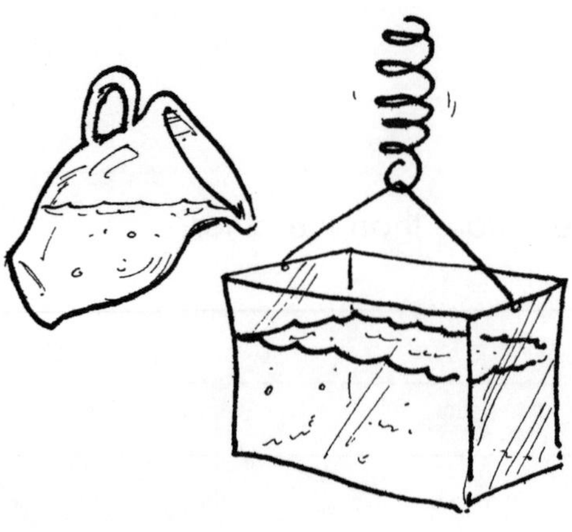

Sciencecheck © HarperCollins*Publishers* Ltd 1998

Sciencecheck	**NAME**	**DATE**
Sc4, Level 3 **Test 18, Series A**	**PHYSICAL PROCESSES** **Types of forces** Pupils should be taught about types of forces.	

1 **Tick the pushes which could knock over the small tree.**

2 **Gayle used a big hammer and a small hammer to knock some pegs into the ground.**

It took three hits to knock in the peg with the big hammer.
It took six hits to knock in the peg with the small hammer.

a. Which hammer knocked the pegs in most easily?

____

b. How many hits do you think a very heavy hammer would need?

____

c. How many hits do you think a very small hammer would need?

____

Sciencecheck	NAME	DATE
Sc4, Level 3 Test 18, Series A	**PHYSICAL PROCESSES** **Types of forces** Pupils should be taught about types of forces.	

3 **Tim is pushing a cart along a flat path at the camp.**

With one push the empty cart goes forward 5 metres.

Fatima gets in.

Now one push moves the cart forward 3 metres.

Why do you think this is?

4 **Which team do you think will win?**

Explain your idea each time.

a.

b.

c.

 Sciencecheck © HarperCollinsPublishers Ltd 1998

Sciencecheck	**NAME**	**DATE**
Sc4, Level 3	**PHYSICAL PROCESSES**	
Test 19, Series A	**Direction of forces** Pupils should be taught that forces act in particular directions.	

1 **Join each sentence to the correct drawing.**

The dog is pulling with more force.

The pulling force of the dog and the boy are equal.

The force of the boy is more than the pull of the dog.

a.

b.

c.

2 **Draw an arrow to show the direction of the force made by the person on these things.**

a.

b.

c.

3 **What will happen to the can when these forces press it?**

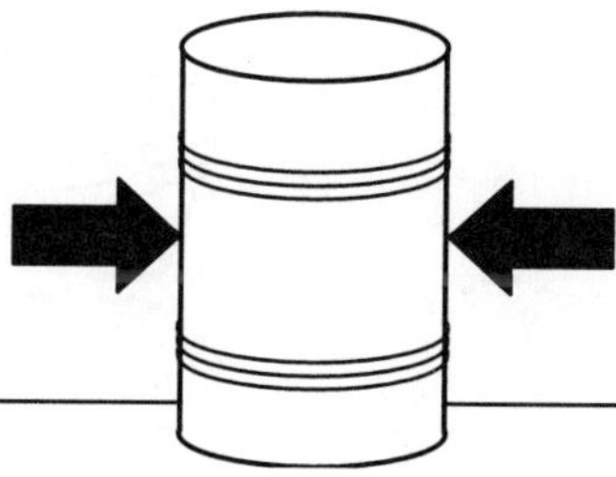

____

____

____

Sciencecheck	NAME	DATE
Sc4, Level 3	**PHYSICAL PROCESSES**	
Test 19, Series A	**Direction of forces** Pupils should be taught that forces act in particular directions.	

4 **a.** What might happen to the thin cotton if this big force pulls it?

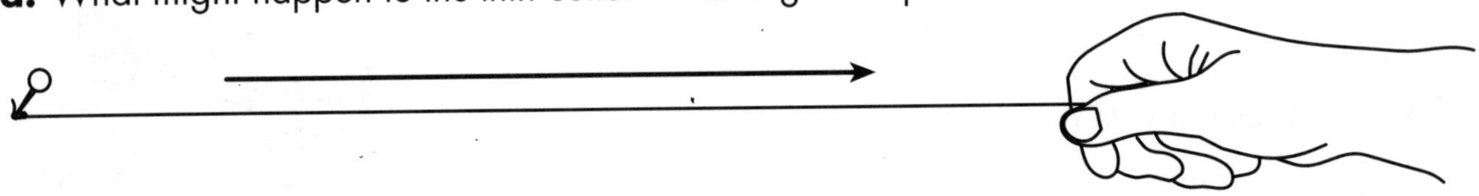

____

b. What might happen to this thick rope?

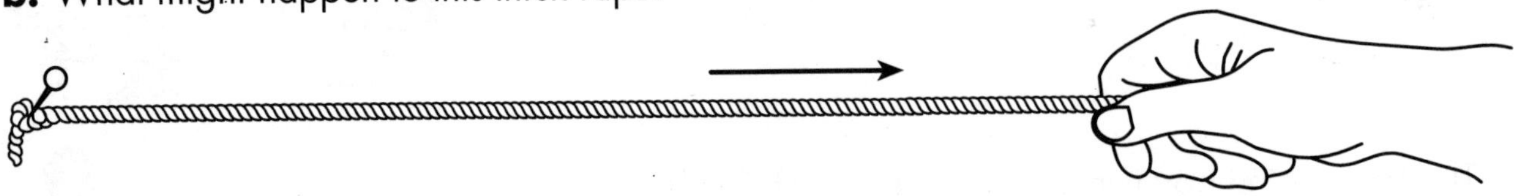

____

5 **Draw a rubber ball and a stone in this tank of water.**

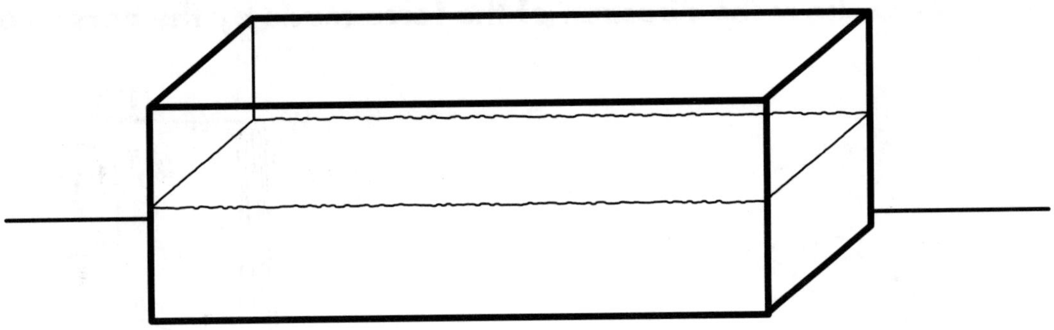

Will they be floating or sunk?

____

6 **a.** Which of these boats is loaded with cargo?

____

b. How can you tell?

____

Sciencecheck © HarperCollins*Publishers* Ltd 1998

Sciencecheck	**NAME**	**DATE**
Sc4, Level 3 **Test 20, Series A**	**PHYSICAL PROCESSES** **Light** Pupils should be taught about seeing and the everyday effects of light.	

1 **Tick the materials in this list which light can go through.**

glass

wood

steel

clingfilm

2 **Match the word to the object.**

transparent

translucent

opaque

tin

bubble wrap

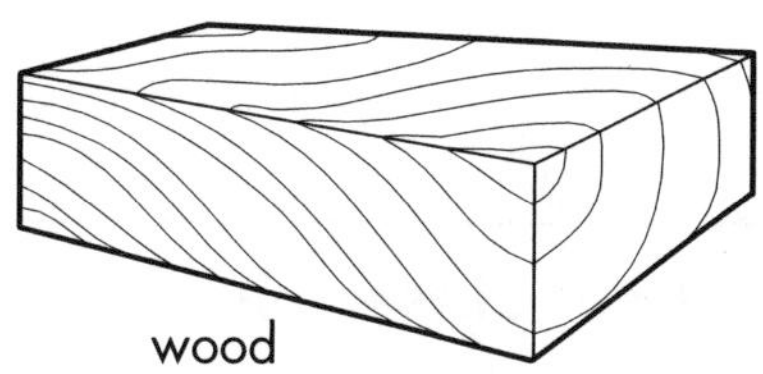

wood

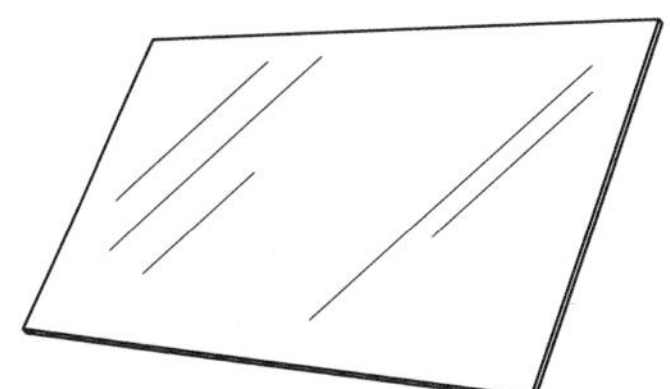

clear plastic

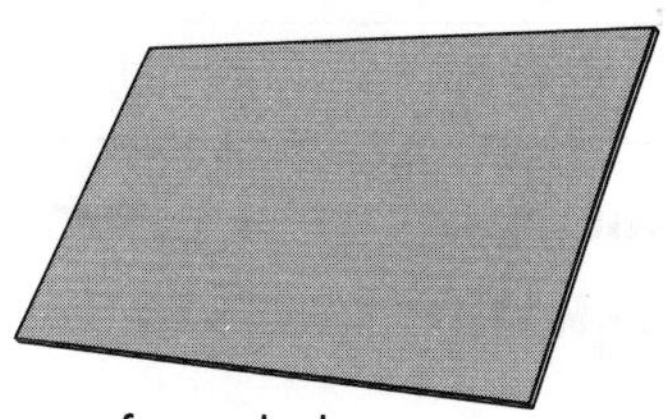

frosted glass

glass

3

Explain why Kate can read her book easily while Emma cannot.

____

____

Sciencecheck © HarperCollins*Publishers* Ltd 1998

Sciencecheck	**NAME**	**DATE**
Sc4, Level 3	**PHYSICAL PROCESSES**	
Test 20, Series A	**Light** Pupils should be taught about seeing and the everyday effects of light.	

4 **Draw a line connecting the object to its shadow.**

5 **Why does Devika wear sunglasses in the summer?**

____

6 **Jo's candle looks bright in an unlit room at night.**

It does not look so bright by daylight.

Explain why.

____

7 **Why is it hard to see things in a dark cave?**

____

8 **List these light sources in order of brightness.**

a pen torch   football-ground floodlights   a car headlight

____

Sciencecheck © HarperCollins*Publishers* Ltd 199

Sciencecheck	**NAME**	**DATE**
Sc4, Level 3 **Test 21, Series A**	**PHYSICAL PROCESSES** **Sound** Pupils should be taught about the way sounds are made by vibrating objects.	

1

Why do these people wear ear protectors?

____

2 **Emma thinks that sound does not travel through bricks.**

a. How could she test her idea?

____

b. Why do you think her idea is right?

____

3 **Draw a line from the sentence to the correct box.**

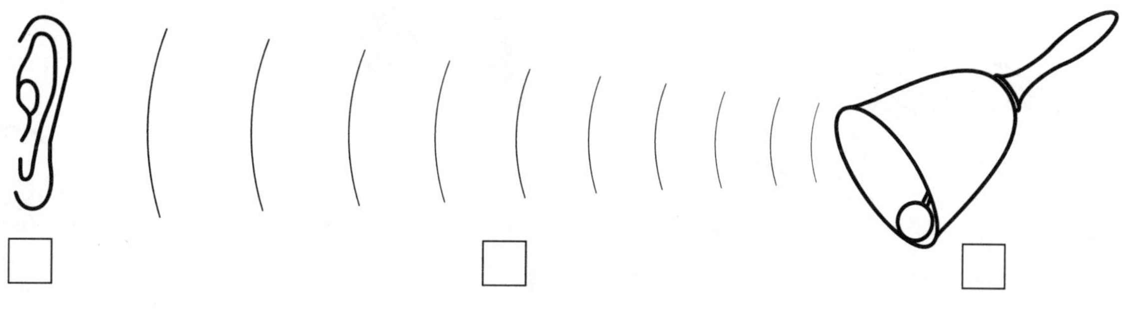

The sound enters the person's ear.

The bell vibrates.

The sound travels through the air.

4 **Tick the sounds you could hear across the playground.**

someone whispering   someone shouting   a mouse squeaking   teacher's whistle

Sciencecheck	**NAME**	**DATE**
Sc4, Level 3	**PHYSICAL PROCESSES**	
Test 21, Series A	**Sound** Pupils should be taught about the way sounds are made by vibrating objects.	

5 **Jon taps very gently on a rail.**
Helen can hear it clearly if she puts her ear to the rail.

Tick the sentence which is correct.

Sound travels through the rail. ☐

Sound does not travel through solid things. ☐

Sound only travels through the air. ☐

6

Karen can hear the sound made by the kitten.

Why can't Richard hear it?

____

7

Colour blue the instruments which are played by hitting.

Colour green the instruments which are played by blowing.

Colour red the instruments which make a sound with strings.

Sciencecheck © HarperCollins*Publishers* Ltd 1998

Sciencecheck	**NAME**	**DATE**
Sc4, Level 3	**PHYSICAL PROCESSES**	
Test 22, Series A	**The Earth and beyond** Pupils should be taught about some of the periodic changes in the position of the Earth, Moon and Sun.	

1 **What shape is the Sun?**

Tick one box.

a circle ☐

a sphere ☐

flat ☐

a cube ☐

2 **Clouds are nearer to you than the Sun.**

How do you know?

____

3 **Draw a line from the sentence to the correct box.**

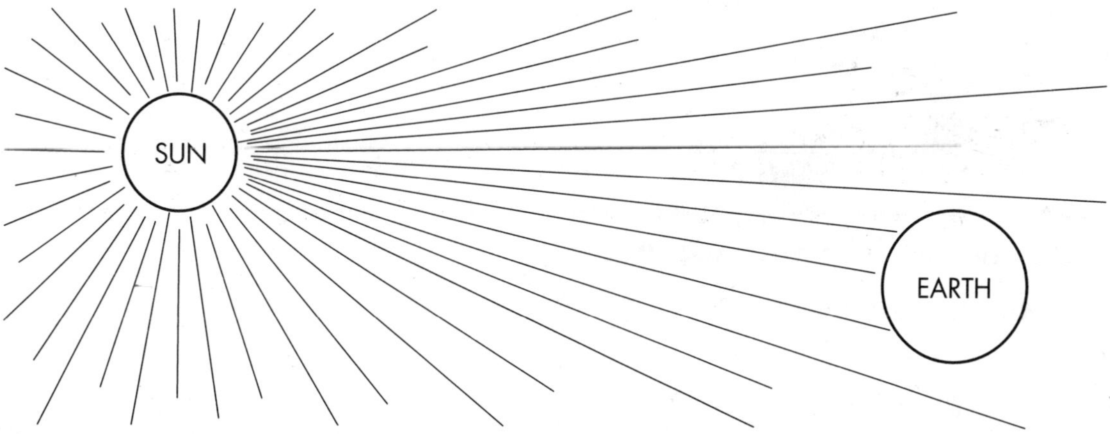

☐ ☐ ☐

The Sun's light hits the Earth.

The light travels through space.

The Sun is a source of light.

4 Write **true** or **false** next to each sentence.

a. You can see many stars in the sky at lunchtime. ____________

b. The Sun is low in the sky in the early morning. ____________

c. The Sun mainly shines during the day. ____________

d. It is dark at night because the Sun is shining on the other side of the Earth. ____________

Sciencecheck	**NAME**	**DATE**
Sc4, Level 3 / **Test 22, Series A**	**PHYSICAL PROCESSES** **The Earth and beyond** Pupils should be taught about some of the periodic changes in the position of the Earth, Moon and Sun.	

5 **Look at the table below.**

At what time of day is the stick's shadow shortest? ____________

Time of day	Length of shadow
10 am	20 cm
11 am	15 cm
3 pm	30 cm

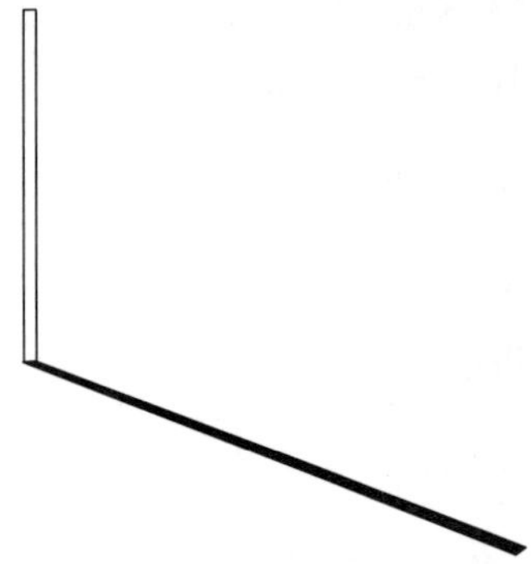

6 **Do you think a spaceship could land on the Sun and return to Earth?**

Explain your idea.

____

____

____

____

____

7 **See where the sun is in each picture.**

Draw a shadow for each tree.

 Sciencecheck © HarperCollins*Publishers* Ltd 1998

Sciencecheck	**NAME**	**DATE**
Sc1, Level 3 **Test 1, Series B**	**EXPERIMENTAL AND INVESTIGATIVE SCIENCE** **Planning investigations** Pupils should be taught to plan experimental work.	

1 **Tim wants to find out if he can see better with his right eye or his left eye.**

a. What test could he do?

____

b. How could he make his test fair?

____

2 **Aisha thinks that plants grow best if the soil is very wet all the time.**

How could she find out if her idea is right?

____

3 **Class 3 want to see if stirring sugar helps it to dissolve quickly.**

a. Write down how they could do their test.

____

b. Write down two things they should keep the same in each test.

1) ______________________________

2) ______________________________

4 **Simon is testing how well his friends can hear sounds.**

He thinks that they should wear a blindfold.

Why this is a good idea?

____

5 **Class 3 are seeing who is the best thrower.**

How could they make the test fair?

____

____

____

Sciencecheck	NAME	DATE
Sc1, Level 3 **Test 2, Series B**	**EXPERIMENTAL AND INVESTIGATIVE SCIENCE** **Obtaining evidence** Pupils should be taught to obtain evidence from measurements and observations.	

1 **Match the apparatus on the left to the activity on the right.**

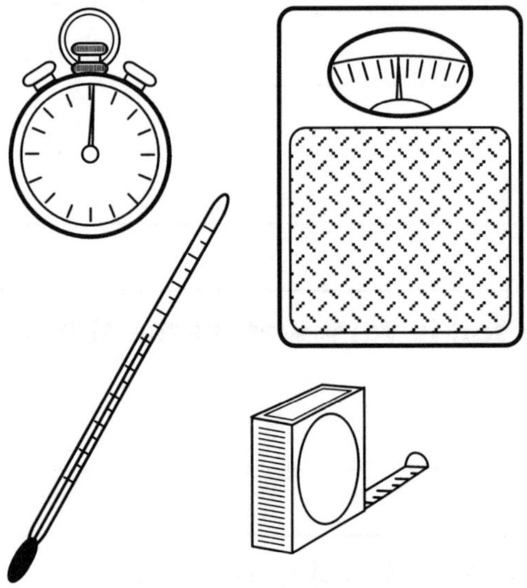

measuring temperature

measuring length

measuring weight

measuring time

2 **Tim is measuring the temperature in three different places.**

He writes down three readings.

4°C   45°C   20°C

Fill in the table by putting the temperatures in the correct place.

Place	Temperature
in a room	
in a fridge	
on a radiator	

3 **Class 3 made three pieces of cloth wet.**

They put them in different places to see where they would dry first.

a. When should they first check the cloth?

Tick one box.

after one hour ☐   after one day ☐   after one week ☐   after half a day ☐

b. Where do you think a piece of cloth would dry quickest in your classroom?

____

c. Give one reason for your idea.

____

Sciencecheck © HarperCollins*Publishers* Ltd 1998

Sciencecheck	**NAME**	**DATE**
Sc1, Level 3 **Test 3, Series B**	**EXPERIMENTAL AND INVESTIGATIVE SCIENCE** **Considering evidence** Pupils should be taught to consider evidence from experimental work.	

1 **Robert and his friends put a piece of old carpet on some grass.**

They also pegged out a piece of clear plastic on the grass.
They left them for two weeks.
After two weeks, the grass under the carpet was yellow.
The grass under the clear plastic was still green.

a. Why was the grass under the carpet yellow?

____

b. Why was the grass under the plastic still green?

____

c. What would happen to the yellow grass if it was left uncovered?

____

2 **Jon bounced different balls on the playground.**

A rubber ball bounced 10 times.
A golf ball bounced 8 times.
A sponge ball bounced 5 times.

a. Which ball bounced best?

____

b. Which ball bounced least well?

____

c. How many times would you expect a plasticine ball to bounce?

____

3 **This pie-chart shows the food eaten by a horse.**

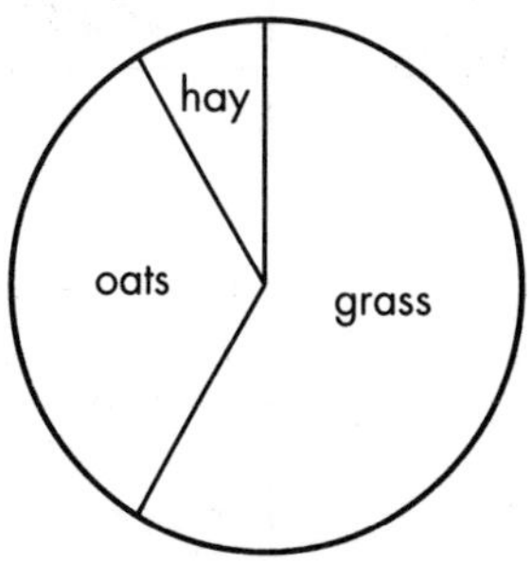

a. What was the main food eaten by this horse?

____

b. Is the horse a **carnivore** or a **herbivore**?

____

Sciencecheck	NAME	DATE
Sc1, Level 3	**EXPERIMENTAL AND INVESTIGATIVE SCIENCE**	
Test 3, Series B	**Considering evidence** Pupils should be taught to consider evidence from experimental work.	

4 **Tim rolls two different cars down a ramp.**

He measures how far each one goes.

Here are the results.

Height of ramp	Blue car	Red car
2 cm	10 cm	6 cm
4 cm	14 cm	8 cm
6 cm	18 cm	10 cm

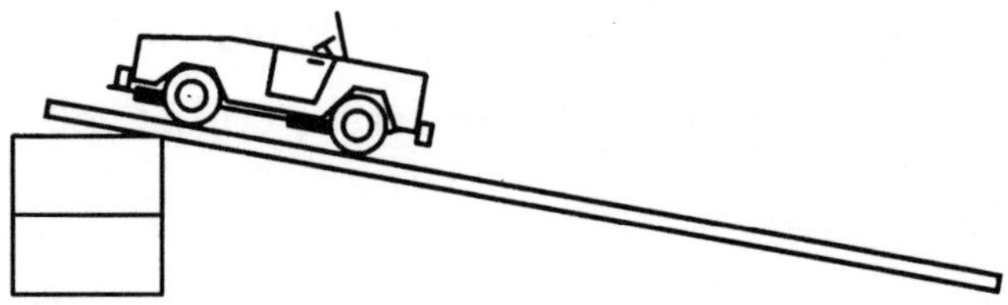

Write about the patterns you can see in these results.

____

____

5 **Hannah made some parachutes.**

She made them all the same size but added different amounts of paperclips to each one.

She timed how long each one took to fall with a stopwatch.

She then drew this bar chart.

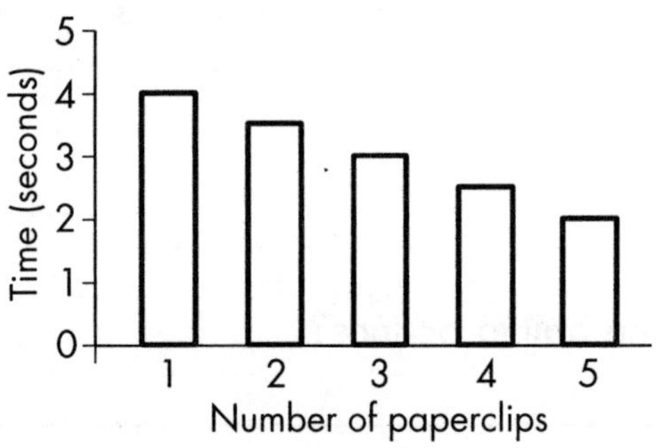

a. Use the bar chart to fill in this table.

Number of paperclips	Time to fall (seconds)
1	4
2	
3	
4	$2\frac{1}{2}$
5	

b. Give the table a title. ________________________

c. What pattern do you notice from these results?

____

 Sciencecheck © HarperCollins*Publishers* Ltd 1998

Sciencecheck	**NAME**	**DATE**
Sc2, Level 3 / **Test 4, Series B**	**LIFE PROCESSES AND LIVING THINGS** **Life processes** Pupils should be taught that there are life processes common to plants and animals.	

1

Rob went for a walk in the farmyard.

He made a list of all the things he could see.

Look at the picture and write down four things which are alive and four things which are not alive.

Alive	Not alive
1	1
2	2
3	3
4	4

2

Write two things that tell you that plants are alive.

1) ____________________

2) ____________________

Sciencecheck	NAME	DATE
Sc2, Level 3 Test 4, Series B	**LIFE PROCESSES AND LIVING THINGS** **Life processes** Pupils should be taught that there are life processes common to plants and animals.	

3 **Put ticks to show what these things can do.**

	Grow	Move by itself	Reproduce (have young)
cow			
daisy			
beetle			
piece of wood			

4 **a.** Write about the life cycle of a duck.

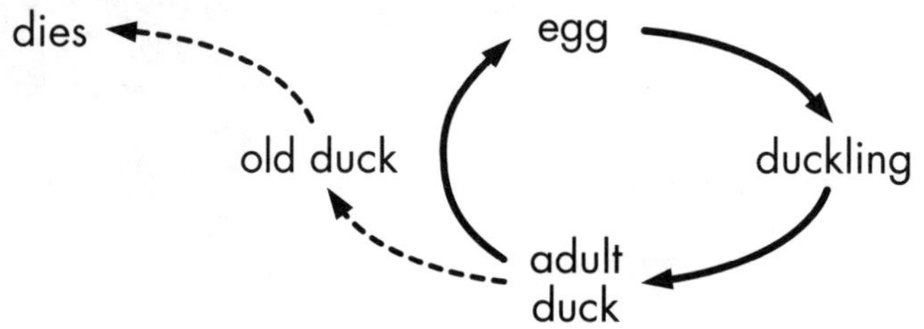

____

____

____

b. Write about the life cycle of a butterfly.

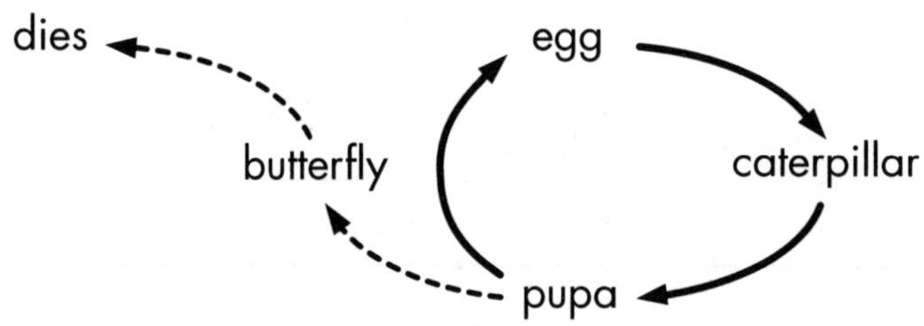

____

____

____

5 **Link the animal to the way it begins life.**

cat	spawn
hen	born alive from its mother
frog	egg with a hard shell
moth	caterpillar/pupa

Sciencecheck © HarperCollins*Publishers* Ltd 1998

Sciencecheck	NAME	DATE
Sc2, Level 3 **Test 5, Series B**	**LIFE PROCESSES AND LIVING THINGS** **Humans as organisms** Pupils should be taught about humans as organisms.	

1 **Jack likes to keep fit.**

Join his pulse rate to the type of activity he does.

Activity		Pulse rate
sitting		fast
swimming		slow
walking		very fast

2 **Underline all the senses Sam uses to stay safe as he rides his bike along the road.**

hearing   smell   sight   feel   taste

3 **Draw a line to link the parts of the body to the job they do.**

skin		protect the ends of fingers
teeth		keeps the body warm and protects the head
fingernails		break up food
hair		covers and protects the body

4 Write **true** or **false** next to each of these sentences.

Your skull protects your brain. ________

Your backbone is made up of many small bones. ________

Your spine protects your feet. ________

Your bones are made from hard skin. ________

Your muscles are attached to your bones. ________

5 **What would happen to you if you did not drink anything for a week?**

____

6 **Why would you feel very tired if you did not eat for a week?**

____

7 **What do you think would happen if you did not sleep for a week?**

____

 © HarperCollins*Publishers* Ltd 1998 One sheet only

Sciencecheck	**NAME**	**DATE**
Sc2, Level 3	**LIFE PROCESSES AND LIVING THINGS**	
Test 6, Series B	**Healthy living** Pupils should be taught about nutrition, circulation and health.	

1 **The doctor has told Alan's dad not to eat fatty food.**

Circle the foods he should not eat too often.

cheese chips apples crisps bread pasta peas

pork pies chicken margarine chocolate carrots

2 **a.** Why does Jon's mum say he should not eat so many sweets?

____

b. Why does Jon's mum tell him to eat fruit and vegetables?

____

3 **Using the list, complete the table to show Jenny how she can stay fit and healthy.**

Drink lots of alcohol Walk Eat fruit Eat good food

Eat lots of crisps Wear a hat on sunny days Swim

Brush teeth Wash every day Watch TV all day

Do these things	Don't do these things

3 **Write about three good ways to exercise.**

1) ______________________________

2) ______________________________

3) ______________________________

 Sciencecheck © HarperCollins*Publishers* Ltd 1998

Sciencecheck	**NAME**	**DATE**
Sc2, Level 3 **Test 7, Series B**	**LIFE PROCESSES AND LIVING THINGS** **Green plants** Pupils should be taught about the growth and nutrition of plants.	

1 **What is the job of each of these parts of a tree?**

Seeds ______________________

Trunk ______________________

Roots ______________________

2 **Parmi planted some new plants in a tub.**

Connect the picture of the plant with how he treated each one.

He forgets to water it for a week. He waters it. He forgets to water it for two weeks.

3 **Jenny grew cress plants in different places.**

The cress plants grown next to the window were healthy.
The cress plants grown in a cupboard were yellow and very weak.

Why do you think there was a difference between the two sets of seeds?

____

4 **Kate put a black plastic bag on some grass.**
She put a clear plastic bag next to it.
She weighed them down with bricks.
She left them for two weeks.

a. What colour will the grass be under the black plastic bag?

____

b. What colour will the grass be under the clear plastic bag?

____

c. What colour will the grass be under the bricks?

____

5 **What two things do all plants need to grow?**

1) ______________________

2) ______________________

Sciencecheck	**NAME**	**DATE**
Sc2, Level 3	**LIFE PROCESSES AND LIVING THINGS**	
Test 8, Series B	**Variation and classification** Pupils should be taught how animals and plants can be assigned to groups.	

1 **a.** Some of these animals eat plants (herbivores) and some eat meat (carnivores). Write them under the correct headings.

sheep kestrel dog cow slug lion

Carnivore	Herbivore

b. Add one more animal to each list.

2 **Look carefully at these pictures of minibeasts.**

Use the key to match the animal to the letter A, B, C or D.

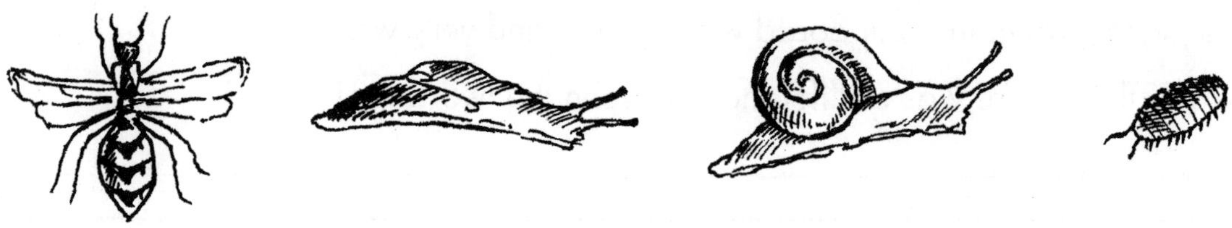

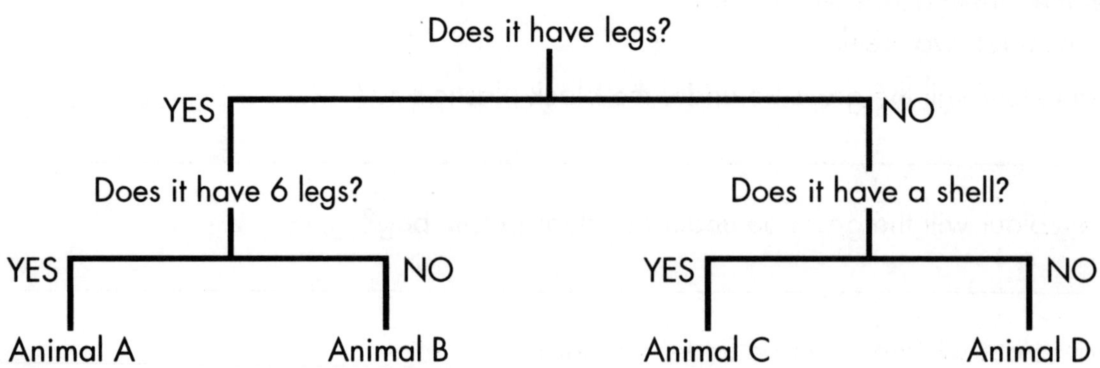

Animal A is a ______________

Animal B is a ______________

Animal C is a ______________

Animal D is a ______________

 Sciencecheck © HarperCollins*Publishers* Ltd 1998

LIFE PROCESSES AND LIVING THINGS

Variation and classification

Pupils should be taught how animals and plants can be assigned to groups.

3 **Look carefully at these pictures of plants.**

Use the key to match the plant to the letter A, B, C or D.

daisy

daffodil

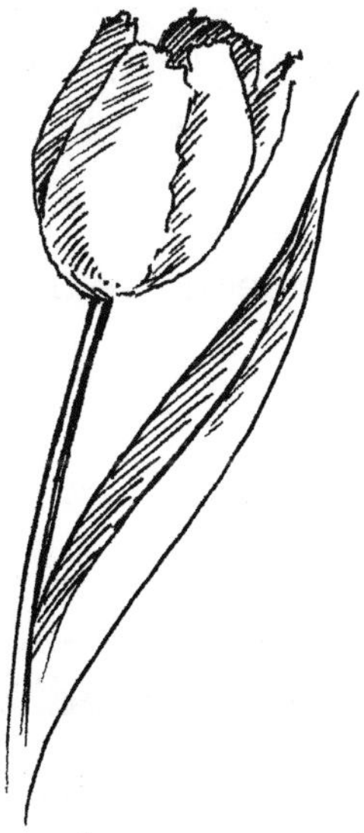

tulip

dandelion

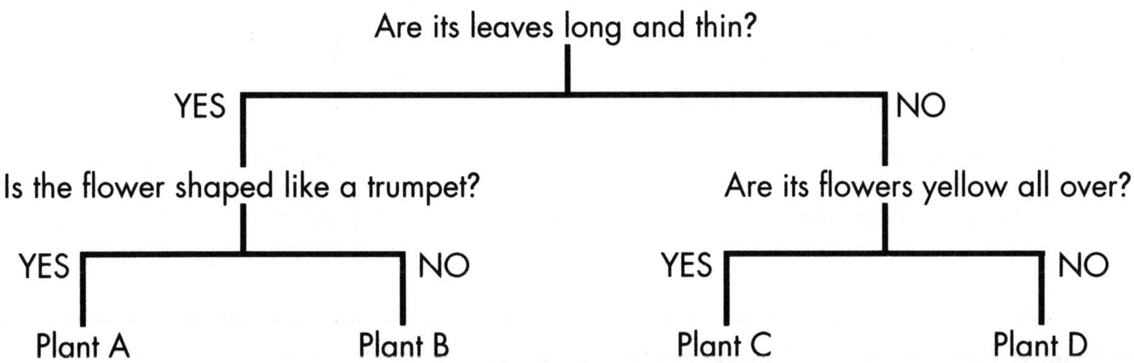

Plant A is a ____________

Plant B is a ____________

Plant C is a ____________

Plant D is a ____________

Sciencecheck	**NAME**	**DATE**
Sc2, Level 3 **Test 9, Series B**	**LIFE PROCESSES AND LIVING THINGS** **Living things in their environment (adaptation)** Pupils should be taught how animals and plants are suited to their environment.	

1 **Give two reasons why ducks are suited to living on water.**

1) ______________________________

2) ______________________________

2 Polar bears have thick coats that keep them warm in very cool conditions. They have claws which help them to grip on to ice and to catch seals to eat. They are very large so do not get cold easily.

Give two reasons why polar bears are able to survive in very cold places.

1) ______________________________

2) ______________________________

3 **Jill lifted a stone and found woodlice under it.**

Give two reasons why you think woodlice like to live under stones.

1) ______________________________

2) ______________________________

4 **Draw lines connecting the start and finish of each sentence.**

Cats have sharp claws	to hold their prey.
Birds have wings	to gnaw hard food.
Kangaroos have strong back legs	to fly.
Fish have fins	to hop long distances.
Rats have sharp teeth	to swim.

5 **Write about how each of these animals catches its food.**

Eagle ______________________________

Crocodile ______________________________

Tiger ______________________________

Sciencecheck © HarperCollins*Publishers* Ltd 1998

Sciencecheck	**NAME**	**DATE**
Sc3, Level 3 **Test 10, Series B**	**MATERIALS AND THEIR PROPERTIES** **Grouping and classifying** Pupils should be taught to group and classify materials.	

1 **Sort these materials.**

Write each material in the correct box.

sawdust   cotton cloth   soil   metal   paper   plastic   glass

Soaks up water	Does not soak up water

2 **Jack bends these things to see which will break.**

a. Tick the ones you think he will be able to break.

biscuit   old bike tyre   electrical wire   matchstick   potato crisp

b. Circle the word which describes a pencil rubber.

see-through   soft   flexible   stiff   hard

3 **Ann wants to keep her bread fresh.**

a. Circle the bag she should use.

plastic bag   paper bag   hand bag   cloth bag

b. Explain why it is best.

____

____

____

4 **Kerry plays hopscotch.**

Tick the one she should use to draw on the ground.

pencil   felt tip   chalk   crayon

Sciencecheck **NAME** **DATE**

Sc3, Level 3

Test 10, Series B

MATERIALS AND THEIR PROPERTIES

Grouping and classifying

Pupils should be taught to group and classify materials.

5 Why are a baby's toys made from these materials?

A rattle is made from plastic because ______________________________

A toy dog is made from cloth because ______________________________

Building bricks are made from wood because ______________________________

6 Put these things in order from the hardest to the softest.

cotton wool wood iron card

7 Draw an arrow from the rubbish to the correct bin.

milk bottle drink can bean can yoghurt pot foil pie dish

margarine tub jam jar sardine tin polythene bag

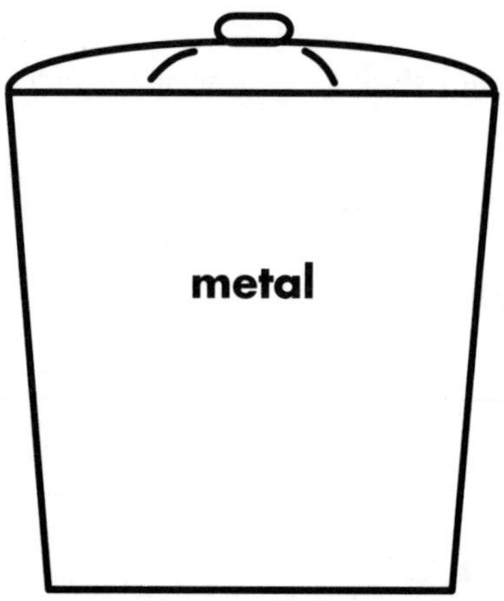

Sciencecheck © HarperCollins*Publishers* Ltd 1998

Sciencecheck	**NAME**	**DATE**
Sc3, Level 3 **Test 11, Series B**	**MATERIALS AND THEIR PROPERTIES** **Changing materials** Pupils should be taught that materials can be changed.	

1 **Joe puts a block of ice in a warm oven for an hour.**
James puts cold water in a warm oven for the same length of time.

What will happen to each?

a. Ice in the oven ______________________________

b. Cold water in the oven ______________________________

2 **Tick three materials which will not dissolve in water.**

cork   wood   salt   icing sugar   paper

3 **a.** What word describes ice turning to water? Circle the correct word.

freeze   melt   dissolve   run

b. When does ice turn to water? Tick the correct sentence.

When its temperature is above 0°C.   When the ice has got thinner.   When the ice is lost.

4 **Daniel is making bread.**

a. How does the dough feel as he mixes it?

____

b. How does the crust feel when it is cooked?

____

c. Could he turn it back into dough again?

____

5 **What happens to cornflakes when you add milk?**

____

6 **Why is plastic a good material for a raincoat?**

____

7 **a.** What changes happen inside eggs when you boil them?

____

b. Can eggs be made raw again after cooking?

____

Sciencecheck	**NAME**	**DATE**
Sc3, Level 3 **Test 12, Series B**	**MATERIALS AND THEIR PROPERTIES** **Separating mixtures** Pupils should be taught about separating mixtures.	

1 **Zak's dad has got some muddy potatoes.**

How does he separate the mud from the potatoes?

____

2 **Jerry has a bin of nails and sawdust.**

What can he use to separate them?

____

3 **Jade drops a mixture of polystyrene chips and large nails into water.**

a. How does this help to separate them?

____

b. What will happen to the nails if they stay in the water?

____

4 **Tick the sentences which are true.**

Magnets can attract brass screws.

Only things made of iron and steel are attracted to a magnet.

Glass is sometimes attracted to a magnet.

Magnets can be used to pick up steel pins.

Pencil shavings are attracted to a magnet.

5 **Simon has made some mixtures.**

Tick those he can separate with a sieve.

- nuts and flour ☐
- beaten egg and milk ☐
- salt and water ☐
- sand and pebbles ☐

6 **What would be the best way to separate a mixture of shells from sand?**

____

 Sciencecheck © HarperCollins*Publishers* Ltd 1998

Sciencecheck	NAME	DATE
Sc3, Level 3 **Test 13, Series B**	**MATERIALS AND THEIR PROPERTIES** **Using materials** Pupils should be taught to relate the properties to the everyday uses of materials.	

1 **Match each material to a use.**

Material	**Use**
glass	doors
copper	mirror
cotton	electrical wire
steel	clothes
wood	scissors

2 **List two materials you can see in your classroom.**

Write what they are used for.

1) ________________________________

2) ________________________________

3 **List two materials you might see in a bathroom.**

Write what they are used for.

1) ________________________________

2) ________________________________

4 **List two materials you might see in a bedroom.**

Write what they are used for.

1) ________________________________

2) ________________________________

5 **a.** What are credit cards made from?

____

b. Why are they not made from metal?

Give two reasons.

1) ________________________________

2) ________________________________

Sciencecheck	**NAME**	**DATE**
Sc3, Level 3	**MATERIALS AND THEIR PROPERTIES**	
Test 13, Series B	**Using materials** Pupils should be taught to relate the properties to the everyday uses of materials.	

6 **Sarah is looking at a car.**

a. Draw a line from the material to its use in the car.

Material
cloth
rubber
steel
glass

Use
tyres
roof
windscreen
carpets

b. Why isn't metal used to make the seat covers?

Give one reason.

____

7 **Match the material to the musical instrument.**

metal

school recorder

wood

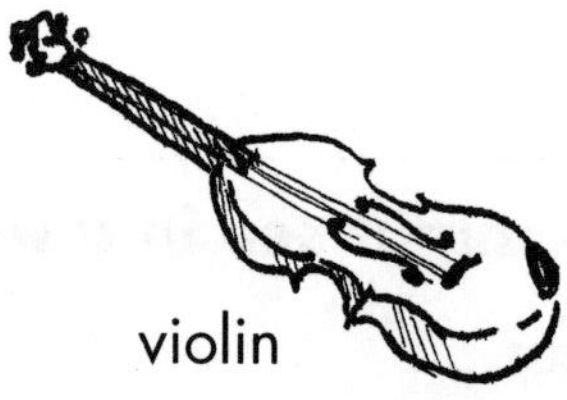

violin

plastic

trumpet

8 **Circle the materials which could be used to make a teapot.**

chocolate glass paper wax pottery metal jelly

9 **Circle the materials which could be made into a spoon.**

wood straw plastic cloth card metal jelly

Sciencecheck © HarperCollins*Publishers* Ltd 1998

Sciencecheck	NAME	DATE

Sc4, Level 3

Test 14, Series B

PHYSICAL PROCESSES

Electricity

Pupils should be taught about simple electric circuits.

1 **The bulb won't light in each of these circuits. Write the reason why next to each circuit.**

a.

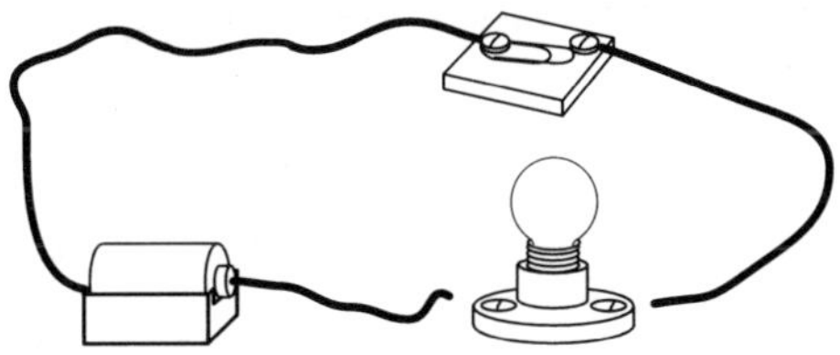

____

____

b.

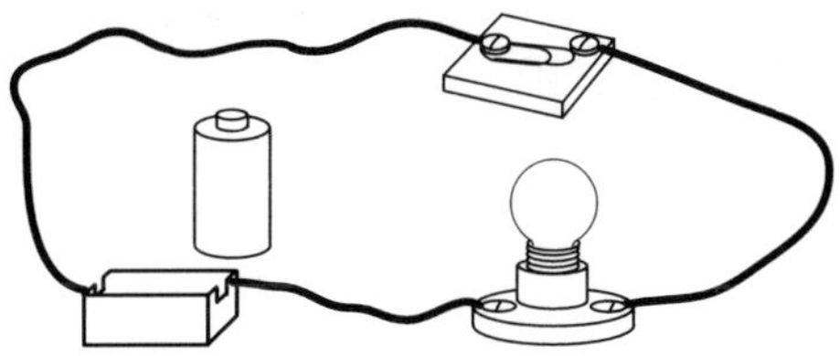

____

____

c.

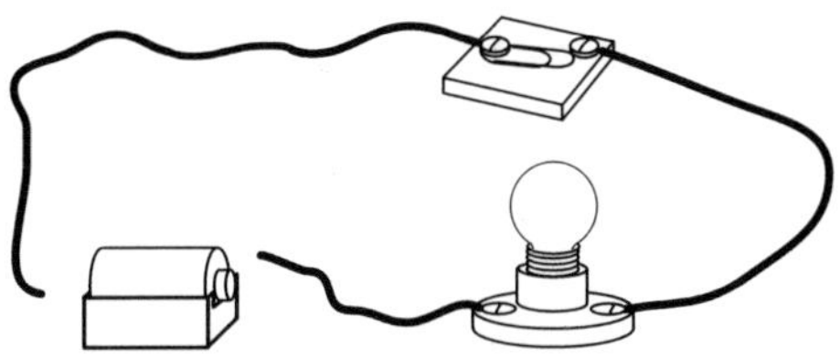

____

____

d.

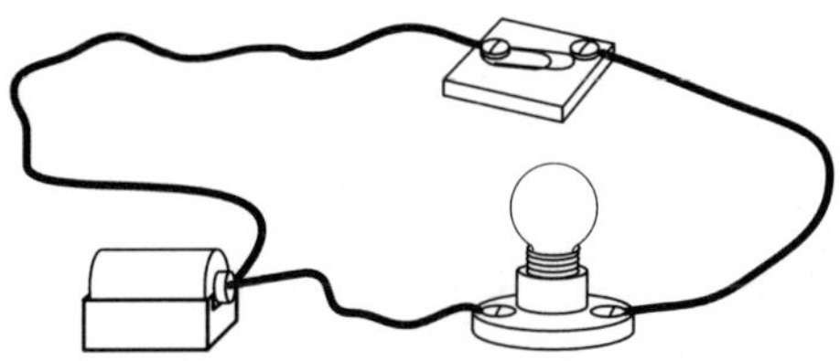

____

____

2 **What happens when each of these switches is turned on?**

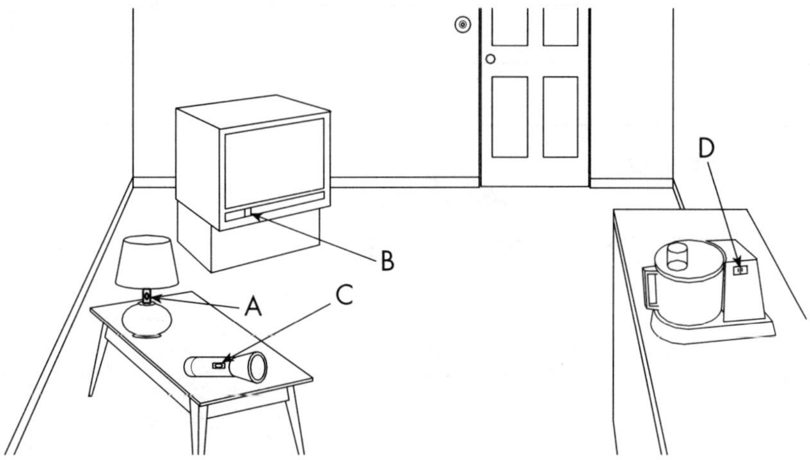

Switch A ____

Switch B ____

Switch C ____

Switch D ____

Sciencecheck © HarperCollins*Publishers* Ltd 1998

Sciencecheck	NAME	DATE
Sc4, Level 3 Test 14, Series B	**PHYSICAL PROCESSES** **Electricity** Pupils should be taught about simple electric circuits.	

3 **Jon has tried to make this bulb light. He has used four different batteries.**

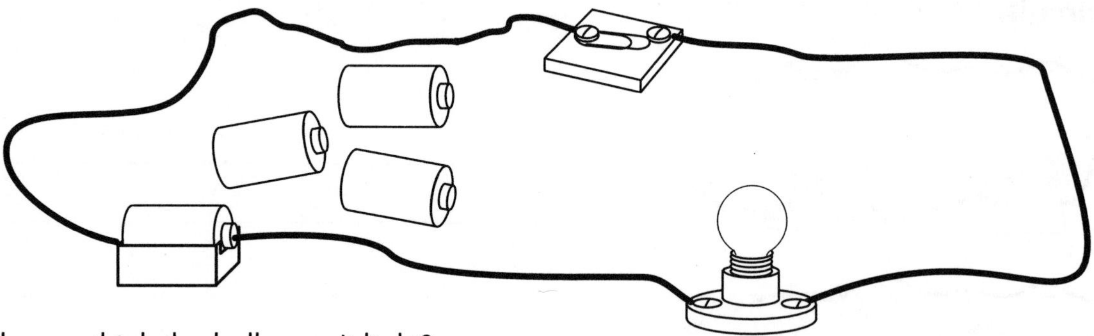

Why do you think the bulb won't light?

____

4 **Jan plays with her torch for an hour. Then the light begins to dim.**

What do you think has happened?

____

5 **Tick the things which are safe to play with.**

torch	table lamp	battery car	toaster
foodmixer	watch	hair dryer	calculator

Explain why some are dangerous.

____

____

6 **The television will not work.**

What might be wrong?

____

Sciencecheck © HarperCollinsPublishers Ltd 1998

Sciencecheck	**NAME**	**DATE**
Sc4, Level 3 / **Test 15, Series B**	**PHYSICAL PROCESSES** **Gravity and magnetism** Pupils should be taught about gravity and magnetism as forces.	

1 **Which one of these boxes would be the hardest to pick up?**

Circle the drawing.

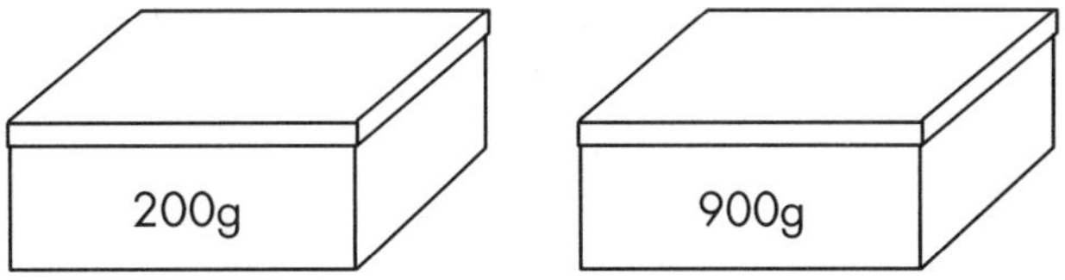

2 **Circle the drawing which shows the pull of gravity.**

3 **a.** Draw arrows to show how each apple will fall.

b. Why will each apple fall in the way you have drawn?

____

4 **Tick the sentences about magnets which are true.**

Magnets attract iron. ☐

Magnets attract all metals. ☐

Magnets attract wood. ☐

Magnets attract steel. ☐

5 **a.** Do you think magnets work through paper?

____

b. How could you find out?

____

Sciencecheck	**NAME**	**DATE**
Sc4, Level 3 **Test 16, Series B**	**PHYSICAL PROCESSES** **Friction and air resistance** Pupils should be taught about friction and air resistance as forces which slow moving objects.	

1 **Jim made two parachutes the same size.**

He put different weights on them.

Which parachute do you think will fall faster?

____

____

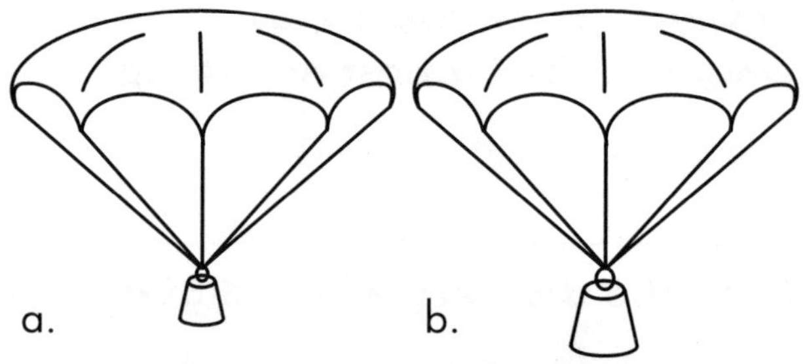

2 **Julie has made a ramp for her toy car.**

a. What will happen if she makes the slope steeper?

____

____

b. She put a piece of card on her car.

It slowed it down.

Why did this happen?

____

____

3 **It is a windy day.**

Why is it so difficult for Sarah to walk with an open umbrella?

____

4 **Julie tests how much force is needed to make her shoes slide on the kitchen floor.**

Here are her results.

	Trainer	**Boot**
Force needed to pull the shoe on the kitchen floor	4 N	2 N

a. Which shoe has the most friction?

____

b. She made the floor wet. What do you think happened to the force needed to move the shoes?

____

Sciencecheck © HarperCollins*Publishers* Ltd 1998

Sciencecheck	**NAME**	**DATE**
Sc4, Level 3 / **Test 17, Series B**	**PHYSICAL PROCESSES** **Springs and elastic bands** Pupils should be taught about the forces on springs and elastic bands.	

1 **Becky is hanging weights from springs.**

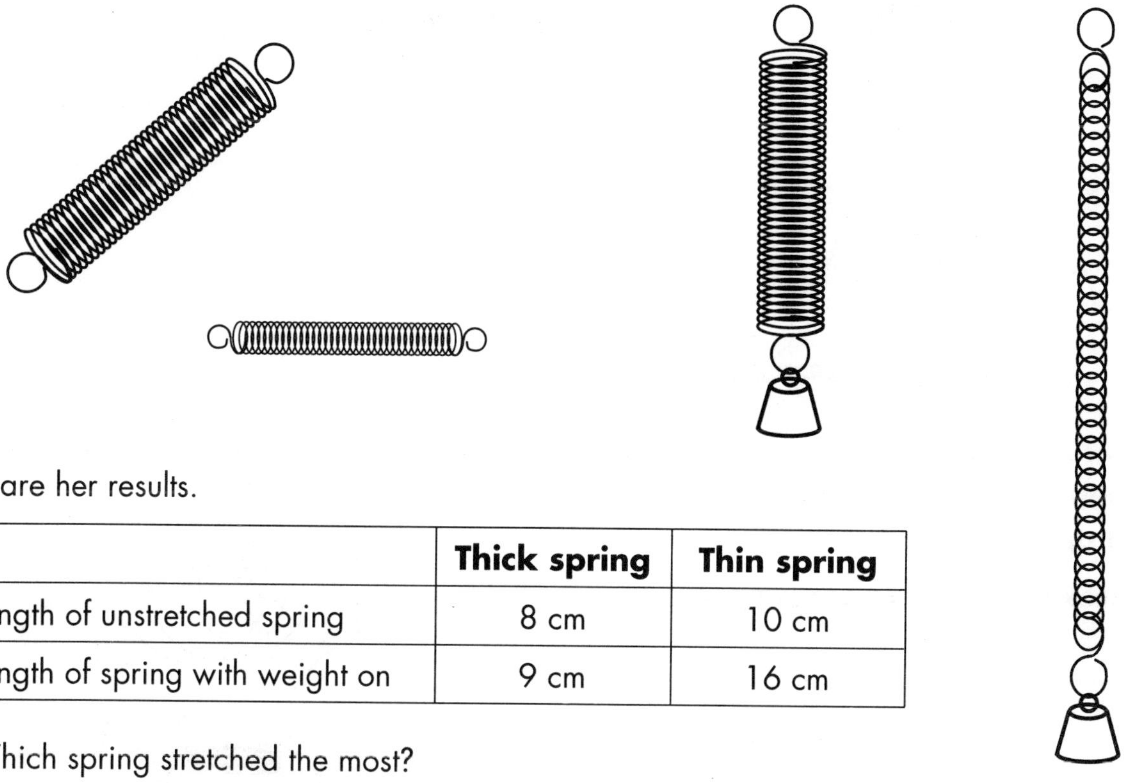

Here are her results.

	Thick spring	Thin spring
Length of unstretched spring	8 cm	10 cm
Length of spring with weight on	9 cm	16 cm

a. Which spring stretched the most?

____

b. Which spring do you think she could squash most easily?

____

2 **Becky puts some weights into two socks from the same pair.**

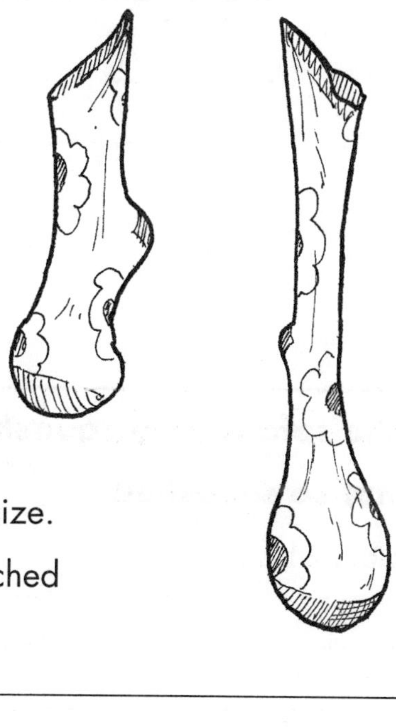

At first the socks were the same size.

Why do you think one sock stretched more than the other?

____

Sciencecheck	**NAME**	**DATE**
Sc4, Level 3	**PHYSICAL PROCESSES**	
Test 17, Series B	**Springs and elastic bands** Pupils should be taught about the forces on springs and elastic bands.	

3

What will happen to this elastic band when Ali lets go?

____

____

4 **Ali opens the box lid and a Jack-in-a-box jumps up.**

What makes the Jack-in-a-box jump up?

____

____

5

What will happen to this elastic band if more sand is added to the pot?

____

____

6 **The place where Dad sits on the sofa is very squashed.**

The place where Mum sits is not so squashed.

Think of two reasons that might explain why.

1) ______________________________

2) ______________________________

Sciencecheck © HarperCollins*Publishers* Ltd 1998

Sciencecheck	**NAME**	**DATE**
Sc4, Level 3	**PHYSICAL PROCESSES**	
Test 18, Series B	**Types of forces** Pupils should be taught about types of forces.	

1 Which of these pushes could move the trailer?

2 Bruno is holding the horse with a rope.

Which arrow shows the direction of the horse's pull? __________

Sciencecheck	**NAME**	**DATE**
Sc4, Level 3 **Test 18, Series B**	**PHYSICAL PROCESSES** **Types of forces** Pupils should be taught about types of forces.	

3 **Jim pushes an empty cart along a flat path.**

With one push the cart moves 10 metres.

He loads it with heavy bricks.

Will the loaded cart go as far with one push?

______

4 **Which team do you think will win?**

Explain your idea each time.

a.

Team A   Team B

______

______

b.

Team A   Team B

______

______

c.

Team A   Team B

______

______

Sciencecheck © HarperCollins*Publishers* Ltd 1998

Sciencecheck	**NAME**	**DATE**
Sc4, Level 3	**PHYSICAL PROCESSES**	
Test 19, Series B	**Direction of forces** Pupils should be taught that forces act in particular directions.	

1 **Join the sentence to the correct drawing.**

The car is pulling with more force.

a.

The pulling force of the strongman and the car are equal.

b.

The force of the strongman is more than the pull of the car.

c.

2 **Draw an arrow to show the direction in which these things are moving.**

a.

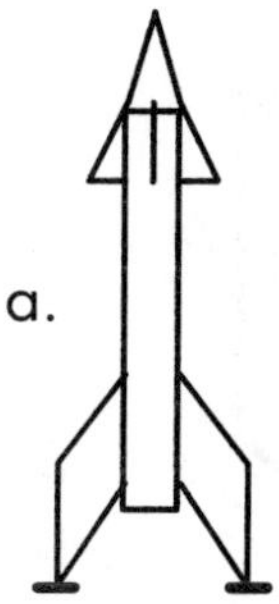

b.

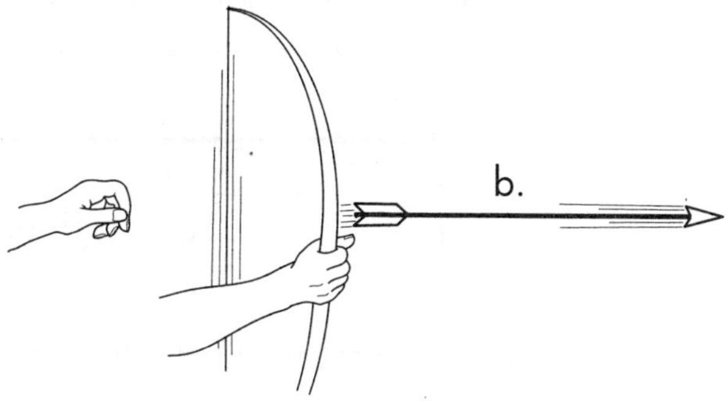

c.

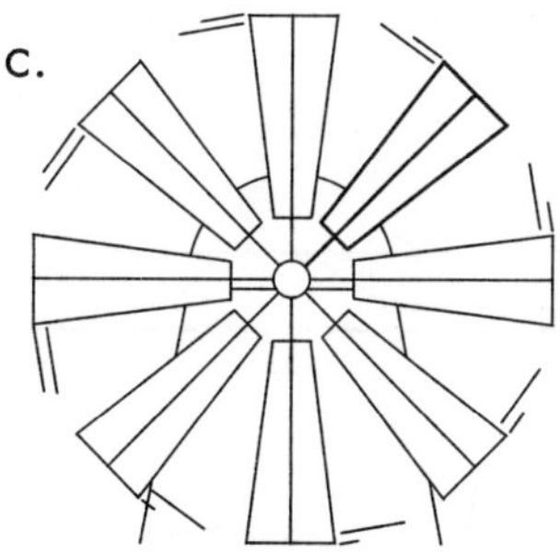

3 **What will happen to the wet sponge when it is pressed?**

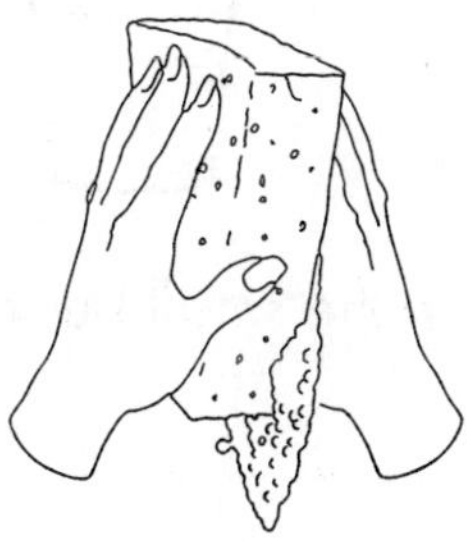

____

____

Sciencecheck	NAME	DATE
Sc4, Level 3	**PHYSICAL PROCESSES**	
Test 19, Series B	**Direction of forces** Pupils should be taught that forces act in particular directions.	

4 **Which of these bottles will fall over first?**

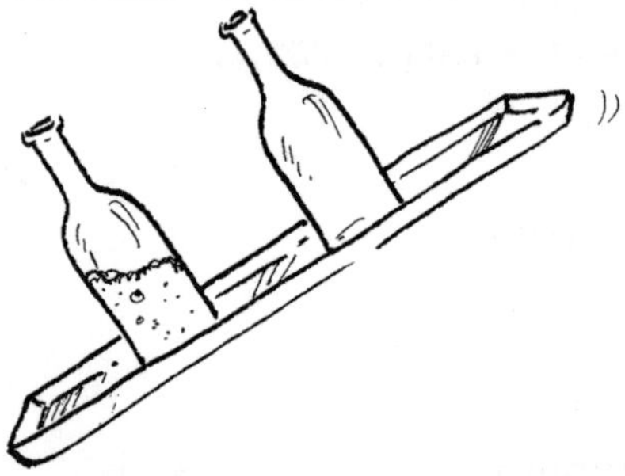

____

5 **A cork floats in water.**

Circle the best explanation.

It is cork. It is light for its size. It is smooth. It is made of wood.

6 **Plastic boxes make good boats to play with.**

a. Which of these plastic boxes is loaded with marbles?

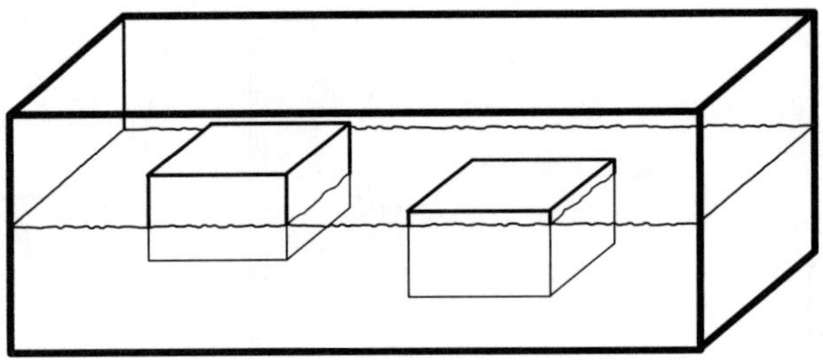

____

b. How can you tell?

____

7

a. What will happen to the spring when the small bucket is hung from it?

____

b. What will happen to the spring when the big bucket is hung from it?

____

Sciencecheck © HarperCollins*Publishers* Ltd 199

Sciencecheck	NAME	DATE
Sc4, Level 3	**PHYSICAL PROCESSES**	
Test 20, Series B	**Light** Pupils should be taught about seeing and the everyday effects of light.	

1 **Tick the materials in this list that do not let light pass through.**

glass   wood   steel   clingfilm

2 **Match the word to the explanation.**

transparent	not see-through at all
translucent	completely see-through
opaque	partly see-through

3

Who can see Jim?

____

4 **Draw a line connecting the shadow to the object.**

Sciencecheck	**NAME**	**DATE**
Sc4, Level 3	**PHYSICAL PROCESSES**	
Test 20, Series B	**Light** Pupils should be taught about seeing and the everyday effects of light.	

5 **Why does Jim wear his baseball cap on a sunny day?**

____

6 **Jim's torch shows up well in his bedroom at night.**

It does not show up well by day.

Explain why.

____

7 **Why is it hard to see things in a dark country lane at night?**

____

8 **List these light sources in order of brightness.**

a torch   the Sun   a street lamp

____

9 **Sharma has some coloured sweet wrappers and a torch.**

How could he change the colour of the torchlight?

____

10 **Match the light to where you might see it.**

bike   kitchen   living room   car   street

Sciencecheck © HarperCollins*Publishers* Ltd 199

Sciencecheck	**NAME**	**DATE**
Sc4, Level 3	**PHYSICAL PROCESSES**	
Test 21, Series B	**Sound** Pupils should be taught about the way sounds are made by vibrating objects.	

1 **What are these people doing to protect their ears from loud noises?**

____

2 **Emma thinks that sound travels through the floor.**

a. How could she test her idea?

____

b. Do you think her idea is right?

____

3 **Write about how Claire hears the sound from the radio.**

____

____

4 **Put these sounds in order from the loudest to the quietest.**

a. road drill bird singing big dog barking

____

b. bike car lorry

____

Sciencecheck	**NAME**	**DATE**
Sc4, Level 3	**PHYSICAL PROCESSES**	
Test 21, Series B	**Sound** Pupils should be taught about the way sounds are made by vibrating objects.	

5 **Jon puts his head under water at the swimming pool.**

He can hear someone tapping on the sides of the pool.

a. Do you think sound travels through water?

___

b. How do you know?

___

6

Andrew can hear the sound made by the mouse.

Why can't Amy hear it?

___

7 Colour blue the instruments which are played by hitting.

Colour green the instruments which are played by blowing.

Colour red the instruments which make a sound with strings.

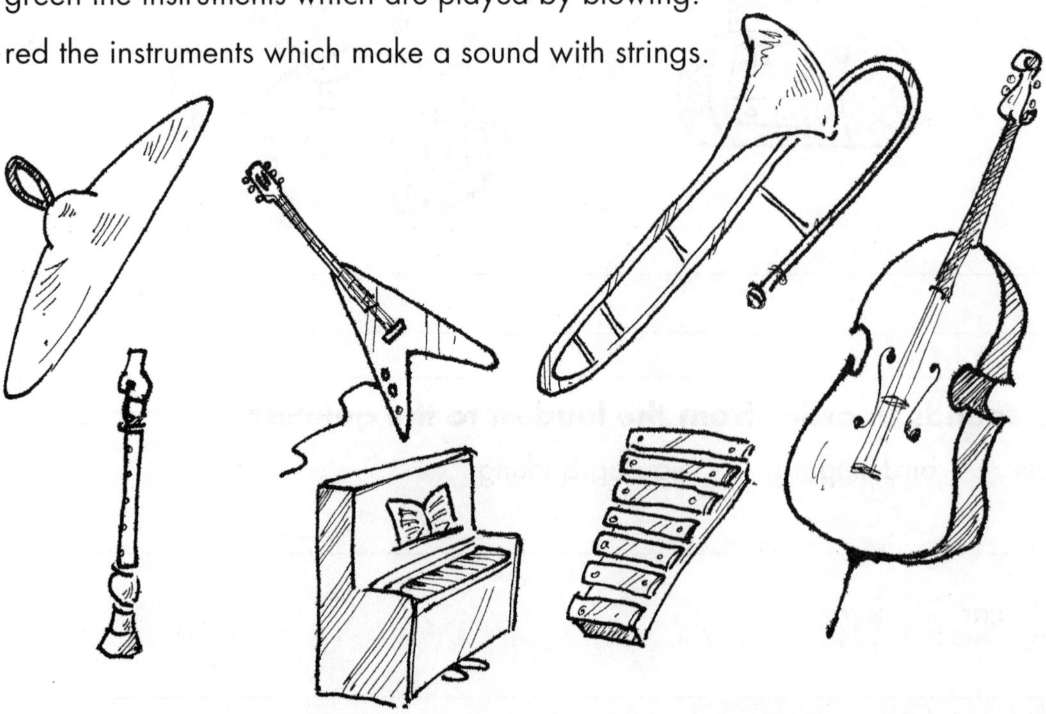

 Sciencecheck © HarperCollins*Publishers* Ltd 1998

Sciencecheck	**NAME**	**DATE**
Sc4, Level 3	**PHYSICAL PROCESSES**	
Test 22, Series B	**The Earth and beyond** Pupils should be taught about some of the periodic changes in the position of the Earth, Moon and Sun.	

1 **What shape is the Earth?**

Tick one box.

a circle ☐

a sphere ☐

flat ☐

a cube ☐

2 **Clouds are nearer to the Earth than the stars.**

How do you know?

____

3 **During the day, what is our main source of light?**

____

4 **Look at this table.**

a. At what time of day is the stick's shadow shortest? __________

Time of day	Length of shadow
2 pm	20 cm
3 pm	26 cm
6 pm	47 cm

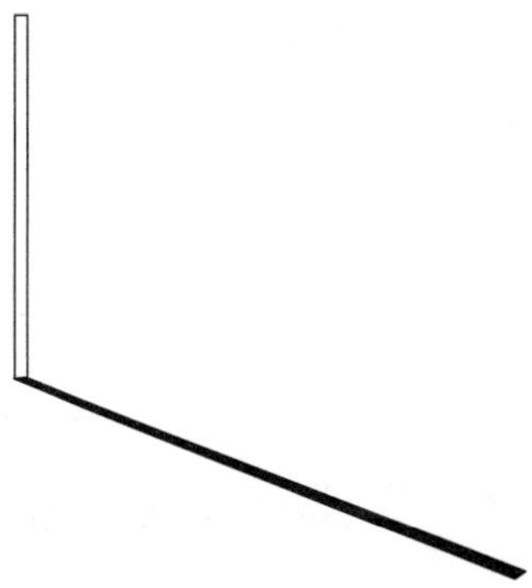

b. Why is the shadow getting longer?

____

5 **Write these three things in order of size:**

Earth Moon Sun

____

6 **How long does it take for the Earth to do one turn on its axis?**

____

7 **How long does it take for the Earth to go all the way round the Sun?**

____

Sciencecheck © HarperCollins*Publishers* Ltd 1998

One sheet only

Test 1 Planning investigations

1 **a.** A timed writing test with both hands.
b. Write the same words for each test using the same writing tools.

2 **a.** Windowsill and cupboard **b.** The windowsill pot

3 **a.** They could time how long it takes to dissolve small amounts of both types in water keeping all factors the same except for the type of sugars.
b. The amount of water and sugar, the temperature of the water, the time of stirring or the number of stirs.

4 To make sure that they do not pick their favourite colour, but their favourite taste.

Test 2 Obtaining evidence

1
stopclock	measuring time
spring balance	measuring weight
thermometer	measuring temperature
ruler	measuring length

2
Cup	Temperature
warm water	20°C
hot water	60°C
cold water	5°C

3 **a.** One week **b.** The wide one (A).
c. It has the largest surface area from which the water can evaporate.

Test 3 Considering evidence

1 **a.** The plant in the box did not get enough light.

2 **a.** On the wooden floor. **b.** On the carpet. **c.** No

3 **a.** Mice **b.** A meat-eater

4 The more bricks she uses, the further the car goes, or the distance travelled increases by 5 cm for each brick.

5 **a.** 9 **b.**

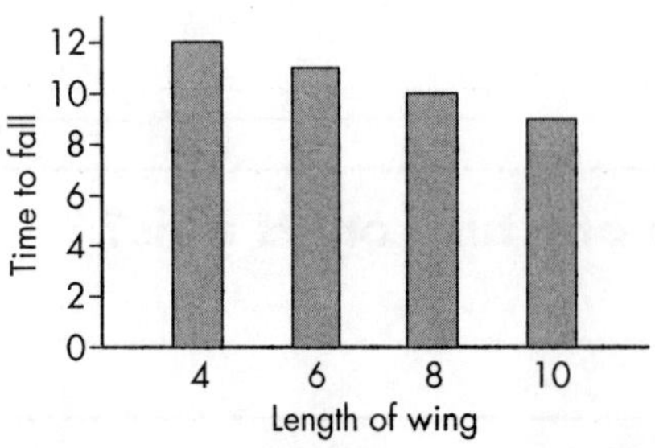

c. Chart to show how the size of a spinner wing affects the time it takes to fall
d. shorter **e.** slowly

Test 4 Life processes

1

Alive	**Not Alive**
1 people	1 boats
2 dog	2 beach ball
3 crab	3 stones/pebbles/sand
4 bird	4 tractor
Could also include seaweed and mussels.	Could also include buckets and spades.

2 We know the animals are alive because they: breathe, feed, move and may have babies and they respond to stimulus such as light or noise.

3

	Breathe	**Feed**	**Grow**
dog	✓	✓	✓
doll			
tree	✓ Children may tick here. This is correct since plants exchange gases and respire in a way similar to animals, but this does not need to be taught at this level.	✓ Plants make food from sunlight, water and carbon dioxide, so plants could be said to 'feed' on these.	✓
aeroplane			

4 **a.** Expect the children to write about the way that people grow larger and become adult. Mothers give birth to children. The mother eventually becomes old and dies.
b. Children should write about the way that tadpoles hatch from an egg. They should describe how the tadpoles change as they become adults.
c. The human is born looking like its mother but the tadpole does not look much like its mother/the human is born alive and not from an egg.

5
human — born live from its mother
bird — egg with a hard shell
frog — tadpole
butterfly/moth — caterpillar/pupa

Butterflies and moths start life as an egg but the adult emerges from a pupa.

Test 5 Humans as organisms

1 He can brush them / eat fruit / drink milk and eat cheese or foods rich in calcium / avoid sugary foods / visit the dentist regularly.

2 **a.** incisors
b. molars

3 Hearing and sight should be underlined. (Smell is not important although traffic does smell.)

4

brain	breathe
lungs	digests food
stomach	thinks

5 The skull, ribs and backbone should be correctly labelled.

Test 6 Healthy living

1

Activity	Pulse rate
sleeping	fast
skipping	slow
walking	very fast

2 fruit juice
apple
cheese sandwich
low fat yoghurt
carrot sticks

Do these things
Drink plenty of water
Use protection cream in the sun
Eat fruit
Get a good night's sleep
Take regular exercise
Eat good meals

Don't do these things
Smoke
Eat lots of toffee
Take drugs
Eat lots of fat

Test 7 Green plants

1

Roots	take up water and nutrients and hold the plant in the soil.
Leaves	make food from sunlight (water and carbon dioxide), evaporate water and exchange gases.
Flowers	attract insects to pollinate and produce seeds.
Seeds	they grow into new plants.
Flower stem	supports the flowers, leaves and seeds.

2

He watered one and kept it in a bright place.	It grew well.
He forgot to water one.	It shrivelled, went brown and died.
He watered one but kept it in a dark cupboard.	It went yellow and died.

3

Box	Growth of cress
B	tall and strong
A	tall and spindly
C	growing to one side

4 **a.** The grass will be yellow.
b. It does not get sunlight *(green chlorophyll is not produced by the plant)*.
c. She should move her hutch to a different place every few days or prop it up on bricks.

5 Water and sunlight should be circled. All the others can be substituted with other materials – pond plants, for example, do not need soil.

6 **a.** The first pot grew best.
b. It was taller and had more fruit
c. The fertiliser helped it grow better.

Test 8 Variation and classification

1

Eats meat	Eats plants
owl	cow
cat	rabbit
dog	sheep
	snail

2 **a.**

No legs	Six legs	More than six legs
earthworm	wasp	millipede
snail	ant	woodlouse

b. The children should add one other small animal to each column.
c. Bee/wasp, worm or snake, millipede or centipede.

3

Conifer	Deciduous
pine, fir, cedar	oak, sycamore, birch

4 Animal A is a sheep.
Animal B is a cat.
Animal C is a fish.
Animal D is a snake.

Test 9 Living things in their environment (adaptation)

1 Fish have fins and gills. They are shaped for moving easily through water.

2 Camels can live easily in the desert because they can store water, their feet do not sink in the sand and their eyelashes stop sand getting into their eyes.

3 **a.** A Polar bear has a thick warm coat which is white for camouflage.
b. An otter is a good swimmer / it has webbed feet / it has a flat tail / it has a waterproof coat.
c. A lion can run fast / it is good at ambushing animals / it has sharp claws / it has sharp teeth / it is very large and strong.

4

Polar bears have thick coats…	…to stop animals eating them.
Eagles have sharp claws…	…to keep them warm.
Blackberries have thorns…	…to catch earthworms.
Moles dig through the earth…	…to hold on to their prey.

5

Spider	traps food in web (some pounce on prey)
Wildcat	creeps up on its prey and grabs it with claws
Hawk	drops on prey and grabs with talons

Test 10 Grouping and classifying

1 Does conduct electricity: tin can, metal scissors, gold ring
Does not conduct electricity: wood, wool, cotton, stone, fur

2 **a.** These should be ticked: paper, thin card, wooden twig.
b. It is stiff. It will not bend when it is pushed and pulled.

3 **a.** Examples include plastic ruler, plastic bag.
b. Examples include Lego bricks, cases of computers and televisions.
c. Various answers e.g. plastic beaker or food container or plastic bag.
d. Various answers e.g. plastic computer casing.

4 **a.** These should be ticked: scissors, pin, spoon, paperclip.
b. iron or steel (do not accept metal)

5 Her car is made of metal because, for example, it is strong, hard and shiny.
Her teddy is made of fabric because, for example, it is soft and cuddly.
Her boat is made of wood because, for example, it will float.

6 popcorn, flour, butter

7 Flour is a powder. ✓
Some glass is transparent. ✓
Woollen clothes come from animals ✓

Test 11 Changing materials

1 **a.** Zoe's water freezes. **b.** Ann's water goes cold but stays liquid.

2 These should be ticked: salt, sugar.

3 **a.** The word 'freeze' should be circled.
b. Water temperature is below 0°C.
c. They melt and change to water.

4 **a.** It feels soft. (Children might correctly add gritty, heavy, cold, sticky.)
b. It feels hard. (Children might correctly add smooth, light, silky.)
c. She could add water to it / soak it in water.
d. It is darker in colour.
e. She could cover it with a paper towel / a plastic bag or any other sensible idea.

5 **a.** Ice-cream melts in warm weather. **b.** Put it in a freezer / fridge (for a short time only).

6 **a.** Wool soaks up water / it changes shape.
b. Nylon is very stretchy / it can be see-through.

7 These should be ticked: jam, chocolate, butter, jelly.

8 When an egg is fried the white is no longer see-through. The egg becomes harder – it changes from a liquid to a solid.

9 It goes brown and usually softer.

10 Paper, bread, wax, plastic and cloth should be circled.

Test 12 Separating mixtures

1 He can catch the peas in a sieve and let the water fall through the mesh.

2 He can use a magnet to attract the steel paperclips.

3 **a.** The wood floats and the screws sink.
b. The screws will go rusty.

4 Wood shavings are attracted to a magnet.
Magnets attract steel pins. ✓
Plastic is sometimes attracted to a magnet.
All metals are attracted to a magnet.
Iron filings are attracted to a magnet. ✓

5 sweets and sugar ✓
sugar and salt (but some children may suggest coarse salt and icing sugar)
potatoes and water ✓
milk and water

6 Sieving

Test 13 Using materials

1

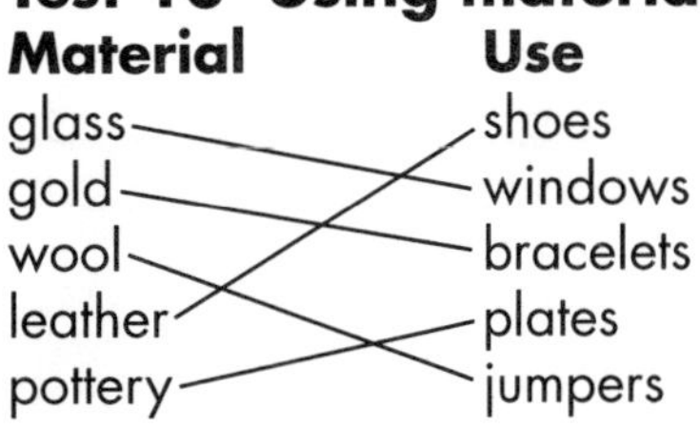

2 Children may write two from (and others)
wool – jumper
leather – belt / shoes
metal – watch
plastic – watch
rubber – shoe soles
cotton – trousers, socks
nylon – top
wood – pencil
plastic – pen

3 **a.** Coins are made from metal.
b. Card would wear out too quickly / get soggy / bend.

4 **a.**

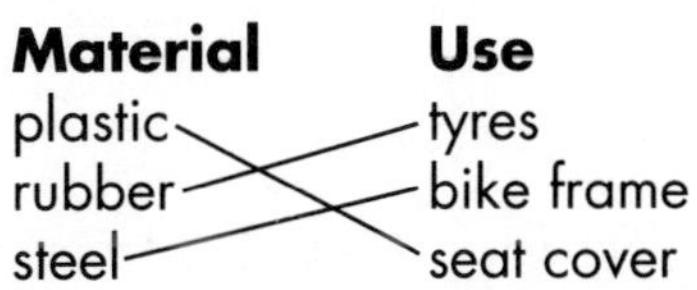

b. Steel is used for the chain because it is strong.

5 It is see-through and it can be made into sheets.

6 Glass and iron should be circled.

Test 14 Electricity

1 **a.** The circuit is incomplete because one of the leads is not connected.
b. The bulb is not in the circuit.
c. There is no battery in the circuit.
d. The circuit is incomplete because both leads go to the same side of the bulb.

2 The battery may be flat / there may be a break in the circuit / the bulb holder might be faulty.

3 Switch A: The light is lit.
Switch B: The TV comes on.
Switch C: The kettle heats up.
Switch D: The radio comes on.

4 The battery is going flat, or the battery is running out of electricity.

Test 15 Gravity and magnetism

1 7 kg

2 The picture with the arrow down should be circled.

3 **a.** The arrows should all point towards the Earth.
b. The pull of gravity is always towards the Earth.

4 North poles attract north poles.
North poles repel south poles.
South poles repel south poles. ✓

5 It showed that the force of magnetism can work through a piece of wood.

6 There is something made from iron or steel inside the matchbox.

Test 16 Friction and air resistance

1 The larger parachute had more air resistance.

2 **a.** The toy will go faster. **b.** The cloak increased the air resistance of the toy.

3 She could time how long she takes to run the same distance with and without wearing her jacket.

4 **a.** The carpet **b.** The tiles

Test 17 Springs and elastic bands

1 **a.** The thin band
b. They will return to their original length.

2 One leg has a heavier mass / weight than the other.

3 It will bounce up and get bigger.

4 It will spring back and get smaller.

5 It will stretch / get longer.

Test 18 Types of forces

1 The bulldozer and bull

2 **a.** The big hammer **b.** One or two hits **c.** Seven or more

3 The cart is heavier with Fatima and won't move as far with the same push.

4 **a.** Team B because they have a bigger pull. **b.** Team A because their load is lighter.
c. Team B because they can produce a bigger pull than A.

Test 19 Direction of forces

1 b The dog is pulling with more force.
c The pulling force of the dog and the boy are equal.
a The force of the boy is more than the pull of the dog.

2 **a.** Arrow pointed upwards.
b. Arrow pointed towards the book.
c. Arrow pointed towards the ball.

3 It will be dented / squashed.

4 **a.** It will probably snap (the long line sugggests a big force).
b. It may stretch a tiny bit / nothing (the short line suggests a small force and the rope can easily withstand that).

5 The ball should be floating at a sensible level (about one-third to two-thirds down) and the stone should be resting on the bottom.

6 **a.** a is loaded
b. It is lower in the water.

Test 20 Light

1 Glass and clingfilm should be ticked.

2

transparent	glass, clear plastic
translucent	frosted glass, bubble wrap
opaque	wood, tin can

3 Emma is trying to read where there is not enough light to see her book.

4 Objects should be connected to the correct shadows.

5 To protect her eyes from strong sunlight.

6 Daylight is stronger than candlelight and so the candle does not seem as bright as it does in the dark. *(Also eyes are more sensitive to light in low light conditions – the pupils are more open.)*

7 Because we need light to see things.

8 football-ground floodlights
a car headlight
a pen torch

Test 21 Sound

1 To prevent loud noises from damaging their ears.

2 **a.** Best idea is:
she could put her ear to a brick wall and try to hear sounds in the next room
or
she could tap one end of a brick gently while she puts her ear to the other end to see if she can hear the taps *(but she would hear the sound through the air anyway).*
b. Answers such as: I have heard sounds through brick walls / I know that sounds travel through solids.

3 Link the bell with ...The bell vibrates.
Link the ear with ...The sound enters the person's ear
Link the air with ...The sound travels through the air.

4 someone shouting ✓
teacher's whistle ✓

5 Sound travels through the rail.

6 Karen is very close to the kitten, Richard is a little distance away.

7 blue (hitting): drum xylophone
green (blowing): whistle trumpet flute
red (strings): violin guitar

Test 22 The Earth and beyond

1 A sphere

2 They can move in front of the Sun.

3 Link the first sentence with Sun.
Link the second sentence with the space between the Sun and Earth.
Link the third sentence with the place where light hits the Earth.

4 **a.** false **b.** true **c.** true **d.** true

5 11 am

6 No, it would melt / burn before it reached the Sun.

7

Test 1 Planning investigations

1 **a.** He could stand a long way from a chart with small and large letters and close one eye at a time to see which eye can read the smallest letters.
Or
He could close his right eye and walk towards a newspaper to see how far away he is when he can see the headline with his left eye. He could then do the same for the other eye.
b. He could use the same chart for both eyes and stay at the same distance for the first test.
He could use the same chart for both eyes in the second test.

2 She could water 3 pots of plants with different amounts of water, keeping one pot soaking wet. She could do this for a week and compare the three plants for colour, height and size of leaves.

3 **a.** They could put some sugar into two different containers with equal volumes of water, only stirring one container. They could then time how long it takes the sugar in each to dissolve.
b. The amount of water, the amount of sugar, the temperature of the water.

4 They will not be influenced by what they can see – they might imagine they can hear something if they see the noise being made.

5 The children should all stand in the same starting place and throw the same weight ball.

Test 2 Obtaining evidence

1

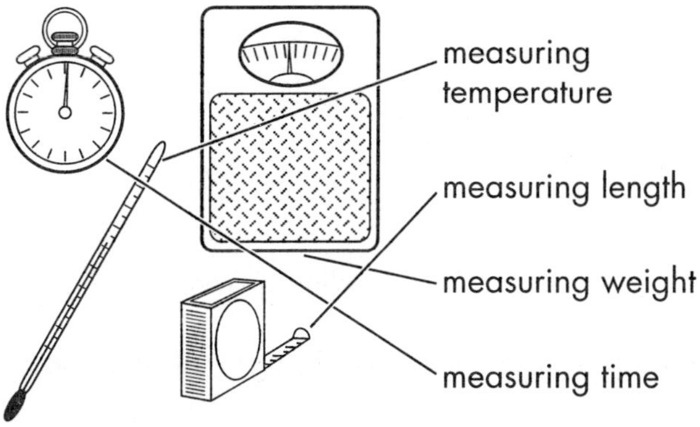

2

Place	Temperature
in a room	20°C
in a fridge	4°C
on a radiator	45°C

3 **a.** one hour
b. By the radiator if the test is done in winter. On the windowsill in the sun might be a better answer in summer. The answers given will be affected by the types of classroom and the season of the year.
c. It is warmest / driest there.

Test 3 Considering evidence

1 **a.** It did not get any light. **b.** It did get light.
c. It would become green again.

2 **a.** The rubber ball **b.** The sponge ball
c. Any answer less than 2 is acceptable since plasticine would simply "splat" rather than bounce.

3 **a.** Grass **b.** Herbivore

4 The higher the ramp, the further the car goes. The blue car always goes further than the red car.

5 **a.**

Number of paperclips	Time to fall (seconds)
1	4
2	$3\frac{1}{2}$
3	3
4	$2\frac{1}{2}$
5	2

b. A table to show how long it took for some parachutes to fall
c. The more paperclips on a parachute, the faster it fell,
or the heavier the parachute, the faster it fell.

Test 4 Life processes

1

Alive	Not Alive
1 cows	1 barn
2 pig	2 scarecrow
3 farmer	3 tractor
4 chickens	4 gate

2 We know that plants are alive because they: make food from sunlight, move, grow, produce new plants / reproduce and they 'breathe' by exchanging gases.

3

	Grow	Move by itself	Reproduce (have young)
cow	✓	✓	✓
daisy	✓	✓ daisies follow the Sun across the sky each day and grow towards the light	✓
beetle	✓	✓	✓
piece of wood			

4 **a.** The adult duck lays an egg. When it hatches the duckling emerges. The duckling grows up to be an adult duck. The adult eventually grows old and dies.
b. The butterfly starts as an egg which hatches into a caterpillar. The caterpillar changes into a pupa. The butterfly comes out of the pupa and then lays eggs.

5

cat	born alive from its mother
hen	egg with a hard shell
frog	spawn
moth	caterpillar/pupa

Moths and caterpillars do originally come from an egg, but the adult emerges from the pupa.

Test 5 Humans as organisms

1

Activity	Pulse rate
sitting	slow
swimming	very fast
walking	fast

2 Hearing and sight should be underlined. (Smell is not important although traffic does smell.)

3

skin	protect the ends of fingers
teeth	keeps body warm and protects the head
fingernails	break up food
hair	covers and protects the body

4

Your skull protects your brain.	true
Your backbone is made up many small bones.	true
Your spine protects your feet.	false
Your bones are made from hard skin.	false
Your muscles are attached to your bones.	true

5 You would probably die if you did not drink (and if you did not eat food which contained a great deal of water).

6 You get all your energy from food, so if you did not eat you would not have any energy.

7 You would get ill / You would fall over and sleep anyway.

Test 6 Healthy living

1 The following foods should be circled:
cheese, chips, crisps, pork pies, margarine, chocolate.

2 **a.** She says he should eat fewer sweets because they will cause his teeth to decay and may make him overweight.
b. Fruit and vegetables have lots of vitamins and will help clean his teeth.

3

Do these things	Don't do these things
Walk	Drink lots of alcohol
Eat good food	Eat lots of crisps
Eat fruit	Watch TV all day
Wear a hat on sunny days	
Swim	
Brush teeth	
Wash every day	

4 swimming, walking, running, aerobics, football training...

Test 7 Green plants

1

Seeds	produce new plants
Trunk	holds up the branches and leaves
Roots	hold the tree in the ground and draw up water

2

He waters it.	healthy
He forgets to water it for a week.	drooping
He forgets to water it for two weeks.	dead

3 The cress seeds grown in the cupboard did not get enough light and so did not grow well.

4 **a.** The grass will be yellow. **b.** The grass will be green. **c.** The grass will be yellow.

5 Water and sunlight. (Plants also need carbon dioxide and oxygen but children are unlikely to say this – some may correctly suggest air.)

Test 8 Variation and classification

1 **a, b.**

Carnivore	**Herbivore**
kestrel	sheep
dog	cow
lion	slug
plus one other	plus one other

2 Animal A is a wasp.
Animal B is a woodlouse.
Animal C is a snail.
Animal D is a slug.

3 Plant A is a daffodil.
Plant B is a tulip.
Plant C is a dandelion.
Plant D is a daisy.

Test 9 Living things in their environment (adaptation)

1 Ducks have webbed feet to help them swim and their feathers are waterproof.

2 Polar bears have very thick coats, they have sharp claws and are very large.

3 Woodlice like cool, damp and dark conditions. They are also protected from predators under stones.

4

Cats have sharp claws	to hold their prey.
Birds have wings	to gnaw hard food.
Kangaroos have strong back legs	to fly.
Rats have sharp teeth	to hop long distances.

5

Eagle	swoops down and grabs animal in its claws
Crocodile	swims quietly up to animal and grabs it in its mouth
Tiger	creeps up and grabs the animal in its claws and teeth.

Test 10 Grouping and classifying

1

Soaks up water	Does not soak up water
sawdust	metal
cotton cloth	plastic
soil	glass
paper	

2 **a.** These should be ticked: biscuit, matchstick, potato crisp.
b. 'Flexible' or 'soft' should be circled.

3 **a.** Plastic bag should be circled.
b. It will not let the bread dry out.

4 chalk

5 ...it makes a sound / it's safe to suck.
...it is soft to cuddle.
...they are light, strong and heavier than plastic / they do not fall over so easily.

6 iron wood card cotton wool

7 These should be in the metal bin: drink can, bean can, foil pie dish, sardine tin.
These should be in the plastic bin: yoghurt pot, margarine tub, polythene bag.
These should be in the glass bin: milk bottle, jam jar.

Test 11 Changing materials

1 **a.** Ice in the oven will melt and then get warm. It might then boil and / or evaporate.
b. Cold water in the oven will get warm. It might then boil and / or evaporate.

2 These should be ticked: cork, wood, paper.

3 **a.** 'Melt' should be circled.
b. When its temperature is above 0°C.

4 **a.** It feels soft / sticky / smooth / bendy / squashy.
b. It feels harder / crisper.
c. No

5 They go soft / squashy.

6 It is waterproof / flexible / does not let water in / cheap and easy to make.

7 **a.** The inside of the egg turns from a liquid to a solid. The white part does not stay see-through.
b. No

Test 12 Separating mixtures

1 He can pick the big pieces of mud off the potatoes then wash off the smaller pieces.

2 He can use a magnet to attract the nails.

3 **a.** The polystyrene floats and the nails sink.
b. They will go rusty.

4 Magnets can attract brass screws.
Only things made of iron and steel are attracted to a magnet. ✓ (apart from cobalt and nickel)
Glass is sometimes attracted to a magnet.
Magnets can be used to pick up steel pins. ✓
Pencil shavings are attracted to a magnet.

5 nuts and flour ✓
beaten egg and milk
salt and water
sand and pebbles ✓

6 Sieving

Test 13 Using materials

1

Material	Use
glass	mirror
copper	electrical wire
cotton	clothes
steel	scissors
wood	doors

2 These might include:
glass – windows
plastic – chair
metal – chair / table frame
wood – floor / table
cloth – curtains

3 Tiles: they are easy to clean
Towels: they soak up water
Soap: it gets you clean
Water: it can be used to wash things

4 Cloth: keeps you warm
Carpet: warm to walk on
Curtain material: keeps out the light

5 **a.** Plastic **b.** Metal would be too stiff and heavy.

6 **a.**

Material	Use
cloth	carpets
rubber	tyres
steel	roof
glass	windscreen

b. Metal would be too cold / hard for a seat cover.

7 metal: trumpet; wood: violin; plastic: school recorder

8 Glass, pottery and metal should be circled.

9 Wood, plastic and metal should be circled.

Test 14 Electricity

1 **a.** The leads are not connected to the bulb.
b. The battery is not inserted into the battery holder.
c. There are no wires from the battery holder to complete the circuit.
d. Both wires are going to one side of the battery holder so there is no complete circuit.

2 Switch A: The light will go on.
Switch B: The TV will switch on.
Switch C: The torch will light.
Switch D: The foodmixer will work

3 The bulb may be broken or there may be a damaged wire or faulty bulb holder.

4 The batteries are getting flat (running out of electricity is acceptable).

5 Torch, battery car, watch, calculator should be ticked.
The others all use mains electricity.

6 It might not be switched on, plugged in, there is a power cut, the fuse has gone, it is broken, the controller's batteries are worn out.

Test 15 Gravity and magnetism

1 900 g

2 The drawing with the arrow pointing downwards should be circled.

3 **a.** The arrows should all point towards the globe.
b. The apple will always be attracted to Earth because gravity is the pull of the Earth.

4 Magnets attract iron. ✓
Magnets attract all metals.
Magnets attract wood.
Magnets attract steel. ✓

5 **a.** and **b.** Yes. You could put something made from iron or steel, such as a paperclip, on one side of a sheet of paper and try to move it using a magnet on the other side.

Test 16 Friction and air resistance

1 The one with the heavier weight (b).
Without the parachute both weights should fall at the same speed. However, using parachutes increases the air resistance on the weights which slows the smaller weight more than the bigger one.

2 **a.** The car will go further.
b. The air resistance increased.

3 The umbrella resists the air as she walks / it increases her air resistance.

4 **a.** trainer
b. She needed less force because the water acted as a lubricant and reduced the friction between the shoes and the floor.

Test 17 Springs and elastic bands

1 **a.** The thin spring **b.** The thin spring

2 One sock has a heavier mass / weight inside it than the other.

3 It will ping away from him when he lets go.

4 A spring which has been compressed by the lid is released when the lid is opened.

5 It will be stretched further.

6 **a.** Dad is heavier than Mum. **b.** Dad sits on his place on the sofa more often than Mum sits on hers.

Test 18 Types of forces

1 The horse and bulldozer.

2 The arrow marked x.

3 When the cart is loaded the same push will only move the cart a short distance.

4 **a.** Team B because team B can push harder. **b.** Team A because team A has only a small weight.
c. Team A because team A can push harder than B.

Test 19 Directions of forces

1 A = The force of the strongman is more than the pull of the car.
B = The car is pulling with more force.
C = The pulling force of the strongman and the car are equal.

2 **a.** Arrow pointing upwards. **b.** Horizontal arrow.
c. Arrow in a circular direction (if referring to sails). However, some children may draw a line to show the direction of the wind which will be towards the sails.

3 It will be squashed / look smaller (some children might say that water will be squeezed out).

4 The empty bottle will fall over first because the quarter-full bottle has a lower centre of gravity / it is more stable / its weight is lower down and it is more stable.

5 It is light for its size.

6 **a.** The one which is lower in the water.
b. It is lower in the water because the load in the box is pushing it further down into the water.

7 **a.** It will stretch a little way when the small bucket is attached.
b. It will stretch more when the big bucket is attached.

Test 20 Light

1 Wood and steel should be ticked.

2

transparent	completely see-through
translucent	partly see-through
opaque	not see-through at all

3 Chris

4 The shadows should match the objects.

5 To protect his eyes/ face from bright sunlight.

6 Daylight is stronger than torchlight and so the torch does not seem as bright as it does in the dark.

7 Because there is so little light / because we need light to see things.

8 the Sun, a street lamp, a torch

9 He could shine the torch through the wrapper.

10
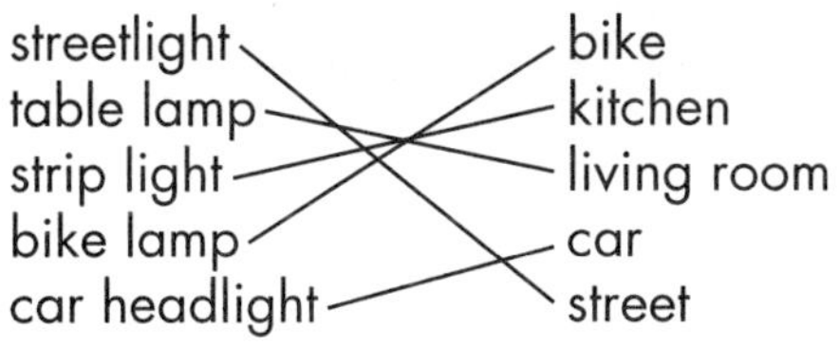

Test 21 Sound

1 They are wearing ear protectors.

2 **a.** She could put her ear to the floor and ask someone to tap on it lightly as far away as possible. She may be able to hear the sound through the air but she would notice that she heard the tapping more clearly through the wood.
b. Yes – sounds travel through solid materials.

3 The sounds waves travel from the radio to her ear.

4 **a.** Road drill, big dog barking, bird singing. **b.** Lorry, car, bike

5 **a.** Yes
b. Personal anecdote or refer to text which says boy can hear the tapping through the water.

6 Andrew is very close to the mouse, Amy is further away.

7 Blue: cymbal, glockenspiel; green: recorder, trombone; red: piano, cello, electric guitar.

Test 22 The Earth and beyond

1 A sphere

2 They can be seen to move in front of them at night.

3 The Sun

4 **a.** 2 pm **b.** The shadow is getting longer because the Sun is getting lower in the sky.

5 Sun Earth Moon

6 24 hours / 1 day

7 A year / $365\frac{1}{4}$ days

Glossary

air resistance	the force which slows objects as they go through the air
battery	this gives a flow of electricity in a circuit
carnivore	an animal which eats other animals
caterpillar	one of the stages in a butterfly's life cycle
circuit	a series of wires and other components which carry electricity
conductor	a material which lets electricity / heat travel through it
evaporate	change from a liquid to a gas
food chain	a food chain shows you which animals eat plants and which animals eat other animals. A food chain always starts with a plant and ends with the animal which nothing else eats.
freeze	change from a liquid to a solid
friction	the force which slows moving objects
gravity	the pull of the Earth on objects
heart	the organ which pumps blood around the body
herbivore	an animal which eats plants
insulator	a material which does not let electricity / heat travel through it
kilograms	the measure of mass
lungs	the organs which take in oxygen from the air
melt	change from a solid to a liquid
muscle	parts of the body which can stretch and get smaller
newtons	the measure of force
petal	these surround the sexual parts of a flower
predator	an animal which hunts other animals
prey	an animal which is hunted by other animals
pulse	the bump caused by each beat of your heart
reflection	the way light is bounced off a surface
seed	part of a plant made by a flower which can grow into a new plant
seedling	a small plant growing from a seed
stomach	part of your body where food is digested
thermometer	used to measure the temperature of an object

Sciencecheck © HarperCollins*Publishers* Ltd 1998

Record sheets

This simple chart can be used to indicate the results of your teacher assessment. It is related to the level descriptions only.
You may decide to indicate that a child has definitely achieved a level by ⊠.
Indicate uncertainty by /.

Name	**Level 2**				**Level 3**			
	AT 1	**AT 2**	**AT 3**	**AT 4**	**AT 1**	**AT 2**	**AT 3**	**AT 4**

Name	Level 4				Level 5			
	AT 1	AT 2	AT 3	AT 4	AT 1	AT 2	AT 3	AT 4

Sciencecheck © HarperCollinsPublishers Ltd 1998

GCSE German for OCR

Teacher's Book

Kirsty Thathapudi

with answers and additional material by:

Lynn Erler
Morag McCrorie
Clare Parker
Dagmar Sauer
Michael Spencer

OCR RECOGNISING ACHIEVEMENT
OXFORD UNIVERSITY PRESS
Official Publisher Partnership

CW01597440

OXFORD
UNIVERSITY PRESS

Great Clarendon Street, Oxford OX2 6DP

Oxford University Press is a department of the University of Oxford.

It furthers the University's objective of excellence in research, scholarship, and education by publishing worldwide in
Oxford New York
Auckland Cape Town Dar es Salaam Hong Kong Karachi
Kuala Lumpur Madrid Melbourne Mexico City Nairobi
New Delhi Shanghai Taipei Toronto

With offices in
Argentina Austria Brazil Chile Czech Republic France Greece Guatemala
Hungary Italy Japan South Korea Poland Portugal Singapore Switzerland
Thailand Turkey Ukraine Vietnam

Oxford is a registered trade mark of Oxford University Press
in the UK and in certain other countries

© Oxford University Press 2009

The moral rights of the author have been asserted

Database right Oxford University Press (maker)

First published 2009

All rights reserved. No part of this publication may be reproduced, stored in a retrieval system, or transmitted, in any form or by any means, without the prior permission in writing of Oxford University Press, or as expressly permitted by law, or under terms agreed with the appropriate reprographics rights organization. Enquiries concerning reproduction outside the scope of the above should be sent to the Rights Department, Oxford University Press, at the address above

You must not circulate this book in any other binding or cover and you must impose this same condition on any acquirer

British Library Cataloguing in Publication Data

Data available

ISBN 978 019 915496 8

10 9 8 7 6 5 4 3 2 1

Printed in Great Britain by Ashford Colour Press Ltd

Paper used in the production of this book is a natural, recyclable product made from wood grown in sustainable forests. The manufacturing process conforms to the environmental regulations of the country of origin.

Acknowledgements

Activity sheets: 16.6 AFP/Getty Images, 16.7 FEDERICO GAMBARINI/epa/Corbis, 17.1 purchased from www.bigstock.com, 43.2 OUP, 43.3 Rex Rover/Shutterstock, 43.4 OUP.

Assessment sheets: 13.6 Sue Cunningham Photographic/Alamy, 13.7 Charles Gullung/zefa/Corbis, 13.8 Michael Paras/www.photolibrary.com, 13.9 ianmurray/ Alamy, 29.1 OUP, 29.2 OUP, 29.3 Gordon Ball LRPS/Shutterstock, 29.4 OUP.

Illustrations for Activity and Assessment sheets by: Barking Dog Art, Stefan Chabluk and Peter Donnelley.

Cover image: Erik Isakson/Getty

Activity and Assessment sheets by: Eleanor Caldwell and Clare Parker

The authors and publisher would like to thank the following people for their help and advice: Frances Reynolds; Marion Dill; Chris Buckland, Tessa Kelly, Helen Smith. Audio recordings studio production: Colette Thomson and Andrew Garrett (Footstep Productions).

Contents

Symbols used in this Teacher's Book:

- a pairwork activity
- a groupwork activity
- a listening activity – audio on accompanying CD
- a speaking activity
- a reading activity
- a writing activity
- X–X reference to a Languages Ladder grade
- PLTS an activity that has been selected as an example of particular Personal Learning and Thinking Skills

Summary of Unit Contents					
Unit	**Contexts**	**Skills**	**Grammar**	**Cross-curricular links**	**Scenario**
1A Mein Leben: *Life at home; family, friends and relationships*	Talk about yourself and your family Describe your daily routine and life at home Household chores	**Speaking** Practising before you speak Asking questions to keep a conversation going **Writing** Correct sentence order with separable verbs	Present tense: regular, reflexive verbs Gender and plurals Possessive adjectives Adjective endings in the accusative	PHSE	• Writing an application to appear on a reality TV show • Preparing for and taking part in an imaginary press conference
1B Wohnort und Umgebung: *Local area, facilities and getting around*	Describe where you live and compare it with other places Find out about a place Find your way around Means of transport	**Reading** Cognates Deducing meaning from context Making clever guesses **Listening** Targeted listening	Comparative/superlative Modal verbs Dates Imperative Prepositions with accusative/dative Introduction to imperfect	Geography, Leisure and tourism, Citizenship	• Preparing a presentation about your home town • Making the case for your home town to be twinned with Münster
2A Gesundheit und Sport: *Sports, outdoor pursuits and healthy lifestyle*	Usual and extreme sports Sporting heroes Healthy living Sport injuries	**Speaking** Using qualifiers and expressions of time Expressing opinions Expressing preferences **Writing** Giving reasons Capital letters	Perfect tense Separable/inseparable verbs Standard word order Time phrases	PE, PHSE	• Preparing and delivering a presentation on a sporting hero • Planning a sporting holiday
2B Essen und trinken: *Food and drink*	Food and drink in different cultures Healthy eating Shopping for food Order food and complain	**Reading** Recognising adjectival nouns Making predictions about meaning Recognising and understanding pronouns **Listening** Listening for detail Making good guesses	Infinitive constructions *Um ... zu* Accusative object pronouns Demonstrative pronouns Adjective endings after indefinite articles	Food technology, PHSE/ Citizenship	• Producing a brochure about healthy eating • Preparing and delivering a presentation about an eating disorder
3A Freizeit: *Socialising, special occasions and festivals*	Make arrangements to go out with friends Shopping Internet usage Compare festivals in different countries	**Speaking** Asking questions and making suggestions Varying tone Giving examples **Listening** Listening for linking words which reverse meaning Use tone for understanding	Present tense with future meaning Dative object pronouns Future tense Imperfect tense	PHSE/Citizenship	• Responding to an e-mail from a German exchange partner • Surveying classmates about how they use computers and presenting the results in an oral report
3B Die Medien: *TV, films and music*	Express views about books, films and music Compare tastes now and in the past Write a film review Talk about celebrities	**Reading** Using contextual clues Inferring meaning Dictionary skills **Writing** Varying structures Justifying opinions	Pluperfect Revision of comparative/ superlative Impersonal verbs Relative clauses	Music, Media studies	• Preparing an interview with a celebrity • Writing a book/film review
4A Urlaub und Austausch: *Holidays and exchanges*	Choose and book a holiday destination Give your opinion of a holiday Plan an exchange Describe past holiday experiences	**Speaking** Making recommendations Varying expressions of opinion Giving opinions of past events **Listening** Recognising different tenses Using transcripts to develop listening skills	Conditional Verbs with *zu* 'If' clauses: present and future	Geography, PHSE	• Planning a stay in Germany, Austria or Switzerland • Producing a brochure for a holiday destination

4B Die Welt und die Umwelt: *Environmental issues and life in other countries*	Talk about threats and dangers to the environment Conservation and recycling Eco-tourism Life in German-speaking countries	**Reading** Revising reading strategies **Listening** Effective note taking Sense checking answers	Compound nouns Prepositions with the genitive Imperfect subjunctive 'If' clauses: imperfect subjunctive	Geography, Citizenship	• Designing an eco-outing or holiday • Making proposals for and discussing the development of a green area
5A Schulleben: *School life in the UK and German-speaking countries*	Exchange information and opinions about school life Describe and compare school and school subjects in different countries Talk about money and part-time jobs	**Speaking** Asking questions: intonation Embellishing answers Adapting questions in answers **Listening** Predicting vocabulary Recognising sound-spelling links	Revision of *weil* Weak nouns Revision: *um ... zu* Revision: dative reflexive pronouns	PHSE	• Preparing an agenda for a school council meeting • Giving a presentation of a part-time job that would be suitable for students while at school
5B Arbeit und Zukunftspläne: *Work experience, future study and jobs, working abroad*	Future career and study plans Work experience Find and apply for a placement Job interviews	**Writing** Checking as you write Word order Writing longer sentences **Reading** Deducing meaning of unknown words and compound words	Revision of future tense Revision of 'if' clauses Revision of forms of address Revision of word order	PHSE/ Citizenship	• Debate concerning work experience and CVs • Writing a story about an interesting work experience placement

Introduction

GCSE German for OCR and the new GCSE specifications

Welcome to **GCSE German for OCR**!

GCSE German for OCR is a broad-ability course for 14-16 year-olds which prepares students for the new OCR GCSE German specifications. The course offers a single-tier **Students' Book** and is accompanied by differentiated **Exam Skills Workbooks**. The course has been written in response to a need for more motivating and relevant content to prepare students for Controlled Assessments and to inspire them to pursue German to GCSE level and beyond.

How does GCSE German for OCR differ from other courses on the market?

GCSE German for OCR has been designed to take account of:

- the introduction of Controlled Assessment to examine speaking and writing
- a renewed emphasis on Personal Learning and Thinking Skills, and cross-curricular links in the new National Curriculum
- a reduction in the uptake of GCSE languages
- a greater range of ability in non-tiered classes
- the findings of the Dearing Review regarding the need for more motivating topic coverage at Key Stage 4
- increased demands on teacher time in terms of planning, presentation and assessment.

To achieve this, **GCSE German for OCR** offers:

- differentiation within the activities on each double-page spread, with material that will be within reach of students of all abilities
- motivating themes and topics that will be of greater relevance to teenagers, presented in a "hands-on" manner and including more real world and vocational links
- activities on every spread that are designed to help students to prepare for the kind of tasks that they will need to perform in a Controlled Assessment
- an emphasis on transferable skills, so that if teachers choose to set Controlled Assessments on topics that are not on the prescribed topic list for listening and reading, students will have the tools to approach them with confidence
- material which will appeal to a variety of different learning styles, flagged up in this Teacher's Book with the PLTS icon
- a more personalised approach to assessment, including on-screen assessment *of* and *for* learning, supported by the **Assessment OxBox CD-ROM**
- Record & Playback activities and a video-based pronunciation guide in an integrated multimedia package (**Resources and Planning OxBox CD-ROM**)
- fully editable lesson plans to allow teachers to customise and deliver exciting structured lessons with minimal hassle (**Resources and Planning OxBox CD-ROM**).

How does GCSE German for OCR make it easier for you to meet the needs of your students?

Firstly, **GCSE German for OCR** provides ***clarity***:

- **a clear structure**
  - There are ten units in total, each pair covering one of the prescribed topics from the OCR GCSE specification.
  - Each unit is designed to cover one half-term's work, with six units being covered in Year 10, and four units covered in Year 11, to allow time for mock exams and Controlled Assessments during teaching time in Year 11.
  - Each unit has five main teaching spreads, and a grammar spread (*Aktive Grammatik*), which makes it easy to teach one double-page spread per week.
  - Additional pages provide further work on skills (*Kompetenzen*), a speaking and writing task which take a similar form to a Controlled Assessment (*Szenario*), additional reading material (*Lesen A/B*), and a vocabulary résumé.
  - The assessment sheets provide material for end-of-term tests at the end of each unit. There are also regular formative and summative assessments on the **Assessment OxBox CD-ROM**.
- **clear presentation**
  - In the Students' Books, scene-setting unit opener pages provide clear contexts and a preview of the skills and grammar that will be covered in each unit.
  - Activities are tagged with listening, speaking, reading, writing, pairwork and groupwork icons, so that students can find their way around a spread easily and know what they will need to do in each activity at a glance.
  - Core grammar and skills are highlighted in *Grammatik* and *Tipp* boxes, and revisited in greater detail on the *Aktive Grammatik* and *Kompetenzen* pages.

- **clear progression**
  - Clear learning objectives for grammar (G), vocabulary (V) and skills (K) at the top of each spread show students exactly what they will learn.
  - Key grammar and skills are presented and practised carefully and systematically.
  - Students are able to check their progress and identify areas for improvement via each unit's *Kompetenzen* page and the *Checklist* page in the **Exam Skills Workbooks**.

In addition, **GCSE German for OCR** provides comprehensive and flexible support to ensure that lesson planning and teaching are as easy as possible:

- This Teacher's Resource Book provides a clear, at-a-glance Lesson Planner page for each core spread, with ideas for starter and plenary activities to help you save preparation time.
- The teaching notes make extensive suggestions for how activities can be differentiated for different ability ranges, and indicate which other course components can be used to reinforce and extend the material covered on a particular spread.
- On the **Resources and Planning OxBox CD-ROM**, you'll find an editable electronic version of these Lesson Planners, with links to the resources required for each lesson, allowing you to build and modify your lessons to suit your students' needs.
- Other useful features on the **Resources and Planning OxBox CD-ROM** include a lesson plan builder, audio recordings in MP3 format, and the facility to incorporate all your own lesson resources, including worksheets and photos.

To find out more about individual components, please read on!

The components of GCSE German for OCR

Students' Book

The 224-page Students' Book consists of ten main units, plus a *Trainingszone* at the start of the book which introduces a range of learning strategies students can employ while studying for their GCSE. This allows roughly one unit per half-term's work. Each unit is divided into an opening page, presenting the themes, skills and grammar coverage of the unit, five core teaching spreads, a grammar spread and a skills page. Each spread offers a range of different activities to suit different levels of ability and the course has been written to enable teachers to select those activities that will suit individual groups and students. **GCSE German for OCR** is designed to build on Key Stage 3 German and provides the necessary programme of teaching, practice, revision and reference materials. Full attention has been given throughout the course to the Subject Criteria for Modern Foreign Languages.

The Students' Book contains the following sections:

Einheiten 1A-5B

There are ten 16-page units structured around the contexts from the OCR prescribed topic list. Each unit has been planned to be interesting and motivating, as well as to provide a coherent and systematic approach to language development in terms of grammar and skills. An outline of the content of each unit is given on pages 4–5 of this book. For a detailed description of the features of a **GCSE German for OCR** unit, see pages 10–11.

Lesen

GCSE German for OCR features a 20-page section of differentiated reading material towards the back of the Students' Book, consisting of one reinforcement page (*Lesen A*) and one extension page (*Lesen B*) for each unit. The *Lesen A* pages provide opportunities for extra practice of core language from the unit, while the *Lesen B* pages provide extension material for students who are confident with the core language.

Aktive Grammatik/Grammar Bank

A grasp of grammar and structure lies at the heart of language learning, but grammar is too often perceived by learners as boring, unnecessary drudgery, rather than as a tool which enables them to express themselves with greater freedom and variety. In **GCSE German for OCR**, grammar is introduced on a 'need' basis, in grammar boxes on each spread, and presented with a clear purpose in mind. Grammar is thus integrated into the core aims and productive outcomes of each spread, rather than being treated as a separate aspect of language learning. A more in-depth treatment of the grammar points covered is then provided in the *Aktive Grammatik* spread at the end of the unit, which focuses on 3-4 core grammar areas. This is supported by a series of detailed grammar presentations on the **Resources and Planning OxBox CD-ROM**, which are designed to provide a point of reference for students who would like to deepen or revise their knowledge of a particular aspect of grammar.

The grammar explanations within the main teaching units are complemented by the detailed grammar reference section at the back of the Students' Book, the *Grammar Bank*. Here, additional grammar practice activities are integrated into the corresponding grammatical explanations, enabling students to consolidate or revise further their knowledge of grammar.

Exam Practice

The *Exam Practice* section at the back of the Students' Book provides students with a complete set of sample exam questions for each of the four key skill areas, which can either be used at the beginning of the course to ascertain the level needed to obtain a GCSE, or close to the end of the course as revision material.

Vokabeln

A German–English and English–German glossary contains useful words from both the Students' Book and the OCR prescribed vocabulary list for students' reference. Vocabulary flashcards for each unit are also provided on the **Resources and Planning OxBox CD-ROM**.

Teacher's Book

Each unit contains the following detailed teaching notes:
- a unit overview grid, providing a summary of the skills, grammar and language coverage of the unit
- notes to accompany the unit opening page, including unit objectives and assessment opportunities
- a Planner section for each core teaching spread for ease of lesson planning, including suggestions for starter and plenary activities
- ideas for presenting and practising new language
- detailed notes on the Students' Book material, including answers to all activities
- suggestions for further activities to reinforce and extend the content of the Students' Book
- cross-references to other course components, indicating where corresponding resources are available on the **Resources and Planning OxBox CD-ROM**, in the **Activity Sheets** supplied with this book or in the **Exam Skills Workbooks**
- transcripts for all listening material from the Students' Book.

Audio CDs and MP3 files

The CDs provide the listening material to accompany the Students' Book and **Activity and Assessment Sheets**. The listening material was recorded by native German speakers. The material is scripted and contains a range of text types, including monologues, dialogues and longer conversations. Sound files are also available in MP3 format on the **Resources and Planning OxBox CD-ROM**. All recorded material may be copied within the purchasing institution for use by teachers and students.

CD contents:

CD 1 Units 1A-2A
CD 2 Units 2B-3B
CD 3 Units 4A-Exam Practice
CD 4 Assessment Papers

Activity and Assessment Sheets

The Activity Sheets, located on the CD that accompanies this Teacher's Resource Book, are designed to be used in parallel with the **GCSE German for OCR** course and there are cross-references to them throughout. Answers for each unit's Activity Sheets are provided on the CD and on the **Resources and Planning OxBox CD-ROM**. The Activity Sheets provide opportunities for further practice and extension of the language, grammar and skills covered in the unit.

Each unit has the following Activity Sheets:
- *Lesen:* a page of reading extension material with comprehension activities
- *Schreiben*: a page of writing activities, offering advice on how to use a range of different expressions and structure writing
- *Hören*: listening activities
- *Sprechen*: speaking activities
- *Aktive Grammatik*: consolidation and practice of key grammar points
- *Kompetenzen*: a page on which students can record their responses to the language learning skills and strategies page at the end of the Students' Book unit
- *Vokabeln*: a list of key vocabulary from the unit, which students can use as a reference or as an aid to learning

Exam Skills Workbooks (Foundation and Higher Tier)

The **Exam Skills Workbooks** are divided into two sections: practical advice and worksheets. The first section offers targeted advice for how students can prepared for and approach the GCSE exams and Controlled Assessments for each skill. There is a detailed pronunciation guide, followed by practice listening material which follows the same format at the listening exam. There then follows a section on strategies for learning vocabulary.
In the worksheets section, the following sheets are provided for each unit of the Students' Book:
- *Aktive Grammatik*: a page focusing on key grammar covered in the unit
- *Szenario:* two worksheets offering advice and strategies for approaching the written and spoken Controlled Assessment-style tasks from the *Szenario* page of each unit of the Students' Book
- *Checklist*: a checklist of the core language and skills covered in the unit, providing an opportunity for students to review their progress and reflect on areas for improvement.

The Workbooks are designed for students to write in, so they are ideal for homework and individual study. Rubrics are provided in English throughout so that students can work independently. The activities can be completed with minimal teacher input.

Grammar Workbook

The **GCSE German for OCR Grammar Workbook** provides comprehensive coverage of the QCA prescribed grammar content for GCSE. It includes:
- clear explanations of all grammar points
- extensive practice activities
- answers (in a detachable answer booklet).

OxBox CD-ROMs

See **An integrated approach: How OxBox works** on page 11 of this book.

Course progression

Review of GCSE specifications

The new specifications for GCSE Modern languages introduced in September 2009 respond directly to the need to make language learning and assessment reflect more closely the needs and interests of students, changing patterns of learning at KS2 and KS3, and the increasing use of ICT to enhance learning.

The specifications impact on the way tasks are assessed – most notably speaking, which is assessed internally; on the selection of topics and contexts for learning – speaking and writing tasks may be selected by teachers and students if they wish, and are no longer tiered; and on the way tasks are submitted – as up to 60% of the final marks can be achieved prior to a terminal exam by using unitised assessment. We include a brief summary of course details, assessment objectives and changes below, but you should refer to the official OCR website http://www.ocr.org.uk/qualifications/gcsefor2009/German for full details.

Course summary		
Unit title and description	**Assessment and duration**	**Weighting**
Listening (tiered)		
Learners: • listen for, identify and note main points, and take details from spoken target language of increasing length, speed and complexity • demonstrate an understanding of target language using a range of non-verbal responses, and some short answers in English.	Written examination Foundation tier – 35 minutes Higher tier – 45 minutes	20% Spoken short course 40%
Speaking (untiered)		
Using target language, learners: • communicate in target language on at least two topics – from a specified list, or of their own choice • interact with target language speakers, expressing and justifying opinions where appropriate.	Controlled assessment	30% Spoken short course 60%
Reading (tiered)		
Learners: • read, identify and note main points, and take details from target language text of increasing length, speed and complexity • demonstrate an understanding of target language using a range of non-verbal responses, and some short answers in English.	Written examination 50 minutes	20% Written short course 40%
Writing (untiered)		
Using the target language, learners: • communicate on at least two topic areas – from a specified list, or of their own choice • express and justify points of view in target language where appropriate.	Controlled assessment	30% Written short course 60%

The above table shows the increased relative value of speaking and writing in the new exams – 60%, as compared to 40% total for reading and listening. The table below summarises all the key changes in the new specification.

	What changes?	**What stays the same?**
Structure	• Speaking tasks are now assessed internally, and externally moderated by OCR. • There are now only two speaking tasks. • Written tasks are all moderated by OCR. • There are now only two written tasks. • GCSE short courses are now available. • Listening and reading remain tiered.	• The four skills – reading, writing, listening and speaking – are still assessed separately.
Content	• Updated choice of topics. • Teachers and learners can now choose your own topics for speaking and writing. • Listening and reading questions are no longer in the target language.	• Most topics cover areas that are essential in language learning contexts.
Assessment	• Speaking no longer needs to be taken as a final exam. • Not all speaking tasks have to be recorded. • Spoken and written work can be submitted via the OCR website repository, a secure website designed specifically for uploading portfolios electronically. • Short courses are available, so learners can choose to be assessed on just their strongest skills.	• The four assessment objectives remain the same.

Completing the GCSE programme in one year

Until recently, the general assumption in course construction was that students benefited from a relatively predetermined course progression over a fixed period of time, typically two years, to ensure that 'prescribed content' was covered in full. The advent of primary languages, fast-tracking, competition for timetable allocation, etc., means that courses may need be delivered over different lengths of time and even in different Key Stages. The revised GCSE specifications, which have a reduced emphasis on pre-defined content (at least for the Controlled Assessments in speaking and writing, which account for the majority (60%) of the total marks), also create opportunities for more streamlined approaches to learning. **GCSE German for OCR** is designed to be used flexibly as regards time allocation, content coverage and also content sequencing. Here are some suggestions to consider if you wish to prepare students for GCSE over one year:

- Encourage learners to identify, analyse and plan responses to their own learning needs from the outset. They can construct personal study plans for regular review.
- Select contexts for Controlled Assessments at the outset by asking students to vote for interest areas – e.g. sport, shopping, music, etc. (Remember only two submissions are required.) Focus on these units.
- Focus on developing and reviewing skills and grammar rather than lots of topics. The introductory section in the Students' Book provides some useful pointers. The **Exam Skills Workbooks** and **Resources and Planning OxBox** provide key points of support and are ideal for independent study.
- Prepare for listening and reading assessments by homing in on the most useful associated skills and strategies: prediction, gist and detail, sound/spelling links, applying grammatical knowledge, personalised vocabulary lists, etc. Avoid lengthy detours through topics not on your priority list and long decontextualised word lists.
- Plan intensive sessions on some/all of the above at regular intervals, with specially timetabled half or whole days to review and embed skills and grammar leading to *Szenario* assessments or other motivating outcomes.

Detailed plans are included on the **Resources and Planning OxBox** so that lesson planning and delivery can be done flexibly and adapted to fit timetable allocations.

Teaching across the ability range using GCSE German for OCR

There is an extensive literature on differentiation, with many excellent ideas available in print and on the internet. The Framework for KS3 supports entitlement and enablement for all learners of a Modern Foreign Language. The purpose here is to provide a few ideas and pointers as to how **GCSE German for OCR** supports the spirit and practice of the new specifications across the ability range. Several of the points have already been made in the precediing section *Completing the GCSE programme in one year* – please refer back to this for further ideas.

Some key points:

- Differentiated teaching and learning is a response to the needs of learners of *all* abilities, to be planned for at the outset once the composition of the teaching group is known, and implicit in each lesson and activity. It should not be seen as a bolt-on activity for remedial work.
- The two OxBoxes provide unique, flexible tools to help with planning, resourcing and assessing your learners at each stage (see page 11).
- 60% of marks are available for Speaking and Writing Controlled Assessments, which are both untiered. As candidates are no longer pre-classified into Foundation and Higher-tier entrants, they can accede to any grade on the day.
- The course is constructed to support untiered whole class teaching and learning using the coursebook, whilst providing for individual needs and independent study in other components, particularly the two **Exam Skills Workbooks**.
- There are now only two Speaking and two Writing tasks, which allows for a greater focus on both content and skills.
- Sharpen your focus through selection: content can be selected at unit and even spread level if desired, and adapted to meet specific interests and local environments.
- Focus on skills: regular and imaginative review of skills and strategies for learning are needed throughout KS4. Make sure your students work through the ideas in the *Trainingszone* section, as well as the *Kompetenzen* pages.

What about the listening and reading exams?

- The focus on skills and strategies should also reduce the need for exhaustive coverage of all content and vocabulary – especially for learners who find memorising vocabulary difficult. There is provision through the course for regular and varied practice of these skills. (See also *Lesen A* and *B* in the reading section.)

And grammar?

- Grammar, traditionally seen as threatening or tedious by some learners (and teachers?) is treated pragmatically through on-the-page help boxes in English, and regular *Aktive Grammatik* reviews designed to be accessible to all students.

Teaching with GCSE German for OCR

Features of a GCSE German for OCR unit

Unit opening page

Each unit begins with an opening page which is designed to set the scene for the unit. A list of contexts, skills and grammar points provides a preview of what is to come, and each opening page encourages students to think ahead to the extended *Szenario* tasks that they will be performing at the end of it. The opening pages can also be used as the basis for plenary activities: at the end of work on each unit, students can return to the opening page to answer the questions, review what they have learned and reflect on areas for improvement. Each unit takes two primary skills as its main focus: listening, speaking, reading or writing.

Activity spreads

There are five activity spreads per unit, via which the key language is presented and practised. Each double-page spread includes:

- a clear statement of what students are going to learn on the spread, given in German to encourage students to reflect on their learning in the target language
- activities in all four skills to practise the key language of the spread: the majority of rubrics on the core spreads are in German; English is used for the *Jetzt seid ihr dran!* section in which students bring all of their acquired knowledge together in two extended tasks
- icons to identify each skill (listening, speaking, reading, writing) and highlight pairwork and groupwork activities
- clearly identified vocabulary and skills panels, providing support and reference for students
- clearly presented grammar boxes to introduce and recap on grammar points. Key grammar is then further developed on the *Aktive Grammatik* spread (see below).

The first activity spread in each unit is designed to review prior knowledge, and draws on language and topics that are likely to have been touched upon in Key Stage 3. These are then taken and translated into more relevant and advanced contexts over the following spreads. Throughout the book, there is an emphasis on the cross-curricular aspects of language learning: how a knowledge of the German-speaking world feeds into students' studies of geography and citizenship, and equips them for the world of work. There is a concerted attempt to demonstrate how a knowledge of German and other foreign languages can be useful for different jobs, lifestyles and travel, and a focus on the cultural differences and similarities between German-speaking countries and the UK.

Aktive Grammatik

Each unit features a *Aktive Grammatik* spread, focusing on key grammar points that have been introduced on the five core teaching spreads. Further grammar practice activities are provided in the grammar reference section (*Grammar Bank*) at the back of the Students' Book, in the **Activity Sheets**, **Exam Skills Workbooks** and **Grammar Workbook**. An overview of the grammar points covered in each unit of **GCSE German for OCR** is provided on pages 4–5 of this book.

Kompetenzen

This page recaps the language learning skills and strategies introduced in the unit. The development of language learning skills is considered to be an integral part of the language learning process and should be given sufficient time during whole-class work. Students who are given opportunities to practise these skills from the start will develop into effective independent language learners. An overview of the skills coverage of **GCSE German for OCR** is provided on pages 4–5 of this book.

Szenario

This page presents two extended tasks or projects of a similar type to those that students will be expected to perform for the GCSE Speaking and Writing Controlled Assessments. Additional support and advice on how to approach these tasks is provided in the **Exam Skills Workbooks**.

Lesen

This section, coming after Unit 5B in the Students' Book, has additional reading material designed to encourage students to work independently and practise their reading strategies. There are two pages per unit, with the first page *Lesen A*, more suited to learners working at Foundation level, and *Lesen B* pitched at Higher-level learners

Vokabeln

This summary of the key language covered on each spread of the unit can be used by students as a reference or as an aid to learning. The *Vokabeln* list is also provided as an **Activity Sheet** and in the **Exam Skills Workbooks**.

An integrated approach: How OxBox works

What is OxBox?

OxBox is a 'toolkit' of electronic resources that is designed to facilitate lesson planning and delivery, and to provide an effective way of assessing students' progress through the **GCSE German for OCR** course. Think of OxBox as a virtual filing cabinet with three main folders: one for lesson plans, one for teaching materials and one for tests.

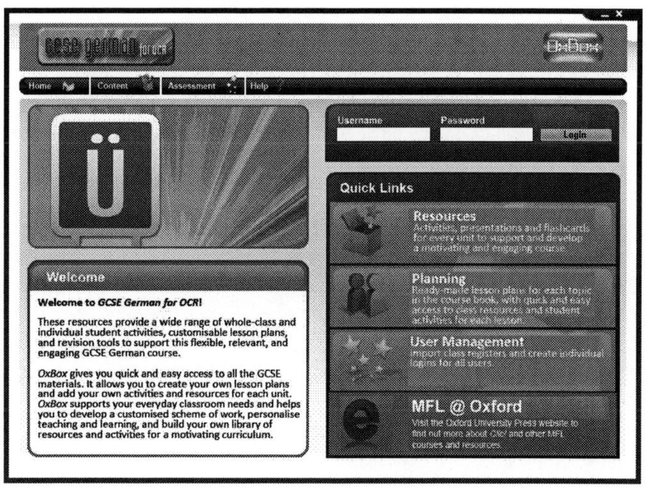

Each folder comes filled with pre-prepared resources to supplement and support the **GCSE German for OCR** course, ranging from electronic lesson plans that make it easy for you to plan and deliver your lesson, to stimulating interactive activities that will motivate your students as they learn. In developing the OxBox resources, the main areas of anxiety and difficulty at GCSE level have been focussed on: speaking, pronunciation, grammar, and vocabulary learning. There are motivating resources to help students to develop their skills in each of these areas (see 'Resources' section below). OxBox also contains a 'User Management' folder, into which you can import class registers and create user accounts for your students.

Fully customisable
OxBox is compatible with all standard Microsoft Office® programs so, as well as being able to create new plans and assessments using the OxBox interface, you can also import your own Word® or Excel®-based lesson plans and materials into OxBox and file them in one centralised location. Many of the resources included in OxBox are themselves fully editable Word® and PowerPoint® files, permitting you to adapt them to the needs of a particular class or combine them with your own materials as you see fit. Because OxBox comes with a site licence, it can be installed on your school's local network, thereby additionally enabling you to share materials with other teachers if you wish to do so.

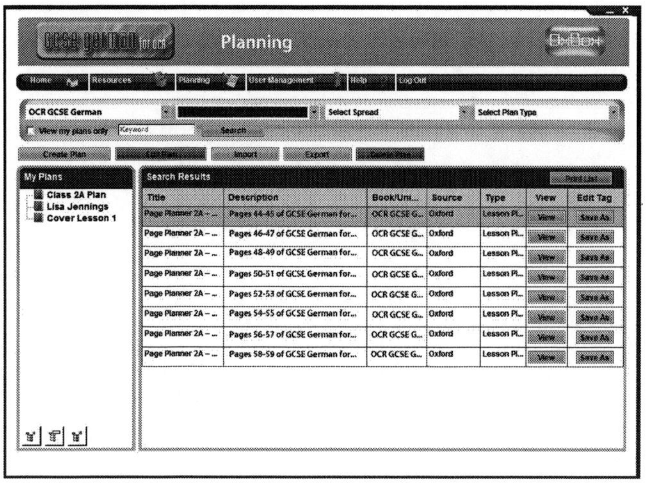

Different access levels for teachers and students
OxBox provides two separate environments, one for teachers and one for students, giving access to different resources. If you log in as a teacher, you have complete access to all of OxBox's resources: you can import class registers, add new exercises and assessments, and assign assessments to particular groups of students. You can also see individual or aggregated test results for any assessments you have set. Students, on the other hand, can only run interactive activities and resources that have been tagged specifically for student access and take the tests that you have assigned to them. This means that students can work on OxBox activities and assessments at individual workstations in the classroom using individual log-in IDs.

Lesson planning
The planning section in the OxBox contains a variety of resources designed to help you teach the **GCSE German for OCR** course, and reduce the burden of time-consuming lesson conception and planning:

- Course overviews and unit plans familiarise you with the objectives and contents of each unit, allowing you to map out the term's work quickly and easily.
- Lesson plans offer ideas and strategies for delivering the **GCSE German for OCR** course, and suggestions on how you can combine the different resources available in the **GCSE German for OCR** Students' Book and on OxBox. They also point to extension activities from the **Exam Skills Workbooks** and **Activity Sheets**. The Lesson Player automatically launches each of the resources required for a lesson, so you don't need to waste any time finding and opening them while teaching.
- The Lesson Planner provides a simple template in which you can write additional lesson plans which link to resources in OxBox. Using the lesson planner, you can also customise existing plans, tailoring them to different classes by changing the materials used in the lesson.

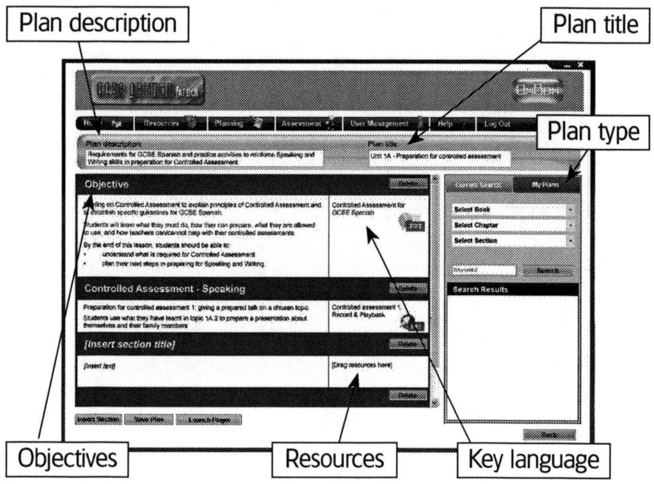

Resources

Record & Playback Activities
On the **Resources and Planning OxBox**, there is one interactive activity to accompany each of the spoken *Jetzt seid ihr dran!* tasks from the main teaching spreads, and each of the spoken *Szenario* tasks from the end of each unit of the Students' Book. The activities, which take three different formats, enable students to record their verbal responses to each task and save them to disc so that they can analyse their own strengths and weaknesses and gain valuable practice for the speaking controlled assessments. The three types of activity available are:

- **Interview** (single user activity)
  Users hear a series of recorded questions, in German, or see a series of English prompts on screen, and record their responses to them. At the end of the activity, users can play back the entire conversation, including the answers they recorded.
- **Role play** (single user activity)
  Users hear a recorded conversation between two people, and are then invited to play the part of one of the two speakers. At the end of the activity, they can play back a new version of the conversation, which includes the parts that they recorded.
- **Debate** (two-user activity)
  Two users take part in a debate on a given topic and record their arguments on alternate screens. At the end of the activity, they can play back a recording of their discussion.

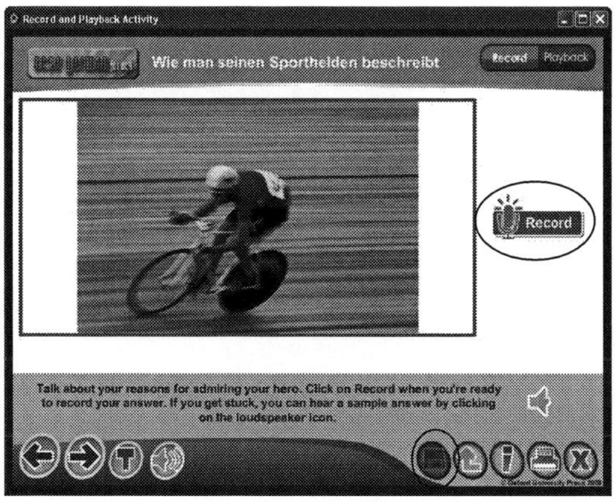

To make use of the record functionality, simply connect a microphone or microphone headset to your student's computer microphone socket, and press the 'Record' button on screen to start recording. Remind students to click on the disc icon at the end of each activity to save all of the recorded audio clips to disc.

The audio files from the Record & Playback activities are saved as MP3s, so can easily be e-mailed from student to teacher, imported back into the OxBox, or saved to disc to create a portfolio of speaking tasks enabling you to monitor students' progress throughout the course.

Pronunciation presentations

On the OxBox, you'll find one pronunciation presentation for each unit of the **GCSE German for OCR** course. Each presentation addresses the main pronunciation issues that arise from the content of the unit. They include clear explanations of how to form the German sounds described, and video clips of native speakers making each sound, offering students a model to emulate.

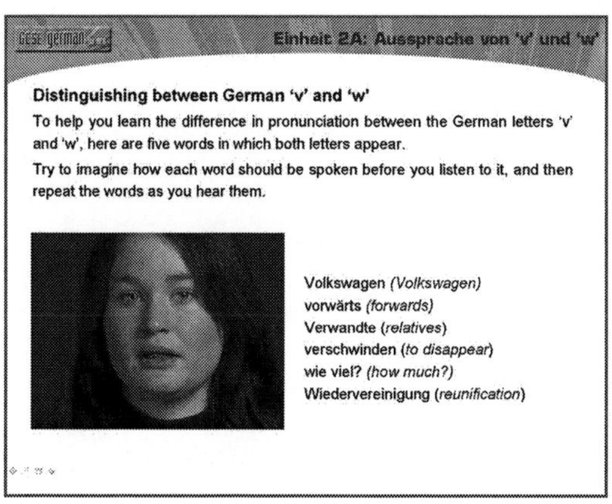

The video clips can be started simply by clicking on the video still on screen.

Grammar reference presentations

The **Resources and Planning OxBox** also contains animated grammar presentations for each unit of the course, covering key grammar topics from the QCA prescribed grammar content for GCSE. These presentations offer clear explanations of each point, with ample examples, and are intended to be used by students for reference and revision. They are best viewed in 'Slide Show' mode.

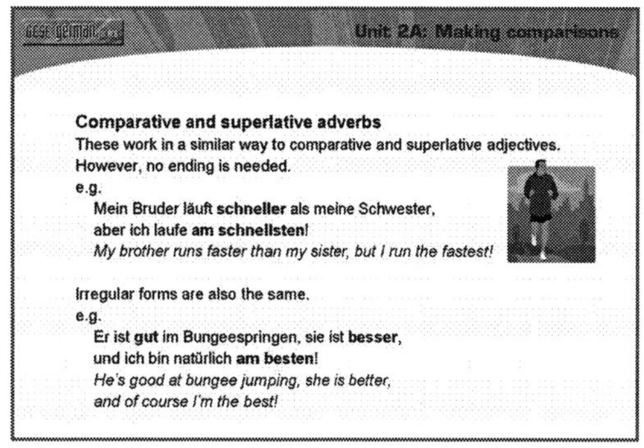

The topics covered in each presentation are:

1A The basics
1B The case system
2A Making comparisons
2B Verbs – the present tense
3A Working with verbs
3B Giving detailed answers
4A Questions, exclamations and orders
4B Past tenses
5A Future and conditional
5B Improving your style

Interactive vocabulary flashcards

The **Resources and Planning OxBox** also provides a set of interactive flashcards for each unit of the course. Each set covers selected vocabulary from the OCR Vocabulary List and contains integrated sound clips so that students can test both their recall and their pronunciation.

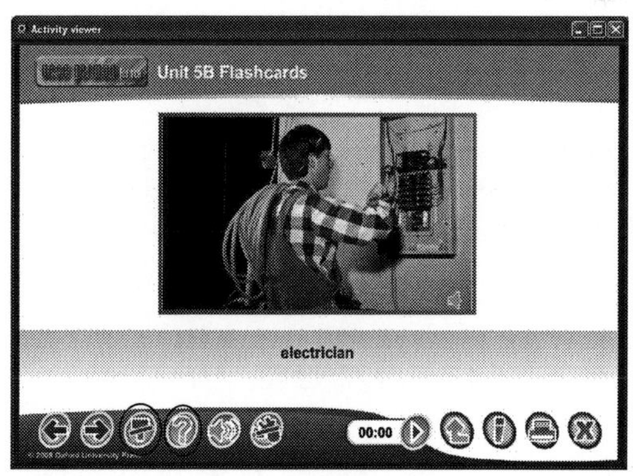

The 'text' and 'clue' features help students to learn words that they are having difficulty with and use the flashcards formatively.

Zoomable opening page presentations

An interactive presentation of the opening page of each unit is provided on the **Resources and Planning OxBox**. Each presentation consists of an image of the relevant page from the Students' Book, which is intended to be displayed on an interactive whiteboard. Key parts of the image have been predefined as zoomable areas. The magnified areas can be taken as the focus of class discussion surrounding the skills and grammar knowledge listed, or used as a springboard for vocabulary extension.

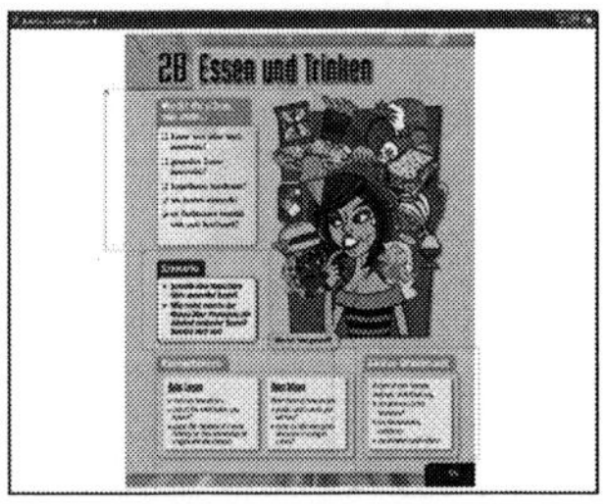

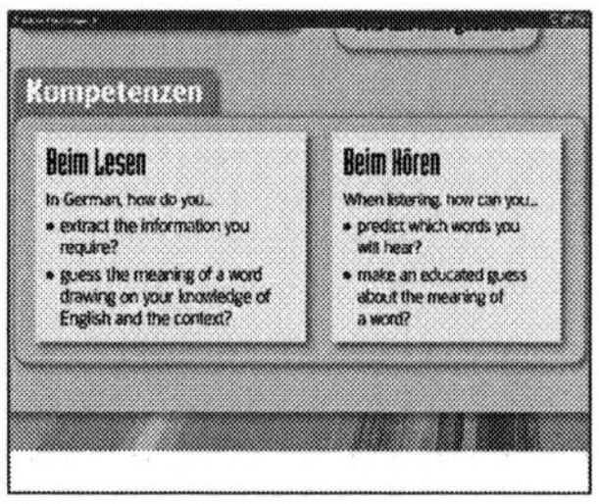

Assessment

The **Assessment OxBox CD-ROM** contains a series of formative and summative tests in each of the key skill areas, many of them auto-marked, for each unit of the course. The tests loosely mirror the structure of the OCR exams in terms of the number of tasks per test, and two different versions of each summative listening and reading test are provided: one for foundation-tier candidates and one for higher-tier candidates.

- **Formative assessments**
  Formative assessments are designed to be completed by students as they progress through the course, helping them to master what they have learned and improve any areas of weakness. In auto-marked tests, students are asked to predict how well they will answer each question before attempting it, and are given two chances to get it right. If they answer incorrectly, they are given feedback on why their answer was wrong and, ultimately, told the right answer. At the end of the test, they are not given an overall score.
- **Summative assessments**
  Summative assessments provide you with a simple and effective way to chart your students' progress at regular intervals throughout the **GCSE German for OCR** course. Summative assessments are provided as end-of-term and end-of-year tests. In the auto-marked summative assessments, students may only attempt each question once and are given an overall result at the end of the test. Once all the members of a class have sat a summative test, the results are aggregated automatically so that you can identify any areas that caused particular difficulty.

Presentation and practice of new language

In the Students' Book, new language is presented via the core spreads in a variety of ways, through photos, illustrations and different types of text. Recorded material is provided on CD or as MP3 files on the **Resources and Planning OxBox CD-ROM**, and may be used for repetition by students in order to ensure the best possible pronunciation and intonation.

Once presented, the key language of each unit is developed through a wide variety of mixed-skill practice, with activities to ensure language development from supported/guided to more open-ended. **GCSE German for OCR** intends each activity to have a purpose for students, and to be interesting and motivating as well as promoting linguistic development. Students should be encouraged to learn by heart on a regular basis, not only items of vocabulary but also short conversations. This promotes good language learning habits and ensures that students are able to transfer language learned to new contexts.

Additional reinforcement and extension activities are provided on the *Lesen* pages, with further consolidation and practice on the **Activity Sheets**, in the **Exam Skills Workbooks** and on the **Resources and Planning OxBox CD-ROM**, in the form of interactive flashcards. Extra grammar practice is available at the end of the Students' Book in the grammar reference section.

Target language in the classroom

GCSE German for GCSE builds on good practice at KS3, providing support through rubrics and examples to maximise the use of German as the means of communication in the classroom. Comprehension questions for listening and reading activities are given in English, however, mirroring the style of the OCR exams, as are the more complicated instructions for the Controlled Assessment-style tasks in the *Jetzt seid ihr dran!* and *Szenario* sections.

It is worth spending time on a regular basis revising classroom language, so that students are reminded of the key phrases and encouraged to use them as much as possible.

Differentiation

Particular features of **GCSE German for OCR** that make it easier to differentiate work include:

- Two levels of **Exam Skills Workbooks** and foundation and higher-level *Lesen* pages in the Students' Book for fast- and slow-tracking learners.
- Record & Playback activities including examples of sample answers at different levels, with activities that will be accessible to all ranges of ability.
- The earlier activities on each core teaching spread of the Students' Book provide more accessible tasks for less able students. The activities towards the end of the spread are more challenging.
- The teaching notes for individual activities often provide suggestions for differentiation, e.g. varying the amount of support offered and adapting the tasks slightly to suit different students.

Independent learning

The following features of **GCSE German for OCR** are designed to encourage learner independence:

- The *Aktive Grammatik* and *Lesen* pages in each unit are ideal for independent work.
- Each unit's *Kompetenzen* page/Activity Sheet and the Checklist worksheet in the **Exam Skills Workbooks** encourage students to take responsibility for their own learning by providing opportunities for them to review what they have learned and reflect on areas for improvement.
- The *Vokabeln* pages at the end of each unit and on an Activity Sheet can be used independently by students as a reference source or as an aid to learning.

- The *Grammar Bank* section at the back of the Students' Book provides full explanations of all the grammar points in English together with additional practice activities, so that students are able to use it independently as a reference source.
- A strong emphasis on language learning strategies throughout (via the *Tipp* boxes and pages in the Students' Book and associated Activity Sheets) encourages students to progress as independent learners.
- Thc **Exam Skills Workbooks** are designed for independent work, with rubrics in English throughout.

PLTS and creativity

One of the key aims of **GCSE German for OCR**, and indeed of the new National Curriculum, is that students should be able to learn in a meaningful way. This means, for example, thinking flexibly, analysing language and problem-solving, justifying answers, and making predictions based on previous knowledge. It encourages students to move towards becoming independent learners. Once students take a more active role in their language learning, they make quicker progress and the thinking skills learned can be applied to other curriculum areas.

Creativity in language learning is not simply imaginative use of language, such as poetry, creative writing, etc. It also refers to resourcefulness, e.g. finding ways to express oneself using only a limited range of language, taking risks and experimenting with language.

See **Independent learning** above for examples of features of **GCSE German for OCR** that encourage students to take a more active role in their learning. In addition, the following types of activity used in the course help to promote thinking skills and creativity:

- Encourage students to deduce new language for themselves (e.g. verb endings, adjective endings) by working from what they already know.
- Ask students to spot the odd-one-out in a group of words/phrases, giving a reason. All appropriate answers should be accepted, provided that students can justify them, e.g. answers may be based on meaning, grammar, pronunciation, etc.
- Encourage students to apply previously learned language in different contexts.
- Provide opportunities for students to use language spontaneously. This promotes the development of coping strategies, since students need to find ways of communicating when they don't know the word for something, dealing with unpredictable situations, etc.
- Ask students to write something within an exact word count, e.g. 100 words exactly. This type of task encourages students to experiment with language and take risks, because in order to arrive at the precise word count they will need to paraphrase.
- Provide opportunities for students to share their knowledge in pairs/groups or during whole-class feedback.

Assessment

Assessment of learning

Regular assessment of student progress is an integral part of the learning process. **GCSE German for OCR** offers an approach to assessment in line with the National Curriculum and OCR GCSE syllabus.

A range of formative and summative assessment opportunities are provided on the **Assessment OxBox CD-ROM**: for details of this, see *An integrated approach: How OxBox works* on pages 11–12 of this book. In addition, **GCSE German for OCR** provides the following assessment opportunities:

- The *Szenario* page at the end of each unit in the Students' Book can be used as a practice Controlled Assessment task and graded using GCSE marking criteria (included on page 32 of this book).
- At the start of the teaching notes for each unit in this book, the **Assessment opportunities** section suggests activities from the forthcoming unit that may be suitable for formative assessment. Two skills are suggested for assessment in each unit.
- The **Assessment Sheets**, supplied on the CD accompanying this book, provide material for end of unit texts to help you monitor students' progress in the four key skill areas thoughout the course.

Assessment for Learning

Assessment for Learning (AfL) helps students to know and understand the standard they are aiming for, and also to understand what they need to do in order to achieve their objectives. It involves not only sharing learning goals with students, but also involving them in both peer- and self-assessment. AfL stresses the importance of ensuring that the information gained about students' progress is used, by both teachers and learners, to identify the next steps for learning. This might involve giving students opportunities to talk about what they have learned and what they have found difficult.

In **GCSE German for OCR**, each unit's *Kompetenzen* page/ Activity Sheet and accompanying Checklist in the **Exam Skills Workbooks** is specifically designed to encourage students to review their progress and reflect on areas for improvement. Formative assessments on the **Assessment OxBox CD-ROM** also include colour-coded confidence buttons, prompting students to reflect on how well they have absorbed the material covered in the Students' Book as they answer each question.

Further guidance on AfL can be found in *Training Materials for the Foundation Subjects* (Module 1 "Assessment for learning in everyday lessons"), which is available to download from The Standards Site (managed by the Department for Children, Schools and Families) (www.standards.dfes.gov.uk). For further guidance on AfL, see also the website of the Qualifications and Curriculum Authority (QCA) (www.qca.org.uk).

Unit 1A: Mein Leben		Overview grid		
Spread	**Contexts and objectives**	**Skills**	**Grammar**	**Vocabulary**
pages 12–13 **Wie man sich vorstellt**	• Describing personal traits	• Avoiding awkward silences	• The present tense	*das Alter; der Wohnort; faul; freundlich; fröhlich; groß; klein; lustig; also; eigentlich; Lieblings...; nun; wirklich*
pages 14–15 **Wie man seine Freunde und Familie beschreibt**	• Describing friends and family	• Asking questions in a discussion	• Gender of nouns • Adjective endings • Possessive adjectives in the accusative	*das Geschwister; die Frau; der Mann; alt; bekannt; dünn; erfolgreich; geschieden; getrennt; groß; jung; nett; verheiratet*
pages 16–17 **Wie man seine tägliche Routine beschreibt**	• Describing daily routine	• Sentence order	• Reflexive and separable verbs in the present tense	*der Feierabend; das Geschenk; sich anziehen; aufräumen; aufstehen; einschlafen; kochen*
pages 18–19 **Wie man die Hausarbeit einteilt**	• Discussing how to organise housework	• Adverbs of time • Making excuses	• The negative, *kein*	*abtrocknen; bügeln; dann; zuerst; Ich habe keine Lust.*
pages 20–21 **Wie man über das Leben zu Hause spricht**	• Talking about your home life	• Talking about different types of accommodation	• Plurals	*das Badezimmer; der Bungalow; das Doppelhaus; die Dusche; das Einfamilienhaus; das Esszimmer; der Garten; die Küche; das Schlafzimmer; das Schloss; das Schwimmbecken; die Wohnung; das Wohnzimmer; praktisch*
pages 22–23 **Aktive Grammatik**	• Grammar		• Uses of the present tense • Gender of nouns • Adjective endings in the accusative • Possessive adjectives • Reflexive pronouns	
page 24 **Kompetenzen**	• Summarising what you have learnt	• Asking questions to keep a conversation going and for clarification • Using filler words • Feeling confident when speaking • Listening to German • Improving pronunciation • Checking your work carefully for spelling • Looking out for umlauts • Learning gender • Checking verb tenses and verb endings • Using correct word order		
page 25 **Szenario**	• Writing an application to appear on reality TV • Preparing and taking part in a press conference	• Speaking practice • Writing practice		
page 26 **Vokabeln**	• Key language			
pages 171–172 **Lesen**	• Talking about yourself and others • To encourage independent reading and develop reading strategies • To provide alternative class and homework material	• Reading practice		

1A Mein Leben

Unit Objectives

Contexts and cultural focus: you and your life
Skills focus: starting a conversation with confidence; avoiding awkward silences; coping when you don't understand what's been said; improving your accuracy in written German; writing more sophisticated sentences
Grammar: telling the gender of common nouns; making plural forms of nouns; using the present tense of common regular and irregular verbs; using adjectives to show possession; using reflexive pronouns

Controlled assessment opportunities

Speaking: Students' Book, page 13 activity 9a
Speaking: Students' Book, page 15 activity 5b
Writing: Students' Book, page 17 activity 9
Writing: Students' Book, page 19 activity 8
Writing: Students' Book, page 21 activity 8
Writing: Students' Book, page 25 Zum Schreiben, activity 1
Speaking: Students' Book, page 25 Zum Sprechen, activity 3

See also ***GCSE German for OCR Assessment OxBox CD-ROM.***

An introduction to the unit Seite 11

- *Aim*: To introduce the themes of the unit.
- The opening spread of each unit is styled as the contents page of a teenage magazine. Illustrations, captions and skills summaries provide a preview of what is to come:

	Students' Book
Weißt du schon, wie man sich vorstellt?	pages 12–13
Weißt du schon, wie man seine Freunde und Familie beschreibt?	pages 14–15
Weißt du schon, wie man seine tägliche Routine beschreibt?	pages 16–17
Weißt du schon, wie man die Hausarbeit einteilt?	pages 18–19
Weißt du schon, wie man über das Leben zu Hause spricht?	pages 20–21

- Allow time for students to read the questions and cross-refer to the relevant pages of the Students' Book. They could do this individually or in pairs/ groups, followed by whole-class discussion.
- This spread also provides an opportunity for students to recap on familiar language. Ask them to think about language they already know that might be useful when working on the themes of the unit.
- At the end of work on Unit 1A:
  - If time permits, ask students to devise a replacement opening spread. What do they think should be on it, in terms of pictures, captions, etc.? What would they change/keep the same, and why? Ask them to imagine it is the contents page of a teenage magazine: what sort of captions and pictures do they feel would attract people to buy the magazine? This sort of activity encourages students to think about features of a text that make it suitable for a particular audience or purpose.
  - Allow time for students to return to this opening spread to answer the questions, review what they have learned and reflect on areas for improvement. What did they find difficult, interesting, etc.? What do they think are the most important things they have learned in this unit?

Wie man sich vorstellt

Seiten 12–13

Planner

➤ Objectives

- Describing personal traits

➤ Resources

Students' Book, pages 12–13
CD 1, tracks 2–3
Grammar Workbook, page 45

➤ Key language

das Alter; der Wohnort
faul; freundlich; fröhlich; groß; klein; lustig
also; eigentlich; Lieblings…; nun; wirklich

➤ Skills

- Avoiding awkward silences

➤ Grammar

- The present tense

➤ PLTS

Question 9a: Creative thinkers/Reflective learners/Team workers/Self-managers
Question 9b: Reflective learners/Self-managers

➤ Starters

- Display a jumble of key questions and answers, e.g. *Wie heißt du? Wie alt bist du? Wo wohnst du? Ich bin 14 Jahre alt. Ich wohne in X. Ich heiße Anna.* etc. Students race against the clock to match the questions to their corresponding answers.
- Ask a student a simple question, e.g. *Wie alt bist du? Wo wohnst du?* The student answers and asks another student a question. He/She answers, and so on. If necessary, display model questions and answers for support.
- Display the four profiles from page 12 with some key words blanked out. Students supply the missing items. To make this into a competitive activity, divide the class into two teams: teams win a point if they provide the correct word or phrase at their first attempt.

➤ Plenaries

- Call out an answer from the spread, e.g. *Ich wohne in Freiburg, das liegt in Südwestdeutschland.* Students compete to provide the corresponding question, e.g. *Wo wohnst du?* Do this activity in reverse: call out a question and students compete to answer.
- Show the class two photos of people (not famous), taken from magazines. Divide the class into two teams. Team A acts as the person in photo A; team B acts as the person in photo B. Teams build a conversation between the two people, imagining they are meeting each other for the first time. They take turns to ask and answer questions.
- Display some German infinitives with which students will be familiar, e.g. *heißen, wohnen, haben, sein, machen.* Challenge students to write five sentences, using each of the verbs in a different person, e.g. *Ich bin 14 Jahre alt.* etc.

1 Schau dir die Website-Einträge 1–4 und die Bilder a–d an. Was passt zusammen?

- As an introduction to the spread, students read the website profiles and match each of them to the appropriate picture.

Answers:

a 4; **b** 1; **c** 2; **d** 3

2a Du willst dich deinem/deiner Internet-Partner/in beschreiben. Wie bist du? Was passt zusammen?

- Students begin to think about how they would describe themselves.
- They match the English and German adjectives.

Answers:

1 e; **2** a; **3** g; **4** h; **5** f; **6** b; **7** d; **8** i; **9** c

2b Such in einem Wörterbuch noch weitere fünf positive und fünf negative Adjektive, um dich zu beschreiben.

- Students now look in a dictionary to find five more positive and five more negative adjectives to describe themselves.

2c Arbeite mit einem Partner/einer Partnerin und frag ihn/sie: „Wie bist du?“ B ↔ A

- Students work in pairs. They draw upon the vocabulary from the previous three activities to describe themselves.

3 Hör gut zu. Wer spricht hier? Füll die Tabelle aus.

- Students listen to the recording and fill in the table.
- This activity offers two opportunities for differentiation. The first is the extra info in

column 3, the second the adverbs *sehr* and *immer* which some students may know.
- Listen again and draw students' attention to the different ways of greeting people.

CD 1, track 2 **Seite 13, Übung 3**

1
Hallo, ich heiße Florian. Das buchstabiert man F-L-O-R-I-A-N. Ich wohne in Dresden. Das liegt in Ostdeutschland. Ich bin groß und immer fröhlich. Ich möchte mein Englisch verbessern.
2
Hallo, ich heiße Gülçin. Das buchstabiert man G-Ü-L-C-I-N. Meine Freunde sagen, dass ich sehr nett bin, aber meine Mutti sagt, dass ich faul bin. Ich wohne in Frankfurt am Main, das ist in Westdeutschland. Ich finde englische Rockmusik toll.
3
Gruezi, ich heiße Elke. Das buchstabiert man E-L-K-E. Ich wohne in Luzern, das ist in der Schweiz. Und wie ich bin? Also, mittelgroß und sehr freundlich. Ich möchte gern London besuchen.
4
Servus, ich bin der Thomi. Meine Mutti und mein Stiefvater nennen mich Thomas, aber meine Freunde sagen Thomi. Ich wohne in Österreich, in der Stadt Salzburg. Ich bin 1 m 75 groß und meistens ziemlich lustig. Englische Filme sind echt cool.

Answers:

Who?	Home town?	Country?	What is he/ she like?	Why does he/she want an English partner?
Florian	Dresden	in East Germany	tall, always happy	to practise English
Gulcin	Frankfurt am Main	in West Germany	very nice, lazy	finds English rock music great
Elke	Luzern	in Switzerland	medium height, very friendly	to visit London
Thomi	Salzburg	in Austria	(1m75) tall, jovial	English films are cool

4 Buchstabiere zuerst diese Namen und dann deinen und andere Namen. Dein/e Partner/in muss die Namen aufschreiben. Tauscht dann die Rollen.

4–6

- Recap the German alphabet by reciting it.
- Ask students to spell the names listed, their name and other names of their choice for their partner. Their partner writes down what he/she hears. They then swap roles.

5a Lara und ihre englische Internet-Partnerin sprechen zum ersten Mal am Telefon miteinander. Sie stellen sich vor. Hör gut zu und beantworte die Fragen.

4–6

- Students listen to a telephone conversation between Lara and her English Internet partner, Sarah, and answer the questions.
- Encourage students to keep in mind descriptions from previous activities in order to try and predict what they might hear.

CD 1, track 3 **Seite 13, Übung 5**

Lara: Hallo, ich heiße Lara und, äh, ich bin 14, also 14 Jahre alt, und wie heißt du?
Sarah: Hi Lara, ich bin auch 14 und ich heiße Sarah.
Lara: Ah, toll, hallo Sarah, [awkward silence]... ähm, also Sarah, wo wohnst du eigentlich genau?
Sarah: In Loughborough, das liegt in Mittelengland.
Lara: Ah, ja und ich, ich wohne in Freiburg, das liegt in Südwestdeutschland. Also, Loughborough, ist das eine große Stadt? Freiburg ist ziemlich groß und echt toll.
Sarah: Oh, ich habe das nicht verstanden. Noch mal bitte.
[Lara repeats]
Sarah: Ah, danke. Ja, Loughborough ist mittelgroß und ein bisschen langweilig. Lara, hast du Geschwister? Ich habe einen Bruder – er ist ganz nett.
Lara: Mann, das ist ja lustig, ich habe auch einen Bruder, aber er ist soooo doof! [awkward silence]
Sarah: Und wie heißt deine Lieblingsband? Was für Musik magst du?
Lara: Also, ich mag Rockmusik am liebsten, du auch?
Sarah: Ja, ich finde Tokio Hotel ganz toll. Lara, es tut mir Leid, ich muss jetzt Schluss machen, meine Mutti ruft...
Lara: Okay, Sarah, das ist cool, sprechen wir am Samstag wieder?
Sarah: Also, ja, gut, bis Samstag, dann.

Answers:

a 14 years old, Freiburg, in South-West Germany; **b** Freiburg is quite big and really great; **c** one brother; **d** he's quite nice; **e** she finds rock music quite good

5b Schau dir die Ausdrücke in der Tipp-Box an und hör dann nochmal gut zu. Welche Ausdrücke benutzt Lara?

4–6

- Students read through the words and phrases in the *Tipp* section on page 12.
- They then listen to the recording again and note down which of these words and phrases Lara uses.

Answers:

äh, also, ah, toll, ähm, Mann, das ist, Also, ja, gut

6 Partnerarbeit. Wählt eine bekannte Persönlichkeit. A stellt die Fragen von Seite 12 und B antwortet. Weißt du, wer A ist? B ↔ A.

4–9

- This activity is an opportunity for students to use what they have learnt so far about describing themselves and other people.
- Students work with a partner. Partner B chooses a famous person. Partner A asks questions to guess who the person is. They then swap roles.

7 Füll die Tabelle mit den richtigen Verbformen aus.

- Practice of the present tense. Students fill in the table with the correct form of the present tense.
- Remind them to refer back to the *Grammatik* section for support if necessary.

Answers:

Verb in present tense	ich	du	er/sie/es/man	wir	ihr	sie/Sie
sein	bin	bi**st**	ist	sind	seid	sind
haben	habe	hast	ha**t**	haben	habt	haben
heißen	heiße	hei**ßt**	heißt	heißen	heißt	heißen
wohnen	wohn**e**	wohnst	wohnt	wohnen	wohnt	wohnen

8 Schau dir diese Verbendungen an. Zu welcher Person (*ich, du, er/sie/es, wir, ihr, sie/Sie*) gehören sie? Schreib das Subjekt auf.

- More practice of the present tense.
- Students look at the verb endings listed, decide to which person they belong and write down the subject of the verb.

Answers:

a ich; **b** er/sie/es; **c** ihr; **d** ich; **e** wir/sie/Sie; **f** er/sie/es

9a Choose an Internet correspondent from page 12 you'd like to meet and talk to. Work with a partner and prepare the conversation.

- **Write down the questions in German you'd like to ask your correspondent and your own answers to these questions in case he/she asks you them as well.**
- **Practise your conversation in German with your partner. A asks the questions and B answers. B ↔ A. Include some filler expressions.**

- This activity draws together what students have learnt in the spread. It is an ideal assessment opportunity.
- Encourage students to incorporate as much of the vocabulary and as many of the ideas covered in the spread into their conversation as possible.
- Remind them to use filler words to avoid awkward silences and to make the conversation flow.
- This activity encourages students to generate ideas, to communicate previous learning and to work confidently with others to achieve results. It covers the Creative thinkers, Reflective learners, Team workers and Self-managers groups of skills from the framework of personal, learning and thinking skills.

Success criteria:

- ideas communicated
- pronunciation, and intonation and fluency
- range of vocabulary and structures used

9b To make contact with your German correspondent:

a fill in the web form on page 12 in German.

b write a short message to introduce yourself.

- This activity draws together what students have learnt about introducing themselves.
- Encourage students to use vocabulary and structures from the spread in their message.
- This activity encourages students to communicate previous learning and to work towards and achieve goals. It covers the Reflective learners and Self-managers groups of skills from the framework of personal, learning and thinking skills.

Wie man seine Freunde und Familie beschreibt

Seiten 14–15

Planner

➤ Objectives
- Describing friends and family

➤ Resources
Students' Book, pages 14–15
CD 1, track 4
Grammar Workbook, pages 8, 12, 21–23
Activity Sheet 1

➤ Key language
das Geschwister; die Frau; der Mann
(auf die Kinder) aufpassen
alt; bekannt; dünn; erfolgreich; geschieden; getrennt; groß; jung; nett; verheiratet

➤ Skills
- Asking questions in a discussion

➤ Grammar
- Gender of nouns
- Adjective endings
- Possessive adjectives in the accusative

➤ PLTS
Question 5a: Creative thinkers/Reflective learners/Team workers/Self-managers
Question 5b: Creative thinkers/Reflective learners/Team workers/Self-managers

➤ Starters
- Display people and animals from the spread, e.g. *Bruder, Frau, Hund*, etc. Students brainstorm adjectives that could be used to describe them. e.g. *nett*, etc. Make a list of adjectives and keep it to use later.
- Display the list of adjectives from starter activity 1. Go round the class asking students to use any one of them in a simple sentence, beginning with a possessive, e.g. *Meine Mutter ist* ***nett****. Meine Schwester ist* ***geduldig****.* etc. Once all students have said a sentence, ask them where the adjective is positioned in the sentences they have produced (*after the verb*). Then ask them where else adjectives can be positioned in sentences (*before the noun*). Explain that you will be looking in more detail at adjectives positioned before nouns.
- Have a quick class quiz based on the sentences on page 14. Divide the class into two teams. Display two headings: *Michael Schumacher* and *Boris Becker*. How much can each team remember about each of these sports stars?

➤ Plenaries
- Students work in pairs. They take it in turns to choose a famous person or a well-known fictional character and to describe him or her and his or her family to their partner. Their partner tries to guess who it is, e.g.
  Partner A: *Er war ein sehr erfolgreicher Rennfahrer und ist in der ganzen Welt bekannt.*
  Partner B: *Hat er Geschwister?*
  Partner A: *Ja, er hat einen jüngeren Bruder.*
- Play a memory game to practise adjective endings in the accusative. Start by saying a sentence including an adjective in the accusative, e.g.
  Teacher: *Ich habe einen kleinen Bruder.*
  Student 1: *Ich habe einen kleinen Bruder und eine nette Schwester.*
  Student 2: *Ich habe einen kleinen Bruder, eine nette Schwester und* ein *hungriges Kaninchen.*
  etc.
  Display the list of adjectives from starter activity 1 for support.
- Students use vocabulary from the spread to describe the worst family they can imagine, e.g. a naughty little brother, etc. They present their descriptions to the class which votes for the worst imaginary family.

1a Welche Sätze passen zu wem? Mach eine Liste für Michael Schumacher und eine für Boris Becker.

4–6

- As an introduction to the spread, students read the speech bubbles and allocate each to Michael Schumacher or to Boris Becker.

Answers:

Michael Schumacher: a, c, e, f, h, i, l
Boris Becker: b, d, g, j, k

1b Such die Adjektive in den Sätzen a–l. Welche stehen vor einem Nomen? Welche stehen nach einem Verb? Mach zwei Listen. Welchen Unterschied stellst du fest? (Denk an die Endungen!)

4–6

- Students read the sentences again and, this time, note down adjectives that come before a noun and adjectives that come after a verb.
- They then establish the difference between the adjectives in each list.

Answers:

Adjectives before a noun: erfolgreich**er**, jünger**en**, älter**e**,

Adjectives after a verb: bekannt, groß, kräftig, dünn, verheiratet, getrennt, geschieden, sportlich, nett

Difference: when an adjective is positioned before a noun, the ending changes according to number, gender and case.

1c Wie heißen diese Adjektive auf Englisch? Schau im Wörterbuch nach.

- Students write down the English for each of the adjectives in activity 1b.
- They can look in a dictionary if necessary.

Answers:

erfolgreicher – successful; jüngeren – younger; ältere – older; bekannt – known; groß – tall; kräftig – strong; dünn – slim; verheiratet – married; getrennt – separated; geschieden – divorced; sportlich – sporty; nett – nice

2a Lara stellt sich und ihre Familie vor. Hör gut zu und beantworte die Fragen auf Englisch.

- Students listen to Lara describing herself and her family and answer the questions in English.

CD 1, track 4 **Seite 15, Übung 2**

Also, wie ihr wisst, heiße ich Lara Kleiser, bin 14 Jahre alt und wohne in Freiburg in Südwestdeutschland. Ich wohne dort seit 5 Jahren. Meine Familie ist ziemlich groß. Es gibt meine Mutti, meinen Stiefvater, meinen jüngeren Bruder und meine zwei älteren Schwestern. Meine Eltern sind geschieden: mein Vater wohnt also nicht bei uns. Ich habe auch ein süßes, kleines Kaninchen. Es heißt Kniffel. Mein Bruder heißt Jens und ist 12, und meine Schwestern Lisa und Katja, die Zwillinge, sind 17 Jahre alt. Sie sind wirklich nett und wir verstehen uns gut. Aber mein kleiner Bruder geht mir auf die Nerven. Er ist so faul und total doof. Meine beste Freundin heißt Silke. Sie ist so groß wie ich und hat meistens gute Laune. Ich finde meine Familie echt toll, weil wir viel zusammen machen.

Answers:

a it's quite large; **b** three (a brother and 2 sisters); **c** they are twins, they are 17, they are nice and she gets on well with them; **d** he gets on her nerves, he is so lazy and totally stupid; **e** her name is Silke, she is as tall as Lara and is usually in a good mood; **f** she finds her family really great (because they do a lot together).

2b Du willst Lara einige Fragen stellen. Hör noch einmal gut zu und schreib die Fragen zu den folgenden Antworten.

- Students read through the list of answers. They then listen to Lara again and write a question for each of the answers listed.
- If necessary, point out that students can use the wording in the answers to form their questions.

4–6

Answers:

a Wie alt bist du? **b** Wie viele Mitglieder gibt es in deiner Familie? **c** Wie sind deine Schwestern? **d** Wie heißt dein Bruder? **e** Wie groß ist deine Freundin? **f** Wie findest du deine Familie?

3 Schau dir die Grammatik-Box an. Schreib neue Sätze mit den folgenden Adjektiven.

- Students write a sentence, similar to the examples in the *Grammatik* section, for each of the adjectives listed.
- Remind students that when adjectives are positioned before a noun, the adjective endings will change according to the gender of the noun.

A1 Activity Sheet 1 provides additional activities to support students with their work on describing themselves, their friends and their family.

4 Schreib einen Artikel über dich und deine Familie für die *Hallo!*-Webseite. (Wenn du nicht über deine eigene Familie schreiben möchtest, kannst du dir vorstellen, du bist eine berühmte Person!) Benutze die Ausdrücke aus der Wortschatz-Box auf Seite 14.

4–9

- Students write an article about themselves and their family for the *Hallo!* magazine website.
- Encourage them to use the phrases from the vocabulary box.
- Point out to students that they can stretch the truth to make their writing more interesting, for example, pretending that they play in a band.

5a Work in groups of six. Each person chooses a character from the TV series *Beste Freunde* and writes sentences about his/her imaginary family and friends.

4–9

PLTS

- Students begin to think about describing a person in more detail.
- This activity encourages students to generate ideas and explore possibilities whilst communicating their learning in relevant ways. It also encourages them to collaborate with others to work towards goals. It covers the Creative thinkers, Reflective learners, Team workers and Self-managers groups of skills from the framework of personal, learning and thinking skills.

5b In your groups, act out a scene from *Beste Freunde* in which each character talks about themselves and their family. Try to find out as much as you can about the other characters by asking questions. Act out your scene in front of the class. Record it using the OxBox software.

4–9

PLTS

- Students use what they have prepared in activity 9b to act out the scene. This is an ideal assessment opportunity.
- This encourages students to connect their own and others' ideas and expereinces in inventive ways, to communicate their learning in relevant ways, and to collaborate with others to work towards goals. It covers the Creative thinkers, Reflective learners, Team workers and Self-managers groups of skills from the framework of personal, learning and thinking skills.

Success criteria:

- ideas communicated
- pronunciation and intonation and fluency
- range of vocabulary and structures used
- personal opinions given

Wie man seine tägliche Routine beschreibt

Seiten 16–17

Planner

➤ **Objectives**
- Describing daily routine

➤ **Resources**
Students' Book, pages 16–17
CD 1, track 5
Grammar Workbook, pages 41, 43
Activity Sheet 2

➤ **Key language**
der Feierabend; das Geschenk
sich anziehen; aufräumen; aufstehen; einschlafen; kochen

➤ **Skills**
- Sentence order

➤ **Grammar**
- Reflexive and separable verbs in the present tense

➤ **PLTS**
Question 4: Creative thinkers/Reflective learners/ Team workers/Self-managers
Question 8: Creative thinkers/Reflective learners/ Team workers/Self-managers

➤ **Starters**
- Display some activities that students are likely to do as part of their daily routine, e.g. *sich duschen; sich anziehen,* etc. Give students a time limit to put these in the order they usually do them each day. Compare answers as a class.
- Display some of the separable verbs from the spread, e.g. *aufstehen; aufräumen; einkaufen,* etc. Challenge students to use each of them in a sentence on the topic of the spread, e.g. *Ich stehe um 7 Uhr auf.* etc.
- Students brainstorm things they might do on a special day, such as a Birthday, e.g. *Freunde treffen,* etc. Make a list and keep this to use in plenary activities 1 and 2.

➤ **Plenaries**
- The class describes a day – either a normal week day or a special day. Start with an introductory sentence. Then go round the class with each student continuing the description, e.g.
Teacher: *Der Wecker rasselt! Aber es ist doch Wochenende!.*
Student 1: *Ich stehe mich auf, dusche kurz und ziehe mich an.*
Student 2: *Dann, gehe ich frühstücken.* etc.
If necessary, display possible activities and vocabulary from the spread for support.
- Students write a paragraph describing what they usually do on their Birthday. They should include separable and reflexive verbs. Display the list of activities from starter activity 3 for support. Students read out their descriptions to the class who decides which is the best Birthday.
- Students choose a famous person and describe what they think is his/her daily routine. The class tries to guess who they are talking about.

1 Partnerarbeit. Schaut euch Annikas Tagebuch an und beschreibt Annikas Tag.

4–6

- As an introduction to the spread, students look at Annika's diary.
- They work with a partner to describe her day.

2 Schau dir die Bilder von Lutz an. Wie feiert er Fasching? Welche Sätze passen zu welchem Bild?

4–6

- Students look at the pictures of Lutz celebrating *Fasching*.
- They match the pictures to the sentences to create a description of his day.

Answers:

1 g; **2** b; **3** e; **4** f; **5** c; **6** d

3a Hör gut zu. Was für einen Tag beschreiben Ann-Kathrin und Daniel?

4–6

- Students listen to Ann-Kathrin and Daniel.
- They note down what type of day each of them describes.

CD 1, track 5 **Seite 17, Übung 3**

Ann-Cathrin
Hallo, ich bin die Ann-Cathrin. Was ich so jeden Tag mache? Also, normalerweise stehe ich um 7 Uhr auf. Das ist einfach zuuuu früh!! Ich dusche mich schnell, ziehe mich an und um halb acht frühstücke ich dann. Meistens esse ich Brot oder ein Brötchen mit Marmelade und trinke ein Glas Orangensaft. Ich putze mir die Zähne, und danach gehe ich zur Schule. Um Viertel nach eins komme ich nach Hause und esse mein Mittagessen. Nach den Hausaufgaben treffe ich meine Freunde und um 19 Uhr gibt es Abendessen. Dann sehe ich

ein bisschen fern oder chatte im Internet und um zehn Uhr gehe ich ins Bett. Meistens schlafe ich so um elf Uhr ein.

Daniel

Also, ich heiße Daniel und heute ist ein toller Tag. Wir machen heute Abend eine Party, weil ich Geburtstag habe. Aber zuerst wasche ich mich, ziehe mich an und frühstücke mit meiner Familie. Alle singen 'Happy Birthday' und geben mir Geschenke. Ich bekomme eine Digitalkamera, ein Buch und einige CDs. Das ist super. Nach dem Mittagessen kommen meine Freunde und wir machen eine Einkaufsliste für die Party. Wir gehen einkaufen und dann machen wir Platz in meinem Zimmer. Meine Freunde bringen ihre CDs und um acht Uhr kommen die Gäste. Ich bekomme noch mehr Geschenke. Ich liebe Geburtstage!! Wir haben gute Musik – ziemlich laut – und wir tanzen bis Mitternacht.

Answers:

Ann-Cathrin: a normal school day
Daniel: his Birthday

3b Hör noch einmal zu. Wie sagt man auf Deutsch...?

- Students listen again carefully and note down the German for the English phrases listed.

4–6

Answers:

a Ich dusche mich. **b** Ich ziehe mich an. **c** Ich frühstücke. **d** Ich putze mir die Zähne. **e** Ich gehe zur Schule. **f** Ich schlafe...ein. **g** Wir machen eine Party. **h** Ich bekomme eine Digitalkamera. **i** Wir gehen einkaufen.

3c Hör noch einmal zu und füll die Lücken aus.

- Students listen again and pick out more detail to complete the sentences.
- Give students time to read the sentences first to try and predict what the missing words will be.

4–6

Answers:

a 7; **b** trinke; **c** Viertel nach eins; **d** treffe; **e** heute; **f** kommen; **g** Einkaufsliste für die Party; **h** Geschenke

4 Partnerarbeit. Schaut euch die Zeichnungen unter an und beschreibt den Tagesablauf. Schreibt Sätze. Macht einen Wettbewerb in der Klasse. Welches Paar hat die beste Beschreibung?

- Students work with a partner to look at the drawings and write sentences describing the daily routines.
- They present their descriptions to the class which votes for the best one.
- This encourages students to think creatively, to communicate previous learning and to collaborate with others to work towards goals. It covers the Creative thinkers, Reflective learners, Team workers and Self-managers groups of skills.

4–6

PLTS

5 Beschreib jetzt deinen Tagesablauf. Wähl entweder einen normalen Wochentag, ein Wochenende oder einen besonderen Tag.

- Students use the work they have done in activity 4 as a model to describe their own daily routine.
- They choose a normal week day, a weekend or a special day.

4–6

A2 Activity Sheet 2 provides activities on describing daily routine.

6 Übersetze die folgenden Sätze auf Englisch.

- Read the *Grammatik* section on reflexive verbs.
- To ensure that students have understood, ask them to translate the sentences into English.

Answers:

a He has a wash. **b** She has a shower. **c** You get dressed. **d** We dress up. **e** You get changed. **f** They clean their teeth.

7 Setz das passende Reflexivpronomen (*mich, dich, sich*) ein.

- Further practice of reflexive verbs. Students complete the sentences with the appropriate reflexive pronoun.

Answers:

a Ich dusche **mich**. **b** Wir ziehen **uns** an. **c** Er putzt **sich** die Zähne. **d** Du verkleidest **dich**. **e** Sie zieht **sich** aus.

8 You are planning a surprise party for a friend. With a partner, discuss in German all of the things you have to do on the day (e.g. shopping, cooking, decorating the room), and when you will do them.

- This activity draws together what students have practised in the spread.
- It encourages students to generate and explore ideas, to communicate previous learning and to collaborate with others to work towards goals. It covers the Creative thinkers, Reflective learners, Team workers and Self-managers groups of skills.

4–9

PLTS

9 You're spending a day in the *Big Brother* house. Fill in the blog on page 16 to describe what happens. Then read your blog out to the class and decide whose is the best.

- This activity is an ideal assessement opportunity.
- Encourage students to think back to previous activities for ideas and support.

4–9

Success criteria:

- amount of information communicated
- variety of vocabulary and structures used
- number of personal opinions given

Wie man die Hausarbeit einteilt

Seiten 18–19

Planner

➤ Objectives
- Discussing how to organise housework

➤ Resources
Students' Book, pages 18–19
CD 1, track 6
Grammar Workbook, pages 30, 38
Activity Sheet 3

➤ Key language
abtrocknen; bügeln
dann; zuerst
Ich habe keine Lust.

➤ Skills
- Adverbs of time
- Making excuses

➤ Grammar
- The negative, *kein*

➤ PLTS
Question 7: Creative thinkers/Reflective learners/Team workers/Self-managers
Question 8: Creative thinkers/Reflective learners/Self-managers

➤ Starters
- Play a miming game to practise household chores. Mime doing a chore and ask students to guess what it is in German. They should use full sentences, e.g. *Sie bügeln? Sie waschen das Auto?*
- Go round the class asking *Was machst du?* Students reply with household chores that they do. Go round the class again asking, *Was willst du nicht machen?* Students reply with jobs that they don't like doing. With more able classes, expand on this by asking *Warum?* Students reply using *weil…*
- Go round the class asking questions, but explain that they have to answer negatively, i.e. using *nicht, nie* or *kein*, e.g.
  Teacher: *Hast du einen Hund?*
  Student: *Nein, ich habe keinen Hund.*
  Teacher: *Spielst du gern auf der Playstation?*
  Student: *Ich spiele nie auf der Playstation.*

➤ Plenaries
- Display the adverbs of time featured in the spread, *zuerst, dann, danach, anschließend, zum Schluss* and challenge students to use them all in a short paragraph on the theme of the spread. Volunteers read out their paragraph.
- Display some of the expressions used to make excuses, e.g. *Ich habe keine Lust. Ich habe jetzt keine Zeit. Ich habe keinen Bock. Ich mag jetzt nicht*, etc. Go round the class asking *Kannst du mir bitte helfen?* Students reply with an excuse, using *weil*, e.g. *Ich habe keine Zeit, weil ich meine Hausaufgaben mache.* Remind them to watch out for word order.
- Conduct a class survey. What household chores do students do at home? Display the results in the form of a graph or pie chart. Discuss this as a class. What are the most and least popular chores? Why might this be the case?

1a Welcher Text passt zu welchem Bild?

- As an introduction to the spread, students work with a partner to match the captions to the pictures.

4–6

Answers:

a 8; **b** 11; **c** 12; **d** 10; **e** 3; **f** 2; **g** 4; **h** 7; **i** 1; **j** 6; **k** 9; **l** 5

1b Wer macht was in deiner Familien? Schreib Sätze. Überprüfe deine Antworten mit deinem Partner/deiner Partnerin.

- Students continue to work with a partner.
- They build sentences to say who does what in their family. Remind students to watch out for any mistakes their partner might make.

4–6

2a Was für Hausarbeit ist das? Du hast nur eine Minute Zeit, um die Wörter zu entziffern.

- A quick activity to check students' knowledge of household chores in German.
- Students have a minute to unjumble the household tasks. Encourage them to think back to the previous two activites for ideas of what the words are likely to be.

4–6

Answers:

a bügeln; **b** putzen; **c** staubsaugen; **d** aufräumen; **e** abtrocknen; **f** kochen

2b Überleg dir noch andere Arten von Hausarbeit. Schau die Wörter im Wörterbuch nach, bring die Buchstaben durcheinander und lass dann deine Klasse die Wörter entziffern.

- Students think of more household chores. They look these up in a dictionary and then list them, but with the letters all jumbled up.
- The rest of the class tries to decipher the words.

4–6

3 Es gibt bei Lisa in der Küche ein schreckliches Durcheinander. Was muss Lisa alles machen? Arbeite mit einem Partner/einer Partnerin und ergänze die Liste von Lisas Mutti.

- Read the *Tipp* section on adverbs of time.
- Students then work with a partner to complete Lisa's list of chores.
- Encourage them to think back to the chores mentioned in previous activities for support.

4–6

4 Hör gut zu und sieh dir die Bilder oben an. Welche Hausarbeiten sollen diese jungen Leute machen und was sind ihre Ausreden? Füll die Tabelle auf Englisch aus.

- Students listen and fill in the table.
- Encourage them to think about what they might hear.

4–6

CD 1, track 6 — **Seite 19, Übung 4**

1
Vati: Florian, putz bitte den Boden im Bad.
Florian: Ach, Vati, ich habe jetzt keinen Bock, weil ich gerade diesen Krimi sehen möchte.
2
Mutti: Anna, bitte mach jetzt dein Bett.
Anna: Aber Mutti, ich kann jetzt nicht, weil ich gerade meine Fingernägel lackiere.
3
Mutti: Jan, kannst du mir bitte helfen und die Spülmaschine füllen?
Jan: Tut mir Leid, ich habe keine Zeit. Ich spreche gerade mit Ramona am Telefon.
4
Vati: Gülçin, kannst du bitte das Auto waschen?
Gülçin: Ich habe jetzt keine Lust, ich will gerade mit meinem Kaninchen spazieren gehen.
5
Mutti: Thomas, bitte bügle deine Hemden.
Thomas: Aber ich habe jetzt keine Zeit. Ich muss dieses Spiel zu Ende machen.
6
Vati: Sandra, bitte koch jetzt das Abendessen.
Sandra: Ich mag jetzt nicht, weil ich gerade meine Hausaufgaben mache.

Answers:

Name	Which chores?	Excuse
Florian	cleaning bathroom floor	wants to watch a crime thriller
Anna	make the bed	painting finger nails
Jan	load the dishwasher	speaking with Ramona on the phone
Gülçin	wash the car	going to walk his rabbit
Thomas	iron his shirts	finishing playing his game
Sandra	cook evening meal	doing homework

5a Schreib deine eigenen Ausreden zu den folgenden Bitten. Benutze die Ausdrücke aus der Tipp-Box.

- Read through the excuses in the *Tipp* section.
- Students practise writing their own excuses, saying why they can't do the tasks listed.

4–6

5b Macht einen Wettbewerb in eurer Klasse. Wer hat die besten Ausreden? Lest eure Ausreden vor und vergebt Punkte von 1 bis 10: 10 für die besten Ausreden und 1 für die schlechtesten.

- Students read out their excuses from activity 5a.
- The class allocates points from 1 to 10: 10 points for the best excuses, 1 for the worst.
- The student with the most points wins.

4–6

A3 Activity Sheet 3 provides additional activities on household chores.

6 Setz die richtige Form von *kein* ein.

- Read through the *Grammatik* section on negative sentences as a class.
- Students then complete the sentences with the appropriate form of *kein*.

Answers:

a Ich habe **keinen** Hund. **b** Sie hat **kein** Telefon.
c Du kaufst **keine** Bananen. **d** Er hat **keinen** Bock.

7 Work with a partner. A is the parent and B is the son/daughter. B should be helping A with the housework, but B keeps coming up with excuses to get out of helping! B ↔ A.

- An activity to draw together the ideas, and grammar points covered in the spread.
- This encourages students to generate ideas and explore possibilities whilst communicating their learning in relevant ways and to collaborate with others to work towards goals. It covers the Creative thinkers, Reflective learners, Team workers and Self-managers groups of skills.

4–9

PLTS

8 Write a scene in a play entitled *Krise im Haushalt der Meiers* (Crisis in the Meier household). It should include the following characters: grandmother, mother, a baby, a 3-year-old and a 15-year-old.

- A writing activity to draw together the vocabulary, ideas, and grammar points covered in the spread. This is an ideal assessment opportunity.
- This activity encourages students to generate ideas and explore possibilities, setting goals for their development and work and to work towards these goals. It covers the Creative thinkers, Reflective learners and Self-managers groups of skills.

4–9

PLTS

Success criteria:

- amount of information communicated
- variety of vocabulary and structures used

Wie man über das Leben zu Hause spricht

Seiten 20–21

Planner

➤ Objectives

- Talking about your home life

➤ Resources

Students' Book, pages 20–21
CD 1, track 7
Grammar Workbook, page 9
Activity Sheet 4

➤ Key language

das Badezimmer; der Bungalow; das Doppelhaus; die Dusche; das Einfamilienhaus; das Esszimmer; der Garten; die Küche; das Schlafzimmer; das Schloss; das Schwimmbad; die Wohnung; das Wohnzimmer
praktisch

➤ Grammar

- Plurals

➤ PLTS

Question 2a: Independent enquirers/Creative thinkers/Team workers/Self-managers/Effective participators
Question 7: Independent enquirers/Creative thinkers/Reflective learners/Team workers/Self-managers/Effective participators

➤ Starters

- Display the different types of accommodation mentioned in the spread, e.g. *Bungalow, Doppelhaus, Einfamilienhaus*, etc. Next to these display the English translations but in jumbled order. Students race to match the German and the English. Compare answers as a class.
- Display some nouns from the spread, some singular and some plural, e.g. *die Stunde, die Partner, der Garten, die Freundin*, etc. Give students a time limit to categorise these under the headings **Singular** and **Plural**. When they have finished, compare answers as a class. Ask students how they could tell which nouns were in the plural form.
- Display some sentences from the spread all jumbled up, e.g.
  toll Einfamilienhaus finde Ich dieses (*Ich finde dieses Einfamilienhaus ganz toll.*)
  Bungalow den finde echt Ich gut (*Ich finde den Bungalow echt gut.*)
  Weiß ist Bad Unser in ganz (*Unser Bad ist ganz in Weiß.*)
  auch haben Garten Wir vielen mit Blumen schönen einen (*Wir haben auch einen schönen Garten mit vielen Blumen.*)
  Give students a time limit to unjumble the sentences. Compare answers as a class and elicit what the sentences mean in English. If there is time, ask students to rewrite the four sentences, changing certain elements, e.g. *Unsere Küche ist ganz in Rot.*

➤ Plenaries

- Students play a version of consequences to describe a home. Each student writes a statement about a home at the top of a piece of paper, e.g. *Es ist ein Einfamilienhaus.* They then fold over the paper so their sentence can't be seen and pass it on. The next student adds another sentence to describe the home, e.g. *Es hat einen großen, sonnigen Garten.* Pass each piece of paper on in this way five or six times. Each student then opens the piece of paper they have and read out the descripton.
- Challenge students to write five sentences on the theme of the spread, each one containing a plural. Compare sentences as a class and list some of them. Discuss which category (a–g) each of the plurals belongs to.
- Students write a paragraph, describing what they would consider to be a nightmare home. Volunteers read their paragraph out to the class. The class votes for the worst home described.

1 Schau dir die verschiedenen Häuser oben an. Wähl für jedes Bild das richtige Wort.

4–6

- As an introduction to this spread, students look at the pictures and choose the appropriate caption for each one.

Answers:

a 3; **b** 1; **c** 2; **d** 6; **e** 5; **f** 4

2a Familie Steinberger sucht ein neues Haus. Welches Haus wählen sie? Diskutiert zuerst mit einem Partner/einer Partnerin und dann in der Klasse.

a Elke: sie hat eine Katze.
b Elkes Mutter: sie ist ziemlich sportlich.
c Elkes Vater: er arbeitet viel zu Hause am Computer.

- Students work with a partner to decide which of the houses shown would be best for the Steinberger family, considering their needs.
- They then discuss this as a class.
- This activity encourages students to explore issues, events or problems from different perspectives, to try out alternatives or new solutions and to collaborate and negotiate effectively with others to work towards goals. It covers the Independent enquirers, Creative thinkers, Team workers, Self-managers and Effective participators groups of skills from the framework of personal, learning and thinking skills.

4–9 PLTS

2b Hör gut zu. Wer möchte:
a den Bungalow?
b das Einfamilienhaus?
c das Doppelhaus?

- Students listen to the recording and note down which family member would like each of the properties.

4–6

CD 1, track 7 **Seite 20, Übung 2b, 2c und 2d**

Frau Steinberger: Also, was meint ihr? Ich finde dieses Einfamilienhaus ganz toll. Es hat einen großen, sonnigen Garten und das Beste ist natürlich das Schwimmbad. Ahhhh, mein Traum – ich wollte schon als Kind ein Haus mit Schwimmbad. Da kann ich jeden Tag eine Stunde oder länger schwimmen. Das ist ja so gesund und hält mich fit. Das Wohnzimmer ist auch schön groß und unser Sofa und die Sessel passen bestimmt sehr gut.

Elke: Mann, ein Haus mit Schwimmbad ist ja schon total cool, aber ich glaube, das Wasser ist bestimmt zu kalt. Du kannst vielleicht im Juli oder August schwimmen und danach ist es wirklich zu kalt. Ich finde den Bungalow echt gut. Er sieht so modern aus und man kann in der Küche essen, das mag ich, weil es praktisch ist. Und dann, guck 'mal, der Garten ist toll und unser kleines Kätzchen kann direkt vom Wohnzimmer in den Garten. Das ist doch ideal. Bitte – bitte – lass uns diesen Bungalow kaufen!

Herr Steinberger: Hmmmm, tja, und wie ist es denn mit dem Doppelhaus? Das ist nicht so teuer wie das Einfamilienhaus und größer als der Bungalow, und außerdem hat es zwei Badezimmer, das finde ich sehr praktisch. Und was ich besonders gut finde, ist, dass es ein Arbeitszimmer gibt. Da ist Platz für meine Bücherregale. Da kann ich sehr gut arbeiten. Das Haus hat auch einen Keller für den Wein und unsere Fahrräder. Also, ich würde sagen, wir nehmen das Doppelhaus.

Frau Steinberger und Elke: Nein, nein, nicht so schnell!

Frau Steinberger: Ich finde, wir schauen uns alle drei Häuser einmal an, und dann werden wir sehen.

Answers:

a Elke; **b** Frau Steinberger; **c** Herr Steinberger

2c Hör noch einmal zu. Was sagen sie?

- Students listen to the recording again.
- They then complete the sentences with the appropriate phrase.

4–6

Answers:

1 c; **2** a; **3** b

2d Hör noch einmal gut zu und mach Notizen auf Englisch.

- Students listen once more and answer the questions in English.

Answers:

4–6

a swimming pool; her dream; can keep fit; bigger, sunnier garden; big living room; sofa will go well; **b** swimming pool is too cold – can only swim in July or August; **c** bigger than bungalow, cheaper than detached house

3a Steffi beschreibt ihr Zuhause. Ergänze die Lücken mit Wörtern aus dem Kasten.

- Students read Steffi's description and fill in the gaps with the appropriate word from the box.
- Encourage them to read the completed text to check that it makes sense.

4–6

Answers:

1 Zimmer; **2** Hausaufgaben; **3** Küche; **4** nettes; **5** Dusche; **6** Garten; **7** nach; **8** bevor; **9** Zuhause

3b Partnerarbeit. A beschreibt sein/ihr ideales Zuhause. B macht Notizen und beschreibt dann A's Traumwohnung. Hat er/sie gut zugehört? B ↔ A. Benutzt die *schräg gedruckten* Wörter aus Steffis Text.

- Students work with a partner. Partner A describes his/her ideal home; partner B makes notes and then describes A's dream residence. They then swap roles.
- Encourage them to use the italicised words from Steffi's description in order to make their description flow better and sound more authentic.

4–9

4 Stell dir vor: du studierst in Berlin und suchst einen anderen Studenten/eine andere Studentin, der/die eine Wohnung mit dir teilen will. Schreib eine Anzeige für die Zeitung und beschreib die Wohnung.

- Students write an advert to find a flatmate, in which they describe the flat that they will share.
- Encourage students to use vocabulary and structures from the previous activities.

4–6

A4 Further listening/speaking activities practising talking about where you live are provided on Activity Sheet 4.

5 Finde die Pluralformen für die folgenden Wörter.

- To practise forming plurals in German, students write down the plural form of each of the words listed.
- Remind them that they can also refer back to the example in the *Grammatik* section.

Answers:

a Tanten; **b** Küsse; **c** Zimmer; **d** Blumen; **e** Kaninchen; **f** Fernseher

6 **Partnerarbeit. Findet andere Beispiele von Wörtern der Typen a–g. Wo könnt ihr die Pluralformen prüfen?**

- Further practice of plurals. Students work with a partner to find more examples of each type of plural ending (a–g).
- Ask them how they can check that their answers are correct. Allow them to check their answers in a dictionary to check that they are correct.

7 **Work in pairs. You are going on holiday to Switzerland with your German correspondant and you need to phone him/her to exchange information about two possible holiday apartments you've found.**

- **Draw a plan of your apartment and describe the layout and the rooms it has.**
- **Say what is particularly good about your apartment and why you think it is better than the other one.**

4–9

PLTS

- A speaking activity to draw together the vocabulary and grammar students have practised in the spread.
- This activity encourages students to explore issues different perspectives, to generare ideas, to communicate their learning in relevant ways and to collaborate effectively with others to work towards goals, trying to influence them and negotiate with them. It covers the Independent enquirers, Creative thinkers, Reflective learners, Team workers, Self-managers and Effective participators groups of skills from the framework of personal, learning and thinking skills.

8 **Find out about the home of one of your favourite stars on the Internet and write a short article describing it. Use your imagination if necessary! When you've finished, check your text for:**

- **word order**
- **the gender of the nouns**
- **plural forms**

4–9

- Students use the vocabulary, grammar and ideas they have practised in the spread to produce their own article describing a home. This is an ideal assessment opportunity.

Success criteria:

- ideas communicated
- range of vocabulary and structures used
- accuracy of writing

Aktive Grammatik

Seiten 22–23

Planner

➤ **Objectives**
- Using the present tense
- Using the correct gender
- Using adjective endings in the accusative
- Using possessive adjectives
- Using reflexive pronouns

➤ **Resources**
Students' Book, pages 22–23
Exam Skills Workbooks, page 26
Grammar Workbook, pages 8, 12, 21–23, 34, 45
Activity Sheet 5
Resources and Planning OxBox CD-ROM

➤ **Grammar**
- Uses of the present tense
- Gender of nouns
- Adjective endings in the accusative
- Possessive adjectives
- Reflexive pronouns

➤ **PLTS**
All questions: Reflective learners/Self-managers

➤ Uses of the present tense

1 **Fill in the correct form of the verb for each person. If you are not sure, check the endings in the examples.**
- This question focuses on forming the present tense.

Answers:

a sehen; **b** hörst; **c** verstehen sich gut; **d** wäscht sich; **e** gehen spazieren; **f** heißt; **g** wohnt

2 **Read the text and fill in the correct verbs. Think carefully: there are more verbs than gaps!**
- Further practice of the present tense.

Answers:

heiße; wohnen; liegt; ist; verstehen; hat; heißt; sehe...fern; höre; macht; kochen

➤ Gender of nouns

3 **Look at these words and decide whether they are masculine, feminine or neuter, and which are plural.**
- Students note down which nouns are masculine, which are feminine, which are neuter and which are plural and how they can tell.

Answers

a feminine (use of feminine indefinite article *eine*); **b** plural (use of *die* and plural ending of noun); **c** neuter (indefinite article is *ein*; typical neuter ending '-chen'); **d** masculine (indefinate article is *ein*); **e** plural (use of *die* and plural ending of noun)

4 **Make a list of all the new nouns that you have encountered in this unit and learn them by heart, including the gender and how the plural is formed.**
- This question focuses on learning the gender whenever you learn a new noun.

➤ Adjective endings in the accusative

5 **Complete the sentences.**
- This question focuses on using the correct adjective ending according to gender and number.

Answers:

a einen kleinen Hund; **b** einen neuen Fernseher; **c** ein braunes Kaninchen; **d** süße Katzen; **e** einen neuen Computer; **f** ein großes Pferd

➤ Possessive adjectives

6 **Read the sentences and choose the correct form of the possessive adjective for each one.**
- Practice of possessive adjectives.

Answers:

a mein; **b** deine; **c** ihr; **d** unsere; **e** sein; **f** deine

7 **Complete the sentence with the correct possessive adjective (*mein, dein, sein* etc.).**
- Practice of possessive adjectives. *Answers:*

a mein; **b** meinen; **c** meine, ihre; **d** seine

➤ Reflexive pronouns

8 **Match up the reflexive pronoun with the correct subject. One reflexive pronoun matches more than one subject: which one?**
- Practice of reflexive pronouns

Answers:

a 4; **b** 2; **c** 7; **d** 1, 3, 5, 8; **e** 6

9 **Your little brother is not very cooperative. Fill in the correct reflexive pronouns in each sentence.**

a mich, sich, mich; **b** uns; **c** dich; **d** sich, mir; **e** sich

Kompetenzen

Seite 24

Planner

➤ Objectives
- Summarising what you have learnt

➤ Resources
Students' Book, page 24
Exam Skills Workbooks, page 27
Activity Sheet 6
Resources and Planning OxBox CD-ROM

➤ Skills
- Asking questions to keep a conversation going
- Asking questions for clarification
- Using filler words to gain time to think of what you want to say next
- Feeling confident when speaking and having a conversation
- Listening to as much German as possible
- Improving your pronunciation
- Checking your work carefully for spelling
- Looking out for umlauts
- Learning the correct gender of nouns
- Checking verb tenses and verb endings
- Making sure you use the correct word order

➤ PLTS
Question 5, Beim Sprechen: Reflective learners/ Self-managers
Question 1, Beim Schreiben: Reflective learners/ Self-managers

In this unit, students have learnt how to...

➤ Beim Sprechen

1 **Ask questions to keep a conversation going.**
- Students use the verbs, *wohnen*, *haben*, *hören* and *lesen* to form questions.
- Encourage them to try to use one or two questions like this in their roleplays and discussions.

2 **Ask questions for clarification.**
- Students have an imaginary telephone conversation with an estate agent (their partner) who is describing a house to them. The line is bad, so they have to ask if he/she could repeat.
- Encourage them to use as many of the expressions from the tip on page 12 as possible. They then swap roles.

3 **Use filler words to gain time to think of what you want to say next.**
- Students practise using filler words in a conversation with thier partner about what they normally do on a Friday evening.

4 **Feel confident when speaking and having a conversation.**
- Encourage students to try to think as much as possible in German.
- To practise speaking, students prepare five sentences about what they are going to do after school today. They then tell their partner.

5 **Listen to as much German as possible.**

PLTS
- Provide students with some listening comprehensions or encourage them to practise listening from the Exam Skills Workbook CD.
- This activity encourages students to monitor their own performance and progress and to work towards goals, showing initiative, commitment and perserverance. It covers the Reflective learners and Self-managers groups of skills.

6 **Improve your pronunciation.**
- Students work on German sounds such as *u* and *ü*, *o* and *ö*, and *a* and *ä* on the CD-ROM.

➤ Beim Schreiben

1 **Check your work carefully for spelling.**

PLTS
- Students make a list of their main spelling mistakes to refer to, so that they don't repeat the same mistakes.
- This activity encourages students to review progress, acting on the outcomes and to work towards goals, showing initiative, commitment and perseverance. It covers the Reflective learners and Self-managers groups of skills.

2 **Look out for umlauts.**
- Students think about how a word is pronounced to work out if an umlaut is needed. They can check in the dictionary.

3 **Learn the correct gender of nouns.**
- Remind students of the importance of knowing the gender of nouns. Refer them back to page 21 and encourage them to revise endings which are typically masculine, feminine and neuter.

4 **Check verb tenses and verb endings.**
- Students check in the grammar section at the back of this book for the verb endings in the present and perfect tenses.

Szenario

Planner

➤ Objectives
- Writing an application to appear on a reality TV show
- Preparing and taking part in an imaginary press conference

➤ Resources
Students' Book, page 25
Exam Skills Workbooks, pages 24–25
Resources and Planning OxBox CD-ROM

➤ Skills
- Writing practice
- Speaking practice

➤ PLTS
Question 1, Zum Schreiben: Independent enquirers/Creative thinkers/Reflective learners/Self-managers
Question 1, Zum Sprechen: Independent enquirers/Creative thinkers/Self-managers

➤ Zum Schreiben

In this section, students will write an application to appear on a German reality TV show.

It is possible for students to obtain GCSE grades A–F depending on their ability:
Grade F students write a short review using simple sentences and communicate some information.
Grade C students include a variety of structures which may include different tenses or time frames. They communicate information and express personal opinions.
Grade A students include a variety of vocabulary, structures and verb tenses. They convey information, narrate events and express and explain ideas and points of view.

1 **You want to take part in a new reality TV series for teenagers called *Kleiner Bruder*. To apply, you need to write a paragraph for the TV company telling them about yourself and your home life and why you think you are the ideal candidate for the programme. You should mention at least three of the following points listed.**

PLTS
- This activity is an ideal assessment opportunity.
- It encourages students to identify questions to answer, to generate and explore ideas, to communicate their learning in relevant ways and to work towards goals. It covers the Independent enquirers, Creative thinkers, Reflective learners and Self-managers groups of skills from the framework of personal, learning and thinking skills.

2 **Make sure you check your letter carefully for word order, adjectival endings and the gender of nouns.**

➤ Zum Sprechen

In this section, students play a famous person taking part in a press conference where they answer questions about themself and their family. Encourage them to use the Internet for research and to rehearse their material thoroughly. Suggest recording it to help improve their accent and intonation. This could be done using the record/playback facility on the OxBox CD-ROM.

It is possible for students to obtain GCSE grades A–F depending on their ability and they are marked on Communication, Quality of language and Pronunciation and intonation:
Grade F students communicate a limited number of ideas, expressing simple opinions. A few phrases or short sentences are accurate enough to be recognisable. There are very few instances of clear pronunciation and intonation.
Grade C students communicate the essential elements, expressing points of view. They can respond to some unpredictable questions. They use straightforward vocabulary and structures which may contain different tenses or time frames. Pronunciation and intonation is generally accurate.
Grade A students use relevant information to develop and justify individual ideas and points of view. There is no hesitation and they are able to respond to unpredictable questions. They use a wide range of clause types, vocabulary and structures accurately. The presentation is fluent and coherent with just minor errors. Pronunciation and intonation are very accurate with a few minor slips.

1 **Choose a famous person to play: an actor, sportsperson or politician. Prepare the questions and answers that are likely to come up in your next press conference so that you will be able to face the journalists with confidence.**

PLTS
- This activity gives students the opportunity to prepare for activities 2 and 3.
- Encourage them to do research on their famous person, so they are prepared to answer any questions.
- This encourages students to plan and carry out research, and to explore possibilities in order to work towards goals. It covers the Independent enquirers, Creative thinkers and Self-managers groups of skills from the framework of personal, learning and thinking skills.

2 **Practise with a partner, taking turns to ask and answer questions on the points below. Use some of the filler words you have learnt if you find yourself lost for words at any time!**
- Students think in more detail about what they are going to say and practise this.

3 **Now it's time for the press conference itself. Introduce yourself as your chosen character, remembering to mention where you come from, something about your family background and what you like doing. Rehearse what you want to say before you begin and look up any of the words you will need in the dictionary. The rest of the class has to guess who you are. You can record your presentation using the OxBox software.**

- Students use what they have prepared and practised, remembering to include filler words and to concentrate on pronunciation.

Vokabeln

Seite 26

Planner

➤ **Resources**
Students' Book, page 26
Activity Sheet 7

This page provides a summary of the key language covered in each spread of this unit. It could be used as a handy reference for students as they work through the unit. Alternatively, students could use its clear German–English format when learning vocabulary.

Lesen

Seiten 171–172

Planner

➤ Objectives

- To encourage independent reading and develop reading strategies
- To provide alternative class and homework material for students who finish other activities quickly

Page 171 provides a magazine-style quiz in the context of the unit.
Page 172 provides a letter to an agony aunt in the context of the unit.

➤ Resources

Students' Book, pages 171–172

➤ Skills

- Reading practice

➤ PLTS

Question 2 (part 1): Creative thinkers/Reflective learners/Self-managers
Question 3 (part 2): Creative thinkers/Reflective learners/Self-managers

Lesen A: Wie gut kennst du dich?

1 Lies die Fragen. Wie sagt man das auf Deutsch?

- Students read the questions.
- To test comprehension, they then note down the German for the English phrases listed.

4–6

Answers:

a deine zwei besten Charaktereigenschaften; **b** Charakterschwächen; **c** Aussehen; **d** Wie wichtig sind . . .? **e** das Wochenende verbringen; **f** lieber

2 Beantworte die Fragen im Quiz schriftlich.

- Students now write down their answers.
- Encourage them to use the wording in the questions to form their answers and to answer using full sentences.
- This activity encourages students to think creatively and explore different ideas whilst communicating their learning in relevant ways to work towards goals. It covers the Creative thinkers, Reflective learners and Self-managers groups of skills from the framework of personal, learning and thinking skills.

4–9

PLTS

3 Vergleiche deine Antworten mit einem Partner/einer Partnerin. Seid ihr ähnlich oder verschieden?

- Students compare their answers with those of a partner. Encourage discussion with students explaining and justifying their answers.

4–6

Lesen B: Stefans Brief

1 Lies Stefans Brief und die vier Anzeigen. Beantworte dann die Fragen auf Englisch.

- Students read Stefan's letter and the four adverts. They then answer the questions in English.

4–6

Answers:

a 14; **b** he wants to have a Birthday party, but doesn't have a girlfriend to invite; **c** they all have girlfriends who they invite to parties or the cinema; **d** Monika **e** Sylvie; **f** Pia; **g** Käthe

2 Lies Stefans Brief und wähle dann aus den vier Anzeigen die aus, die am besten zu Stefan passen könnte.

4–6

- Students read the letter again and decide which of the girls in the adverts would be best for Stefan.

3 Schreib einen Antwortbrief an Stefan.

- Students write a reply to Stefan's letter.
- This activity encourages students to generate ideas and to communicate previous learning to work towards goals. It covers the Creative thinkers, Reflective learners and Self-managers groups of skills from the framework of personal, learning and thinking skills.

4–9

PLTS

Unit 1B: Wohnort und Umgebung		Overview grid		
Spread	**Contexts and objectives**	**Skills**	**Grammar**	**Vocabulary**
pages 28–29 **Wie man eine Stadt beschreibt**	• Describing buildings and facilities in a town	• Improving listening skills	• The imperfect of *haben* and *sein*	*der Bahnhof; der Berg; der Einwohner; die Fabrik; das Gebäude; die Gegend; die Hauptstadt; der Nachteil; das Stadion; die Stadien; das Verkehrsamt*
pages 30–31 **Wie man Städte vergleicht**	• Comparing towns	• Reading for gist	• The comparative and superlative	*der Dom; das Geschäft; der See; die Sehenswürdigkeiten; der Stadtteil; der Wald; genießen*
pages 32–33 **Wie man sich über eine Gegend informiert**	• Asking for information at the tourist information office	• Reading for gist	• Dates • Modal verbs: *können, wollen* and *mögen*	*der Eintritt; die Jugendherberge; die Schienen; das Tal, die Täler; die Unterhaltung sich entspannen; überqueren; lecker; sicher*
pages 34–35 **Wie man sich in einer Stadt zurechtfindet**	• Asking for directions	• Reading for gist	• The imperative	*die Ampel; der Bahnsteig; die Bauarbeiten; der Fahrplan; das Gleis; die Haltestelle; die Kreuzung; die öffentlichen Verkehrsmittel; die Rückfahrkarte; die S-Bahn; die Straßenbahn; die U-Bahn; der Verkehr; der Zug; abfahren; ankommen; billig; verspätet; entlang; geradeaus; links; rechts; weit*
pages 36–37 **Wie man eine Stadtführung macht**	• Going on a city tour	• Listening for detail	• Prepositions with the dative and the accusative	*die Aussicht; die Brücke; der Brunnen; das Münster; die Umwelt; mieten; Schlittschuh laufen; bequem; einfach; langsam oben; wieder*
pages 38–39 **Aktive Grammatik**	• Grammar		• The imperfect tense • modal verbs • The imperative • The comparative and the superlative • Prepositions with the dative and the accusative	
page 40 **Kompetenzen**	• Summarising what you have learnt	• Making guesses about what words mean • Recognising common sound-spelling links • Listening with the task in mind • Learning about word families • Creating mind maps		
page 41 **Szenario**	• Skills/Scenario • Preparing a presentation about your home town	• Speaking practice • Writing practice		
page 42 **Vokabeln**	• Key language			
pages 173–174 **Lesen**	• Towns and cities • To develop reading strategies • To provide alternative class and homework material for students who finish other activities quickly	• Reading practice		

1B Wohnort und Umgebung

Unit Objectives

Contexts and cultural focus: the area where you live
Skills focus: reading for gist; using context and cognates to understand a German text; answering questions about a German text; improving targeted listening; improving general listening skills
Grammar: using the imperfect tense of *haben*, *sein* and modal verbs; using comparatives and superlatives; using the imperative; using the correct dative and accusative forms after prepositions

Controlled assessment opportunities

Writing: Students' Book, page 29 activity 6
Writing: Students' Book, page 31 activity 5b
Writing: Students' Book, page 33 activity 7
Writing: Students' Book, page 35 activity 7
Speaking: Students' Book, page 37 activity 7
Writing: Students' Book, page 41 Zum Schreiben, activities 1–4
Speaking: Students' Book, page 41 Zum Sprechen, activities 1–4

See also ***GCSE German for OCR Assessment OxBox CD-ROM.***

An introduction to the unit Seite 27

- *Aim*: To introduce the themes of the unit.
- The opening spread of each unit is styled as the contents page of a teenage magazine. Illustrations, captions and skills summaries provide a preview of what is to come:

	Students' Book
Weißt du schon, wie man eine Stadt beschreibt?	pages 28–29
Weißt du schon, wie man Städte vergleicht?	pages 30–31
Weißt du schon, wie man sich über eine Gegend informiert?	pages 32–33
Weißt du schon, wie man sich in einer Stadt zurechtfindet?	pages 34–35
Weißt du schon, wie man eine Stadtführung macht?	pages 36–37

- Allow time for students to read the questions and cross-refer to the relevant pages of the Students' Book. They could do this individually or in pairs/groups, followed by whole-class discussion.
- This spread also provides an opportunity for students to recap on familiar language. Ask them to think about language they already know that might be useful when working on the themes of the unit.
- At the end of work on Unit 1B:
  - If time permits, ask students to devise a replacement opening spread. What do they think should be on it, in terms of pictures, captions, etc.? What would they change/keep the same, and why? Ask them to imagine it is the contents page of a teenage magazine: what sort of captions and pictures do they feel would attract people to buy the magazine? This sort of activity encourages students to think about features of a text that make it suitable for a particular audience or purpose.
  - Allow time for students to return to this opening spread to answer the questions, review what they have learned and reflect on areas for improvement. What did they find difficult, interesting, etc.? What do they think are the most important things they have learned in this unit?

Wie man eine Stadt beschreibt

Seiten 28–29

Planner

➤ Objectives
- Describing buildings and facilities in a town

➤ Resources
Students' Book, pages 28–29
CD 1, tracks 14–15
Activity Sheet 8

➤ Key language
der Bahnhof; der Berg; der Einwohner; die Fabrik; das Gebäude; die Gegend; die Hauptstadt; der Nachteil; das Stadion; die Stadien; das Verkehrsamt

➤ Skills
- Improving listening skills

➤ Grammar
- The imperfect of *haben* and *sein*

➤ PLTS
Question 5: Creative thinkers/Reflective learners/Team workers
Question 6: Creative thinkers/Reflective learners
Question 7: Independent enquirers/Creative thinkers/Reflective learners/Effective participators

➤ Starters
- In pairs, students make up true/false statements about their town/region, e.g. A: *X ist eine sehr historische Stadt.*
  B: *X Richtig. hat heute mehr als 2 Millionen Einwohner.*
  A: *X Falsch – hat heute X Einwohner. Es gibt viele Theater.*
- Display, in German, a list of places in town and adjectives describing these. Next to these, display the English translations but jumbled up. Give students a time limit to match the English to the German. Compare answers as a class. Ask more confident classes to try and use some of the words listed in sentences.
- Start by asking a confident student, *Was gefällt dir an der Stadt?* Once the student has answered, he/she asks another student the same question. Continue around the class.

➤ Plenaries
- Students write a paragraph describing their ideal town. They should include the structures covered in the spread, e.g. *Es wäre gut, wenn die Stadt viele Geschäfte hätte.* A few confident volunteers then present their paragraph to the class who decides which imaginary town they prefer.
- Ask students to tell you how to form the imperfect tense. Ask quick-fire questions, e.g. *present = es gibt… imperfect = es …?* Once you are confident students have all fully understood how to form and use the imperfect, ask them to write a paragraph about how their town used to be in the past. For support, display some example sentences in the imperfect tense, e.g. *Letztes Jahr* ***hatte*** *meine Stadt nur ein altes, kleines Kino.*
- Have a class debate on the town/village where the school is located. You start, e.g. *X ist eine sehr historische Stadt und das finde ich gut. Aber leider gibt es viele Touristen.* Students join in giving their opinion. If necessary, have a quick brainstorming session first, listing what there is in the town/village, how many inhabitants there are, etc. If everyone agrees on what is good and bad, allocate roles, e.g. old person, mother of young children, teenager, etc. to add interest and encourage more debate.

1a Was sagen diese jungen Leute über ihren Wohnort? Finde die passenden Bilder für die Texte.

- As an introduction to the spread, students read the texts and then match each text to the appropriate picture.

4–6

Answers:

a 9; **b** 5, 6; **c** 4, 3, 12; **d** 7, 8; **e** 11, 2, 1

1b Lies die Texte noch einmal. Wie sagt man auf Deutsch…?

- Students read through the texts again and find the German for the English phrases listed.

4–6

Answers:

a restaurierte Gebäude; **b** das Dorf; **c** gibt es nicht viel für junge Leute; **d** Einwohnern; **e** unternehmen; **f** in den Bergen; **g** Fabriken

2 Hör gut zu. Kannst du das Rätsel lösen? Das Lösungswort ist eine deutsche Stadt.

- Students listen to the recording, fill in the crossword and then use the first letter of each answers to find the name of a German town.

4–6

CD 1, track 14 **Seite 28, Übung 2**

Eins waagerecht: Touristen schlafen dort. Man kann Zimmer buchen.
Zwei waagerecht: Es ist eine schnelle Straße, wo Autos über 100 km pro Stunde fahren.
Drei waagerecht: Man kann dort alte historische Dinge sehen.
Vier waagerecht: Man kann von dort mit dem Zug fahren.
Fünf waagerecht: Man kann dort studieren.
Sechs waagerecht: Blumen, die im Park und im Stadtgarten wachsen
Sieben waagerecht: Meine Stadt liegt in den Bergen. Sie liegt in einer sehr schönen …

Answers:

HAMBURG: **1** Hotel; **2** Autobahn; **3** Museum; **4** Bahnhof; **5** Universität; **6** Rosen; **7** Gegend

3a Lies die E-Mail und beantworte die Fragen auf Englisch.

- As a class, read through the *Tipp* section and the *Grammatik* section on the imperfect tense.
- Then ask students to read the e-mail and, to check comprehension, answer the questions in English.

4–6

Answers:

a the Kaiser family; **b** that it is a muscial town; **c** there are too many tourists and too many souvenir shops; **d** The football world cup final was played in Vienna's football stadium.

3b Lies den Text noch einmal und ergänze die Sätze mit dem passenden Wort.

- Students read the e-mail again and then complete the sentences with the appropriate words.

4–6

Answers:

1 a; **2** a; **3** c; **4** c

4a Katja, Jana und Franjo beschreiben ihren Wohnort. Hör gut zu und füll die Tabelle aus.

- Read the *Tipp* section on 'could' and 'should'.
- Students listen to the three young people describing where they live and fill in the table.

4–6

CD 1, track 15 **Seite 29, Übung 4**

Katja: Ich wohne in einem kleinen Dorf in der Nähe von München. Es ist nicht weit von den Bergen und das gefällt mir. Auch die Leute im Dorf sind sehr nett. Was es in unserem Dorf gibt? Also, nicht sehr viel! Es gibt einen ganz kleinen Supermarkt, wo man Lebensmittel kaufen kann, ein Restaurant und eine kleine, ziemlich alte Kirche. Nächstes Jahr soll es ein neues Café geben. Das finde ich gut für junge Leute, weil man sich da mit Freunden treffen kann, statt auf der Straße herumzuhängen.

Jana: Ich wohne in einer Kleinstadt in einem Skigebiet. Das ist natürlich im Winter besonders toll. Ich fahre so gern Ski und ich treffe meine Freunde auf der Skipiste. Das macht total Spaß! Aber leider gibt es viele Touristen, vor allem im Winter. Im Sommer ist es nicht so gut hier. Es gibt kein Schwimmbad und das finde ich schade. Aber die Stadt will nächstes Jahr ein beheiztes Freibad bauen. Das ist meiner Meinung nach klasse!

Franjo: Ich wohne in Berlin, der Hauptstadt Deutschlands. Seit der Wende gibt es viele tolle Einkaufszentren und einen super Kinokomplex. Das gefällt mir. Das Leben hier ist viel besser geworden. Deutschland ist jetzt wieder ein vereintes Land, und ich finde es gut, dass Berlin die Hauptstadt ist. Es sollte ein besseres Freibad geben, weil das alte zu klein ist. Es wäre auch gut, wenn unsere Stadt mehr Tennisplätze hätte.

Answers:

	Type of place?	Advantages	Plans/wishes for the future
Katja	small village	not far from mountains, nice people	a new café
Jana	small town	ski resort	a heated swimming pool
Franjo	big town	great shopping centre super cinema complex	a better pool, more tennis courts

4b Hör noch einmal gut zu. Was sagen diese Jugendlichen, um ihre Meinung auszudrücken?

- Students listen to the three young people again.
- They then fill in the gaps.

4–6

Answers:

a finde; **b** leider; **c** schade; **d** Meinung

5 **Partnerarbeit. Wählt entweder einen Wohnort aus Übung la oder eine andere bekannte Stadt. A muss die Stadt erraten und stellt die folgenden Fragen, B antwortet. B ↔ A.**

4–6

PLTS

- Students choose a German town, either from activity la or another well-known German town. Their partner asks the questions listed to try and guess their town. They then swap roles.
- This activity encourages students to generate and explore ideas, communicate previous learning and to collaborate with others to achieve results. It covers the Creative thinkers, Reflective learners and Team workers groups of skills from the framework of personal, learning and thinking skills.

A8 Activity Sheet 8 provides further activities on buildings and facilities in a town and German-speaking towns.

6 **Your German MSN contact wants to know more about your home town. Send a message saying what you can do there, what advantages and disadvantages it has and what you would change, especially to improve facilities for young people.**

4–9

PLTS

- This activity draws together what students have learnt in the spread.
- It is an ideal assessment opportunity.
- It encourages students to generate and explore ideas whilst communicating previous learning. It covers the Creative thinkers and Reflective learners groups of skills from the framework of personal, learning and thinking skills.

Success criteria:

- information communicated
- variety of vocabulary and structures used
- personal opinions expressed

7 **Where is it better to live: in a country village or in a city? Write a list of the advantages and disadvantages of both (find at least five for each) and decide. Then debate in class. Which is the most popular option?**

4–9

PLTS

- Students use what they have learnt in spread to have a class debate.
- This activity encourages students to plan and carry out research, to generate and explore ideas, to communicate previous learning and to influence others. It covers the Independent enquirers, Creative thinkers, Reflective learners and Effective participators groups of skills from the framework of personal, learning and thinking skills.

Wie man Städte vergleicht

Seiten 30–31

Planner

➤ **Objectives**
- Comparing towns

➤ **Resources**
Students' Book, pages 30–31
CD 1, track 16
Grammar Workbook, pages 25–27

➤ **Key language**
der Dom; das Geschäft; der See; die Sehenswürdigkeiten; der Stadtteil; der Wald; genießen

➤ **Skills**
- Reading for gist

➤ **Grammar**
- The comparative and superlative

➤ **PLTS**
Question 5a: Independent enquirers/Reflective learners/Team workers
Question 5b: Creative thinkers/Reflective learners/ Self-managers

➤ **Starters**
- Split the class into two teams and challenge them to find a German town or village for each letter of the alphabet. Give students a fixed amount of time to write down as many as they can. The teams then compare answers. They score a point for each original town/village they have written down (if both teams have the same town, neither scores a point). The team with the most points wins.
- Have a quick class quiz about a well-known towns (British or German) e.g. London, Cardiff, Edinburgh, Berlin, etc. Split the class into teams and ask questions about these towns e.g. *London ist eine große oder eine kleine Stadt? Berlin ist die Schweizer Hauptstadt – Richtig oder Falsch?*, etc. The first team to answer correctly wins a point. With true/false questions, encourage teams to correct the statement, if it is false, e.g.
– Berlin ist die Schweizer Hauptstadt – Richtig oder Falsch?
– Falsch. ***Bern*** *ist die Schweizer Hauptstadt.*
- Display the key language in one column and the English transations of these words and phrases jumbled up in a second column. Students work in pairs to match each term with its English translation in a set amount of time.

➤ **Plenaries**
- Display pairs of towns that are known to the students (include those from the spread), e.g. Berlin and London; Hamburg and Oxford, etc. Challenge students to write as many sentences as possible comparing these towns. They should use the comparative and the superlative as well as useful expressions they have learned for making comparisons. Compare answers as a class.
- Display a list of adjectives and adverbs featured in the spread and any others. Ask students to write the comparative and the superlative forms of these along with the English translation. Go through the answers as a class.
- Have a class quiz using the reading text from page 30. Divide the class into two teams and ask questions about the text, e.g. *Hamburg ist eine große oder eine kleine Stadt? Hamburg hat mehr oder weniger Einwohnern als Titisee-Neustadt.*

1a Lies die Texte und finde die passenden Wörter für die Sätze.

4–6

- As an introduction to the spread, students read the texts complete each sentence with the appropriate word.

Answers:

1 b; **2** a; **3** b; **4** c; **5** b; **6** b

1b Lies die Texte noch einmal und füll das Formular aus.

4–6

- Students read the texts again and, this time, fill in the table for each of the places mentioned.

Answers:

	Hamburg	**Titisee-Neustadt**
Location	North Germany	Black Forest
Population	almost 2,000,000	about 10,000
Sports	sailing	swimming, bike riding, skiing, golf
Tourist attractions	lake, shopping	forests, meadows

2a Peter und Sonja vergleichen ihre Wohnorte. Hör gut zu. Wer sagt was?

- Students listen to Peter and Sonja comparing where they live.
- They note down who says what.

4–6

CD 1, track 16 **Seite 31, Übung 2**

Peter: Also, Sonja, du kommst aus Bern, der Hauptstadt der Schweiz, nicht?
Sonja: Ja, genau. Bern ist die Schweizer Hauptstadt, aber die Stadt hat weniger als eine halbe Million Einwohner – ich glaube, es sind ungefähr 129 000. Es ist die viertgrößte Stadt der Schweiz.
Peter: Ach, wirklich? Das ist ja echt witzig, denn ich wohne in Köln und das ist auch die viertgrößte Stadt, aber in Deutschland! Köln hat aber mehr als 1 Million Einwohner. Du weißt ja vielleicht, dass der Rhein durch Köln fließt. Die bekannteste Sehenswürdigkeit ist der Kölner Dom, und das ganze Jahr über kommen viele Touristen nach Köln. Liegt Bern auch an einem Fluss?
Sonja: Ja, die Aare verläuft fast um die ganze Stadt. Bern ist eigentlich keine Touristenstadt. Das finde ich besser. Aber es gibt auch eine bekannte Sehenswürdigkeit, und zwar den Bärengraben mit vier Braunbären.
Peter: Wow, echt?
Sonja: Ja, das ist schon toll. Dann gibt es eine Universität, eine Kunsthochschule und viele Museen. Bern ist eine historische Stadt mit vielen historischen Brunnen. Ich wohne gern hier, aber es wäre besser, wenn es mehr Kleidergeschäfte mit Mode für junge Leute gäbe.
Peter: Da musst du nach Köln kommen. Hier gibt es echt gute Einkaufszentren. Am liebsten mag ich die Karnevalszeit in Köln. Da ist so viel los – Partys, Umzüge und so. Gibt es so was auch in der Schweiz?
Sonja: Ja, klar doch, aber bei uns heißt das nicht Karneval. Wir sagen Fastnacht, und die Stadt Basel ist besonders bekannt dafür.

Answers:

a Sonja; **b** Peter; **c** Peter; **d** Sonja; **e** Sonja; **f** Peter

2b Hör noch einmal gut zu. Welche Wörter benutzen Peter und Sonja, um ihre Wohnorte zu vergleichen? Füll die Lücken aus.

- Students listen again and fill the gaps with the words Peter and Sonja use to compare their towns.
- This activity encourages students to listen to the recording in more detail.

4–6

Answers:

a weniger; **b** mehr; **c** besser/mehr; **d** liebsten

3 Füll die Lücken mit den passenden Formen der Adjektive im Kasten aus.

- Read through the *Grammatik* section on the comparative and the superlative as a class and work through the examples to ensure that all students fully understand how to form and them.
- Ask students to complete the sentences with the appropriate form of the adjectives in the box.

Answers:

a viel, mehr, meisten; **b** warmer; **c** bekannt

4a Partnerarbeit. Jeder wählt eine britische Stadt und stellt Fragen zu den folgenden Punkten.

- Students work with a partner. Each chooses a British town and they ask each other questions based on the points in the Students' Book.
- They note down the answers ready to use in the next activity.

4–6

4b Jeder schreibt fünf Sätze im Komparativ oder Superlativ, um die zwei Städte zu vergleichen.

- Students now write five sentences in the comparative or superlative to compare the two towns. The *Tipp* box offers useful expressions.

4–6

5a You are trying to find a town to twin your hometown with. Work with a partner. Choose a town or area in Germany, Austria or Switzerland and research information about it on the Internet, e.g. size, sights, specialities and shops.

- This practises what students have learnt in the spread and acts as preparation for activity 5b.
- Students note down the results in grid-form.
- This activity encourages students to plan and carry out reseach and to analyse and evaluate information. It also encourages them to communicate previous learning and to work confidently with others. It covers the Independent enquirers, Reflective learners and Team workers groups of skills from the framework of personal, learning and thinking skills.

4–9

PLTS

5b Now write a leaflet about the German-speaking town or area you have chosen. Make comparisons with your own town or area and say why you think they should be twin towns (*Partnerstädte*). Use as many expressions from the Tipp box as you can.

- Students draw upon their notes from activity 5a to write a leaflet.
- This activity encourages students to generate and explore ideas, making original connections whilst communicating previous learning and to organise their time and resources effectively. It covers the Creative thinkers, Reflective learners and Self-managers groups of skills.
- This is an ideal assessment opportunity.

4–9

PLTS

Success criteria:

- amount of information communicated
- variety of vocabulary and structures used
- number of personal opinions given

Wie man sich über eine Gegend informiert

Seiten 32–33

Planner

➤ Objectives
- Asking for information at the tourist information office

➤ Resources
Students' Book, pages 32–33
CD 1, tracks 17–18

➤ Key language
der Eintritt; die Jugendherberge; die Schienen; das Tal, die Täler; die Unterhaltung
sich entspannen; überqueren
lecker; sicher

➤ Skills
- Reading for gist

➤ Grammar
- Dates
- Modal verbs: *können, wollen* and *mögen*

➤ PLTS
Question 4: Creative thinkers/Reflective learners/Team workers
Question 7: Creative thinkers/Reflective learners/Self-managers

➤ Starters
- Split the class into two teams. Challenge each team to think of a tourist/holiday-related word in German for each letter of the alphabet. Give them a fixed amount of time in which to do this. Compare answers as a class.
- Go round the class asking each student when is his/her Birthday to practise simple dates. Students answer using full sentences.
- Students work in pairs to think of as many German verbs as possible to say what they like doing on holiday, e.g. *sich entspannen, schwimmen, …besuchen*, etc. Compare answers as a class and keep the list to use later.

➤ Plenaries
- Display some vocabulary from the spread and the list of verbs from starter activity 3, e.g. *Museen, sich entspannen, Broschüren*, etc. Students work with a partner to prepare a conversation between a tourist office worker and a tourist, using as many of the words listed as possible. Remind them to use the modal verbs covered in the spread. Confident volunteers act out their conversation in front of the class.
- Go round the class asking each student to say a sentence on the topic of the spread including one of the modal verbs covered in the spread.
- Play a version of consequences using questions as prompts. Each student starts with a piece of paper. Ask a question, e.g. *Wann möchtest du in Ferien fahren?* Each student writes an answer, e.g. *Ich möchte vom 21. bis 29. März Ferien machen.* They then fold the paper so that their answer can't be seen and pass it on to the student sitting next to them. Ask a second question, e.g. *Wo möchtest du übernachten?* Each student writes their answer on the paper they have just been given, e.g. *Ich möchte gern in einem Hotel übernachten.* Once again they fold it and pass it on. After you have asked several questions, students unfold their paper and volunteers read out what it says.

1a Lies die Anzeigen. Wie sagt man auf Deutsch…?

- As an introduction to the spread, students read the two advertisements and find the German for the English words and phrases listed.

Answers:

a bietet Unterhaltung; **b** das besondere Erlebnis; **c** Seilbrücke; **d** Rodelbahn; **e** für große und kleine Flitzer; **f** mit Schlitten auf Schienen; **g** selbst bestimmen; **h** voller Überraschung

1b Lies die Anzeigen noch einmal und beantworte die Fragen auf Englisch.

- Read through the *Tipp* section as a class.
- Ask students to read through the advertisements again and to answer the questions in English.

Answers:

a the longest rope bridge in the world; **b** the Wildpark; **c** to a self-service restaurant, a restaurant with a terrace or to the kiosk; **d** in Hasenhorn in the Black Forest; **e** you determine the speed yourself; **f** for everyone – old and young

2a Drei Leute rufen beim Verkehrsamt an. Hör gut zu. Kopiere die Tabelle und füll sie auf Englisch aus.

- Students listen to the three people asking for tourist information.
- They fill in the table in English.

CD 1, track 17 **Seite 32, Übung 2**

Herr Krause: Ja, guten Tag, mein Name ist Krause. Wir möchten nächste Woche in Konstanz Ferien machen, also vom 21. bis 29. März. Können Sie uns bitte Informationen über Konzerte und Museen in der Stadt schicken? Wir möchten gern in einem Hotel übernachten. Gibt es ein besonders gutes in der Gegend? Gibt es auch ein Schloss in der Nähe? Wir interessieren uns nämlich für historische Gebäude.

Andreas Pfaff: Hallo, Ich bin Andreas Pfaff. Gibt es in Heidelberg eine Jugendherberge oder einen Campingplatz? Wir wollen im Winter kommen, für eine Woche in den Weihnachtsferien. Können Sie mir bitte eine Broschüre über Wintersport schicken? Wir wollen vor allem rodeln gehen. Gibt es auch billige Restaurants? Wir haben nämlich nicht viel Geld.

Frau Behrens: Mein Name ist Behrens, und ich möchte nächsten Monat vom 14. bis 23. Oktober in Hamburg Urlaub machen. Können Sie mir bitte Informationen über Campingplätze in der Gegend schicken? Gibt es in Hamburg auch Schwimmbäder? Beheizte natürlich – ein See ist mir zu kalt. Welche Spezialitäten und Sehenswürdigkeiten gibt es? Schicken Sie mir doch bitte eine Broschüre. Vielen Dank!

Answers:

Herr Krause: Konstanz – concerts, museums, hotel, castle, historical buildings

Andreas Pfaff: Heidelberg – youth hostel campsite, Winter sports, tobogganing, cheap restaurants

Frau Behrens: Hamburg – campsites; swimming pools; specialities; places of interest – brochure

2b Hör noch einmal gut zu. Wer sagt was?

- Students listen again, and note down who says each of the sentences.

4–6

Answers:

a Andreas Pfaff; **b** Herr Krause; **c** Herr Krause; **d** Frau Behrens; **e** Andreas Pfaff

3 Füll die Lücken mit den passenden Wörtern im Kasten aus.

- Students fill in the gaps with the words from the box.

4–6

Answers:

a Können; **b** Schwarzwald; **c** möchten; **d** Wanderwege; **e** Gegend; **f** Schwimmbäder; **g** Broschüren; **h** hätten

4 Arbeitet mit einem Partner/einer Partnerin. Jeder überlegt sich zuerst Folgendes:

- **Wann möchtet ihr in die Ferien fahren?**
- **Über welche Aktivitäten wollt ihr euch informieren?**
- **Wo wollt ihr übernachten?**
- **Interessiert ihr euch für Sehenswürdigkeiten oder Spezialitäten?**

Setzt euch nun Rücken an Rücken, so dass ihr euren Partner/eure Partnerin nicht sehen, aber hören könnt. A arbeitet im Verkehrsamt und beantwortet die Fragen. B möchte sich informieren und stellt Fragen. B ↔ A.

- Students work with a partner to act out a role play. One partner works in a tourist information office; the other is a tourist asking questions.
- This activity encourages students to generate and explore ideas whilst communicating previous learning and to collaborate with others. It covers the Creative thinkers, Reflective learners and Team workers groups of skills from the framework of personal, learning and thinking skills.

4–6

PLTS

5 Übersetze die Sätze ins Deutsche.

- Read through the *Grammatik* sections on 'dates' and 'the modal verbs, *können, mögen, wollen* as a class.
- Ask students to translate the sentences into German.

Answers:

a Welches Datum ist heute? Heute ist der fünfte September.
b Wir wollen nächsten Sommer kommen.
c Ich möchte bleiben vom erste bis sieb[en]te Oktober.
d Er will nächsten Monat vom zweite bis neunte Januar kommen.

6 Listen to the information from the tourist office and make notes. What does Pfaffenweiler have to offer in the way of the following?

• sports facilities • culture • food

- This listening activity draws together what students have learnt in this spread, and acts as preparation for the next activity.
- Encourage students to make their notes as detailed as possible.

4–6

CD 1, track 18 **Seite 33, Übung 6**

Kommen Sie nach Pfaffenweiler. Hier gibt es das beste Angebot für Leute, die gern aktiv sind oder Sport treiben. Besuchen Sie unseren idyllisch gelegenen Golfplatz. Für die Kleinen oder auch für die ganze Familie gibt es einen Minigolfplatz, wo man nach dem Spielen noch ein Eis essen kann. Es gibt viele Wanderwege durch den Wald und an unserem wunderschönen See entlang. Wenn Sie gern Rad fahren, können Sie für sich und Ihre Freunde Räder leihen.

Wenn Sie sich mehr für Kultur interessieren, bietet Ihnen unsere Stadt auch sehr viel. Jeden Donnerstag gibt es ein Konzert im Park, und einmal im Monat gibt es ein Sommernachtsfest mit dem besten Feuerwerk, das Sie je gesehen haben.

Zum Mittag- oder Abendessen besuchen Sie unsere gemütlichen Restaurants, wo Sie sich die leckeren Spezialitäten der Stadt schmecken lassen können. Wenn Sie gern Italienisch essen, empfehle ich Ihnen die italienische Pizzeria.

7 **Write to the tourist office in your real or imaginary twin town and ask for information about the following points so that you can plan activities with your class when you go on an exchange visit there.**

4–9

PLTS

- This activity draws together the vocabulary and grammar covered in this spread. It is an ideal assessment opportunity.
- It encourages students to generate and explore ideas whilst communicating previous learning to work towards their goal. It covers the Creative thinkers, Reflective learners and Self-managers groups of skills from the framework of personal, learning and thinking skills.

Success criteria:

- amount of information communicated
- variety of vocabulary and structures used
- number of personal opinions given

Wie man sich in einer Stadt zurechtfindet

Seiten 34–35

Planner

➤ Objectives

- Asking for directions

➤ Resources

Students' Book, pages 34–35
CD 1, tracks 19–20
Grammar Workbook, page 59
Activity Sheets 9–10

➤ Key language

die Ampel; der Bahnsteig; die Bauarbeiten; der Fahrplan; das Gleis; die Haltestelle; die Kreuzung; die öffentlichen Verkehrsmittel; die Rückfahrkarte; die S-Bahn; die Straßenbahn; die U-Bahn; der Verkehr; der Zug
abfahren; ankommen
billig; verspätet
entlang; geradeaus; links; rechts; weit

➤ Skills

- Reading for gist

➤ Grammar

- The imperative

➤ PLTS

Question 6: Independent enquirers/Creative thinkers/Reflective learners/Team workers/Effective participators
Question 7: Independent enquirers/Creative thinkers/Reflective learners

➤ Starters

- Display the following words from the spread with the vowels missing: *die Ampel, die Bauarbeiten, der Fahrplan*; *das Gleis, die S-Bahn*; *die Straßenbahn, die U-Bahn*; *der Verkehr, der Zug, abfahren, ankommen, nehmen*. Students race against each other to fill in the missing letters. Elicit the English for these words.
- Play a miming game to practise modes of transport. Mime a mode of transport, e.g. walking along, driving a car, etc. Students try to guess what mode of transport it is. Encourage them to use full sentences when guessing, e.g. *Sie nehmen die U-Bahn? Sie gehen zu Fuß?* etc.
- After working on the imperative, display some jumbled sentences in the imperative, e.g.
  links Straße erste Nehmt die.
  die besten Nehmen am Sie U-Bahn.
  Students race against each other to unjumble them. They then translate them into English.

➤ Plenaries

- Display some imperatives in the *ihr* form, e.g. *Nehmt*. Go round the class asking each student in turn to say a sentence in the imperative, e.g. *Nehmt die U-Bahn!* If necessary for support, also display a list of words from the spread that students could use in their sentences. Repeat this with imperatives in the *du* form and *Sie* form.
- Call out a word from the spread. Students respond by putting it into a sentence, e.g.
  Teacher: *Straße*
  Student: *Nehmen Sie die erste Straße links.*
  Teacher: *ankommen*
  Student: *Wann kommt er in Hamburg an?*
- Students work in pairs. Allocate each student a shopping centre/monument/tourist attraction, etc. in the region. Students then describe to their partner how best to get to the place they have been allocated, how far it is and how long it will take to get there. From this description, their partner tries to guess which place they are talking about.

1a Lies die Dialoge. Welches Bild passt zu welchem Dialog? Warum? Hör dann zu, um deine Antworten zu prüfen.

4–6

- As an introduction to the spread, students read the dialogues.
- They then match the pictures to the dialogues, giving reasons why they have matched them as they have.

CD 1, track 19 **Seite 34, Übung 1a**

A

A: Entschuldige bitte, kannst du mir sagen, wie ich am besten von hier zum Krankenhaus komme?

B: Ja, das ist nicht weit. Sie gehen am besten zu Fuß. Gehen Sie die Nymphenburgerstraße entlang und biegen Sie dann in die dritte Straße rechts ein, das ist die Lachnerstraße. Gehen Sie bis zur Renatastraße, biegen Sie dann rechts ab und gehen Sie die Straße entlang. Das Krankenhaus ist auf der linken Seite an der Ecke.

A: Vielen Dank!

B

A: Entschuldigung, wir wollen zum Olympia-Einkaufszentrum. Wie kommen wir am schnellsten dahin?

B: Also, wir sind hier am Rotkreuzplatz und ihr wollt zum Olympia-Einkaufszentrum. Da nehmt ihr am besten die U-Bahn. Es gibt auch einen Bus, aber mit der U-Bahn seid ihr schneller dort.

A: Danke und welche U-Bahn-Linie ist das, bitte?

B: Tja, da bin ich mir nicht so sicher. Ich glaube, es ist die Linie 3.

A: Danke schön!

C

A: Entschuldigen Sie bitte, ich möchte zur Jugendherberge. Wie komme ich am besten dorthin?

B: Die Jugendherberge, also, fahr mit dem Bus. Das wäre die Nummer 13 oder fahr mit der S-Bahn, mit der Linie S7.

A: Ist es weit?

B: Mit dem Bus etwa 20 Minuten, mit der S-Bahn etwa 15.

A: Danke, dann nehme ich die S-Bahn.

Answers:

1 B – wir = more than 1– ihr = younger
2 C – ich = one person, uses Sie talking to older person, using du = talking to younger person
3 A – using du = younger person – uses Sie = talking to older person

1b Lies die Dialoge noch einmal. Welche Verkehrsmittel gibt es in München? Welche anderen gibt es noch? Mach eine Liste.

- Students read the dialogues again.
- They list the types of transport there are in Munich and then list any other types of transport they can think of.

4–6

Answers:

U-Bahn, S-Bahn, Bus, nicht erwähnt: Zug und Straßenbahn *(+ others that students can think of)*

1c Lies die Dialoge noch einmal. Richtig (R), falsch (F) oder nicht angegeben (N)?

- Students read the dialogue once more and this time note whether the sentences listed are true, false or not mentioned in the text.

4–6

Answers:

a F; **b** R; **c** N; **d** F; **e** R; **f** R

2 Hör gut zu. Wohin wollen diese Leute? Wie kommen sie dorthin? Wie weit ist es?

- Students listen to the recording and note down where the people want to go, how they get there and how far it is.

4–6

CD 1, track 20 **Seite 34, Übung 2**

1

Frau Breuner: Entschuldige bitte, ich suche das historische Museum.
Wie komme ich am schnellsten dorthin?

Boy: Das historische Museum, das ist nicht weit. Wenn Sie mit der U-Bahn fahren, dauert es nur 10 Minuten. Fahren Sie mit der U-Bahn-Linie 3.

Frau Breuner: Vielen Dank. Ach, wo ist die U-Bahn-Station?

Boy: Einfach hier geradeaus – die U-Bahn-Station ist da vorne an der Ampel.

2

Thomas: Hallo, kannst du mir bitte helfen? Ich möchte zum Stadion.

Girl: Also, das Stadion ist ziemlich weit von hier. Du kannst entweder mit dem
Bus oder mit der S-Bahn fahren. Der Bus ist billiger, aber die S-Bahn ist schneller.

Thomas: Und welche S-Bahnlinie ist das, bitte?

Girl: Die Linie 23. Die Fahrt dauert so um die 20 Minuten.

Thomas: Okay, danke.

3

Susi und Anna: Entschuldigen Sie bitte, wir suchen das neue Kino. Können Sie uns bitte helfen?

Woman: Ja, sicher, einen Moment. So, das neue Kino. Also, ihr geht hier an der Kreuzung über die Ampel. Dann die Hauptstraße entlang, biegt in die zweite, ach nein, die dritte Straße links ein und dann in die nächste Straße rechts. Das Kino ist direkt an der Ecke.

Susi und Anna: Wie weit ist es zu Fuß?

Woman: Nun, so etwa 15 bis 20 Minuten.

4

Herr Kleiser: Ich treffe meine Frau am Einkaufszentrum, aber wo ist das Einkaufszentrum? Könnt ihr mir bitte helfen?

2 young people: Na, klar. Am besten fahren Sie mit dem Bus Nummer 5 und dann gehen Sie . . . (is interrupted by 2nd person), aber nein, das ist doch nicht die Nummer 5, zum Einkaufszentrum fährt die Nummer 18.

Herr Kleiser: Die Nummer 18, bist du dir sicher?

Young person: Ja, ganz sicher. Der nächste Bus fährt in fünf Minuten.

Herr Kleiser: Vielen Dank. Ist das weit?

Young person: Ungefähr eine halbe Stunde.

Answers:

Frau Breuner: where?: Museum; **how?**: on the underground; **how far?**: 10 minutes; **further info**: not far, line 3, underground station before the traffic lights
Thomas: where?: Stadium; **how?**: suburban railway or bus; **how far?**: about 20 minutes with train line 23; **further info**: quite far
Susie und Anna: where?: new cinema; **how?**: on foot; **how far?**: between 15–20 minutes; **further info**: junction over traffic lights, along main street, 3rd street left, next right, on corner
Herr Kleiser: where?: shopping centre; **how?**: bus; **how far?**: half an hour; **further info**: bus 18, in 5 minutes

3 Macht eine Liste von Wörten und Ausdrücken, die man braucht, um Anweisungen zu geben.

- Students work with a partner to list useful words for giving instructions.

4 Du möchtest mit dem Zug nach Starnberg fahren. Lies den Fahrplan und ergänze den Dialog.

- Students read the train timetable and then complete the dialogue.

4–6

Answers:

a 10:33; **b** 11:04; **c** nicht; **d** 8; **e** 9,30

A9 Further reading and writing activities on giving directions and describing a town.

A10 Further listening and speaking activities on directions and transport.

5a Lies die Dialoge auf Seite 34 noch einmal und schreib eine Liste mit den Imperativformen.

PLTS

- Read through the *Grammatik* section on 'the imperative' as a class.
- Students read the dialogues on page 34 again and write a list of all of the imperatives.

Answers:

du: fahr; **ihr:** nehmt; **sie:** gehen Sie, biegen Sie … ab, nehmen Sie

5b Was sind die Imperativformen der folgenden Verben? Schreib eine Liste in dein Heft.

- Students write the imperative forms of the verbs listed.

Answers:

gehen: geh; geht; gehen Sie
nehmen: nimm; nehmt; nehmen Sie
fahren: fahr; fahrt; fahren Sie
kommen: komm; kommt; kommen Sie

6 Work in pairs. A wants to buy a train ticket and B works in the ticket office. Act out a dialogue, taking activity 4 as a model. B ↔ A

4–9

PLTS

- Students use what they have learnt in the spread to complete this activity.
- It encourages students to plan what to do and how to go about it, to generate and explore ideas whilst communicating previous learning and to collaborate and negotiate effectively with others. It covers the Independent enquirers, Creative thinkers, Reflective learners, Team workers and Effective participators groups of skills from the framework of personal, learning and thinking skills.

7 Your German exchange partner is coming next week and sends you an email to ask how to get to your house from the train or bus station. Write a reply, saying which form of transport to take or giving directions for how to get to your house on foot.

4–9

- A writing activity to draw together the vocabulary, ideas, and grammar points covered in the spread. This is an ideal assessment opportunity.
- This activity encourages students to carry out research and to generate ideas and explore possibilities whilst communicating previous learning. It covers the Independent enquirers, Creative thinkers and Reflective learners groups of skills from the framework of personal, learning and thinking skills.

Success criteria:

- amount of information communicated
- variety of vocabulary and structures used
- number of personal opinions given

Wie man eine Stadtführung macht

Seiten 36–37

Planner

➤ Objectives

- Giving a guided tour of one's town/city

➤ Resources

Students' Book, pages 36–37
CD 1, tracks 21–22
Grammar Workbook, page 16
Activity Sheet 11

➤ Key language

die Aussicht; die Brücke; der Brunnen; der Fluss; das Münster; die Umwelt
mieten; Schlittschuh laufen
bequem; einfach; langsam
oben; wieder

➤ Skills

- Listening for detail

➤ Grammar

- Prepositions with the dative and the accusative

➤ PLTS

Question 6: Independent enquirers/Creative thinkers/Reflective learners/Team workers/Self-managers/Effective participators
Question 7: Creative thinkers/Reflective learners/Self-managers

➤ Starters

- Display a list of modes of transport in German, e.g *zu Fuß*, etc. and ask students to order these with what they consider to be the most environmentally friendly at the top, and the least environmentally friendly at the bottom. Compare answers as a class. Choose a few volunteers to justify their choices.
- Students brainstorm as many places of interest in their town/village as possible, e.g. *der Münster, die Brücke*, etc. They then think of as many adjectives as possible to describe these. Compile a list and keep this to use later.

➤ Plenaries

- Display the prepositions, *an, auf, hinter, in, neben, über, unter, vor, zwischen*. Students choose one of these and use it in an accusative and a dative sentence. Compare answers as a class, asking students to explain when you use the dative and when you use the accusative.
- Challenge students to write five sentences on the themes of this spread using the prepositions from plenary activity 1.
- Ask students to imagine their ideal town. They write a paragraph describing it: the buildings and places, the types of public transport and how environmentally friendly the transport is. Display the list from starter activity 3.

1a Lies die Meinungen der vier Schüler und Schülerinnen und beantworte die Fragen.

- As an introduction to this spread, students read the four opinions and answer the questions.

Answers:

4–6

a Nick; **b** Asli; **c** Ann-Cathrin and Nick; **d** Jamie; **e** Asli; **f** Nick; **g** Ann-Cathrin; **h** Jamie

1b Diskutiert mit einem Partner/einer Partnerin. Was sind die Vor- und Nachteile jedes Verkehrsmittels? Mach Notizen.

4–6

- Students work with a partner to discuss advantages and disadvantages of each mode of transport.
- They read the four opinions again for ideas.

2a Hör gut zu. Was sagen diese Leute über die verschiedenen öffentlichen Verkehrsmittel? Mach Notizen.

- Read through the *Tipp* section on listening for detail as a class.
- Students try to put into practise what they have read. They listen to the recording and make notes.

4–6

CD 1, track 21 **Seite 37, Übung 2**

Frau Klein: Ich fahre immer mit dem Bus. Die Busse fahren alle 20 Minuten. Das finde ich sehr gut, weil man nie lange auf einen Bus warten muss. Früher musste ich mit dem Zug fahren, und ich musste immer lange warten.

Herr Gipfel: Ich fahre manchmal mit der Straßenbahn und manchmal mit dem Bus. Beides ist bequem, aber die Straßenbahn ist natürlich besser für die Umwelt. Am liebsten fahre ich mit dem Rad, obwohl es langsamer ist. Als Student konnte ich jeden Tag mit dem Rad fahren, aber heute habe ich nicht so viel Zeit.

Frau Schneider: Ich fahre fast immer mit dem Auto in die Stadt, obwohl Parken ein Problem ist. Aber ich wohne in einem kleinen Dorf, und es gibt nur zwei Busse pro Tag, einen um 9.00 Uhr und der zweite dann erst wieder um 17.00 Uhr. Früher gab es einen Bus um 12 Uhr – das war viel praktischer und auch besser für die Umwelt – und ich brauchte nicht mit dem Auto zu fahren.

Herr Weiß: Wenn ich in die Stadt gehe, gehe ich meistens zu Fuß oder ich fahre mit dem Rad, weil ich fit bleiben will und weil beides gut für die Umwelt ist. Wenn es regnet, nehme ich aber die Straßenbahn. Als Kind wollte ich immer Straßenbahn fahren – es hat mir immer Spaß gemacht.

2b Hör noch einmal zu. Wer sagt was?

4–6

- Students listen again and this time note down who said what.
- Remind students that they may not hear exactly the same phrases and that they need to think about the context and the meaning of the phrases.

Answers:

a Frau Schneider; **b** Herr Weiß; **c** Herr Gipfel; **d** Frau Klein; **e** Herr Weiß; **f** Frau Schneider; **g** Herr Gipfel

3 Welche Sätze passen zu welchen Fotos?

- For further practise of the vocabulary in the spread, students match the texts to the photos.

4–6

Answers:

1 c; **2** d; **3** a; **4** b

4a Hör gut zu. Anja beschreibt ihre Stadt. Welche Gebäude und Plätze nennt sie und mit welchen Verkehrsmitteln kommt man dorthin? Mach Notizen.

4–6

- Read through the *Tipp* section.
- To put into practise what they have read, students listen to the recording and make notes.

CD 1, track 22 **Seite 37, Übung 4**

Hallo, ich bin die Anja, und ich möchte euch gern durch meine Stadt führen. Fangen wir beim Theater an. Das Theater ist nicht sehr groß und es ist ziemlich modern. Manchmal gibt es hier auch Konzerte, meistens klassische Musik. Das interessiert mich nicht so sehr – ich finde Rockmusik viel besser. Am Theater mieten wir ein Rad und fahren durch den Park zur Universität. Nach dem Abitur möchte ich hier gern studieren. Die Universität ist sehr bekannt, besonders für Sport. Wir fahren weiter zum Stadion. Hier trainiere ich jeden Donnerstagabend. Vom Stadion nehmen wir den Bus und fahren zum alten Schloss. Gegenüber dem Schloss gibt es ein Museum. Es ist ziemlich interessant. Hier gibt es auch ein kleines Café, wo man etwas essen und trinken kann. Anschließend gehen wir zu Fuß zum Fluss. Ich gehe gern am Fluss entlang, besonders wenn das Wetter schön ist. Wir gehen über die Brücke und dort ist eine Bushaltestelle. Mit der Straßenbahn fahren wir wieder zurück zur Stadtmitte. Wir nehmen die Linie 15, weil sie vor dem Kino hält, und ich möchte jetzt gern einen Film sehen. Also, tschüs dann!

Answers:

Gebäude/Plätze: Theater, Park, Universität, Stadion, Schloss, Museum, Café, Fluss, Brücke, Bushaltestelle, Kino
Verkehrsmittel: Rad, Bus, zu Fuß, Straßenbahn

4b Hör noch einmal gut zu und beantworte die Fragen auf Englisch.

- Students listen to the recording again and this time answer the questions in English.

4–6

Answers:

a not very big, quite modern; **b** famous especially for sport; **c** old; **d** quite interesting; **e** nice to walk along in good weather

A11 Activity Sheet 11 provides further speaking activities on describing your town and environmental issues.

5 Partnerarbeit. Diskutiert den Unterschied zwischen den Sätzen a und b in der Grammatik-Box. Wann benutzt man den Dativ und wann benutzt man den Akkusativ?

- Read the *Grammatik* section on Prepositions with the dative and the accusative as a class.
- In pairs, students discuss what differences there are between example sentences 'a' and 'b'. They try to come up with a rule saying when you use the dative and when you use the accusative.

6 Work with a partner. Choose a German, Austrian or Swiss town and research it on the Internet.

4–9

PLTS

- This activity draws together what students have learnt in the spread. It also acts as preparation for the next activity.
- It encourages students to plan and carry out research, to generate and explore ideas, to communicate previous learning, to collaborate and negotiate effectively with others and to organise time and resources effectively. It covers the Independent enquirers, Creative thinkers, Reflective learners, Team workers, Self-managers and Effective participators groups of skills from the framework of personal, learning and thinking skills.

7 Design and present a virtual tour through your chosen town, thinking about the environment and the different means of transport available there. Use your notes from activity 6 and the text *Eine Führung durch Freiburg* to help you.

4–9

PLTS

- Students use their research from activity 6 to design and present a tour through their chosen town.
- This activity encourages students to generate and explore ideas, making original connections whilst communicating previous learning and to organise time and resources effectively. It covers the Creative thinkers, Reflective learners and Self-managers groups of skills from the framework of personal, learning and thinking skills.
- This is an ideal assessment opportunity.

Success criteria:

- ideas communicated
- pronunciation and intonation and fluency
- range of vocabulary and structures used
- number of personal opinions given

Aktive Grammatik

Seiten 38–39

Planner

➤ Objectives
- Using the imperfect tense
- Using modal verbs
- Using the imperative
- Using the comparative and the superlative
- Using prepositions with the dative and the accusative

➤ Resources
Students' Book, pages 38–39
Exam Skills Workbooks, page 30
Grammar Workbook, pages 16, 25–27, 39, 53, 59
Activity Sheet 12
Resources and Planning OxBox CD-ROM

➤ Grammar
- The imperfect tense
- Modal verbs
- The imperative
- The comparative and the superlative
- Prepositions with the dative and the accusative

➤ PLTS
All questions: Reflective learners/Self-managers

➤ Introduction to the imperfect tense

1 Translate the following sentences into English.
- This question focuses on the imperfect tense.

Answers:

a The town was once very small.
b There were lots of tourists on the train.
c The Steinwasen park had lots of attractions.
d The people in Titisee-Neustadt were very nice.
e The young people had lots of fun on the toboggan run.

2 Fill in the gap with words from the box.
- This question provides further practice of the imperfect tense.

Answers:

a gab; **b** war; **c** hatte; **d** hatten; **e** waren

➤ Modal verbs

3 Fill in the gaps in the table to complete the modal verbs, following the pattern of *können*.
- This question focuses on using the correct form of modal verbs.

Answers:

missing words:
[ich] darf; mag; soll; will
[du] darfst; musst; sollst; willst
[er/sie/es] mag; muss
[wir] mögen; sollen; wollen
[ihr] dürft; müsst; wollt
[sie/Sie] dürfen; mögen; müssen; sollen

4 Translate the following sentences into German.
- This question focuses on using the correct form of modal verbs.

Answers:

a Wir wollen nächtsten Sommer kommen.
b Du kannst mit dem Bus in die Stadt fahren.
c Sie sollen Hamburg besuchen.
d Ihr mögt mit der Straßenbahn fahren?
e Sie können den Dreiuhrzug nehmen / mit dem Dreiuhrzug fahren.
F Ich darf nicht zum Steinwasen Park gehen.

➤ The imperative

5 Change these sentences into the instructions using the imperative form.
- This question focuses on using the imperative form.

Answers:

a Nimm die erste Straße links.
b Fahren Sie mit dem Bus.
c Geh zu Fuß.
d Fahrt über die Brücke.
e Kaufen Sie einen Stadtplan.
f Nehmt die U-Bahn.

➤ The imperfect tense of modal verbs

6 **Fill in the imperfect form of the verbs in brackets.**
- This question focuses on using modal verbs in the imperfect.

Answers:

a mochte; **b** wollten, war; **c** musste; **d** konnte; **e** wollten; **f** durften

➤ The comparative and superlative

7 **Comparative or superlative? Complete the sentences.**
- This question focuses on using the comparative and superlative correctly.

Answers:

a wärmer; **b** höher; **c** beste; **d** hoch, höher, am höchsten

➤ Prepositions with the dative and the accusative

8 **Read the sentences carefully: dative or accusative? Fill in the correct definite article.**
- This question provides further practice of prepositions with the dative and accusative.

Answers:

a Gegenüber **dem** Bahnhof gibt es ein neues Einkausfszentrum.
b Du musst nach **der** nächsten Haltestelle aussteigen.
c Geh zuerst nach rechts, dann nach links und das Rathaus ist gleich um **die** Ecke.
d Ohne **das** alte Stadion ist die Stadt viel schöner.
e Wenn Sie mit **dem** Bus fahren, können Sie bis zu **der** Kirche fahren.
f Der Bus fährt von **der** Universität bis zu **den** Geschäften.

Kompetenzen

Seite 40

Planner

➤ Objectives
- Summarising what you have learnt

➤ Resources
Students' Book, page 40
Exam Skills Workbooks, page 31
Activity Sheet 13
Resources and Planning OxBox CD-ROM

➤ Skills
- Practising making clever guesses about what unknown words mean
- Recognising common sound-spelling links
- Listening with the task in mind
- Learning about word families
- Creating mind maps using pictures or words/questions
- Writing vocabulary on sticky notes

➤ PLTS
Question 2, Beim Lesen: Reflective learners/Self-managers
Question 1, Beim Lernen: Creative thinkers/Reflective learners

➤ Beim Lesen

1 **Practise making clever guesses about what unknown words mean.**
- Students look at the text on page 173 for two seconds and use strategy 'a' to try to guess what it is about.
- They then use strategy 'b' to explain the words listed.

Answers:

Auto = motor/car, Bahn = road – Autobahn = road for cars or motorway
Halte = stop, Stelle = place – Haltestelle = place where you stop or bus stop
Park = parking, Platz = place – Parkplatz = place where you park or car park

2 **Recognise common sound-spelling links**

PLTS
- Students find some more words to fit into the categories listed in the Students' Book.
- This activity encourages students to reflect upon what they have learnt and build on this. It covers the Reflective learners and Self-managers groups of skills from the framework of personal, learning and thinking skills.

➤ Beim Hören

1 **Listen with the task in mind.**
- Students brainstorm 10 German words they might hear for each of the topics listed.

➤ Beim Lernen

1 Learn about word families

PLTS
- Students list the vocabulary of a topic area, for example 'Meine Stadt', into categories such as verbs, nouns and adjectives.
- Before they begin, brainstorm possible topic areas and categories as a class.
- This activity encourages students to think creatively and explore different ideas whilst communicating previous learning. It covers the Creative thinkers and Reflective learners groups of skills from the framework of personal, learning and thinking skills.

2 Create mind maps using pictures or words/questions.
- Students look at the mind map in the Students' book.
- Encourage them to choose a different topic and to create their own mind map.

3 Write vocabulary on sticky notes.
- Students make a list of new words they have come across in this unit and organise them in the way that they find most helpful. They could stick them on their walls, desk, folders or anywhere else in their room.

Szenario

Seite 41

Planner

➤ Objectives
- Preparing a presentation about your home town

➤ Resources
Students' Book, page 41
Exam Skills Workbooks, pages 28–29
Assessment Sheets 1–8
Resources and Planning OxBox CD-ROM

➤ Skills
- Writing practice
- Speaking practice

➤ PLTS
Zum Schreiben: Independent enquirers/Creative thinkers/Reflective learners/Team workers/Self-managers/Effective participators
Zum Sprechen: Creative thinkers/Reflective learners/Team workers/ Effective participators

➤ Zum Schreiben

In this section, students will prepare a presentation about thier home town in order to win a competition to be twinned with the German town of Münster.

It is possible for students to obtain GCSE grades A–F depending on their ability:
Grade F students write a short review using simple sentences and communicate some information.
Grade C students include a variety of structures which may include different tenses or time frames. They communicate information and express personal opinions.
Grade A students include a variety of vocabulary, structures and verb tenses. They convey information, narrate events and express and explain ideas and points of view.

1 Work in a group. Brainstorm the most interesting buildings, places and events in your town, and any green transport initiatives it has. Then write down suitable adjectives to describe each of them in German.

2 Each member of the group chooses one of the locations, events or initiatives and does some research into its background on the Internet. Make notes in German.

3 Each person then writes a paragraph of 150–300 words about the item they have researched.

4 Find pictures on the Internet to illustrate your paragraph and then put them together to create a brochure about your town for your group's competition entry.
- These four activities make up complete task. Encourage students to draw upon what they have learnt in the unit. This is an ideal assessment opportunity.

PLTS
- This encourages students to identify questions to answer and to plan and carry out research, to generate and explore ideas, to reflect upon what they have learnt, to collaborate and negotiate effectively with others, and to organise time and resources effectively to achieve goals. It covers the Independent enquirers, Creative thinkers, Reflective learners, Team workers, Self-managers and Effective participators groups of skills from the framework of personal, learning and thinking skills.

➤ Zum Sprechen

In this section, students act out a meeting with the committee deciding which town will be Münster's twin. Some groups must play the parts of committee members and ask questions about the town. The others must present convincing arguments for why their town should be chosen. Suggest recording the debate using the record/playback facility on the OxBox CD-ROM.

It is possible to obtain GCSE grades A–F depending on ability and students are marked on Communication, Quality of language and Pronunciation and intonation:
Grade F students communicate a limited number of ideas, expressing simple opinions. A few phrases or short sentences are accurate enough to be recognisable. There are very few instances of clear pronunciation and intonation.
Grade C students communicate the essential elements, readily expressing points of view. They occasionally hesitate and can respond to some unpredictable questions. They use straightforward vocabulary and structures which may contain different tenses or time frames. Pronunciation and intonation is generally accurate.
Grade A students use relevant information to develop and justify individual ideas and points of view. There is no hesitation and they are able to respond to unpredictable questions. They use a wide range of clause types, vocabulary and structures accurately. The presentation is fluent and coherent with just minor errors. Pronunciation and intonation are very accurate with a few minor slips.

1 **The time has come to meet the committee and tell them why you think your town should be chosen.**
2 **Divide into small groups. In your group, write two lists: one containing questions that you think the committee are likely to ask you about your town, and one containing reasons why you think it should be chosen. Try to flesh out your arguments as much as possible, using plenty of adjectives, adverbs, comparatives and superlatives.**
3 **Work with another group. One group is the Münster selection committee and the other is the delegation from your town. Then swap roles.**
4 **Which group do you think had the most convincing arguments? Who do you think should have won?**

PLTS

- These four activities make up a complete task and concentrate on speaking skills. Encourage students to draw upon what they have learnt in the unit. This is an ideal assessment opportunity.
- This encourages students think creatively, generating and exploring ideas, to use what they have learnt to achieve goals and to collaborate and negotiate effectively with others. It covers the Creative thinkers, Reflective learners, Team workers and Effective participators groups from the framework of personal, learning and thinking skills.

Vokabeln

Seite 42

Planner

➤ Resources
Students' Book, page 42
Activity Sheet 14

This page provides a summary of the key language covered in each spread of this unit. It could be used as a handy reference for students as they work through the unit. Alternatively, students could use its clear German–English format when learning vocabulary.

Lesen

Seiten 173–174

Planner

➤ Objectives

- To encourage independent reading and develop reading strategies
- To provide alternative class and homework material for students who finish other activities quickly

Page 173 provides a magazine-style reading text in the context of the unit.
Page 174 provides a magazine-style quiz, again in the context of the unit.

➤ Resources

Students' Book, pages 173–174

➤ Skills

- Reading practice

➤ PLTS

Question 4 (part 1): Creative thinkers/Reflective learners/Team workers
Question 1c (part 2): Reflective learners/Self-managers

Lesen A: Die langweiligste Stadt!

1 Lest den Text, ohne mit dem Wörterbuch zu arbeiten. Benutzt die Lesestrategien auf Seite 40. Arbeitet mit einem Partner/einer Partnerin und helft euch gegenseitig.

- This activity practises reading strategies. Students read the text and work with a partner to work out any words they aren't sure of.

2 Mach eine Liste mit den Problemen, die Herr Weber nennt. Warum ist die Stadt langweilig?

- Students list the problems mentioned by Herr Weber and explain why the town is boring.

3 Mach eine Liste, wie man die Stadt attraktiver machen kann.

- Students make a list saying how the town could be made nicer.
- This activity practises some of the vocabulary and grammar points they have covered in the spread.

4 Macht ein Interview. A ist Herr Weber und stellt die Fragen. B ist der Städteplaner und sagt, wie man die Stadt verbessern kann.

- Students work in pairs conduct an interview. Partner A is Herr Weber; B is the town planner.
- This activity encourages students to think creatively and explore different ideas whilst communicating previous learning and to collaborate effectively with others. It covers the Creative thinkers, Reflective learners and Team workers groups of skills from the framework of personal, learning and thinking skills.

5 Mach nun eine Broschüre über die Stadt, die jetzt nicht mehr langweilig ist.

- Students use what they have done in previous activities to produce a brochure on the town.

Lesen B: Ein Städtequiz

1a Lies die Texte. Benutze die Lesestrategien auf Seite 40. Wie heißen die Städte und die Gegend?

- Students read the texts, using the reading strategies on page 40 for support. They match the photos of towns or regions to each text.

Answers:

1 Salzburg; **2** Frankfurt; **3** Basel; **4** Stuttgart; **5** Zürich

1b Welche Stadt oder Gegend ist es? Schreib nur den Namen.

- Students read the sentences and say which town or region they refer to.

Answers:

a Basel; **b** Stuttgart; **c** Salzburg; **d** Zürich; **e** Frankfurt

1c Lies die Texte und beantworte die Fragen auf Deutsch.

- To check they fully understand the texts, students answer the questions in English.
- This activity encourages students to communicate previous learning to work towards goals. It covers the Reflective learners and Self-managers groups of skills from the framework of personal, learning and thinking skills.

Answers:

a Frankfurt; **b** Basel; **c** Frankfurt; **d** Salzburg

Unit 2A: Gesundheit und Sport		Overview grid		
Page reference	**Contexts and objectives**	**Skills**	**Grammar**	**Vocabulary**
pages 44–45 **Wie man über Sport redet**	• Discussing sport • Planning a sporting holiday	• Using longer sentences	• The perfect tense • Separable verbs	*das Endspiel, der Held, die Heldin, die Liga, die Mannschaft, der Pokal, das Spiel, der Torwart, die Vorgabe, gucken, loben, aufregend, bekannt, beliebt, enttäuscht, erfolgreich, selbstständig, ab und zu, unter dem Par*
pages 46–47 **Wie man seinen Sporthelden beschreibt**	• Describing sporting heroes	• Giving your opinion	• Word order	*die Weltmeisterschaft, der Weltrekord, der Zweite Weltkrieg*
pages 48–49 **Wie man gesund lebt**	• Discussing how to live healthily	• Using capital letters	• In order to...	*die Essgewohnheiten, der Früchtetee, das Gemüse, die Kekse, das Obst, der Schlaf, die Süßigkeiten, aufstehen, rauchen, stark*
pages 50–51 **Wie man Abenteuer findet!**	• Discussing extreme and unusual sports	• Using intensifiers	• Time phrases	*das Abseilen, die Anspannung, die Aussicht, die Einweisung, das Erlebnis, das Gleitschirmfliegen, die Hingabe, das Paragliding, begleiten, erhalten, erleben, Kayak fahren, ängstlich, atemberaubend, einmalig, furchtbar, gefährlich, psychisch, unvergesslich, zur Verfügung stehen*
pages 52–53 **Wie man eine Verletzung beschreibt**	• Describing sports injuries	• Using reflexive pronouns	• Subordinating conjunctions: word order	*das Fußgelenk, verletzt, die Schmerzen, ausgerutscht, gestoßen, hingefallen, überfahren, verdreht, weh tun*
pages 54–55 **Aktive Grammatik**	• Grammar		• Word order • Subordinating conjunctions • The perfect tense	
page 56 **Kompetenzen**	• Speaking • Writing	• Expressing opinions • Changing word order to add emphasis • Using description and linking words • Using quantifiers • Capital letters • Using umlauts		
page 57 **Szenario**	• Prepare and deliver a presentation on your favourite sporting hero • Planning a sporting holiday	• Writing practice • Speaking practice		
page 58 **Vokabeln**	• Key language from the unit			
pages 175–176 **Lesen**	• Extreme sports • To encourage independent reading and develop reading strategies • To provide alternative class and homework material for students who finish other activities quickly	• Reading practice		

2A Gesundheit und Sport

Unit Objectives

Contexts and cultural focus: sport, health
Skills focus: saying what you like and dislike; giving opinions in a variety of ways; using word order to change emphasis; writing longer sentences using conjunctions; adding detail to descriptions; varying sentence structure
Grammar: the perfect tense; conjunctions (with the correct word order); adverbs of time and place

Controlled assessment opportunities

Writing: Students' Book, page 45, activity 8
Writing: Students' Book, page 47, activity 7
Speaking: Students' Book, page 49, activity 6
Writing: Students' Book, page 51, activity 8
Writing: Students' Book, page 53, activity 7
Speaking: Students' Book, page 57, *Zum Sprechen*, activity 5

See also ***GCSE German for OCR Assessment OxBox CD-ROM.***

An introduction to the unit Seite 43

- *Aim*: To introduce the themes of the unit.
- The opening spread of each unit is styled as the contents page of a teenage magazine. Illustrations, captions and skills summaries provide a preview of what is to come:

	Students' Book
Weißt du schon, wie man über Sport redet?	pages 44–45
Weißt du schon, wie man seinen Sporthelden beschreibt?	pages 46–47
Weißt du schon, wie man gesund lebt?	pages 48–49
Weißt du schon, wie man Abenteuer findet?	pages 50–51
Weißt du schon, wie man eine Verletzung beschreibt?	pages 52–53

- Allow time for students to read the questions and cross-refer to the relevant pages of the Students' Book. They could do this individually or in pairs/groups, followed by whole-class discussion.
- This spread also provides an opportunity for students to recap on familiar language. Ask them to think about language they already know that might be useful when working on the themes of the unit.
- At the end of work on Unit 2A:
  - If time permits, ask students to devise a replacement opening spread. What do they think should be on it, in terms of pictures, captions, etc.? What would they change/keep the same, and why? Ask them to imagine it is the contents page of a teenage magazine: what sort of captions and pictures do they feel would attract people to buy the magazine? This sort of activity encourages students to think about features of a text that make it suitable for a particular audience or purpose.
  - Allow time for students to return to this opening spread to answer the questions, review what they have learned and reflect on areas for improvement. What did they find difficult, interesting, etc.? What do they think are the most important things they have learned in this unit?

Wie man über Sport redet

Seiten 44–45

Planner

➤ Objectives
- Discussing sport
- Planning a sporting holiday

➤ Resources
Students' Book, pages 44–45
CD 1, tracks 26–27
Grammar Workbook, page 48
Activity Sheet 15

➤ Key language
die Mannschaft, das Spiel, bekannt, beliebt, loben, enttäuscht, erfolgreich, selbstständig, ab und zu

➤ Skills
- Using expressions of time and frequency

➤ Grammar
- The perfect tense
- Separable verbs

➤ PLTS
Question 2b: Independent enquirers
Question 8: Creative thinkers/Reflective learners/ Self-managers

➤ Starters
- Students brainstorm all the German words they know for sports e.g. *Fußball.* Display these so that the class can seet them. Once they have finished, display a list of various sports stars, e.g. *Wayne Rooney*, and ask students to race against the clock to match the sports stars with their sport.
- Ask a confident volunteer to mime a sport. The class tries to guess what it is in German.
- Start by asking a confident student, *Hast du einen Lieblingssport?* Once the student has answered, he/she asks another student the same question. Continue around the class. With more confident classes, continue with other questions.

➤ Plenaries
- Give students a couple of minutes, working in pairs, to list as many different types of sport as they can, giving an opinion for each. When the time is up, they compare their list with another pair, scoring a point for each type of sport not mentioned by the other pair.
- Play a version of Word Tennis with the class divided into two teams. The aim is to build extended sentences expressing opinions on sporting activities, e.g.
  Team A: *Mein Lieblingsport ist...*
  Team B: *... Tennis...*
  Team A: *... und mein Held ist Roger Federer...*
  Team B: *... weil ich Roger Federer einen sehr guten Spieler finde...*
  Team A: *... Ich sehe sehr gern Tennis im Fernsehen*
- Students choose a celebrity and imagine what his/her favourite sport is, whether he/she practises a sport, who his/her sporting hero is, and whether he/she watches sport on the television. They then write a paragraph on behalf of the celebrity.

As an introduction to the spread, students answer the questions on page 44 for themselves.

1 Lies die Texte auf Seite 44 und füll die Tabelle aus.

- Students read the texts on page 44 of the Students' Book and fill in the table.

4–6

Answers:

	Watches which sport	Hero/Heroine	Participates in which sport?
Thorsten	football	Michael Ballack	football
Tania	tennis	Roger Federer	occasionally swims; jogging
Meike	N/T	N/T	aikido
Michael	handball	Christian Zeitz	handball

2a Wie beschreibt man Sport und Sportler? Finde die deutschen Wörter in den Texten auf Seite 44.

- Students find the German equivalents in the texts on page 44 of the Students' Book for the English words listed.

1–3

Answers: **a** toll; **b** anstrengend; **c** erfolgreich; **d** aufregend/ spannend; **e** launisch; **f** eine Schande

2b Such in einem Wörterbuch weitere fünf positive und negative Adjektive, um Sport und Sportler zu beschreiben.

PLTS

- Students look in a dictionary to try and find five more postive and five more negative adjectives that could be used to describe sportspeople.
- This activity encourages students to analyse and evaluate information, judging its relevance and value. It covers the Independent enquirers group of skills from the framework of personal, learning and thinking skills.

3 Jens stellt sich vor. Hör gut zu und beantworte die folgenden Fragen auf Englisch.

4–6

- Students listen to Jens and then answer the questions in English.

CD 1, track 26 **Seite 45, Übung 3**

Interviewer/in:
Jugendmagazin wollte auch mit Jens über seine Sporterfahrung reden. Leider konnte er nicht ins Studio kommen. Er hat aber Folgendes für uns auf Tonband aufgenommen.
Jens:
Hallo! Ich heiße Jens, bin sechzehn Jahre alt und wohne in Hamburg. Ich spreche über Sport. Ich liebe Sport und am liebsten mag ich Golf. Sonntags spiele ich mit meinem Vater im Golfklub. Mein Vater ist sehr fit and kann sehr gut spielen. Letzte Woche spielte er mit fünf Schlägen unter dem Par. Das kann ich nicht. Leider spielte ich mit einer Vorgabe von vier Schlägen. Mein Held zurzeit ist Martin Kaymer. Er kommt aus Düsseldorf und ist erst dreiundzwanzig Jahre alt, aber letzten Monat hat er die BMW International in München gewonnen. Man lobte ihn sehr und meinte, dass er gut genug sei, einen Platz im Europa-Team für den Ryder Cup zu bekommen. Von sowas kann ich nur träumen! Ansonsten schwimme ich dreimal pro Woche und im Winter fahre ich Ski. Ich glaube, ich bin ziemlich fit.

Answers:

a 16, Hamburg; **b** golf; **c** golf club, with his father; **d** Martin Kaymer; **e** at only 23, won BMW International, will possibly be in Ryder Cup-Team; **f** swimming/skiing

A15 Activity Sheet 15 provides further activities on sport.

4 Hör gut zu. Wie finden sie Sport? Schreib die Tabelle in dein Heft ab und füll sie aus.

4–6

- Students listen to the opinions on sport, copy the table into their exercise books and fill it in.

CD 1, track 27 **Seite 45, Übung 4**

Interviewer/in: *Jugendmagazin* hat viele junge Leute über Sport befragt. Hier reden wir persönlich mit Thorsten und Tania. Wie findest du Sport, Thorsten?
Thorsten: Ich finde Sport toll, aber auch anstrengend. Ich mag besonders Fußball.
Interviewer/in: Spielst du denn auch?
Thorsten: Ja, ich spiele in einer Mannschaft und ich bin ein ziemlich guter Spieler. Ich spiele zweimal die Woche. Ich habe letzte Woche am Samstag gespielt, aber leider haben wir verloren.
Interviewer/in: Ah, wie schade Thorsten. Und du, Tania? Wie findest du Sport?
Tania: Ich finde Sport okay, wenn auch ein bisschen anstrengend.
Interviewer/in: Treibst du auch Sport?
Tania: Ja, ich treibe ein bisschen Sport. Ich schwimme manchmal – und dreimal pro Woche gehe ich joggen. Letzte Woche waren wir im Park joggen und ein Hund ist mir nachgejagt! Ich hatte Angst!
Interviewer/in: Vielen Dank, Thorsten und Tania. Und jetzt...

Answers:

	opinion of sport?	which sport?	how often?	last week
Thorsten	great, tiring	football	2 × a week	lost game
Tania	OK, tiring	swimming, jogging	sometimes 3 × a week	dog chased her

5a Hör noch einmal zu. Wie sagt man auf Deutsch:

- Students listen again and find the German for the phrases listed.

Answers: **a** Ich habe am Samstag gespielt. **b** Leider haben wir verloren. **c** Ein Hund ist mir nachgejagt.

5b Mach andere Sätze im Perfekt mit den Verben (in Klammern).

- Practice of forming the perfect tense.

Answers: **a** Er hat den Pokal gewonnen. **b** Wir haben das Spiel im Fernsehen gesehen. **c** Sie sind am Sonntag Rad gefahren.

6a Finde die deutschen trennbaren Verben für:

- Students find the German separable verbs for the English verbs listed.

Answers: **a** fernsehen; **b** aussehen; **c** skifahren

6b Finde die deutschen untrennbaren für:

- Students find the German inseparable verbs for the English verbs listed.

Answers: **a** bekommen; **b** verlieren; **c** bewundern

7 Work in groups. Imagine you are doing an interview for *Jugendmagazin*. Use the questions on page 44 to interview each other. Which is the favourite sport? Remember to use expressions from the *Tipp* box.

4–6

- This mini-project encourages students to put together all that they have learnt on this spread about describing sport and giving opinions.

8 You are writing an article about sport for *Jugendmagazin*. Answer the questions on page 44 about yourself and then write them up into a report. Try to use as many words and expressions from this spread as possible.

PLTS

4–6

- Encourage students to use vocabulary presented on these pages.
- This activity encourages students to generate and explore ideas for their article whilst setting goals, communicating previous learning and managing their time and resources effectively. It covers the Creative thinkers, Reflective learners, Self-managers groups of skills from the framework of personal, learning and thinking skills.

Success criteria:

- information communicated
- variety of vocabulary and structures used
- different tenses or time frames used

Wie man seinen Sporthelden beschreibt

Seiten 46–47

Planner

➤ Objectives
- Describing sporting heroes

➤ Resources
Students' Book, pages 46–47
CD 1, track 28
Grammar Workbook, page 61
Activity Sheets 16–17

➤ Key language
die Weltmeisterschaft, der Weltrekord

➤ Skills
- Giving your opinion

➤ Grammar
- Word order

➤ PLTS
Question 2: Creative thinkers
Question 6: Independent enquirers/Self-managers

➤ Starters
- Give students a couple of minutes to think of as many famous sports stars as possible. Display this list. Next ask them to brainstorm German adjectives that could be used to describe sports stars. Display the list of adjectives. Students then allocate the adjectives listed to each of the sports stars listed.
- Divide the class into two teams. Call out statements about famous sports stars, e.g. *Roger Federer ist Schwimmer. Richtig oder falsch?* Each team writes *R* or *F* on a piece of paper/mini-whiteboard and holds it up. They score a point for a correct answer. The team with the most correct answers wins.
- Choose a sports star and go around the class asking each student to say an adjective that describes him/her e.g. *Er/Sie ist stark*. Continue until they can't think of any more and then choose a different sports person. Display the list of adjectives from starter activity 1 for support if necessary.

➤ Plenaries
- Display jumbled sentences about sport e.g. *Boris Becker – 1986 – wieder der Sieger – von Wimbledon – war* and give students a set amount of time to unjumble the sentences, reminding them to watch out for the time-manner-place rule. Ask volunteers to come to the front and put the sentences in the correct order and to explain why this is the 'correct' order.
- Display a few words and phrases from the spread and challenge students to use them all in a short paragraph based on the theme of the spread. They exchange their paragraphs with a partner and suggest improvements to each other's work.
- Choose a sports star as in starter activity 3, but this time go round the class asking students to describe him/her using some of the terms from the *Tipp* box, e.g. *Meiner Meinung nach ist er/sie....* Encourage more able students to use longer sentences beginning with a time expression, e.g. *2007 war Roger Federer wieder der Sieger von Wimbledon.*

Kennst du diese Helden? Wer hat was gemacht und wann?
- As an introduction to the spread, students read about the sports stars and answer the questions.

Answers:

1 Franziska van Almsick; **2** Carl Lewis; **3** Bernhard Carl (Bert) Trautmann; **4** 6. September 1994, Rom; **5** Wembley-Stadion, London, 5. Mai 1956; **6** Olympische Spiele der XXIII. Olympiade, Los Angeles Memorial Coliseum, August 1984

1a Schau dir die Bilder und Infos auf Seite 46 an. Sind die folgenden Sätze richtig oder falsch?
- Students look at the pictures and information presented on page 46 and state whether the sentences are true or false.

Answers:

a F – Carl Lewis ist Amerikaner. **b** R; **c** F – 1994 war die 7. Weltmeisterschaft in Italien. **d** F – 1956 war die FA-Cup-Finale in London. **e** R **f** F – Trautmann war Deutscher.

1b Korrigiere die falschen Sätze. Schreib die sechs richtigen Sätze a–f in dein Heft auf.
- Students correct any false sentences and write out the correct sentences from activity 1a.

2 Wie findest du diese Sportler. Wer hat dir am meisten imponiert? Warum? Schreib mindestens sechs Sätze und benutze dabei die Ausdrücke aus der Tipp-Box.
- Read the *Tipp* box as a class and encourage students to use these phrases in their writing.
- Students write six sentences saying what they think of the sports heroes from activity 1 and why.
- This activity encourages students to think

creatively and to make original connections. It covers the Creative thinkers group of skills from the framework of personal, learning and thinking skills.

3a Hör gut zu und beantworte die folgenden Fragen auf Englisch.

4–6

- Students listen to the recording and answer the questions.

CD 1, track 28 **Seite 47, Übung 3**

Hallo! Ich heiße Paul und ich bin 16 Jahre alt. Ich möchte über meinen Helden sprechen. Er heißt Bernhard Carl Trautmann (in England Bert Trautmann), und er war Fußballprofi. Zwischen 1949 und 1964 war er Torwart für eine englische Mannschaft – Manchester City. 1949 war das problematisch, weil Trautmann Deutscher war, und es war erst kurz nach dem Zweiten Weltkrieg. 1956 wurde Trautmann zur Legende, als Manchester City das FA-Cup-Finale in Wembley, London, drei zu eins gewann. Trautmann war der Torwart und spielte in den letzten Minuten mit gebrochenem Hals. Er wurde zum „Spieler des Jahres" und sogar als erster Ausländer zum englischen „Fußballer des Jahres" ernannt. Ich glaube, er ist ein richtiger Held und ein fantastisches Beispiel von internationaler Zusammenarbeit.

Answers:

a Bernhard Carl (Bert Trautmann); **b** Football; **c** goalkeeper; **d** Manchester City; **e** he was German **f** 1949–1964; **g** Manchester City won the FA Cup Final 3–1. **h** a broken neck

3b Hör noch einmal zu und füll die Lücken mit den richtigen Jahreszahlen aus.

- Students listen to the recording again and fill in the gaps with the correct year.

Answers:

4–6

a zwischen 1949 und 1964; **b** 1949; **c** 1956

4 Anna beschreibt ihre Heldin. Füll die Lücken mit den Wörtern aus dem Kasten unten aus.

- Students fill in the gaps with the words from the box.

Answers:

4–6

Heldin, Deutsche, Schwimmen, 1994, Rom, 200 m, Weltrekord, spitze

5 Schreib diese Sätze in der richtigen Reihenfolge auf. Pass auf die korrekte Wortstellung auf!

- Read the *Grammatik* section as a class.
- Students then put the sentences into the correct order. Display an example German sentence for support if needed.

Answers:

a 1972 gewann Deutschland die Europameisterschaft in Brüssel.
b 1986 war Boris Becker wieder der Sieger von Wimbledon.
c 2004 gewann Deutschlands Handballteam die Europameisterschaft in Slowenien.

A16 A17 Activity Sheets 16 and 17 provide further activities on sport and sportspeople.

6 Choose a famous sporting hero or heroine from the past and find out as much as possible about his or her life. Why is he or she famous? What do you think? Is he or she really a hero or heroine? Do an oral presentation about your hero for the class in German.

PLTS

- This activity draws together what students have learnt in the spread
- It encourages students to plan and carry out research and manage their time and resources effectively. It covers the Independent enquirers and Self-managers groups of skills from the framework of personal, learning and thinking skills.

4–9

7 Using the above information write a report about your hero or heroine. Use as many expressions from this spread as possible.

- Students use the information from activity 6 to write a report about the hero or heroine they have chosen. Encourage them to use as many of the ideas and as much of the vocabulary presented on these pages as possible in their writing.
- This is an ideal assessment opportunity.

4–9

Success criteria:

- ideas communicated
- range of vocabulary and structures used
- tenses or time frames used

Wie man gesund lebt

Seiten 48–49

Planner

➤ Objectives

- Discussing how to live healthily

➤ Resources

Students' Book, pages 48–49
CD 1, track 29
Grammar Workbook, page 58
Activity Sheet 18

➤ Key language

das Gemüse, der Keks, das Obst, der Schlaf, die Süßigkeiten, aufstehen, rauchen, stark

➤ Skills

- Using capital letters

➤ Grammar

- In order to…

➤ PLTS

Question 6: Team workers/Effective participators

➤ Starters

- Divide the class into two teams. Give them a couple of minutes to try and come up with a food or drink item in German for each letter of the alphabet. When the time is up, the teams compare what they have. Each team scores a point for each word they have. If both teams have the same item, neither team scores a point. The team with the most points wins.
- Display the phrase, *Ich esse/trinke gern…* and go round the class asking each student to complete the sentence. If there is time, continue with the sentences *Ich esse/trinke lieber…*and finally, *Ich esse/trinke am liebsten….* With the final sentence, remind students that they can alter the word order and begin with *Am liebsten esse ich…*
- Display the titles *gesund* and *ungesund* and ask students to put each of the food and drink items from starter activity 1 in the appropriate column.

➤ Plenaries

- Students work in pairs and interview each other about their lifestyles using sentences containing *um…zu*, e.g.
  A: Was machst du, um gesund zu bleiben?
  B: Um gesund zu bleiben, …
  They should use the vocabulary presented in the spread.
- Students pretend to be a celebrity – a sports star, actor, pop star, etc. and write about their daily routine using a similar format to the two texts in activity 1. They then swap work with a partner who decides how healthy they are and tries to guess which celebrity they are pretending to be.
- Students create their own survey to find out how healthy the class is. Once the class has decided on questions to include, all students fill it in and collate the results to see how healthy the class is.

Was ist gesund? Was ist ungesund? Schreib die Tabelle ab und füll sie aus.

4–6

- As an introduction to the spread, students read the two texts and fill in the grid with examples of what is healthy and unhealthy.

gesund	ungesund
Müesli	Kekse
Wasser	Kaffee
Salat	Hamburger
Orangensaft	Pommes
Hähnchen	Bier
Obst	Pizza
früh ins Bett gehen	spät ins Bett gehen
trainieren	kein Training
viel Schlaf bekommen	zu wenig Schlaf bekommen/ müde
wenig Kaffee und Schokolade	viel Schokolade

1a Lies die Texte über die tägliche Routine von Roger und Bill und beantworte die folgenden Fragen.

4–6

- Students read about Roger Federer and Bill Kaulitz's daily routine and answer the questions.

Answers:

a Um 11 Uhr; **b** Um 6 Uhr; **c** Müesli; **d** Hamburger und Pommes; **e** Bier; **f** Wasser oder Orangensaft; **g** Joggen, Schwimmen, Tennis; **h** nichts

1b Diskutiert mit einem Partner/einer Partnerin über gesundes Essen. Was esst ihr gern oder nicht gern? Was ist gesund, was ist nicht gesund?

4–9

- Students work with a partner to discuss healthy eating. They should include what they like/don't like to eat and which foods are healthy/unhealthy.

2 Hör gut zu! Wer ist das? Schreib die Sätze ab und setz die Namen von Heinrich, Mario oder Brigitte ein.

4–6

- Students listen to the recording and complete the sentences with the appropriate name.

CD 1, track 29 **Seite 49, Übung 2**

Bravo:	*Bravo* interviewt drei junge Leute über ihre Essgewohnheiten.
Bravo:	Also, Heinrich, was isst du gern?
Heinrich:	Ich esse leidenschaftlich gern alles, was süß ist. Schokolade, Kekse, Kuchen...
Bravo:	Aber ist das gut für deine Gesundheit? Mario, was isst du gern?
Mario:	Ich glaube, ich esse sehr gesund. Ich esse viel Gemüse und Obst. Ich hasse Schokolade.
Bravo:	Das hört sich gut an! Und du Brigitte?
Brigitte:	Ich finde, ich esse ziemlich gesund. Ich esse gern Schokolade, aber ich esse lieber Gemüse, weil das gesund ist. Am liebsten esse ich Obst, weil das auch sehr süß ist.
Bravo:	Sehr gut! Und was trinkst du gern, Heinrich?
Heinrich:	Ich trinke gern Cola und auch gern süßen Sprudel, aber am liebsten trinke ich Kaffee.
Bravo:	So viele Süßes und Koffein! Wie ist es mit dir, Mario? Was trinkst du gern?
Mario:	Ich trinke gern Früchtetee, aber am liebsten trinke ich Wasser, weil es überhaupt keine Kalorien hat.
Bravo:	Prima! Und du, Brigitte?
Brigitte:	Ich trinke gern Wasser, aber am liebsten trinke ich Tee.
Bravo:	Danke euch allen.

Answers:

- **a** Brigitte trinkt am liebsten Tee.
- **b** Heinrich isst gern Schokolade.
- **c** Brigitte isst lieber Gemüse.
- **d** Heinrich trinkt am liebsten Kaffee.
- **e** Mario trinkt gern Früchtetee.
- **f** Mario hasst Schokolade.

3 Was isst und trinkst du gern? Füll die Lücken mit deinen eigenen Wörtern aus.

- Students fill in the gaps in the paragraph for themselves saying what they like to eat and drink.

4–6

4 Übersetze die folgenden Sätze.

- Work through the *Grammatik* box on liking and preferring with the class, before asking then to translate the sentences.

Answers:

- **a** Ich esse gern Kekse.
- **b** Ich trinke lieber Kaffee.
- **c** Am liebsten esse ich Eis.
- **d** Ich trinke gern Orangensaft aber ich trinke nicht gern Apfelsaft.
- **e** Ich esse lieber Pommes als Salat.

5 Wie bleibt man fit? Erfinde Sätze, indem du die folgenden Ausdrücke mit *um... zu...* benutzt. Schreib die Sätze mit Übersetzungen auf Englisch in dein Heft.

- Students use the phrases to write sentences using *um... zu...* meaning 'in order to'. They then translate these into English. Before asking them to attempt this activity, work through the *Grammatik* box on *um...zu...* as a class.

Answers:

- **a** Um schlank zu bleiben, esse ich gesund. – *I eat healthily in order to stay slim.*
- **b** Um gesund zu bleiben, esse ich viel Obst. – *I eat a lot of fruit in order to stay healthy.*
- **c** Um stark zu werden, gehe ich ins Sportzentrum. – *I go to the sports centre in order to become strong.*
- **d** Um fit zu bleiben, rauche ich nicht. – *I don't smoke in order to stay fit.*
- **e** Um fit zu werden, trainiere ich viel. – *I do a lot of training in order to become fit.*

A18 Activity Sheet 18 (activities 1a and 1 b) provides further practice on healthy living.

6 What do you do to keep fit and what do you like eating? Discuss your lifestyle with a partner – is it healthy or unhealthy?

PLTS

- Students use the ideas and vocabulary presented on this spread in a discussion with a partner. This is an ideal assessment opportunity.
- This activity encourages students to work confidently with others reaching agreements, managing discussions and showing fairness and consideration. They should also negotiate and balance views. It covers the Team workers and Effective participators groups of skills from the framework of personal, learning and thinking skills.

4–9

Success criteria:

- amount of information communicated
- good pronunciation, information and fluency
- variety of vocabulary and structures used
- personal opinions given

7 Complete the survey on page 48 and find out if you are as healthy as you think you are!

- Students fill in the survey and calculate their score. They then consult the *Gesundheitsstand* box to discover their level of health.

4–6

Wie man Abenteuer findet!

Seiten 50–51

Planner

➤ Objectives

- Discussing extreme and unusual sports

➤ Resources

Students' Book, pages 50–51
CD 1, track 30
Grammar Workbook, page 30
Activity Sheet 18

➤ Key language

die Aussicht, erhalten, ängstlich, furchtbar, gefährlich

➤ Skills

- Using intensifiers

➤ Grammar

- Time phrases

➤ PLTS

Question 4b: Independent enquirers/Reflective learners/Self-managers
Question 7a: Team workers/Effective participators
Question 8: Creative thinkers

➤ Starters

- Display a list of extreme or unusual sports in German. Next to this, display, in random order, the English translations. Give students a few minutes to match the German and English words. Go through the answers as a class.
- Go round the class, asking students to use the sports listed in starter activity 1 in a simple sentence, e.g. *Ich möchte (nicht) gern (Kayakfahren) ausprobieren.* For classes who need more support, display example sentences.
- Display some phrases of time and ask students if they know what they mean. Display the English translation next to each one. With more able classes, display an example sentence using a time phrase, e.g. *Letztes Jahr habe ich Bungee-Springen gemacht*, and choose volunteers to replace it with one of the other time phrases from the list to make a new sentence, e.g. *Vor zwei Jahren habe ich Bungee-Springen gemacht.*

➤ Plenaries

- Display a few words and phrases from the spread and challenge students to use them all in a short paragraph based on the themes of the spread.
- Display the following sports numbered 1–5: 1 = *Rafting*; 2 = *Paragliding*; 3 = *Bungee-Springen*; 4 = *Abseilen*; 5 = *Kayakfahren*. Add number 6 with a dash beside it. In pairs, students take turns to throw a die. If they throw 1–5, they make up a sentence about the corresponding sport; if they throw 6, they make up a sentence about a sport of their choice, e.g.
  Student A: (throws a 2) *Ich möchte nicht gern Rafting ausprobieren, weil es mir sehr gefährlich erscheint.*
  Student B: (throws a 6) *Mein Lieblingssport ist Handball, weil es total aufregend ist.*
  Encourage students to use intensifiers and, if possible, adverbial time phrases in their sentences. Display a list of these, if necessary, for support.
- Students work in pairs to prepare and perform a role-play. Student A loves extreme sports; student B hates them. Each tries to persuade the other that they are right, giving reasons why they find these sports good/bad.

1 Welche dieser Sportarten möchtest du ausprobieren? Warum? Warum nicht?

7–9

- Students read the texts about extreme sports and then discuss which they would/wouldn't like to try and why. Read through the example sentences in the Students' Book as a class before they begin.

2 Schreib jetzt deine Antworten und deine Gründe auf.

7–9

- Students now write up their answers and reasons from activity 1.

3 Lies die Texte auf Seite 50 und beantworte die Fragen auf Englisch.

- Students read through the articles again and answer the questions.

4–6

Answers:

a in Nepal; **b** as a gift; **c** you don't fly alone; **d** the different heights of water; **e** in Germany

4a Lies die Texte und finde die folgenden Wörter.

- Students find the German in the texts for the English words listed.

4–6

Answers:

a ein Erlebnis; **b** die Berge; **c** begleiten; **d** erleben, erfahren; **e** die Aussicht; **f** unvergesslich; **g** einmalig; **h** Höhe

4b Lies die Texte noch einmal und finde andere Wörter, die du nicht kennst. Mach eine Liste in deinem Heft und schau die unbekannten Wörter im Wörterbuch nach.

4–6 PLTS

- Students read the texts again and find any words that they do not know. They list these in their exercise book and look them up in a dictionary.
- This activity encourages students to reflect on what they have learnt and to organise themselves. It covers the Reflective learners and Self-managers groups of skills from the framework of personal, learning and thinking skills.

5a Junge Leute sprechen über Extremsportarten. Hör gut zu und füll die Tabelle aus.

7–9

- Students listen to the recording and fill in the table.

CD 1, track 30 **Seite 51, Übung 5**

Interviewer/in:	Wir fragen junge Leute, „Hast du je einen Extremsport gemacht?" Was kannst du uns dazu sagen, Laura?
Laura:	Letztes Jahr war ich mit meinen Eltern in der Schweiz und wir sind Abseilen gegangen. Das war fantastisch. Ich fand es **total** aufregend, aber ich war auch **ein bisschen** ängstlich.
Interviewer/in:	Danke, Laura, und du, Lars?
Lars:	Vor zwei Jahren bin ich mit meiner Freundin nach Nepal gefahren und wir sind dort Wildwasser gefahren. Meine Freundin fand es furchtbar, aber ich fand es einmalig. Es war **sehr** spannend und es gab sehr viel Wasser. Die verschiedenen Höhen waren **einfach** toll. Nächstes Jahr hoffe ich wieder in Nepal Wildwasser zu fahren, aber es ist **ziemlich** teuer.
Interviewer/in:	Super, Lars und jetzt ist Maria dran! Was kannst du uns zu diesem Thema sagen?
Maria:	Ich habe sowas noch nie gemacht – ich habe **so viel** Angst, aber mein Bruder war vor drei Jahren in Österreich, und er hat dort Bungee-Springen gemacht. Für ihn war das super. Er fand es echt spitze und er hatte **überhaupt** keine Angst.
Interviewer/in:	Vielen Dank, Maria, und zuletzt haben wir Andreas. Na, Andreas, hast du je einen Extremsport gemacht?
Andreas:	Ja sicher, ich habe vor drei Monaten hier in Deutschland Paragliding gemacht. Was für ein Erlebnis! Das war **so** atemberaubend. Ich habe mich auch sicher gefühlt, da wir es zu zweit gemacht haben. Ich möchte das auf jeden Fall wieder machen. Nächsten Monat mache ich es zum zweiten Mal. Ich kann es **kaum** erwarten!

Answers:

	When?	What?	Where?	How was it?
Laura	last year	abseiling	in Switzerland	fantastic, exciting, a bit scary
Lars	two years ago	white water rafting	Nepal	really fantastic, exciting, great, expensive
Marias Bruder	three years ago	bungee jumping	Austria	super, great, not scary
Andreas	three months ago	paragliding	Germany	breathtaking, safe

5b Hör noch einmal zu und finde so viele Adjektive wie möglich. Schreib sie auf und übersetze sie auf Englisch.

4–6

- Students listen again and note down as many adjectives as possible. They then translate them into English.

Answers:

außergewöhnlich – *unusual*, fantastisch – *fantastic*, aufregend – *exciting*, ängstlich – *scared*, furchtbar – *dreadful*, spannend – *thrillling*, toll – *terrific*, verschieden – different, super – *super*, spitze – *the best*, atemberaubend – *breathtaking*, sicher – *safe*

A18 Activity Sheet 18 (activities 2 and 3) provides further practice of speaking about and listening to texts about sports.

5c Lies die Tipp-Box und hör noch einmal zu. Welche Wörter benutzen…?

4–6

- Students read the *Tipp* box on intensifiers.
- They listen again and note down any intensifiers and which speaker says these.

Answers:

a Laura – total, ein bisschen; **b** Lars – sehr, einfach, ziemlich; **c** Maria – so viel, überhaupt; **d** Andreas – so, kaum

6a Wie sagt man auf Deutsch…?

- Read the box on adverbial time phrases.
- Students write the German for the phrases.

Answers:

a vor sechs Wochen; **b** letzten Monat; **c** vor zehn Jahren

6b Schreib einen Satz für jeden Ausdruck. Sag welche Sportarten du gemacht hast und wann.

- Students write a sentence for each expression.

7a In groups of four, choose an extreme sport and work together to produce a report about it. Use as much information from this spread as possible. Remember to use the expressions in the *Tipp* box.

7–9 PLTS

- Students prepare a report on extreme sport which they will then present to the class.
- This activity encourages students to collaborate with others, managing discussions, negotiating when necessary and acheiving results. It covers the

Team workers and Effective participators groups of skills from the framework of personal, learning and thinking skills.

7b Do an oral presentation of your report to the class. Remember to give your own opinion. You can record your presentation using the OxBox software.

- Students now present their sport to the class. Remind them to give their own opinion.
- They can record their presentation using the OxBox software.

8 Now write your own advert for an unusual sport. Mention where you can do it and what the attractions of this sport are.

7–9 PLTS

- Students write their own advertisement for an unusual sport.
- This activity encourages students to think creatively and explore different ideas. It covers the Creative thinkers group of skills from the framework of personal, learning and thinking skills.

Success criteria:

- amount of information communicated
- variety of vocabulary and structures used
- different tenses or time frames used
- personal opinions given

Wie man eine Verletzung beschreibt

Seiten 52–53

Planner

➤ Objectives

- Describing sports injuries

➤ Resources

Students' Book, pages 52–53
CD 1, track 31
Grammar Workbook, pages 34, 63
Activity Sheet 18

➤ Key language

das Fußgelenk, verletzt, die Schmerzen, hingefallen, überfahren, weh tun

➤ Skills

- Reflexive pronouns

➤ Grammar

- Subordinating conjunctions: word order

➤ PLTS

Question 6a: Team workers
Question 7: Creative thinkers

➤ Starters

- Display some words from the key language of the spread with the vowels missing. Students race against each other to fill in the missing letters. Elicit the English for the words included.
- Play a version of the game 'Simon Says'. Explain to students that you will call out an injury in German and they should mime the injury, e.g. holding their head for a head injury, limping for a sprained ankle, etc.
- Ask students to tell you what they already know about German word order. They should be able to talk about the 'time – manner – place' rule. Ask for examples of this. Explain that in this spread you will be looking at word order after *weil*.

➤ Plenaries

- Choose a volunteer to play the role of a doctor on a German television show. The rest of the class 'phone in' and describe sports injuries they have, giving as much information as possible. The 'doctor' gives advice on what they should do. Once the volunteer has answered a few callers, choose a new volunteer.
- Ask students to work in pairs to explain to each other why they are unable to play sports, using the subordinating conjunction, *weil*, e.g. *Ich kann nicht Tennis spielen, weil ich mir das Bein gebrochen habe*. Before they begin, elicit what the word order should be following *weil* and work through a couple of examples.
- Call out a word from the spread. Students respond by putting it into a sentence, e.g.
  Teacher: *Rücken!*
  Student: *Mein Rücken tut weh!*
  Teacher: *Vorgestern!*
  Student: *Vorgestern habe ich Fußball gespielt.*

- As an introduction to the spread, students read the paragraph about Roger Federer and answer the questions.

4–6

Answers:

1 letztes Jahr; **2** im Park; **3** drei Wochen; **4** Er hat seinen Schlägerarm nicht verletzt. **5** joggen

1a Was gehört zusammen? Verbinde die Texte A–D mit den Bildern 1–4 oben.

- Students read the texts and match each to the corresponding picture.

Answers:

1 c; **2** a; **3** d; **4** b

1b Lies noch einmal die vier Texte und füll die Tabelle aus.

- Students read the four texts again and fill in the table.

4–6

	When?	Which Sport?	Injury	When do sport again?
A	last week	tennis	leg	three weeks
B	yesterday	rugby	broken arm	four weeks
C	two weeks ago	paragliding	ankle	last time
D	last Saturday	bungee-jumping	head	next month

2 Finde die deutschen Wörter in den vier Texten und schreib sie auf.

- Students find the German words in the texts that correspond to the English words listed.

4–6

Answers:

a verletzt; **b** gebrochen; **c** knöchel; **d** es tat weh/es hat wehgetan; **e** gefährlich; **f** hingefallen; **g** ernst; **h** Schmerzen; **i** verstaucht; **j** ausgerutscht

3 Hör gut zu und beantworte die Fragen.

- Students listen to the recording and answer the questions.

4–6

CD 1, track 31 **Seite 53, Übung 3**

Nummer 1

Arzt: So, Frank, kommen Sie herein. Was ist mit Ihnen los?
Frank: Guten Tag, Herr Doktor. Mir geht es nicht gut. Mein Rücken tut so weh!
Arzt: Was haben Sie denn gemacht?
Frank: Vorgestern bin ich im Fluss Kajak gefahren. Ich bin mit dem Kajak an einen Stein gestoßen und ins Wasser gefallen. Ich habe mir irgendwie den Rücken verrenkt. Seitdem tut er sehr weh und ich kann nicht schlafen.
Arzt: Oje – das klingt aber schlimm! Lassen Sie mich mal sehen... Ja, ich kann es fühlen. Die Stelle hier ist ein bisschen entzündet. Hier ist eine Salbe. Tragen Sie sie dreimal pro Tag auf, und ich verschreibe Ihnen auch drei Tage Bettruhe. Und einen Monat lang kein Kajakfahren!

Nummer 2

Arzt: Hallo Christiane, komm herein, Was kann ich für dich tun?
Christiane: Guten Morgen, Herr Doktor. Ich habe schlimme Kopfschmerzen.
Arzt: Was hast du denn gemacht?
Christiane: Gestern bin ich Rad gefahren. Ich musste einem Hund ausweichen und dabei bin ich hingefallen und mit dem Kopf auf dem Boden aufgeschlagen.
Arzt: Gut. Lass mich mal in deine Augen sehen. Alles halb so schlimm! Bleib zwei Tage zu Hause, nimm diese Tabletten zweimal pro Tag und kein Radfahren für eine Woche.

Nummer 3

Arzt: Guten Tag, Carl, was ist heute los mit Ihnen?
Carl: Guten Tag, Herr Doktor. Mein Hals tut weh.
Arzt: Was haben Sie gemacht?
Carl: Heute Morgen habe ich Fußball gespielt. Ich war im Tor, und ein Spieler der anderen Mannschaft hat mir in den Nacken geschlagen. Es tut furchtbar weh.
Arzt: Darf ich mal sehen... Oh, das ist aber schlimm. Das gefällt mir gar nicht. Sie müssen sofort ins Krankenhaus.

Answers:

a his back; **b** day before yesterday; **c** riding bike; **d** stay at home for two days and take tablets; **e** his neck; **f** this morning

4 Verbinde diese Sätze mit *weil*.

- Students connect the phrases with the word *weil*, meaning 'because'.
- Before beginning this activity, read the *Grammatik* box, 'Subordinating conjunctions: word order'.

Answers:

a Ich darf nicht Fußball spielen, weil ich Kopfschmerzen habe.
b Ich kann nicht Tennis spielen, weil mein Arm wehtut.
c Ich darf nicht Rad fahren, weil ich mir das Bein gebrochen habe.
d Ich kann nicht schwimmen gehen, weil ich mir den Kopf verletzt habe.

A18 Activity Sheet 18, activity 4, provides further practice on speaking about sports injuries.

5 Verbinde die Probleme mit den Anordungen des Arztes.

- Students match the problems with the doctors orders.

Answers:
1 e; **2** a; **3** d; **4** c; **5** b

6a Work in groups. Imagine you have injured yourself doing sport. Discuss what happened in German, mentioning when and how, and which sport you were doing.

PLTS

7–9

- Students work in groups. They think of sports injuries. They then imagine that they have a sports-related injury and note down when they did it, how, in which sport they were participating and how long it will take to get better.
- This activity encourages students to collaborate with others, managing discussions and acheiving

results. It covers the Team workers group of skills from the framework of personal, learning and thinking skills.

6b Work in pairs. One of you is the doctor, the other the patient. A describes the injury and B gives advice.

- Students work with a partner to perform a role-play. Student A is a patient; student B, a doctor. Student A describes a sport-related injury and student B gives advice. They then swap roles.

7 Write an advice page for *Jugendmagazin*, giving advice for what to do if you get injured in different ways.

- Encourage students to use the ideas and vocabulary presented in the spread in their writing and to refer to the *Grammatik* and *Tipp* boxes when necessary.
- This activity encourages students to think creatively and explore different ideas. It covers the Creative thinkers group of skills from the framework of personal, learning and thinking skills.

Success criteria:

- variety of vocabulary and structures used
- different tenses or time frames used
- personal opinions given

Aktive Grammatik

Seiten 54–55

Planner

➤ Objectives

- Word order
- Subordinating conjunctions
- The perfect tense

➤ Resources

Students' Book, pages 54–55
Exam Skills Workbook, page 34
Grammar Workbook, pages 48, 61, 63
Activity Sheet 19
Resources and Planning OxBox CD-ROM

➤ Grammar

- Word order
- Subordinating conjunctions
- The perfect tense

➤ PLTS

All questions: Reflective learners/Self-managers

➤ Word order

1 Translate these sentences into German, watching out for the word order.

- This question focuses on simple sentences in German.

Answers:

a Ich hasse Tennis. **b** Ich mag Fußball. **c** Er liebt Rugby.

2 Rewrite these sentences, putting the phrase in brackets at the beginning of the sentence and altering the word order appropriately.

- This question focuses on the idea that the verb in German sentences must always be the 'second idea' and putting time phrases at the beginning of the sentence can slightly change the emphasis.

Answers:

a Jeden Tag geht sie schwimmen. **b** Er spielt nächste Woche gegen Bayern München. **c** Sonntags spiele ich Federball. **d** Wir treiben jede Woche Sport. **e** Niemals esst ihr gesund! **f** Die Schüler trinken tagsüber nicht genug.

3 Rewrite these jumbled-up sentences in the right order.

- This question focuses on using adverbial phrases of time, manner and place. Remind students to take particular care with the word order.

Answers:

a 2004 waren die Olympischen Spiele in Athen.
b 2012 kommen sie nach London.
c In vier Jahren fahre ich mit dem Zug nach London.

➤ Subordinating conjunctions

4 Put these sentences together using the conjunctions in brackets.

- Question four focuses on subordinating conjunctions which send the main verb to the end of the sentence or clause.

Answers:

a Ich esse viel Obst, damit ich gesund bleibe.
b Ich finde Michael Ballak toll, weil er ein guter Fußballspieler ist.
c Ich trinke keinen Alkohol, wenn ich ein Spiel habe.
d Ich weiß, dass er gut spielen kann.
e Ich weiß nicht, ob sie schwimmen kann.

5 Translate the sentences from activity 4 into English.

- Further practice of subordinating conjunctions.

Answers:

a I eat lots of fruit so that I stay healthy.
b I think Michael Ballack is great because he is a good football player.

c I don't drink any alcohol if I have a game.
d I know that he can play well.
e I don't know whether she can swim.

➤ The perfect tense

6 **Put these sentences into the perfect tense using the auxiliary and the past participle provided.**
- Practice of the perfect tense.

a Ich bin ins Krankenhaus gegangen.
b Sie ist für England geschwommen.
c Wir haben Bungee-Springen gemacht.
d Meine Mannschaft hat den Pokal gewonnen.
e Ich habe Paragliding toll gefunden.
f Er ist Fußballprofi geworden.

7 **Translate your sentences from activity 6 into English.**
- Students translate the sentences into English.

Answers:

a I went to the hospital. **b** She swam for England. **c** We did a bungee jump. **d** My team won the cup. **e** I found paragliding great. **f** He became a professional footballer.

Kompetenzen

Seite 56

Planner

➤ Objectives
- Summarising what you have learnt

➤ Resources
Students' Book, page 56
Exam Skills Workbooks, page 35
Activity Sheet 20
Resources and Planning OxBox CD-ROM

➤ Skills
- Expressing your opinion
- Using word order to change emphasis
- Writing longer, more colourful sentences
- Using the correct grammar in time expressions
- Using capital letters correctly
- Using umlauts correctly

➤ PLTS
Question 1, Beim Sprechen: Reflective learners/ Self-managers
Question 1, Beim Schreiben: Independent enquirers/Reflective learners/Self-managers

In this unit, students have learnt how to...

➤ Beim Sprechen

1 **Use key phrases needed for giving opinions.**

PLTS
- Students think about the expressions for giving opinions that they have met in this unit and try to remember five different ways in which they can express their opinion. Refer them back to page 47, if necessary.
- This activity encourages students to reflect upon what they have learnt and build on this. It covers the Reflective learners and Self-managers groups of skills from the framework of personal, learning and thinking skills.

2 **Use word order to change emphasis.**
- Students find examples of different word order used for emphasis. Provide them with relevant transcripts for listening activities.

➤ Beim Schreiben

1 **Use description and linking words to avoid short sentences.**

PLTS
- Students write the English translation for five different conjunctions they have learnt in this unit. They then look up any more English conjunctions that they don't know in German and add them to their list.
- This activity encourages students to reflect upon what they have learnt and build on this. It covers the Independent enquirers, Reflective learners and Self-managers groups of skills from the framework of personal, learning and thinking skills.

2 **Use adverbs and expressions of time and frequency to add colour to writing.**
- Students note down how many extra words they remember and what the words listed mean.

Answers: ziemlich – *quite*; natürlich – *naturally*; ein bisschen – *a bit*

3 **Use correct grammar in expressions of time.**
- Students translate the time expressions listed into English. Refer them to page 44 if necessary for support.

Answers:

on Sunday – *sonntags*; last week – *letzte Woche*; next year – *nächstes Jahr*

4 **Use capital letters correctly.**
- Students look through the Students' Book to check that they know when to use capital letters and when not. They share their theory with the class to ensure that they understand correctly.

Answer: In German all nouns must begin with a capital letter.

5 **Use umlauts and work out where they go.**
- Remind students of the importance of accents: they can change the meaning of a word. Ask students to translate *schon* and *schön* to illustrate this.

Answers:

schon – *already*; schön – *beautiful*

➤ Beim Lernen
Students try using the strategies listed for learning vocabulary.

Szenario

Seite 57

Planner

➤ Objectives
- Planning a sporting holiday
- Preparing and delivering a presentation on a favourite sporting hero

➤ Resources
Students' Book, page 57
Exam Skills Workbooks, pages 32–33
Resources and Planning OxBox CD-ROM

➤ Skills
- Writing practice
- Speaking practice

➤ PLTS
Question 2, Writing: Team workers/Creative thinkers/Reflective learners
Question 3, Speaking: Creative thinkers/Reflective learners/Self-managers

➤ Zum Schreiben GCSE A–F
Students will plan a sporting holiday, e.g. a skiing holiday. Encourage them to think about the country, the sport, what they will need as equipment and to use the Internet for ideas, especially www.google.de and www.luftsport.de.

It is possible for students to obtain GCSE grades A–F depending on their ability:
Grade F students write a short plan using simple sentences and communicate some information.
Grade C students include a variety of structures which may include different tenses or time frames. They communicate information and express personal opinions.
Grade A students include a variety of vocabulary, structures and verb tenses. They convey information, narrate events and express and explain ideas and points of view.

1 **In a group, brainstorm all the decisions you will need to take before planning the holiday and make a mind map of them.**
- This activity serves as an introduction to the task. Encourage students to use the ideas presented in the unit.

2 **In pairs, discuss the different options for each of the things on your mind map in German and make decisions for each one.**

PLTS
- This activity allows students to think in more detail about the task.
- It encourages students to collaborate with others, think imaginatively and to reflect upon what they have learnt to acheive goals. It covers the Team workers, Creative thinkers and Reflective learners groups of skills from the framework of personal, learning and thinking skills.

3 **Write down your holiday plan (150–300 words), explaining where you are going and what you are going to do there. Say why you took the decisions you did and describe how you imagine a typical day on this holiday would be. Try to give as much detail as possible.**
- Students use the ideas and vocabulary from activities 1 and 2 to write a holiday plan. Remind them to keep in mind the grammar points covered in the unit, in particular word order.

➤ Zum Sprechen GCSE A–F
Students will prepare and deliver a presentation on their favourite sporting hero. Encourage them to use the Internet for research (www.sportheld.de has some useful material) and to rehearse their material thoroughly. Suggest recording it to help improve their accent and intonation. This could be done using the record/playback facility on the OxBox CD-ROM.

It is possible for students to obtain GCSE grades A–F depending on their ability and they are marked on communication, quality of language and prounciation and intonation:
Grade F students communicate a limited number of ideas, expressing simple opinions. Only a few phrases or short sentences are accurate enough to be recognisable. There are very few instances of clear pronunciation and intonation.
Grade C students communicate the essential elements, readily expressing points of view. They occasionally hesitate and can respond to some unpredictable questions. They use straightforward vocabulary and structures which may contain different tenses or time frames. Pronunciation and intonation is generally accurate.
Grade A students use relevant information to develop and justify individual ideas and points of view. There is no hesitation and they are able to respond to unpredictable questions. They use a wide range of clause types, vocabulary and structures accurately. The presentation is fluent and coherent with just minor errors. Pronunciation and intonation is very accurate with a few minor slips.

1 **In groups of 3–4, choose the sportsperson you would like to nominate for sports personality of the year. You will have to present him/her to the panel of judges so that they can vote on the winner.**
- This activity serves as an introduction to the task. Encourage students to use the ideas presented in the unit.

2 **Start by brainstorming your ideas for what you would like to include in your presentation and how to structure it.**
- This activity allows students to think in more detail about the task. Again, encourage them to look back at the work they have done in this unit for ideas and support.

3 **Split up and research each of the points that you decided to include in your presentation on the Internet.**
- Students use German search engines to find German articles containing useful vocabulary.

4 **Prepare your presentation using visual aids, handouts, etc. Let the rest of the class know who you will be talking about so that they can prepare questions and think about possible answers to questions that might come up.**

PLTS
- Students use the work they have done in activities 1, 2 and 3 to prepare a presentation.
- This activity encourages students to think creatively and explore new ideas, to use what they have learnt to achieve goals and to organise time and resources effectively. It covers the Creative thinkers, Reflective learners and Self-managers groups of skills from the framework of personal, learning and thinking skills.

5 **Deliver your presentation to the class and record it using the OxBox software. As a class, decide who you think should be chosen as sports personality of the year.**
- Students finally present to the class and answer any questions. Encourage them to use ICT to enhance their presentation. This activity is an ideal assessment opportunity.

Vokabeln

Seite 58

Planner

➤ **Resources**
Students' Book, page 58
Activity Sheet 21

This page provides a summary of the key language covered in each spread of this unit. It could be used as a handy reference for students as they work through the unit. Alternatively, students could use its clear German–English format when learning vocabulary.

Lesen

Seiten 175–176

Planner

➤ Objectives

- To encourage independent reading and develop reading strategies
- To provide alternative class and homework material for students who finish other activities quickly

Page 175 provides a reading text in the context of the unit.
Page 176 provides a newspaper article-style text, again in the context of the unit.

➤ Resources

Students' Book, pages 175–176

➤ Skills

- Reading practice

➤ PLTS

Question 3 (parts 1 and 2): Creative thinkers/ Reflective learners/Self-managers

Lesen A: Abseilen in der Schweiz

1 Wie sagt man auf Deutsch…?

4–6

- Students read the text on abseiling in Switzerland and find German equivalents for the English words listed.

Answers:

a öffentliche Verkehrsmittel; **b** der Wasserfall; **c** herrlich; **d** der Blick; **e** selbstständig; **f** der Führer

2 Lies den Artikel und beantworte die folgenden Fragen auf Englisch.

4–6

- Students read the text again and answer the questions in English.

Answers:

a abseiling; **b** in Amden in Switzerland; **c** by car or public transport; **d** the waterfall; **e** tie the belt correctly and abseil independently

3 Was hältst du von Abseilen? Bist du daran interessiert? Schreib fünf Sätze über diese Sportart und deine Meinung dazu.

PLTS

7–9

- Students write five sentences about this sport, giving their opinion of it.
- This activity encourages students to think creatively and explore new ideas, to use what they have learnt to achieve goals, and to organise time and resources. It covers the Creative thinkers, Reflective learners and Self-managers groups of skills from the framework of personal, learning and thinking skills.

Lesen B: Olympiasieger Matthias Steiner

1 Lies den Artikel und beantworte die folgenden Fragen.

4–6

- Students read the text about Matthias Steiner and then answer the questions.

Answers:

a 25 Jahre; **b** Obersulz, Österreich; **c** Er ist Deutscher. **d** Er hat eine Goldmedaille im Gewichtheben gewonnen. **e** Er hob 258 kg. **f** das erste Gold für Gewichtheben seit 16 Jahren; **g** seine Frau – gestorben in einem Autounfall

2 Finde im Text möglichst viele Verben im Imperfekt. Schreib sie auf und übersetz sie auf Englisch.

4–6

- Students read the text again and find as many verbs in the imperfect as possible. They translate them into English. Refer them to the relevant grammar section on the imperfect, if necessary.
- As an extension task, ask them to note the infinitives of these verbs in German and English.

Answers:

gewann – *won*; nahm… teil – *took part*; hob – *lifted*; hatte – *had*; wollte – *wanted*; gab – *gave*; wurde – *became*

3 Wie findest du Matthias Steiner? Ist er ein Held? Schreib einen kurzen Artikel, indem du deine Meinung äußerst.

PLTS

7–9

- Students write a short article about Matthias Steiner in which they express their opinion.
- This activity encourages students to think creatively and explore new ideas, to use what they have learnt to achieve goals, and to organise time and resources. It covers the Creative thinkers, Reflective learners and Self-managers groups of skills from the framework of personal, learning and thinking skills.

Unit 2B: Essen und Trinken		Overview grid		
Spread	**Contexts and objectives**	**Skills**	**Grammar**	**Vocabulary**
pages 60–61 **Wie man Essen aus aller Welt beschreibt**	• Describing food	• Listening for key phrases	• Adjectival nouns	*das Gericht; der Geschmack; das Hähnchen; die Kartoffel; der Ofen; die Soße; der Topf; frisch; etwas Leichtes*
pages 62–63 **Wie man gesundes Essen beschreibt**	• Describing allergies	• Understanding new vocabulary	• Using *um…zu*	*der Blutdruck; aufpassen; Bescheid wissen; riechen; meiden; allergisch gegen*
pages 64–65 **Wie man Essprobleme beschreibt**	• Discussing eating disorders	• Giving advice	• Sentences with …*zu* and *wenn*	*die Kneipe; die Spritze; abnehmen; aufhören; bestrafen; sich um etwas Sorgen machen; glücklich; nötig; satt; betrunken; erlaubt*
pages 66–67 **Wie man am besten einkauft**	• Discussing shopping for food	• Comparing advantages and disadvantages	• Object pronouns in the accusative	*die Auswahl; die Bäckerei; die Metzgerei; Öffnungszeiten; der Ruhetag; aufmachen; zumachen; preiswert; teuer; geschlossen*
pages 68–69 **Wie man im Restaurant bestellt und sich beschwert**	• Ordering food in a restaurant	• Targeted listening	• *dieser, diese, dieses*	*die Gabel; grüne Bohnen; der Lachs; der Messer; die Soße; die Suppe; die Vorspeise; vergessen; kostenlos; Verzeihung!*
pages 70–71 **Aktive Grammatik**	• Grammar		• Adjective endings • Verbs with …*zu* • Object pronouns in the accusative	
page 72 **Kompetenzen**	• Summarising what you have learnt	• Getting an overview • Extracting information • Using cognates • Listening for gist/detail		
page 73 **Szenario**	• Producing a brochure about healthy eating • Preparing and delivering a presentation about an eating disorder	• Writing practice • Speaking practice		
page 74 **Vokabeln**	• Key language			
pages 177–178 **Lesen**	• Food, diet and nutrition • To encourage independent reading and develop reading strategies • To provide alternative class and homework material for students who finish other activities quickly	• Reading practice		

2B Essen und Trinken

Unit Objectives

Contexts and cultural focus: food; drink
Skills focus: extracting information; finding relationships between words; predicting words you will hear; guessing the meaning of a word
Grammar: pronouns in the accusative; demonstrative adjectives; infinitive constructions

Controlled assessment opportunities

Writing: Students' Book, page 61, activity 7
Writing: Students' Book, page 63, activity 6
Speaking: Students' Book, page 65, activity 6
Speaking: Students' Book, page 67, activity 6
Writing: Students' Book, page 69, activity 11
Writing: Students' Book, page 73, Zum Schreiben, activity 3
Speaking: Students' Book, page 73, Zum Sprechen, activity 4

See also ***GCSE German for OCR Assessment OxBox CD-ROM***.

An introduction to the unit Seite 59

- *Aim*: To introduce the themes of the unit.
- The opening spread of each unit is styled as the contents page of a teenage magazine. Illustrations, captions and skills summaries provide a preview of what is to come:

	Students' Book
Weißt du schon, wie man Essen aus aller Welt beschreibt?	pages 60–61
Weißt du schon, wie man gesundes Essen beschreibt?	pages 62–63
Weißt du schon, wie man Essprobleme beschreibt?	pages 64–65
Weißt du schon, wie man am besten einkauft?	pages 66–67
Weißt du schon, wie man im Restaurant bestellt und sich beschwert?	pages 68–69

- Allow time for students to read the questions and cross-refer to the relevant pages of the Students' Book. They could do this individually or in pairs/groups, followed by whole-class discussion.
- This spread also provides an opportunity for students to recap on familiar language. Ask them to think about language they already know that might be useful when working on the themes of the unit.
- At the end of work on Unit 2B:
  – If time permits, ask students to devise a replacement opening spread. What do they think should be on it, in terms of pictures, captions, etc.? What would they change/keep the same, and why? Ask them to imagine it is the contents page of a teenage magazine: what sort of captions and pictures do they feel would attract people to buy the magazine? This sort of activity encourages students to think about features of a text that make it suitable for a particular audience or purpose.
  – Allow time for students to return to this opening spread to answer the questions, review what they have learned and reflect on areas for improvement. What did they find difficult, interesting, etc.? What do they think are the most important things they have learned in this unit?

Wie man Essen aus aller Welt beschreibt

Seiten 60–61

Planner

➤ Objectives
- Describing food

➤ Resources
Students' Book, pages 60–61
CD 1, track 36
Grammar Workbook, pages 21–23
Activity Sheet 25

➤ Key language
das Gericht, der Geschmack, das Hähnchen, die Kartoffel, der Ofen, die Soße, der Topf, frisch, etwas Leichtes

➤ Skills
- Listening for key phrases

➤ Grammar
- Adjectival nouns

➤ PLTS
Question 6: Creative thinkers/Reflective learners
Question 7: Creative thinkers/Reflective learners/ Self-managers

➤ Starters
- Students brainstorm all the German words they know for food and drink e.g. *Hähnchen, Tee.* Display these so that the class can see them. Next, display a list of countries e.g. *Deutschland, Indien,* etc. and ask students to try to categorise the foods according to where they originate from.
- Ask students to think of as many German adjectives as they can, first to describe food or drink and then any other adjectives. List these and explain that later in the unit, you will be looking at adjective nouns.
- Start by asking a confident student, *Was isst du gern?* Once the student has answered, he/ she asks another student the same question. Continue around the class. With more confident classes, continue with other questions.

➤ Plenaries
- Give students a couple of minutes, working in pairs, to try and list in German an item of food or drink for each letter of the alphabet. The pair that has the most items wins. You could play this as a game, going around the class and asking each student to say an item of food and drink beginning with the appropriate letter of the alphabet, e.g.
  A: *Ich esse gern Äpfeln.*
  B: *Ich esse gern Brot.*
- Students brainstorm a list of adjectives to describe the food and drink items listed in plenary activity 1. Ask them to try to use each adjective in a sentence, remembering to add the correct ending, e.g. *Ich esse lieber grüne Äpfel.*
- Students choose a celebrity and imagine what his/her eating habits are, e.g. whether he/she eats breakfast, what his/her favourite food is, whether he/she is vegetarian, etc. They then write a paragraph on behalf of the celebrity.

As an introduction to the spread, students look at the pictures, identify the food and say where it comes from.

4–6

Answers:

1 *Wurst mit Sauerkraut* – Germany; **2** shepherd's pie –UK; **3** *Apfelstudel* – Germany; **4** tandoori – India; **5** *Brezeln* – Germany; **6** Roast chicken – UK; **7** *Bienenstich* – Germany

1a Lies die Texte und finde die deutschen Ausdrücke.
- Students read through the text again, this time to find the German for the English phrases listed.

4–6

Answers:

a Gewürze; **b** etwas Leichtes; **c** selbst gebackene; **d** Brathähnchen; **e** Essgewohnheiten; **f** Gemüse; **g** Soßen

1b Lies die Texte auf Seite 60 noch einmal durch und beantworte die Fragen auf Englisch.
- Students read the text once again and answer the questions in English.

4–6

Answers:

a Paul lives in London. **b** lamb and potatoes **c** tea **d** roast chicken **e** Uschi is 15. **f** bread, sliced cold sausage and cheese **g** at home **h** Her grandmother comes for coffee and cake. **i** Kanha lives in Amritsar, northern India. **j** using a tandoor – a red clay oven **k** at lunchtime **l** He does not like eating meat.

2a Arbeitet mit einem Partner/einer Partnerin. Spielt die Rolle von Paul, Uschi oder Kanha. Fragt und beantwortet die folgenden Fragen.

4–6
- To practise discussing eating habits, students perform a role play in pairs. Each partner takes on the role of Paul, Uschi or Kanha.

2b Beantworte jetzt die Fragen für dich selbst. Schreib mindestens sechs Sätze. Benutz die Ausdrücke aus der Wortschatz-Box.

- Students answer the questions for themselves.

3 Hör gut zu. Was essen und trinken sie (nicht) gern? Schreib die Tabelle in dein Heft und füll sie aus.

- Students listen to Uschi speaking about food and personal eating habits.
- Students copy the table and fill it in.

CD 1, track 36 **Seite 61, Übung 3**

Interviewer/in: Jugendmazin interviewt Uschi aus Berlin über ihre **normalen** Essgewohnheiten. Guten Tag, Uschi. Was essen und trinken Sie am liebsten?
Uschi: Guten Tag, also ich esse am liebsten **gekochten** Schinken und Frischkäse. Ich esse überhaupt nicht gern **rohes** Gemüse. Ich mag den Geschmack nicht. Ich trinke am liebsten **kalten** Orangensaft.
Interviewer/in: Und wie ist das mit Ihren Geschwistern?
Uschi: Heinrich, mein **jüngerer** Bruder, isst gern Wurst, und Uwe, mein **älterer** Bruder, isst gern Schweinefleisch. Beide mögen kein Lammfleisch. Sie trinken gern Milch, aber sie trinken nicht gern Wasser.
Interviewer/in: Und was mag Ihre Mutter?
Uschi: Meine Mutter, Miriam, isst nicht gern Nudeln. Sie isst lieber Reis und Kartoffeln. Sie trinkt gern **schwarzen** Tee.

Answers:

	Likes eating	Dislikes eating	Likes drinking
Uschi	ham, cottage cheese	raw vegetables	orange juice
Heinrich	sausage	lamb	milk
Uwe	pork	lamb	milk
Miriam	rice, potatoes	noodles	black tea

A25 Activity Sheet 25 provides further activities on eating habits.

4 Diskutiert zu zweit.

- Students work in pairs to discuss the questions listed.

5 Vervollständige die folgenden Sätze mit den richtigen Adjektivendungen.

- Students complete the sentences with the correct adjective endings.

Answers:

a gebraten**es** (*neut*); **b** frisch**e** (*neut*); **c** kalt**e** (*fem*); **d** grün**en** (*fem pl*); **e** Kalt**es** (*neut*)

6 Discuss your personal eating habits with your partner. Interview him or her using the questions from activity 2.

- Students work with a partner. Each pair interviews each other using the questions from activity 2. Encourage them to use as many adjectives as they can in their answers.
- This encourages students to generate and explore ideas whilst communicating previous learning. It covers the Creative thinkers and Reflective learners groups of skills from the framework of personal, learning and thinking skills.

4–9 PLTS

7 Write a report about your eating habits following the example of the interviews on page 60. Use as many adjectives as possible and watch out for the endings!

- Students write a report. Remind them to use as many adjectives as possible and to refer back to the *Grammatik* section for the endings if necessary.
- This encourages students to generate and explore ideas for their report whilst setting goals, communicating previous learning and managing their time and resources effectively. It covers the Creative thinkers, Reflective learners and Self-managers groups of skills from the framework of personal, learning and thinking skills.

4–9 PLTS

Success criteria:

- information communicated
- variety of vocabulary and structures used
- personal opinions expressed

Wie man gesundes Essen beschreibt

Seiten 62–63

Planner

➤ Objectives
- Describing allergies

➤ Resources
Students' Book, pages 62–63
CD 1, track 37
Grammar Workbook, page 56
Activity Sheet 22

➤ Key language
der Blutdruck
aufpassen; Bescheid wissen; riechen; meiden
allergisch gegen

➤ Skills
- Understanding new vocabulary

➤ Grammar
- Using *um…zu*

➤ PLTS
Question 5b: Creative thinkers/Reflective learners/Team workers
Question 6: Creative thinkers/Reflective learners/Independent enquirers/Self-managers

➤ Starters
- Display a list of food and drink items, e.g. *Brot, Erdbeeren, Schokolade, Zucker, Wasser*. Also display two headings: *Gesund* and *Ungesund*. Ask volunteers to suggest which column each food should be in. Encourage some discussion, as with some items, it may be a matter of opinion. Keep the final lists to use later.
- Divide the class into two teams. Display a list of German words to do with technology and science, e.g. *Ärzte, Fett, Kalorien, Pestizide, Diät, Blut* (you can adjust the number and difficulty of the words listed depending on the ability of the class). Give each team a fixed amount of time to write what they think each of the words means. When the time is up, compare answers. The team with the most correct answers wins.
- Divide the class into two teams. Call out statements about food, e.g. *Schokolade macht dick! Richtig oder falsch?* Each team writes *R* or *F* on a piece of paper/mini-whiteboard and holds it up. They score a point for a correct answer. The team with the most correct answers wins. Encourage some discussion, as in some cases the answer may be subjective.

➤ Plenaries
- Display a list of German jumbled sentences about food in the future tense e.g. *zu leben – Ich werde Nüsse – um gesund – immer meiden* and give students a set amount of time to unjumble the sentences, reminding them to watch out for word order. Ask volunteers to come to the front and put the sentences in the correct order and to explain why this is the 'correct' order. Also include sentences with the *um…zu* structure.
- Display a few words and phrases from the spread and challenge students to use them all in a short paragraph based on the theme of the spread. They exchange their paragraphs with a partner and suggest improvements to each other's work.
- Look at the lists from starter activity 3 again. Do students still agree with all their choices, or is there anything they would change? If so, why? Encourage them to justify their opinions in German, e.g. *Zucker ist nicht gesund! Das stimmt nicht, aber man muss Zucker mit Maßen essen.*

Richtig oder falsch? Was passt zusammen?

4–6

- As an introduction to the spread, students read the headlines about food and drink and match the sentences to the headlines.

Answers:

1 c, **2** b, **3** f, **4** a, **5** e, **6** d

1a Lies die Texte und finde die deutschen Wörter.

4–6

- Students read the headlines again and find the German equivalents to the English words listed.

Answers:

a Ärzte; **b** Kreislauf; **c** Honig; **d** gefährlich; **e** Kohlenhydrate; **f** Fett; **g** Kalorien; **h** Pestizide; **i** Eiweiß; **j** Energie

1b Welches Essen ist gesund? Welches Essen enthält viel Zucker? Welches Essen hat viel Eiweiß? Mach eine Liste. Wie viele Begriffe kannst du in 5 Minuten aufschreiben?

1–3

- Students think of as many healthy and unhealthy foods as possible and write them into the correct column of the grid.

2a Lest die Texte. Ratet was die folgenden Wörter bedeuten, ohne im Wörterbuch nachzuschauen.

- Students read the text and guess the meaning of the words listed without using a dictionary.

4–6

1 itching; **2** airway; **3** to smell; **4** injection; **5** to avoid; **6** hypersensitive

2b Diskutiert und wählt eine Definition für jedes Wort aus dem Kasten.

- Students write a definition for each word in the box.

3 Lies die Texte noch einmal und beantworte die folgenden Fragen.

4–6

- Students read the text and answer the questions.

Answers:

a quite healthy; **b** fruit and vegetables; **c** strawberries; **d** gets a rash and itching; **e** normal; **f** nut allergy; **g** gets anaphylactic shock/constricted airway/drop in blood pressure; **h** needs adrenaline injection

4 Hör gut zu und beantworte die Fragen auf Englisch.

4–6

- Students listen to the recording and then answer the questions in English to check comprehension.

CD 1, track 37 **Seite 63, Übung 4**

Interviewer/in:	Jugendmagazin interviewt Jasmine über ihre Ernährung. Hallo Jasmine, wie geht's?
Jasmine:	Danke, es geht mir gut.
Interviewer/in:	Erzählen Sie mir etwas über Ihre Ernährung.
Jasmine:	Ich esse ziemlich gesund, glaube ich. Meine Eltern kommen aus China, und wir essen viel Reis mit Gemüse und Fleisch.
Interviewer/in:	Haben Sie irgendwelche Probleme in Bezug auf Ihre Ehrährung?
Jasmine:	Ja, ich habe eine Laktose-Intoleranz. Ich vertrage also keinen Milchzucker.
Interviewer/in:	Können Sie das weiter erklären?
Jasmine:	Ja, es ist normal für Leute aus Asien. Genetisch fehlt uns das Enzym Laktase, und das bedeutet, dass man keinen Milchzucker zu sich nehmen kann; anderfalls wird man krank. Deshalb findet man in chinesischen, andernfalls wird man Restaurants wenig Käse und Milchprodukte.
Interviewer/in:	Und was bedeutet das für Ihr Leben hier in Deutschland?
Jasmine:	Das kann problematisch werden. Zu Hause ist es ganz einfach, da wir fast keine Milchprodukte benutzen, aber in Restaurants und im Imbiss ist es schwierig, weil es überall Milchprodukte gibt. Ich kann keine Milchschokolade essen, ohne dass ich krank werde, und ich muss daher wirklich aufpassen und alle Milchprodukte vermeiden.
Interviewer/in:	Ist es da nicht schwierig, ein normaler Teenager zu sein?
Jasmine:	Ja, ein bisschen schon, aber meine Freunde verstehen mein Problem und helfen mir, solches Essen zu vermeiden. Sie denken an mich und an meine Gesundheit. Deshalb sind sie meine Freunde!
Interviewer/in:	Danke, Jasmine.

Answers:

a China; **b** a fairly healthy diet – rice, vegetables and meat; **c** She is lactose intolerant; **d** It's genetic – she is missing an enzyme, which is normal for Chinese people; **e** She feels ill. **f** avoid milk products

A22 Activity Sheet 22 provides further activities on food and allergies

5a Work in pairs. Take the roles of Jürgen and Birgit and ask and answer these questions.

4–9

- Students work with a partner. Each takes the role of Jürgen or Brigit and asks and answers the questions listed.
- Encourage them to draw upon the vocabulary presented on these pages.

5b Now ask and answer the questions about yourselves.

4–9

PLTS

- Students ask and answer questions about themselves. Encourage them to answer as fully as possible – they can make up imaginative answers if they want to.
- This activity encourages students to generate and explore ideas whilst communicating previous learning and to work confidently with others. It covers the Creative thinkers, Reflective learners and Team workers groups of skills from the framework of personal, learning and thinking skills.

6 With a partner, write an article about Jasmine for *Jugendmagazin*, following Jürgen and Brigit's articles as a model.

4–9

PLTS

- Students work with a partner to write an article. Encourage them to use sentences with …*zu* and, if possible, sentences in the future tense. This is an ideal assessment opportunity.
- This activity encourages students to generate and explore ideas whilst communicating previous learning and to support conclusions, using reasoned arguments and evidence. It also encourages students to organise their time and resources effectively. It covers the Creative thinkers, Reflective learners, Independent enquirers and Self-managers groups of skills from the framework of personal, learning and thinking skills.

Success criteria:

- amount of information communicated
- variety of vocabulary and structures used
- number of personal opinions given

Wie man Essprobleme beschreibt

Seiten 64–65

Planner

➤ Objectives
- Discussing eating disorders

➤ Resources
Students' Book, pages 64–65
CD 1, track 38
Grammar Workbook, page 58

➤ Key language
die Kneipe; die Spritze; abnehmen; aufhören; bestrafen; sich um etwas Sorgen machen; glücklich; nötig; satt; betrunken; erlaubt

➤ Skills
- Giving advice

➤ Grammar
- Sentences with …*zu* and *wenn*

➤ PLTS
Question 6: Creative thinkers/Reflective learners
Question 7: Creative thinkers, Reflective learners and Self-managers

➤ Starters
- As a class play a word game using German food and drink vocabulary. Start by saying a food item, e.g. *Brot*. The student closest to you must say a word beginning with the last letter of your word, i.e. 't' and so it continues around the class. If a student hesitates or can't think of a word, he/she is out. The winner is the last student left.
- Display a list of German vocabulary that students will meet in this spread and the English translations. Ask students to match up as many as they can, using the knowledge they already have. Keep the lists for them to revisit once you have worked through the spread.

➤ Plenaries
- Students work in pairs and note down as many *wenn* sentences as they can in a set amount of time. They should try to use ideas and vocabulary from the spread. Compare the sentences as a class. Remind students to watch out for word order and encourage them to use *wenn* at the beginning of sentences as well.
- Students work in pairs and interview each other on their eating habits, using the *zu* + infinitive structure, e.g.
  A: *Was machst du um gesund zu bleiben?*
  B: *Ich versuche, gesünder zu essen.*
- Students pretend to be a celebrity and write a letter to a problem page about an eating problem they have. They should try to use the expressions and ideas presented on these pages. They could them swap letters with a partner who writes a reply.

Lies die Briefe und die Antworten. Was gehört zusammen? Wer bekommt welchen Rat?

4–6

- As an introduction to the spread, students read the letters to a problem page and match them to the advice given.

Answers:

a Johann; **b** Maria; **c** Anna; **d** Martin

1a Lies die Texte. Wer…

4–6

- Students read the letters and the advice given and answer the questions.

Answers:

a Johann; **b** Maria; **c** Anna; **d** Martin; **e** Johann; **f** Anna; **g** Anna; **h** Maria

1b Lies die Texte noch einmal durch und beantworte die Fragen auf Englisch.

- Students read the letters again and answer the questions in English.

4–6

Answers:

a He is vegetarian, but hasn't told his girlfriend's mother.
b have an insulin injection
c She is diabetic.
d She thinks she is fat.
e only salad and fruit
f He eats too much.

2 Arbeitet mit einem Partner/einer Partnerin. Spielt die Rollen von Anna und Martin und beantwortet die folgenden Fragen.

4–6

- Students work with a partner. Each plays the role of either Anna or Martin and answers the questions.
- Encourage them to use the vocabulary and structures from the letters in their answers.

3a Hör gut zu. Finde die vier Ausdrücke mit *zu* + Infinitiv. Schreib sie auf.

4–6

- Students listen to the recording and note down four examples of the '*zu* + infinitive' structure.

CD 1, track 38 **Seite 65, Übung 3**

Interviewer/in: Hallo, Martin. Wie geht es dir?
Martin: Gut, danke.
Interviewer/in: Martin, wie alt bist du?
Martin: Ich bin fünfzehn Jahre alt.
Interviewer/in: Was ist dein Problem Martin?
Martin: Ich finde, ich bin zu dick. Ich wiege über hundert Kilo und das ist viel zu viel.
Interviewer/in: Warum wiegst du so viel?
Martin: Das ist einfach – ich esse zu viel. Ich esse gern Kekse und Schokolade und ich habe immer Hunger.
Interviewer/in: Welche anderen Probleme bringt das mit sich?
Martin: Ich finde es schwierig, modische Kleidung zu kaufen. Alles, was mir passt, ist hässlich und altmodisch.
Interviewer/in: Hast du es schon mit einer Diät versucht?
Martin: Ja, ich habe versucht, gesünder zu essen, aber ich hasse Salat und Gemüse – sie schmecken nach nichts und das finde ich nicht gut.
Interviewer/in: Willst du etwas gegen dein Übergewicht machen?
Martin: Manchmal denke ich schon, dass ich was dagegen machen will, aber das Problem ist auch, dass ich nur glücklich bin, **wenn ich esse.** Ich finde Trost, **wenn ich Schokolade esse**. Ich hoffe, in der Zukunft eine passende Diät zu finden.
Interviewer/in: Ist das nur eine Sache von Diät?
Martin: Nein, nicht nur das. Das ist auch eine Frage von Bestrafung, glaube ich. Ich versuche, das alles zu verstehen, aber ich glaube, dass ich mich bestrafe, **wenn ich ungesund esse**. **Wenn ich bereit bin**, und **wenn ich mich besser fühle**, werde ich gesünder essen.
Interviewer/in: Martin, vielen Dank und viel Glück.

Answers:

modische Kleider zu kaufen; gesünder zu essen; eine passende Diät zu finden; das alles zu verstehen

3b Hör noch einmal zu und finde fünf *wenn*-Sätze.

- Students listen again and this time note down five sentences which include *wenn*.

4–6

Answers:

Manchmal denke ich schon, dass ich was dagegen machen will, aber das Problem ist auch, dass ich nur glücklich bin, **wenn** ich esse.

Ich finde Trost, **wenn** ich Schokolade esse.

Ich versuche, das alles zu verstehen, aber ich glaube, dass ich mich bestrafe, **wenn** ich ungesund esse.

Wenn ich bereit bin, und **wenn** ich mich besser fühle, werde ich gesünder essen.

3c Hör zum dritten Mal zu und beantworte die folgenden Fragen auf Englisch.

- Students listen a third time and, to check comprehension, answer the questions.

4–6

Answers:

a Martin finds it difficult to find fashionable clothes in his size.
b He's tried dieting but he doesn't like salad and vegetables.
c He finds comfort in eating and feels better when doing so.
d He thinks that it is a form of self-punishment. He punishes himself when he eats unhealthily.

4 Ergänze die Sätze mit *zu* und mit den Ausdrücken aus dem Kasten unten.

- Read the *Grammatik* section.
- Ask students to complete the sentences, using *zu* and the words in the box.

Answers:

a Ich versuche, gesünder zu essen.
b Ich hoffe, ein Gleichgewicht zu finden.
c Ich bin zu jung, Bier zu kaufen.
d Ich finde es schwierig, abzunehmen.
e Sie helfen mir, gesund zu essen.

5a Schreib einzelne Sätze mit *wenn*. Pass auf die Wortstellung auf.

- Ask students to put the sentences together using *wenn*. Remind them to check word order.

Answers:

a Ich bin glücklich, wenn ich betrunken bin.
b Ich esse, wenn ich Trost brauche.
c Ich fühle mich besser, wenn ich Schokolade esse.
d Ich bestrafe mich, wenn ich ungesund esse.

5b Schreib jetzt die Sätze aus Übung 5a mit *wenn* am Satzanfang. Wie ändert sich die Wortstellung?

- Students now turn the sentences from 5a around so that they begin with *wenn*. Ask them what happens to the word order.

Answers:

a Wenn ich betrunken bin, bin ich glücklich.
b Wenn ich Trost brauche, esse ich.
c Wenn ich Schokolade esse, fühle ich mich besser.
d Wenn ich ungesund esse, bestrafe ich mich.

6 Work with a partner. A is the interviewer and B plays the role of Maria. Carry out an interview with Maria, inventing questions about her problem. Then play out the interview in front of the class.

- Students work in pairs. One plays an interviewer, the other, Maria, from the opening text. This is an ideal assessment opportunity.
- This activity encourages students to generate and explore ideas whilst communicating previous learning and to work confidently with others. It covers the Creative thinkers, Reflective learners and Team workers groups of skills from the framework of personal, learning and thinking skills.

4–9

PLTS

Success criteria:

- ideas communicated
- pronunciation and intonation and fluency
- range of vocabulary and structures used
- tenses or time frames used

7 **Imagine you have a problem with eating or drinking. Write a letter to a problem page. Use as many expressions as possible from these two pages. Swap letters with a partner and write the agony aunt's reply.**

- Students write a letter to a problem page and then write some advice for their partner.
- Encourage them to re-read the letters at the beginning of the spread and to draw upon the vocabulary and structure of these to write their letter and reply.

4–9

PLTS

- This activity encourages students to generate and explore ideas whilst communicating previous learning and to support conclusions. It also encourages students to organise their time and resources effectively. It covers the Creative thinkers, Reflective learners and Self-managers groups of skills from the framework of personal, learning and thinking skills.

Wie man am besten einkauft

Seiten 66–67

Planner

➤ Objectives

- Discussing shopping for food

➤ Resources

Students' Book, pages 66–67
CD 1, track 39
Grammar Workbook, pages 25, 32–35
Activity Sheet 23

➤ Key language

die Auswahl; die Bäckerei; die Metzgerei; Öffnungszeiten; der Ruhetag; aufmachen; zumachen; preiswert; teuer; geschlossen

➤ Skills

- Comparing advantages and disadvantages

➤ Grammar

- Object pronouns in the accusative

➤ PLTS

Question 5: Creative thinkers/Reflective learners/ Team workers

➤ Starters

- Display a list of different places to buy food (apart from the supermarket) in German, e.g. *die Bäckerei, die Metzgerei, der Obst- und Gemüsehandler.* Now display a shopping list, e.g. *Erdbeeren, Brot*, etc. and give students a time limit to match the items on the list to each shop. Students could work in teams and score a point for each word they match correctly. The team with the most point wins.
- Go round the class, asking students where they like to buy food, the supermarket or small shops, e.g. *Gehst du in die Stadt oder fährst du lieber zum Supermarkt?* Students reply, e.g. *Ich gehe in die Stadt.* or *Ich fahre zum Supermarkt.* What do most students do?
- Display the headings, *Märkte und kleine Läden* and *Supermärkte* and ask students to think of advantages and disadvantages of each in German. Compare these with the lists on page 66 of the Students' Book.

➤ Plenaries

- Display a few words and phrases from the spread and challenge students to use them all in a short paragraph based on the themes of the spread. Confident students present their paragraph to the class.
- Display sentences from the spread, e.g. *Ich brauche Orangensaft. Ich kann den Orangensaft im Supermarkt kaufen.* Ask students to rewrite them using object pronouns to avoid repeating the name of the thing mentioned in the sentence.
- Students work in pairs to prepare and perform a role-play. Student A loves shopping in supermarkets; student B hates them and prefers small shops in town. Each tries to persuade the other that they are right, giving reasons why they find these shops good/bad, e.g.
Student A: *Ich gehe lieber zum Supermarkt. Beim Supermarkt könnten wir ja besser parken.*
Student B: *Das stimmt, aber da sind die Produkte nicht immer frisch. Man bekommt frischere Produkte in den kleinen Läden* etc.

1 Was sind die Vor- und Nachteile von Märkten und Läden gegenüber Supermärkten? Mach eine Liste. Gibt es noch andere Vor- und Nachteile? Diskutiere die Vor- und Nachteile in der Klasse und trage sie in die Tabelle ein.

- As an introduction to the spread, students consider the advantages and disadvantages of market stalls/small shops and supermarkets.
- As a class they then discuss these and think of any further advantages / disadvantages of each. They add these to the grid.

4–6

2a Lies den Dialog. Was bedeuten die fett gedruckten Wörter? Diskutiert zu zweit.

4–9

- Students read the dialogue and then discuss with a partner what the text in bold means.

2b Übersetze die folgenden Sätze.

- Students translate the sentences.

Answers:

4–6

a Mum takes me in the car.
b We could also take you.
c I find it/them better.
d I can get it at the supermarket.
e Mum gets us to the supermarket quickly.
f I'll take you.

3 Vervollständige die Sätze mit den richtigen Pronomen.

- Students complete the sentences with the correct pronoun.

Answers:

a ihn; **b** sie; **c** sie; **d** sie

Answers:

a In den kleinen Läden; **b** Im Supermarkt; **c** Im Supermarkt; **d** In den kleinen Läden **e** Im Supermarkt

4 Du hörst jetzt zwei Gespräche zum Thema Einkaufen. Hör zu und beantworte die folgenden Fragen auf Englisch.

- Students listen to the recording and then answer the questions in English.

CD 1, track 39 **Seite 67, Übung 4**

Gespräch 1

Mutti: Gehst du bitte für mich einkaufen, Gabi?
Gabi: Ja, aber Mutti, es ist schon achtzehn Uhr. Die Läden sind alle schon geschlossen.
Mutti: Es ist viel später, als ich dachte! Das ist ja schade! Ich brauche frisches Gemüse für die Suppe morgen.
Gabi: Wenn das Gemüse für eine Suppe ist, muss es nicht unbedingt frisch sein, oder? Warum gehe ich nicht zum Supermarkt am Stadtrand?
Mutti: Das ist eine gute Idee, aber wie kommst du dahin? Du kannst nicht zu Fuß gehen – es ist ein weiter Weg!
Gabi: Das ist doch kein Problem, Mutti. Ich höre Papa mit dem Auto kommen. Ich werde ihn bitten, mich zum Supermarkt zu fahren. Bis später!

Gespräch 2

Uschi: Bist du fertig, Sonia? Wir gehen einkaufen!
Sonia: Ja, ich bin fertig. Also wo gehen wir hin?
Uschi: Das kommt darauf an! Was brauchen wir?
Sonia: Ich brauche ein paar Lebensmittel. Meine Mutter sagt, dass ich für mich selber einkaufen soll, da ich jetzt einen Job habe und Geld verdiene.
Uschi: Was willst du denn kaufen?
Sonia: Ich will frisch gebackenes Brot, frisches Obst und Schinken.
Uschi: In Ordnung. Bringt uns dein Vater zum Supermarkt?
Sonia: Zum Supermarkt? Nein – ich will frische Sachen. Ich gehe lieber zu Fuß in die Stadt. Es ist viel näher und wir brauchen die Bewegung.
Uschi: Da hast du Recht, und man bekommt frischere Sachen und eine persönlichere Bedienung in der Stadt, aber die Preise sind ein bisschen höher. Ist das in Ordnung?
Sonia: Ja das ist okay – es lohnt sich!...

Answers:

Gespräch 1

a Gabi's mother needs vegetables for soup.
b It is 6pm.
c The shops are closed.
d Gabi goes to the supermarket with her father by car.

Gespräch 2

a Sonia needs to buy some food – bread, fruit and ham
b in town
c fresher produce, they need the exercise, personal service
d higher prices

A23 Activity Sheet 23 provides a writing activity on preparing and shopping for a special meal.

5 Write and conduct a survey of shopping habits in your class. Where do people shop and what do they buy there? What are the advantages and disadvantages? Use as many expressions from this spread and as many comparatives as possible.

- Students write a survey of shopping habits in their class and then ask other students to complete it.
- This activity encourages students to generate and explore ideas whilst communicating previous learning. It also encourages them to collaborate with others to achieve results. It covers the Creative thinkers, Reflective learners and Team workers groups of skills from the framework of personal, learning and thinking skills.

4–9 PLTS

6 Write up your findings from the survey and present them to the class.

- Students write up the results of the survey and present them to the class.

4–9

Success criteria:

- ideas communicated
- pronunciation and intonation and fluency
- range of vocabulary and structures used
- tenses or time frames used

Wie man im Restaurant bestellt und sich beschwert

Seiten 68–69

Planner

➤ Objectives

- Ordering food in a restaurant

➤ Resources

Students' Book, pages 68–69
CD 1, tracks 40–42
Grammar Workbook, page 13
Activity Sheet 24

➤ Key language

die Gabel; grüne Bohnen; der Lachs; der Messer; die Soße; die Suppe; die Vorspeise; vergessen; kostenlos; Verzeihung!

➤ Skills

- Targeted listening

➤ Grammar

- *dieser, diese, dieses*

➤ PLTS

Question 8: Creative thinkers/Reflective learners/Team workers
Question 10a: Creative thinkers/Reflective learners/Team workers
Question 11: Creative thinkers/Reflective learners/Self-managers

➤ Starters

- Display some words from the key language of the spread with the vowels missing. Students race against each other to fill in the missing letters. Elicit the English for the words included.
- Play a word game with restaurant vocabulary. Explain to students that you will start with one item and the next person must repeat this item and add another of his/her own, and so on, e.g.
  A: *Ich habe eine Gabel.*
  B: *Ich habe eine Gabel und einen Messer.*
- Act out some complaints in German, using the appropriate actions and tone of voice, e.g. *Meine Suppe ist kalt.* Students say what the complaint is in English. Make a list of 'complaint' words.

➤ Plenaries

- Choose a volunteer to play the role of a waiter in a restaurant. The rest of the class are diners. Each student complains about some aspect of the meal/service and the waiter responds accordingly, e.g.
  Student: *Meine Suppe ist kalt.*
  Waiter: *Oh, das tut mir leid. Ich bringe sie fort. Ich komme gleich zurück.*
  Once the waiter has responded to a few complaints, choose a new vounteer.
- Display a couple of example sentences including *diese* in its various forms. Give students a couple of minutes to come up with as many sentences containing *diese* as possible, using *diese* in as many forms as possible. Compare sentences.
- Call out a word from the spread. Students respond by putting it into a sentence, e.g.
  Teacher: *Fisch!*
  Student: *Ich möchte Fisch, glaube ich!*

1 Wer bestellt was? Hör gut zu, lies den Dialog und füll die Tabelle aus.

- Read through the *Tipp* section on listening comprehensions as a class.
- Students listen to the recording and use the advice given in the *Tipp* section to fill in the grid.

4–6

CD 1, track 40 **Seite 68, Übung 1**

Mutter: Herzlichen Glückwünsch zum Geburtstag, Maria! Na, was wollen wir als Vorspeise essen?
Vater: Ja, heute ist ein schöner Tag, Maria.
Kellner: Hallo. Was kann ich für Sie tun?
Vater: Ich möchte die Suppe. Was für Suppe haben Sie heute?
Kellner: Heute gibt's Tomatensuppe.
Vater: Fabelhaft – meine Lieblingssuppe! Ich nehme sie.
Sohn (Stefan): Ich nehme auch die Suppe, danke.
Tochter (Maria): Nein, Suppe will ich nicht! Ich möchte lieber diesen Salat hier, bitte – den Salat „Bravissima".
Mutter: Und ich möchte Fisch, glaube ich. Haben Sie Lachs?
Kellner: Ja, sicher. Und als Hauptgericht? Was hätten Sie gern?

Vater:	Für mich Spaghetti mit Tomatensoße, bitte.
Sohn (Stefan):	Ich nehme das Steak mit Kartoffeln und grünen Bohnen.
Kellner:	Also, einmal Spaghetti und einmal Steak. Und für die Damen?
Mutter:	Ich möchte das Lammfleisch mit Reis und Gemüse. Das hört sich gut an!
Tochter (Maria):	Ich nehme das Omelett mit Pommes und Erbsen, aber bitte sagen Sie dem Koch, dass es nicht mit Milch zubereitet werden darf, da ich keinen Milchzucker vertrage.
Kellner:	Kein Problem, ich sage ihm sofort Bescheid.

Answers:

	Mother	Father	Stefan	Maria
Starter	fish (salmon)	tomato soup	tomato soup	salad
Main course	lamb, rice, vegetables	steak, potatoes, green beans	spaghetti with tomato sauce	Omelette, chips, peas

2 Hör noch einmal zu und finde die deutschen Wörter.

- Students listen again and find the German for the English words listed.

4–6

Answers:

a Lammfleisch; **b** Fisch; **c** Suppe; **d** Hauptgericht; **e** Vorspeise; **f** Koch; **g** Erbsen; **h** Kartoffeln; **i** Reis

3a Hör noch einmal zu. Wie bestellt man Essen? Finde zwei verschiedene Ausdrücke. Schreib sie auf.

- Students listen to the recording again and find two similar expressions used when ordering food.
- Read through the *Tipp* section with students again, if necessary.

4–6

Answers:

ich möchte; ich nehme

3b Wie antwortet der Kellner? Finde vier Ausdrücke. Schreib sie auf.

- Students listen again and find four expressions that the waiter uses to answer the customers' questions.

Answers:

ja, sicher; einmal...; sehr gut; kommt gleich

4–6

4 Hör gut zu und beantworte die folgenden Fragen.

- Read the second *Tipp* section.
- Play the recording and ask them to answer the questions.

4–6

CD 1, track 41 **Seite 69, Übung 4**

Kellner:	So, hier ist Ihre Bestellung. Also, drei Suppen und einen Salat.
Mutter:	Nein, das stimmt nicht. Wo ist mein Fisch? Ich habe Fisch bestellt, keine Suppe.
Kellner:	Sie haben Recht. Verzeihung! Der Fisch kommt sofort.
Vater:	Igitt, die Suppe ist kalt. Das geht nicht! Wie ist deine Suppe, Stefan?
Sohn (Stefan):	Meine Suppe ist auch kalt, Vati.
Vater:	Herr Ober, wir haben hier ein Problem.
Kellner:	Ja, mein Herr. Hier ist Ihr Fisch, meine Dame.
Mutter:	Ja, danke, aber die beiden Suppen sind kalt.
Kellner:	Oh, das tut mir Leid. Ich nehme sie mit zurück in die Küche. Bin gleich wieder da ...
Kellner:	So, hier haben wir die Suppen. Hoffentlich sind diese jetzt besser!
Vater:	Ja, diese Suppe ist viel besser. Deine auch, Stefan?
Sohn (Stefan):	Ja, diese schmeckt gut, danke!

Answers:

a fish (salmon); **b** soup; **c** It is cold. **d** brings two fresh bowls of soup

5 Hör noch einmal zu. Wie sagt man auf Deutsch...?

- Students listen again and note down the German phrases used for the English expressions listed.

4–6

Answers:

a Das tut mir Leid. **b** Das stimmt nicht. Das geht nicht! **c** Sie haben Recht. **d** Wir haben ein Problem. **e** Ich nehme sie mit zurück in die Küche.

6 Hör gut zu und beantworte die Fragen auf Deutsch.

- Students listen to the recording and then answer the questions in German.

CD 1, track 42 **Seite 69, Übung 6**

Kellner:	Und hier sind die Hauptgerichte. Wer bekommt dieses Steak?
Sohn (Stefan):	Er ist für mich, danke.
Kellner:	Und dieses Omelett?
Tochter (Maria):	Das ist für mich, danke!
Mutter:	Ich bekomme das Lammfleisch, danke.
Vater:	Und die Spaghetti sind für mich, danke.
Kellner:	Guten Appetit!
Mutter:	Moment bitte, ich habe kein Messer! Könnten Sie mir ein Messer bringen?
Kellner:	Natürlich, kommt sofort.
Vater:	Diese Gabel ist aber schmutzig. Bitte bringen Sie mir eine saubere Gabel.
Kellner:	Natürlich, sofort.
Tochter (Maria):	Mutti, mir ist schrecklich schlecht. Ich bin krank. Ich weiß genau: in dem Omelett war Milch.
Mutter:	Herr Ober, meine Tochter fühlt sich nicht gut. Können Sie mir sagen, ... ob Milch in diesem Omelett war?

Kellner:	Oh, es tut mir Leid! Ich habe total vergessen, es dem Koch zu sagen. Wir sind gerade voll im Stress. Es tut mir wirklich fürchterlich Leid. Sie bekommen sofort ein Omelett ohne Milch. Und als Entschädigung bekommen Sie alle einen kostenlosen Nachtisch. Hoffentlich können Sie uns verzeihen?
Vater:	Ich möchte mit dem Geschäftsführer sprechen, bitte! Wir sind nicht zufrieden und wir wollen uns beschweren!
Kellner:	Natürlich, das kann ich ja irgendwie verstehen …

Answers:

a Die Mutter hat kein Messer.
b Sie ist schmutzig.
c Maria fühlt sich krank.
d Es gab Milch im Omelett. Der Kellner hat vergessen, dem Koch Bescheid zu sagen.

7a Hör noch einmal zu! Wie hat er/sie sich beschwert?

- Students listen again and note down the phrases the customers used to complain.

4–6

Answers:

Ich möchte mit dem Geschäftsführer sprechen.
Wir sind nicht zufrieden.
Wir wollen uns beschweren!

7b Was bedeutet…?

- Students now translate the German phrases into English.

4–6

Answers:

a I don't have a knife. **b** But this fork is dirty. **c** I would like to speak to the manager. **d** We are not happy. **e** Can you forgive us? **f** We want to complain.

8 Spielt in Gruppen von fünf Personen die Rollen von Mutter, Vater, Stefan, Maria und dem Kellner. Wie geht das Gespräch weiter?

4–9

PLTS

- Students work in groups of five to play the parts of the mother, father, son, daughter and waiter. They act out how they think the scene continues and ends.
- This activity encourages students to think creatively and explore different ideas whilst collaborating with others to work towards a common goal and communicating previous learning. It covers the Creative thinkers, Reflective learners and Team workers groups from the framework of personal, learning and thinking skills.

A24 Further listening activities on ordering food in restaurants are provided on Activity Sheet 24.

9a Ergänze die Sätze mit *dieser*, *diese* und so weiter.

- Read the *Grammatik* section, *this or these.*
- Students complete the sentences with the appropriate form of *dieser*.

Answers:

a diese; **b** dieses; **c** dieser; **d** diese; **e** dieses; **f** dieser

9b Uberprüft eune Sätze aus Übung 9a mit einem Partner/ einer Partnerin.

- Students work with a partner to check their sentences from activity 9a.

10a In groups of five or more, write a dialogue set in a restaurant like the one above. Try to use as many different forms of *dieser* as possible, and include some comparatives.

4–9

PLTS

- Students work in groups to write a dialogue similar to those above.
- This encourages students to think creatively and explore different ideas whilst collaborating with others to work towards a common goal and communicating previous learning. It covers the Creative thinkers, Reflective learners and Team workers groups of skills from the framework of personal, learning and thinking skills.

10b Perform your scene in front of the class. Vote on which restaurant has the worst service and which the best. You can record your scene using the OxBox software.

4–9

- Students perform their dialogues.
- The class votes on which restaurant has the worst service and which has the best.

11 Write a letter of complaint to the restaurant, describing what was wrong and asking for some form of compensation. You might want to use some of the words in the box below.

4–9

PLTS

- Students write a letter of complaint to the restaurant. Encourage them to use some of the words from the tip box as well as other ideas and vocabulary from these pages.
- This activity encourages students to think creatively and explore different ideas whilst communicating previous learning in order to acheive their goal. It covers the Creative thinkers, Reflective learners and Self-managers groups of skills from the framework of personal, learning and thinking skills.

Success criteria:

- variety of vocabulary and structures used
- different tenses or time frames used
- number of personal opinions given

Aktive Grammatik

Seiten 70–71

Planner

➤ Objectives
- To practise adjective endings
- To practise using verbs with …*zu*
- Object pronouns in the accusative

➤ Resources
Students' Book, pages 70–71
Exam Skills Workbooks, page 38
Grammar Workbook, pages 21–23, 32–35, 56, 58
Activity Sheet 26
Resources and Planning OxBox CD-ROM

➤ Grammar
- Adjective endings
- Verbs with …*zu*
- Object pronouns in the accusative

➤ PLTS
All questions: Reflective learners/Self-managers

➤ Adjective endings

1 **Use the tables of adjective endings to complete the following sentences in German, explaining the number, gender, case and which table you used.**
- This question focuses on using the correct adjective ending depending on number, gender and case.

Answers:

a gut**en** alt**en** (*masc, acc, Table C*); **b** italienisch**en** (*masc, acc, Table A*); **c** heiß**e** (*fem, nom, Table B*); **d** frischer**e** klein**en** (*masc pl, acc, Table C; masc pl, dat, Table A*); **e** gebraten**es** (*neut, acc, Table C*); **f** speziell**en** rot**em** (*masc, dat, Table B; masc, dat, Table C*); **g** persönlich**e** (*fem, acc, Table A*); **h** kostenlos**en** (*masc, acc, Table B*); **i** schwarz**en** *(masc, acc, Table C)*; **j** grün**e** *(masc pl, acc, Table C)*; **k** Chinesisch**er** *(masc, nom, Table C)*; **l** Kalt**er** *(masc, nom, Table C)*; **m** braun**e** *(masc, nom, Table A)*; **n** rote *(masc, nom, Table A)*; **o** italienisch**en** *(fem pl, nom, Table A)*

2 **Look at your answers for activity 9a on page 69. For each sentence, explain your use of *dieser, diese, dieses,* etc. with reference to number, gender and case.**
- This activity checks students' understanding of which ending to use with *dieser*.

Answers:

a diese – fem, sing, nom; **b** dieses – neut, sing, nom; **c** dieser – fem, sing, nom; **d** diese – pl, acc; **e** dieses – neut, sing, acc; **f** dieser – masc, sing, nom

➤ Verbs with … *zu*

3 **Join each pair of phrases to make one longer sentence using *zu*.**
- This question focuses on creating longer sentences using *zu*.

Answers:

a Ich verspreche, kein Alkohol mehr zu trinken.
b Ich versuche, weniger zu essen.
c Ich habe vergessen, dem Chef zu sagen.
d Meine Freunde helfen mir, dieses Essen zu meiden.
e Sie hat vor, gesünder zu essen.

4 **Translate the following sentences into German.**
- This question focuses on using sentences with …*zu*.

Answers:

a Ich hoffe, abzunehmen.
b Sie vergisst immer, gesund zu essen.
c Er hat aufgehört, soviel zu essen.
d Wir essen Obst und Gemüse, um gesund zu bleiben.
e Sie können keinen Fisch essen, ohne sich krank zu fühlen.

5 **Complete these sentences using constructions with *zu*.**
- Further practice of using sentences with *zu*.

Answers:

b Es kann helfen, abzunehmen.
c Ohne eine Adrenalinspritze zu bekommen, steigt mein Blutdruck nicht.
d Es ist schwierig, Milchprodukte zu meiden.
e Wir essen viele Kohlenhydrate, um Energie zu bekommen.
f Ich kann keine Erdbeeren essen, ohne mich krank zu fühlen.

➤ Object pronouns in the accusative

6 **Rewrite these sentences replacing the noun in brackets with the correct object pronoun.**
- Practice of using object pronouns.

Answers:

a ihn; **b** sie; **c** sie; **d** es; **e** es

7 **Unjumble these sentences with object pronouns.**
- Question 4 focuses on object pronouns

a Er isst sie jeden Tag.
b Ich backe sie zu Weihnachten.
c Mein Bruder hat es schon gegessen.
d Wir fahren euch hin.
e Ihr habt es nie getrunken?

Kompetenzen

Seite 72

Planner

➤ Objectives

- Summarising what you have learnt

➤ Resources

Students' Book, page 72
Exam Skills Workbooks, page 39
Activity Sheet 27
Resources and Planning OxBox CD-ROM

➤ Skills

- Getting an overview when reading
- Extracting relevant information
- Using cognates
- Listening for gist and detail
- Listening for key opinions and phrases

➤ PLTS

Question 3, Reading: Independent enquirers/ Reflective learners/Self-managers
Question 3, Listening: Independent enquirers/ Reflective learners/Self-managers

In this unit, students have learnt how to...

➤ Beim Lesen

1 **Get an overview when reading.**
- Students read the passage on page 177, and describe what it is about in five words or fewer.

2 **Extract the information they require.**
- Students look at each of the questions listed and jot down the sort of information they would look for in a comprehension text.

3 **Use cognates to help them.**

PLTS
- Students find at least ten examples of German words which are related closely to English.
- This encourages students to reflect upon what they have learnt and build on this. It covers the Independent enquirers, Reflective learners and Self-managers groups of skills from the framework of personal, learning and thinking skills.

➤ Beim Hören

1 **Listen for gist.**
- Students work with a partner. Their partner reads the second reading passage on page 178 and they try to summarise it in as few words as possible.

2 **Listen for detail.**
- Provide students with copies of transcripts so that they can practise picking out single words or phrases.

3 **Listen for key opinions and phrases.**

PLTS
- Students find as many ways of expressing opinions as they can in this unit.
- This activity encourages students to reflect upon what they have learnt and build on this. It covers the Independent enquirers, Reflective learners and Self-managers groups of skills from the framework of personal, learning and thinking skills.

Szenario

Planner

➤ Objectives
- Producing a brochure about healthy eating
- Preparing and delivering a presentation about an eating/drinking disorder

➤ Resources
Students' Book, page 73
Exam Skills Workbooks, pages 36–37
Assessment Sheets 9–16
Resources and Planning OxBox CD-ROM

➤ Skills
- Writing practice
- Speaking practice

➤ PLTS
Question 1, Writing: Team workers/Creative thinkers/Reflective learners/Effective participators
Question 2, Speaking: Independent enquirers/Reflective learners/Self-managers

➤ Zum Schreiben

In this section, students produce a brochure about healthy eating, using all the material in this unit. Encourage them to use the Internet for ideas.

It is possible for students to obtain GCSE grades A–F depending on their ability:
Grade F students write a short plan using simple sentences and communicate some information.
Grade C students include a variety of structures which may include different tenses or time frames. They communicate information and express personal opinions.
Grade A students include a variety of vocabulary, structures and verb tenses. They convey information, narrate events and express and explain ideas and points of view.

1 Work in groups to decide what healthy eating involves, and make a list to be included in the brochure.
- This activity serves as an introduction to the task.
- It encourages students to collaborate with others, think imaginatively, to reflect upon what they have learnt to acheive goals and to negotiate. It covers the Team workers, Creative thinkers, Reflective learners and Effective participators groups of skills from the framework of personal, learning and thinking skills.

PLTS

2 Make up questions for the Frequently Asked Questions section of the brochure and write short replies.
- Students think in more detail about the task.

3 Interview each other about your own eating habits, write up the interviews and include them in the brochure.
- Students use the ideas and vocabulary from activities 1, 2 and 3 to describe their own eating habits. Remind them to keep in mind the grammar points covered in the unit when writing up their interviews. This is an ideal assessment opportunity.

➤ Zum Sprechen

In this section, students will prepare and deliver a presentation about an eating disorder. Encourage them to use the Internet for research and to rehearse their material thoroughly. Suggest recording it to help improve their accent and intonation. This could be done using the record/playback facility on the OxBox CD-ROM.

It is possible for students to obtain GCSE grades A–F depending on their ability and they are marked on Communication, Quality of language and Pronunciation and intonation:
Grade F students communicate a limited number of ideas, expressing simple opinions. A few phrases or short sentences are accurate enough to be recognisable. There are very few instances of clear pronunciation and intonation.
Grade C students communicate the essential elements, expressing points of view. They can respond to some unpredictable questions. They use straightforward vocabulary and structures which may contain different tenses or time frames. Pronunciation and intonation is generally accurate.
Grade A students use relevant information to develop and justify individual ideas and points of view. There is no hesitation and they are able to respond to unpredictable questions. They use a wide range of clause types, vocabulary and structures accurately. The presentation is fluent and coherent with just minor errors. Pronunciation and intonation is very accurate with a few minor slips.

1 In a group, brainstorm ideas to help you choose the eating problem you are going to talk about.
- This activity serves as an introduction to the task. Encourage students to use the ideas presented in the unit for support.

2 **In pairs, read through the articles in this unit and then do your own research. Search for general information about allergies and problems on the Internet, e.g. on www.wikipedia.de.**

PLTS

- Students think in more detail about the task.
- This activity encourages students to plan and carry out research and evaluate information, to use what they have learnt to achieve goals and to organise time and resources effectively. It covers the Independent enquirers, Reflective learners and Self-managers groups of skills from the framework of personal, learning and thinking skills.

3 **Prepare your presentation well. Think carefully about what you want to say. Focus on the three main areas listed. You might want to prepare your presentation using PowerPoint and make handouts. Let your classmates know the subject of your talk in advance so that they can prepare questions to ask in German.**

- Students use the work they have done in activities 1 and 2 to prepare a presentation.

4 **Now it's time for the presentation itself. Rehearse exactly what you want to say before you begin. Give your presentation and answer any questions at the end. Your teacher may grade you using exam criteria.**

- Students finally present to the class and answer any questions. Encourage them to use ICT to enhance their presentation. This activity is an ideal assessment opportunity.

Vokabeln

Seite 74

Planner

➤ **Resources**
Students' Book, page 74
Activity Sheet 28

This page provides a summary of the key language covered in each spread of this unit. It could be used as a handy reference for students as they work through the unit. Alternatively, students could use its clear German–English format when learning vocabulary.

Lesen

Seiten 177–178

Planner

➤ **Objectives**
- To encourage independent reading and develop reading strategies
- To provide alternative class and homework material

Pages 177–178 provide magazine-style reading texts in the context of the unit.

➤ **Resources**
Students' Book, pages 177–178

➤ **Skills**
- Reading practice

➤ **PLTS**
Question 1 (parts 1 and 2): Reflective learners/Self-managers

Lesen A: Was essen die Stars?

1 Lies den Text und beantworte die folgenden Fragen auf Englisch.

4–6 PLTS

- Students read the text and answer the questions.
- This activity encourages students to use what they have learnt to achieve goals. It covers the Reflective learners and Self-managers groups of skills from the framework of personal, learning and thinking skills.

Answers:

Peter:
a He is on the piste for hours at a time; **b** two chocolate bars and two bottles of Coke; **c** meat with vegetables and potatoes; **d** fat

Hanne:
e she must stay slim for concerts and television; **f** chocolate; **g** crispbread, salad, vegetables, fruit; **h** she ate praline chocolates and felt ill

2 Was bedeuten diese Wörter auf Englisch?
- Students translate the German words into English.

Answers:

a a bar; **b** only; **c** slim; **d** ill; **e** little; **f** to expect

3 Und du? Wie ist deine Ernährung? Isst du gesund?
- Students think about their own diet.

Lesen B: Ernährung für Sportler

1 Lies den Artikel und beantworte die Fragen auf Englisch.

4–6 PLTS

- Students read the text and answer the questions.
- This activity encourages students to use what they have learnt to achieve goals. It covers the Reflective learners and Self-managers groups of skills from the framework of personal, learning and thinking skills.

Answers:

a Sportspeople need more and specialised foods.
b The blood flows better, the heart pumps more strongly, breathing gets quicker.
c They don't need much more food than any normal person.
d A few rolls with cheese or curry sausages.
e The right type of food – lots of carbohydrates, good quality protein, plenty of vitamins, not much fat and sufficient liquid.

2 Verbinde die deutschen und englischen Wörter.
- Students match the German and English words.

Answers:

1 i; **2** g; **3** j; **4** a; **5** c; **6** h; **7** b; **8** l; **9** k; **10** d; **11** f; **12** e

Unit 3A: Freizeit	Overview grid			
Spread	**Contexts and objectives**	**Skills**	**Grammar**	**Vocabulary**
pages 76–77 **Wie man sich mit Freunden verabredet**	• Making arrangements with friends	• Using tone • Making suggestions	• The present tense to talk about the future	*der Treffpunkt, erlauben; verbieten; vorhaben; vorschlagen; leider; schade*
pages 78–79 **Wie man einkaufen geht**	• Buying clothes in German	• Predicting the answers	• Dative pronouns	*das Geschenk; die Quittung; der Schmuck; die Umkleidekabine anprobieren; brauchen; einladen; sich entscheiden; sich interessieren; umtauschen; zahlen; teuer*
pages 80–81 **Wie man seine Freizeit plant**	• Discussing going out, and buying tickets	• Asking for information	• The future tense	*die Ausstellung; die Einladung; der Eintritt; die Ermäßigung; der/ die Erwachsene; die Mannschaft; das Theaterstück; die Vorstellung aufmachen; zumachen insgesamt; ausverkauft*
pages 82–83 **Wie man über das Internet spricht**	• Discussing the Internet	• Using conjunctions • Giving examples	• The imperfect tense	*das Internet; die Sache benutzen; buchen; verbringen einfach; gefährlich; vorsichtig trotzdem; ungefähr*
pages 84–85 **Wie man Feste feiert**	• Discussing festivals in Germany	• Listening	• Word order with the perfect and future tenses	*das Fest feiern; zelten*
pages 86–87 **Aktive Grammatik**	• Grammar		• The present tense of irregular verbs • Imperfect tense • Dative pronouns • The future tense	
page 88 **Kompetenzen**	• Summarising what you have learnt	• Using intonation both to understand what you hear and to add variety to what you say • Using tone to work out if something is a question or a statement • Listening out for linking words • Asking questions in a variety of different ways • Adding examples to extend your answers and make what you say more interesting		
page 89 **Szenario**	• Responding to an e-mail from a German exchange partner • Surveying classmates about how they use computers and presenting the results in an oral report	• Writing practice • Speaking practice		
page 90 **Vokabeln**	• Key language from the unit			
pages 179–180 **Lesen**	• The Internet • Festivals • To encourage independent reading and develop reading strategies • To provide alternative class and homework material for students who finish other activities quickly	• Reading practice		

3A Freizeit

Unit Objectives

Contexts and cultural focus: celebrations/parties; the Internet
Skills focus: asking questions and making suggestions; using tone to vary your speech; giving examples to illustrate your point; using tone to help your understanding; making sure you understand linking words; predicting what the correct answers will be
Grammar: irregular verbs in the present tense; the imperfect tense; dative pronouns; the future tense

Controlled assessment opportunities

Speaking: Students' Book, page 77, activity 6
Writing: Students' Book, page 79, activity 7
Writing: Students' Book, page 81, activity 5
Speaking: Students' Book, page 83, activity 4b
Writing: Students' Book, page 85, activity 5
Writing: Students' Book, page 89, Zum Schreiben, activity 2
Speaking: Students' Book, page 89, Zum Sprechen, activity 3

See also ***GCSE German for OCR Assessment OxBox CD-ROM.***

An introduction to the unit Seite 75

- *Aim*: To introduce the themes of the unit.
- The opening spread of each unit is styled as the contents page of a teenage magazine. Illustrations, captions and skills summaries provide a preview of what is to come:

	Students' Book
Weißt du schon, wie man sich mit Freunden verabredet?	pages 76–77
Weißt du schon, wie man einkaufen geht?	pages 78–79
Weißt du schon, wie man seine Freizeit plant	pages 80–81
Weißt du schon, wie man über das Internet spricht?	pages 82–83
Weißt du schon, wie man Feste feiert?	pages 84–85

- Allow time for students to read the questions and cross-refer to the relevant pages of the Students' Book. They could do this individually or in pairs/groups, followed by whole-class discussion.
- This spread also provides an opportunity for students to recap on familiar language. Ask them to think about language they already know that might be useful when working on the themes of the unit.
- At the end of work on Unit 3A:
  - If time permits, ask students to devise a replacement opening spread. What do they think should be on it, in terms of pictures, captions, etc.? What would they change/keep the same, and why? Ask them to imagine it is the contents page of a teenage magazine: what sort of captions and pictures do they feel would attract people to buy the magazine? This sort of activity encourages students to think about features of a text that make it suitable for a particular audience or purpose.
  - Allow time for students to return to this opening spread to answer the questions, review what they have learned and reflect on areas for improvement. What did they find difficult, interesting, etc.? What do they think are the most important things they have learned in this unit?

Wie man sich mit Freunden verabredet

Seiten 76–77

Planner

➤ Objectives
- Making arrangements with friends

➤ Resources
Students' Book, pages 76–77
CD 2, tracks 1–3
Activity Sheets 29–31

➤ Key language
der Treffpunkt, erlauben; verbieten; vorhaben; vorschlagen; leider, schade

➤ Skills
- Using tone
- Making suggestions

➤ Grammar
- Using the present tense to talk about the future

➤ PLTS
Question 4: Creative thinkers/Reflective learners/Team workers
Question 6: Creative thinkers/Reflective learners/Team workers/Effective participators

➤ Starters
- Students brainstorm places in German where young people might arrange to go and activities that they might do, e.g. *ins Kino gehen.* Challenge students to write a couple of simple sentences using this vocabulary e.g. *Ich will ins Kino gehen.* Keep the list of vocabulary to use in the next starter activity.
- Display the phrases, *Hast du Lust . . .? Wie wäre es mit . . .? Ich habe nichts vor. Was läuft . . .? Ich habe keine Ahnung. Wann treffen wir uns? Sagen wir mal . . ., leider, Möchtest du mitkommen? Wie schade!* in one column and the English translations for these in a second column. Students race against one another to match the German with the English. They then work with a partner to use some of these phrases in sentences. Display the vocabulary from starter activity 1 for support, e.g.
  Partner A: *Ich will ins Kino gehen. Möchtest du mitkommen?*
  Partner B: *Ja. Ich habe nichts vor. . .*
- Go round the class asking students, *Wir gehen ins Kino/in die Eisbahn, etc. Wann und wo treffen wir uns?* Students reply with an appropriate time and place.

➤ Plenaries
- Display some vocabulary from the spread and challenge students to work with a partner to act out a role-play using this vocabulary.
- Display some sentences from the spread. To practice using tone to help with understanding, choose a student to read out the sentence sadly, angrily, etc. The class guesses if they are sad, angry, etc.
- Students work in pairs. One imagines that they are inviting a celebrity of their choice to be the star guest the school fete. He/She prepares a list of reasons why he/she should come. The other pretends to be the celebrity and prepares a list of reasons why he/she can't make it. The first student tries to persuade the celebrity to try to fit it in.

1a Hör zu und lies mit.
- Students listen to and read the conversation between Thomas and Katja.

CD 2, track 1 **Seite 76, Übung 1a**

Thomas: Hallo, Katja. Hier Thomas. Wie geht's?
Katja: Hi, Thomas. Was gibt's Neues?
Thomas: Hast du Lust, morgen Abend ins Kino zu gehen?
Katja: Es tut mir Leid, Thomas. Meine Großeltern kommen morgen zu Besuch und ich kann nicht. Wie wäre es mit Samstag?
Thomas: Ach nein, am Samstag muss ich leider arbeiten. Aber am Sonntag habe ich Zeit.
Katja: Ja, am Sonntag habe ich auch nichts vor. Also gehen wir am Sonntag. Was läuft? Ich habe keine Ahnung!
Thomas: Es gibt einen Actionfilm, ‚Hitman 3' und einen Horrorfilm, ‚Der Schatten der Bestie'.
Katja: Ich sehe lieber Actionfilme – sehen wir ‚Hitman 3'an? Wann treffen wir uns?
Thomas: Der Film beginnt um 19.30. Also treffen wir uns um 19.15 vor dem Kino.
Katja: Wie wäre es mit ein bisschen früher? Sagen wir mal um 18.30 Uhr? Dann können wir vorher noch ins Eiscafé gehen.
Thomas: Tolle Idee!
Katja: Und nächsten Samstag gehe ich auf Tanjas Party. Möchtest du mitkommen?
Thomas: Nein, leider muss ich dann wieder arbeiten.
Katja: Wie schade! Aber bis Sonntag. Tschüs!

1b Finde die deutschen Ausdrücke im Text.

- Students read through the conversation again, to find the German for the English phrases listed.

4–6

Answers:

a Hast du Lust ...? **b** Wie wäre es mit ...? **c** Ich habe nichts vor. **d** Was läuft ...? **e** Ich habe keine Ahnung. **f** Wann treffen wir uns? **g** Sagen wir mal ...; **h** leider; **i** Möchtest du mitkommen? **j** Wie schade!

1c Beantworte die Fragen auf Deutsch.

- Students read the conversation once again and, to check that they have fully understood it, they answer the questions in German.

4–6

Answers:

a Er will ins Kino gehen.
b Ihre Großeltern kommen zu Besuch.
c Er musst arbeiten.
d einen Actionfilm, ‚Hitman 3' und einen Horrorfilm, ‚Der Schatten der Bestie'
e Sie will ins Eiscafé gehen.
f Sie geht auf Tanjas Party.

2 Finde die passenden Bilder für die Sätze.

- This activity introduces excuses for not going out.
- Students match the excuses and the pictures.

4–6

Answers:

a 1; **b** 3; **c** 2; **d** 4; **e** 5; **f** 6

3a Hör gut zu und notiere Einzelheiten.

- Students listen to the conversations.
- They then copy the table into their exercise books and fill it in.

4–6

CD 2, track 2 **Seite 77, Übung 3a**

1
Sonia: Hallo, Daniel. Hast du am Montag was vor? Ich gehe auf die Eisbahn. Du gehst auch gern dahin, nicht wahr? Kommst du mit?
Daniel: Ich möchte schon, aber ich bin am Montag leider schon verabredet.
Sonia: Wie schade!

2
Sven: Hi, Elke! Wie geht's? Ich gehe am Freitagabend auf ein tolles Konzert von „Toter Tintenfisch". Hast du Lust, mitzukommen?
Elke: Ja gerne – ich liebe diese Band. Wann und wo treffen wir uns?
Sven: Das Konzert ist im Stadion und beginnt um 20 Uhr. Treffen wir uns um 19.30 an der U-Bahn-Station vor dem Stadion?
Elke: Super! Bis dann.

Answers:

	Suggestion	Yes/no? Excuse	When?	Where?
1	go to icerink	no: already got something on	Monday	
2	go to a great concert	yes	begins at 8pm; meet at 7.30pm	at the underground station in front of the stadium

3b Hör dir diese beiden Gespräche an und finde die Satzhälften, die zusammenpassen.

- Following on from 3a, students listen to two more conversations about making arrangements.
- They then match the sentence halves.

4–6

CD 2, track 3 **Seite 77, Übung 3b**

1
Verena: Hi, Ingo. Hier ist Verena. Ich gehe morgen schwimmen. Kommst du mit?
Ingo: Wann gehst du?
Verena: Nach der Schule um 14 Uhr.
Ingo: Ich muss zuerst Hausaufgaben machen. Wie wäre es mit ein bisschen später?
Verena: Okay, dann gehen wir um 16 Uhr, ja?
Ingo: Prima. Wo treffen wir uns?
Verena: An der Bushaltestelle am Marktplatz.
Ingo: Super – darf ich Markus auch einladen? Er geht auch gern schwimmen und möchte sicher mitkommen.
Verena: Das ist kein Problem aber ich kenne Markus nicht. Wer ist das?
Ingo: Markus ist mein Cousin und gerade bei uns zu Besuch.
Verena: Ja, super. Ich freue mich.
Ingo: Ich mich auch. Bis dann, Verena. Tschüs.

2
Karsten: Hallo, Susi: Hast du am Samstagabend was vor? Ich gehe mit Freunden auf ein Fußballspiel. Das ist dein Lieblingssport, nicht wahr? Kommst du mit?
Susi: Ich möchte gern, Karsten, aber meine Eltern erlauben das nicht, und ich habe sowieso kein Geld für die Karten.
Karsten: Ach, wie schade. Wir können ja was anderes zusammen machen. Hast du einen Vorschlag?
Susi: Am Montag bekomme ich mein Taschengeld. Wir könnten dann vielleicht auf die Eisbahn gehen.
Karsten: Ah, Susi, es tut mir Leid, aber ich kann nicht Schlittschuh laufen. Ich war einmal auf der Eisbahn und es war eine Katastrophe. Aber ich spiele gern Tennis – du doch auch, oder?
Susi: Ja, sehr gern. Und ich bin Mitglied im Tennisklub, also das kostet nichts.
Karsten: Prima, dann treffen wir uns am Dienstag nach der Schule und spielen zusammen Tennis.
Susi: Okay – bis dann!

Answers:

Verena und Ingo: **1** b; **2** d; **3** a; **4** c
Karsten und Susi: **1** b; **2** a; **3** f; **4** g; **5** c; **6** d; **7** e

4 Partnerarbeit. Kommst du mit? A möchte B einladen, aber B kann nicht. B ↔ A. Benutzt die Vokabeln aus Übung 1b.

- Read the *Tipp* section on using intonation to help understanding. If necessary, listen to the recording from activities 3a and 3b again.
- Students work in pairs. Partner A starts by inviting partner B to go somewhere. Partner B can't and gives an excuse. They then swap roles.
- This activity encourages students to think creatively, whilst communicating previous learning and to work confidently with others. It covers the Creative thinkers, Reflective learners and Team workers groups of skills from the framework of personal, learning and thinking skills.

A29 A31 Activity Sheet 29, activity 1 and Activity Sheet 31 provide further practice of making arrangements with friends.

5 Read the email and write a reply. Use the ideas given in either A or B.

- This activity draws together what students have learnt in this spread.
- Encourage students to think creatively and to use the vocabulary and structures from previous activities in their reply.

6 Role-play. Work in pairs to create dialogues between two friends discussing party invitations. Record your dialogues on OxBox.

- Students work with a partner. Encourage them to use the vocabulary and the structures presented on these pages. This is an ideal assessment opportunity.
- This activity encourages students to think creatively, generating and exploring ideas whilst communicating previous learning and to work confidently and negotiate with others. It covers the Creative thinkers, Reflective learners, Team workers and Effective participators groups of skills from the framework of personal, learning and thinking skills.

Success criteria:

- ideas communicated
- pronunciation and intonation and fluency
- range of vocabulary and structures used
- tenses or time frames used

Wie man einkaufen geht

Seiten 78–79

Planner

➤ Objectives

- Buying clothes and presents in German

➤ Resources

Students' Book, pages 78–79
CD 2, tracks 4–7
Grammar Workbook, page 46
Activity Sheet 32

➤ Key language

das Geschenk; die Quittung; der Schmuck; die Umkleidekabine; anprobieren; brauchen; einladen; sich entscheiden; sich interessieren; umtauschen; zahlen
teuer

➤ Skills

- Predicting the answers

➤ Grammar

- Dative pronouns

➤ PLTS

Question 6: Creative thinkers/Reflective learners/Team workers/Self-managers
Question 7: Creative thinkers/Reflective learners/Self-managers

➤ Starters

- Students brainstorm items people might buy for themselves or as a present for somebody, e.g. *ein T-shirt, ein Handy*. They then think of things that could be wrong with these items, e.g. *es funktioniert nicht*. Compile a list and keep it to use later.
- Divide the class into small groups. Display the phrases: *Ich probiere es an. Die Farbe gefällt mir nicht. Die Umkleidekabine ist in der Ecke. Er steht mir sehr gut. Ich nehme ihn. Es passt mir nicht. Es ist zu eng.* Next to these, display possible questions e.g. *Wie findest du den Rock? Nimmst du auch das T-shirt?* Groups match the questions with the answers. Point out that there could be more than one possible answer for each question. Remind them that they must look at gender: *Er steht mir sehr gut* couldn't be the answer if referring to a T-shirt.
- Ask students if they can tell you when dative pronouns would be used. Explain that these are used to convey the idea of 'to someone' and that you will study these in this spread.

➤ Plenaries

- Display dative pronouns, e.g. *mir, dir, ihm, ihr, ihm, uns, euch, ihnen, Ihnen*. Challenge students to use each of these in a sentence on the theme of the spread. Compare sentences as a class.
- Display the list from starter activity 1. Students work in pairs to create dialogues using the items and problems listed. They decide on their own solutions to the problems. Choose volunteers to act out their dialogue in front of the class.
- As a class, have a quick look through some of the dialogues from the spread (read through the transcripts to remind students of the listening texts). Display some of the useful phrases and vocabulary. The class then creates a dialogue along the same lines. You start, e.g.
  Teacher: *Ich brauche ein Geschenk für Anja.*
  Student 1: *Gehen wir zu Kaufhof. Dort findet man immer alles.*
  Student 2: *Ich glaube, Anja hört gern Musik.*

1a Hör gut zu und lies mit.

4–6

- As an introduction to the spread, students listen to and read the conversation.

CD 2, track 4 **Seite 78, Übung 1a**

Katja:	Tanja gibt eine Party am Wochenende und ich brauche etwas Neues.
Anke:	Ich weiß – sie lädt die ganze Klasse ein und ich gehe auch hin.
Katja:	Prima. Was ziehst du an?
Anke:	Meine neuen Jeans, und ich möchte ein neues T-Shirt kaufen.
Katja:	Siehst du das T-Shirt dort drüben? Es ist echt toll.
Anke:	Stimmt! Ich probiere es an. Siehst du etwas, was dir gefällt?
Katja:	Der Rock ist schön, aber die Farbe gefällt mir nicht. Entschuldigen Sie, haben Sie diesen Rock in Schwarz?
Verkäuferin:	In welcher Größe?
Katja:	Größe 36.
Verkäuferin:	Hier bitte. Die Umkleidekabine ist in der Ecke…
Anke:	Wie findest du den Rock, Katja?
Katja:	Super – er steht mir sehr gut. Ich nehme ihn. Nimmst du das T-Shirt?
Anke:	Nein, es passt mir leider nicht. Es ist zu eng.
Katja:	Schade…
Verkäuferin:	Gefällt Ihnen der Rock?
Katja:	Ja, was kostet er?
Verkäuferin:	25 Euro. Zahlen Sie bitte an der Kasse…
Anke:	Katja, ich muss auch noch ein Geburtstagesgeschenk für Tanja kaufen, aber ich habe keine Ahnung was. Hast du eine Idee?
Katja:	Tanja trägt gern Schmuck. Du könntest Ohrringe für sie kaufen.
Anke:	Gute Idee!

1b Finde die deutschen Ausdrücke im Text.

- Students read the conversation again and find the German for the English words listed.

4–6

Answers:

a Ich probiere es an. **b** Die Farbe gefällt mir nicht. **c** Die Umkleidekabine ist in der Ecke. **d** Er steht mir sehr gut. **e** Ich nehme ihn. **f** Es passt mir nicht. **g** Es ist zu eng.

1c Beantworte die Fragen auf Deutsch.

- Students read the conversation once more and answer questions in German.

4–6

Answers:

a Weil Tanja am Wochenende eine Party gibt.
b Sie zieht ihre neuen Jeans.
c Sie möchte ein neues T-shirt kaufen.
d Weil die Farbe ihr nicht gefällt.
e Sie möchte Schwarz.
f Es passt ihr nicht. Es ist zu eng.
g Sie kauft Ohrringe für Tanja.
h Weil Tanja gern Schmuck trägt.

1d Partnerarbeit. Macht Dialoge beim Einkaufen. A ist der Kunde/die Kundin. B ist der Verkäufer/die Verkäuferin. Spielt die Dialoge unten. B ↔ A.

4–9

- Students act out shopping scenarios a–d.
- Encourage them to use vocabulary and structures from the conversation in activity 1a.

A32 Activity Sheet 32 provides further activities on buying clothes in Germany.

2a Ergänze die Sätze mit dem richtigen Dativpronomen.

- Read the *Grammatik* section on dative pronouns.
- Students then complete the sentences with the appropriate dative pronoun.

4–6

Answers:

a Ihnen; **b** dir; **c** ihm; **d** mir; **e** uns; **f** ihnen

2b Übersetze die Sätze aus Übung 2a auf Englisch.

- Students translate the sentences from 2a into English.

Answers:

4–6

a Can I help you? **b** Do the trousers fit you? **c** Does he like the T-Shirt? **d** Does the shirt suit me? **e** He showed us the photos. **f** I gave them the money.

3 Katja und Anke gehen weiter einkaufen. Hör zu und entscheide, welche Satzhälften zusammenpassen.

- Work through the *Tipp* section on listening.
- Students listen to Katja and Anke and match the sentence halves. Had they guessed any correctly?

4–6

CD 2, track 5 **Seite 79, Übung 3**

Katja:	Also, jetzt habe ich meinen Rock und du hast ein Geschenk für Tanja. Was brauchen wir noch?
Anke:	Du brauchst doch noch ein Geschenk für Tanja, oder?
Katja:	Das stimmt – gehen wir zu Kaufhof. Dort findet man immer alles.
Anke:	Gut, Kaufhof. Ich glaube, Tanja liest gern. Wie wäre es mit einem Buch?
Katja:	Das ist eine gute Idee, aber ich weiß nicht, was sie schon alles hat.
Anke:	Also dann Musik – ich glaube sie mag die *Prinzen*. Es ist ihre Lieblingsgruppe.
Katja:	Stimmt, aber die neueste CD hat sie schon. Aber hier ist ein Buch über die *Prinzen*. Das wäre dann ideal, nicht wahr?
Anke:	Tolle Idee. Brauchst du noch was?
Katja:	Ja, mein Vater hat auch bald Geburtstag und ich muss auch noch was für ihn kaufen. Er ist großer Fan von Formel 1. Siehst du ein Buch darüber?
Anke:	Ja, hier, aber es kostet 80 Euro.
Katja:	Nee, das ist viel zu teuer. Aber schau mal, hier ist eine DVD darüber. Es gibt Interviews und Geschichten über berühmte Rennfahrer.
Anke:	Das ist perfekt. Und sie kostet nur 15 Euro.
Katja:	Ich nehme sie.

Answers:

1 b; **2** f; **3** e; **4** a; **5** c; **6** d; **7** h; **8** g

4 **Welche Geschenke würdest du für deine Familie kaufen? Schreib eine Liste. Benutze Dativpronomen.**

- This consolidates what students have learnt about irregular verbs in the present tense.
- Students note down presents they would like to buy for their family, using as many irregular verbs as possible.

5a **Katja und Anke entdecken ein Problem! Hör gut zu. Was ist es?**

4–6

- Students listen to Katja and Anke and note down what the problem is.

CD 2, track 6 **Seite 79, Übung 5a**

Katja:	Ach nein Anke, sieh doch mal! Der Rock hat einen Fleck! Wir müssen zurück ins Kaufhaus.
Im Kaufhaus	
Katja:	Entschuldigen Sie. Ich habe gerade diesen Rock hier gekauft, aber er hat einen Fleck.
Verkäuferin:	Haben Sie Ihre Quittung? Ach ja, ich sehe den Fleck. Es tut mir Leid. Möchten Sie Ihr Geld zurück oder einen anderen Rock?
Katja:	Ich möchte einen anderen Rock ohne Fleck. Danke!

Answer:

Skirt has a stain on it.

5b **Welche Probleme haben diese Kunden? Füll die Tabelle aus.**

4–6

- Students listen to customers complaining. They then fill in the table.

CD 2, track 7 **Seite 79, Übung 5b**

1

Kunde:	Guten Tag. Ich habe letzte Woche dieses Handy hier gekauft, aber es funktioniert nicht.
Angestellte:	Es tut mir sehr Leid. Möchten Sie Ihr Geld zurück?
Kunde:	Nein, ich möchte ein neues Handy.
Angestellte:	Selbstverständlich.

2

Kunde:	Guten Tag. Am Samstag habe ich dieses Hemd hier gekauft, aber es hat ein Loch. Ich möchte mein Geld zurück.
Angestellte:	Es tut mir Leid. Haben Sie Ihre Quitting?
Kunde:	Leider nicht
Angestellte:	Ohne Quittung können Sie ihr Geld nicht zurückbekommen. Aber Sie können das Hemd umtauschen.
Kunde:	Okay, dann nehme ich ein neues Hemd.

3

Kunde:	Ich habe diese Hose am Wochenende hier gekauft, aber sie hat einen Fleck.
Angestellte:	Es tut mir Leid. Möchten Sie die Hose unmtauschen?
Kunde:	Nein, ich möchte mein Geld zurück. Hier ist meine Quittung.
Angestellte:	Selbstverständlich. Kein Problem.

Answers:

1 **what:** a mobile phone; **problem:** doesn't work; **solution:** have a new mobile phone
2 **what:** a shirt; **problem:** a hole in it; **solution:** exchange shirt
3 **what:** trousers; **problem:** stain on them; **solution:** money back

6 **Create a shopping dialogue with a partner. Mention the points listed.**

4–9

PLTS

- This activity draws together what students have learnt in the spread.
- It encourages students to generate and explore ideas, to communicate previous learning and to work confidently with others to work towards goals. It covers the Creative thinkers, Reflective learners, Team workers and Self-managers groups of skills from the framework of personal, learning and thinking skills.

7 **Write an e-mail to a friend suggesting a shopping trip. Include the points listed.**

4–9

PLTS

- This activity draws together what students have covered in the spread. This is an ideal assessment opportunity.
- This encourages students to generate and explore ideas, to communicate previous learning and to work towards goals. It covers the Creative thinkers, Reflective learners and Self-managers groups of skills from the framework of personal, learning and thinking skills.

Success criteria:

- amount of information communicated
- variety of vocabulary and structures used
- number of personal opinions given

Wie man seine Freizeit plant

Seiten 80–81

Planner

➤ Objectives
- Discussing going out, and buying tickets

➤ Resources
Students' Book, pages 80–81
CD 2, tracks 8–9
Grammar Workbook, page 56
Activity Sheet 31

➤ Key language
die Ausstellung; die Einladung; der Eintritt; die Ermäßigung; der/die Erwachsene; die Mannschaft; das Theaterstück; die Vorstellung
aufmachen; zumachen; insgesamt; ausverkauft

➤ Skills
- Asking for information

➤ Grammar
- Future tense

➤ PLTS
Question 5: Independent enquirers/Creative thinkers/Reflective learners/Self-managers
Question 6: Independent enquirers/Creative thinkers/Reflective learners/Team workers/Effective participators

➤ Starters
- Brainstorm in German useful words for making plans/asking for information. Make a list of these to use in Starter activity 2.
- Call out a place or event that you would need a ticket to go to, e.g. *Konzert*. Students use this in a sentence in keeping with the theme of the spread, e.g. *Ich möchte Karten für das Konzert von den Ärzten am 22. Oktober.*
- Brainstorm in German possible problems when buying tickets, e.g. *es ist ausverkauft*.

➤ Plenaries
- Display some key words and phrases from the spread. Students work in pairs to use these words to write a short dialogue on the topic of buying tickets.
- Students write sentences on the theme of the spread. They swap these with a partner who reads them aloud.
- Students create a dialogue as a class, e.g.
  Teacher: *Guten Abend. Hier die Stadthalle.*
  Student 1: *Guten Abend. Ich möchte…*
  Student 2: *zwei Karten für Harry Potter…*
  Student 3: *am 27. Januar.*
  Students should try to incorporate structures and vocabulary from the spread.

1a Hör gut zu und lies mit.

4–6

- As an introduction to the spread, students listen to and read the conversations about buying tickets.

CD 2, track 8 — **Seite 80, Übung 1a**

Jan ruft in der Konzerthalle an

Angestellte:	Guten Abend. Hier Stadthalle.
Jan:	Guten Abend. Ich möchte Karten für das Konzert von den *Ärzten* am 22. Oktober.
Angestellte:	Es tut mir Leid, das Konzert am 22. ist schon ausverkauft, aber ich habe noch Karten für den 23.
Jan:	Gut, das geht.
Angestellte:	Wie viele Karten wollen Sie?
Jan:	Ich komme mit zwei Freunden, also drei Karten insgesamt.
Angestellte:	Wollen Sie Karten zu 70 Euro?
Jan:	Nein, das ist zu teuer. Haben Sie billigere Karten?
Angestellte:	Ja, wir haben auch Karten zu 50 Euro.
Jan:	Prima, die nehme ich.

Jutta ruft das Kino an

Jutta:	Guten Abend. Ich möchte zwei Karten für „Harry Potter" morgen Abend reservieren. Wann fängt der Film an?
Angestellte:	Die erste Vorstellung ist um 19 Uhr.
Jutta:	Was kosten die Karten?
Angestellte:	12 Euro.
Jutta:	Gibt es eine Ermäßigung für Schüler?
Angestellte:	Nicht am Wochenende.
Jutta:	Das ist schade, aber ich nehme die Karten trotzdem.

1b Ergänze die Sätze mit Wörtern aus dem Kasten unten.

- Students read the conversations again and fill in the gaps with the words from the box.

4–6

Answers:

a Karten; **b** Ärzte; **c** billigeren; **d** beginnt; **e** teuer; **f** billiger

2 Hör gut zu und füll die Tabelle aus.

- Students listen and fill in the table.

4–6

CD 2, track 9 **Seite 80, Übung 2**

1
– Guten Abend. Kann ich Ihnen helfen?
– Ja, ich möchte Karten für das Theaterstück am Freitag.
– Es tut mir Leid, am Freitag ist es ausverkauft, aber ich habe Karten für Donnerstag.
– Gut, ich nehme zwei Karten zu zwanzig Euro, bitte.

2
– Guten Tag, ich möchte vier Karten für das Fußballspiel am Samstag.
– Gerne, wie ist die Nummer Ihrer Kreditkarte?
– Oh, ich habe keine Kreditkarte.
– Dann können Sie telefonisch leider keine Karten kaufen. Aber Sie können Karten hier am Stadion kaufen.
– Gut, dann komme ich vorbei.

3
– Guten Tag, ich möchte zwei Karten für das Konzert am Samstag.
– Am Samstag habe ich nur Karten zu 60 Euro.
– Nein, die sind zu teuer. Wann haben Sie billigere Karten?
– Ich habe für Montag Karten zu 25 Euro.
– Prima! Ich nehme sie.

Answers:

What?	Problem?	Solution?
theatre tickets	Friday is sold out	buy tickets for Thursday
four tickets for the football game	can't buy tickets over the phone without a credit card	buy tickets at the stadium
two tickets for the concert	Only 60-euro tickets for Saturday	buy 25-euro tickets for Monday

3a Lies die Anzeigen und beantworte die Fragen.

- Students read the announcements.
- They then answer the questions.

Answers:

4–6

A
a Fußballbundesliga **b** Hamburg St. Pauli und SVR Mainz spielen. **c** Das Spiel beginnt um 15 Uhr. **d** Es kostet 30 Euro oder 20 Euro für Jugendliche.
B
a J. W. von Goethe hat das Theaterstück geschrieben. **b** Man kann Michael Timm in der Hauptrolle sehen. **c** Man kann das Stück sonntags nicht sehen.
C
a 8.00; **b** 21.00; **c** Er zahlt 2 Euro 50
D
a Man kann Puppen und Spielzeuge aus den letzten 50 Jahren sehen. **b** Es ist Kostenlose für alle Kinder. **c** Sie sollten mit zwei Kinder in die Ausstellung gehen.

3b Wie sagt man auf Deutsch…?

- Students translate the words into German.

Answers:

a geöffnet; **b** Eintritt; **c** Vorstellung; **d** Täglich; **e** außer

3c Wohin möchtest du gehen und warum? Mit wem? Was wirst du machen? Schreib ein paar Sätze.

- Students look at the four announcements from 3a again and write a couple of sentences saying which of the places/events they would like to go to, with who and why.

4–6

A31 Further activities on going out and buying tickets are provided on Activity Sheet 31.

4a Partnerarbeit. Was sind eure Pläne für das Wochenende? Fragt einander gegenseitig.

- Students work with a partner to discuss their plans for the weekend.

4–9

4b Schreib Sätze, um deine Pläne und die Pläne von deinem Partner/deiner Partnerin zu beschreiben.

- Students now write sentences describing their partner's plans for the weekend.

4–9

5 You receive this e-mail from a friend, but you'd like to find out more before you decide whether to go to the concert with him.

- This activity draws together what students have learnt in the spread. This is an ideal assessment opportunity.
- This encourages students to identify questions to answer, to generate and explore ideas, to set goals with success criteria for their development and to work towards goals. It covers the Independent enquirers, Creative thinkers, Reflective learners and Self-managers groups of skills from the framework of personal, learning and thinking skills.

4–9

PLTS

Success criteria:

- amount of information communicated
- variety of vocabulary, structures and questions used
- number of personal opinions given

6 **Work in pairs. You're planning an evening out with a friend and need to decide where to go. A has information about a concert and a disco. B has information about a play at the theatre and the leisure centre. Ask each other questions about the different options and make a decision Use the future tense to say what action you will take.**

- This activity draws together what students have learnt in this spread.

4–9

PLTS

- It encourages students to explore issues or problems from different perspectives and to explore different possibilities. It also encourages them to communicate previous learning, to work confidently with and to negotiate with others to reach agreements. It covers the Independent enquirers, Creative thinkers, Reflective learners, Team workers and Effective participators groups of skills from the framework of personal, learning and thinking skills.

Wie man über das Internet spricht

Seiten 82–83

Planner

➤ **Objectives**
- Discussing the Internet

➤ **Resources**

Students' Book, pages 82–83
CD 2, track 10
Grammar Workbook, page 48
Activity Sheet 30

➤ **Key language**

das Internet; die Sache; benutzen; buchen; verbringen; einfach; gefährlich; vorsichtig; trotzdem; ungefähr

➤ **Skills**
- Using conjunctions
- Giving examples

➤ **Grammar**
- The imperfect tense

➤ **PLTS**

Question 4a: Creative thinkers/Reflective learners/Team workers/Self-managers/Effective participators
Question 5: Creative thinkers/Reflective learners/Self-managers

➤ **Starters**
- Display a list of German words for things you can do or buy on the Internet. Next to these display the English translations jumbled up. Students have a fixed amount of time to match them up. Check the answers as a class.
- Go round the class, asking students: *Was hast du diese Woche schon im Internet gemacht?* Display the list from starter activity 1 for support, but explain to students that they must answer in full sentences, e.g. *Ich habe meine E-Mails gelesen.* What did most students do?
- Students brainstorm linking words that they have seen in the spread, e.g. *trotzdem, aber*. Display these. Also display pairs of sentences and ask students to link each these using a different linking word each time. Compare answers as a class.

➤ **Plenaries**
- Display a few words and phrases from the spread and challenge students to use them all in a short paragraph based on the themes of the spread. Confident students present their paragraph to the class.
- Create a survey using the questions from activity 4a:
  - *Hast du zu Hause Internet?*
  - *Wozu benutzt du das Internet?*
  - *Was hast du letzte Woche im Internet gemacht?*
  - *Hast du schon im Internet eingekauft? Was?*
  - *Wie findest du das Internet?*

  Record the results in a graph to display in the classroom.
- Students work in pairs to prepare and perform a role-play. Student A loves the Internet; student B hates it. Each tries to persuade the other that they are right, giving reasons why they find the Internet good/bad.

1a Wozu benutzen Jugendliche das Internet? Lies die Texte.

4–6

- As an introduction to the spread, students read the texts about what young people use the Internet for.

1b Wer hat das im Internet gemacht – Bernd, Carola oder Stefan?

- Students read the texts again and match the young people to the activities listed.

Answers:

4–6

a Bernd, Carola; **b** Bernd; **c** Bernd, Carola; **d** Stefan; **e** Bernd, Stefan; **f** Stefan **g** Bernd, Carola

1c Wer findet, dass es diese Probleme mit dem Internet gibt?

- Students read the text again and match each problem with the young person who mentioned it.

Answers:

4–6

a Stefan; **b** Carola; **c** Bernd

2a Hör zu. Was ist positiv und was ist negativ im Internet? Füll die Tabelle aus.

- Read the *Tipp* section as a class.
- Students listen to the recording and fill in the table with positive and negative aspects of the Internet and any linking words.

4–6

CD 2, track 10 **Seite 82, Übung 2a**

1
– Dirk, Was hältst du vom Internet?
– Es ist schon nützlich für die Schule, aber nicht alles, was man im Internet findet, ist richtig. Man muss vorsichtig sein.

2
– Sonia, was hältst du vom Internet?
– Es ist sehr gut fürs Einkaufen. Man findet Bücher und DVDs, die viel billiger sind. Trotzdem finde ich Chatseiten sehr gefährlich, besonders für Kinder.

3
– Max, was hältst du vom Internet?
– Auf der einen Seite finde ich die Spiele im Internet toll. Ich bin ein großer Fan von Computerspielen. Auf der anderen Seite zeigen manche Spiele zu viel Gewalt und das ist problematisch.

4
– Sara, was hältst du vom Internet?
– Es gibt viele tolle Sachen. E-Mail macht das Leben viel einfacher und man kann problemlos recherchieren. Aber trotz dieser positiven Aspekte gibt es Probleme. Kinder verbringen zu viel Zeit am Computer und das ist ungesund. Sie sollten mehr Sport treiben.

Answers:

	Positive	Negative	Key words
1	useful for school	not all information is correct	however
2	good for shopping; books and DVDs are much cheaper	chat rooms are very dangerous	although
3	great games on the Internet	some games are too violent	but
4	email; easy to do research	children spend too much time at the computer	despite

2b Findest du das Internet positiv oder negativ? Mit wem bist du einer Meinung – mit Dirk, Sonia, Max oder Sara? Warum? Diskutiert zu zweit.

- Students decide which of the four speakers they agree with and why.
- Encourage them to use the previous activities for ideas.

4–6

A30 Activity Sheet 30 provides further reading and writing activities on the subject of the Internet.

3a Screib Sätze mit Verben im Imperfekt.

- Students write sentences in the imperfect tense.

Answers:

a Ich schrieb viele E-Mails.
b Du arbeitetest an deiner Webseite.
c Er spielte ein neues Computerspiel.
d Ihr machtet eure Hausaufgaben.
e Wir buchten die Karten im Internet.

3b Wozu hast du diese Woche das Internet gebraucht? Schreib sätze mit diesen Verben.

- Students write their own sentences.

4a Work in groups. You're taking part in a debate that's going to be recorded for a documentary about how young people use the Internet. One person plays the presenter, and the others answer his/her questions.

- This activity draws together what students have learnt in the spread.
- It encourages students to ask questions to extend their learning, to communicate their learning and to invite feedback from others. It also encourages them to work confidently with others to work towards common goals and to try and influence others, negotiating and balancing diverse views to reach workable solutions. It covers the Creative thinkers, Reflective learners, Team workers, Self-managers and Effective participators groups of skills from the framework of personal, learning and thinking skills.

4–9

PLTS

4b At the end of the debate, the group has to decide whether they are collectively in favour of the Internet or against it. Present your conclusion to the rest of the class and explain why.

- This is an ideal assessment opportunity.
- Encourage students to use as much of the vocabulary and as many of the structures from the spread in their conclusion as possible.

4–9

Success criteria:

- ideas communicated
- pronunciation and intonation and fluency
- range of vocabulary and structures used
- tenses or time frames used

5 Write up your conclusions in an article for the leaflet that is going to accompany the documentary. In general, do you think that the Internet is a good thing or is it dangerous?

PLTS

- Students use what they have discussed and presented in activities 4a and 4b to produce an article.
- This activity encourages students to connect their own and others' ideas in inventive ways, to communicate previous learning and to work towards goals. It covers the Creative thinkers, Reflective learners, and Self-managers groups from the framework of personal, learning and thinking skills.

Wie man Feste feiert

Seiten 84–85

Planner

➤ Objectives
- Discussing festivals

➤ Resources
Students' Book, pages 84–85
CD 2, track 11
Grammar Workbook, page 56
Activity Sheet 29

➤ Key language
das Fest; feiern; zelten

➤ Skills
- Listening

➤ Grammar
- Word order with the perfect and future tenses

➤ PLTS
Question 3: Reflective learners/Team workers/Effective participators
Question 6: Independent enquirers/Creative thinkers/Reflective learners/Team workers/Self-managers

➤ Starters
- Display some words from the key language of the spread with the vowels missing. Students race against each other to fill in the missing letters. Elicit the English for the words included.
- Go round the class asking, *Was ist dein Lieblingsfest? Warum?* Students reply accordingly, e.g. *Mein Lieblingsfest ist Weihnachten, weil ich die Geschenke mag., etc.* Make a note of all the favourite festivals to see which is the most popular amongst the class.
- Call out words associated with each of the festivals, e.g. *Geschenke; 'Stille Nacht'; Christbaum* or *München; Oktoberfest,* etc. Students try to guess which festival you are describing before you get to the end of the list of words.

➤ Plenaries
- Students work in pairs. Each chooses their favourite festival (these must be different) and, using some of the vocabulary and phrases they have met in the spread, they try to persuade each other that their festival is the best, e.g.
Partner A: *Mein Lieblingsfest ist Ostern, weil wir schulfrei haben und das Wetter besser ist.*
Partner B: *Ostern finde ich nicht so gut. Meine Familie feiert nicht groß. Mein Lieblingsfest ist Weihnachten. Letztes Jahr haben wir…*
- Students pretend to be a celebrity and imagine how they might celebrate Christmas, or any other festival, next year. They write a paragraph saying how they will celebrate, who with, etc. They should try to make it as exciting as they can, but the point of this is to practise word order with the future tense.
- Call out a word from the spread. Students respond by putting it into a sentence, e.g.
Teacher: *München*
Student: *Ich war letztes Jahr auf dem Oktoberfest in München.*

1a Lies die Texte.

- As an introduction to the spread, students read the texts.

1b Welches Fest ist das?

- To test comprehension, students read the definitions and note down which festival each refers to.

Answers:

a der Oktoberfest; **b** Weihnachten; **c** Fastnacht; **d** Weihnachten; **e** Der Rock im Park; **f** der Oktoberfest **g** Weihnachten; **h** Fastnacht; **i** Fastnacht; **j** Der Rock im Park

1c Arbeitet mit einem Partner/einer Partnerin. A beschreibt ein Fest. B muss sagen, welches Fest das ist. B ↔ A. Welches Fest findet ihr am besten?

- Students work with a partner. Partner A describes a festival; B guesses which one it is. They then swap roles.
- Which festival do they think is best?

2 Hör zu. Tobias beschreibt Feste in Deutschland. Sind die Sätze unten richtig oder falsch? Korrigiere die falschen Sätze.

- Read the *Tipp* section on listening as a class.
- Students listen and decide whether the sentences are true or false. They correct any false sentences.
- Students then complete the activity at the end of the *Tipp* section.

CD 2, track 11 **Seite 85, Übung 2**

Woman: Tobias, was ist dein Lieblingsfest?
Tobias: Mein Lieblingsfest ist Weihnachten. Ich besuche meine Großeltern in Salzburg und wir fahren Ski. Das ist mein Lieblingssport. Natürlich mag ich auch die Geschenke. Dieses Jahr wünsche ich mir einen neuen Computer.
Woman: Und wie findest du Ostern?
Tobias: Ostern finde ich nicht so gut. Meine Familie ist nicht religiös, und wir feiern nicht groß. Mein kleiner Bruder mag Ostern, weil er viele Schokoladeneier bekommt. Aber wir haben keine Schule und das Wetter ist um die Zeit schon besser.
Woman: Feierst du Fasching?
Tobias: Ja, ich wohne in Köln. Hier heißt das Karneval. Ich liebe Karneval, weil es so viele Partys gibt.
Woman: Warst du schon auf dem Oktoberfest?
Tobias: Ja, ich war einmal da. Es war sehr lustig, obwohl ich natürlich noch kein Bier trinken darf.
Woman: Und warst du schon auf einem Musikfest?
Tobias: Ja, ich war letztes Jahr zum ersten Mal mit meinem älteren Bruder auf dem Rock im Park. Er geht in Nürnberg auf die Uni und ich habe bei ihm gewohnt – zum Glück mussten wir nicht zelten. Ich habe meine Lieblingsgruppe Metallica gesehen und das Fest hat mir sehr viel Spaß gemacht.

Answers:

a True; **b** F – He would like a new computer this year; **c** True; **d** True; **e** True; **f** True **g** True; **h** F – He is not allowed to drink beer; **i** F – He went to the 'Rock im Park' concert for the first time last year; **j** F – He stayed with his older brother.

3 Welche Feste magst du? Wie feierst du? Diskutiert die Fragen unten mit einem Partner/einer Partnerin.

- Students think about festivals in more detail.
- They work with a partner and discuss the questions listed in the Students' Book.
- This activity encourages students to communicate their learning and to collaborate with and try to influence others in order to work towards a common goal. It covers the Reflective learners, Team workers and Effective participators groups of skills from the framework of personal, learning and thinking skills.

4–9

PLTS

A29 Activity Sheet 29, activities 3 and 4, provides further practice of writing about festivals.

4 Mach Sätze im Futur, um deine Pläne für Weihnachten zu beschreiben.

- Read the *Grammatik* section.
- Students complete the sentences in the future tense.

Answers:

a Im Dezember, **werden** wir den Weihnachtsbaum **schmücken**.
b Ich **werde** Geschenke für meine Familie **kaufen**.
c ... **wird** mein Vater Weihnachtsessen **kochen**.
d Wir **werden** zu viel **essen** und **trinken**.
e Zu Weihnachten **wird** die ganze Familie zusammen **feiern**.

5 Write an article for *Spaß! Das Stadtmagazin* about your favourite festival. Include the points listed.

- This activity draws together what students have learnt in the spread.
- It is an ideal assessment opportunity.

4–9

Success criteria:

- variety of vocabulary and structures used
- different tenses or time frames used
- number of personal opinions given

6 Interview other students in your class to find out:
- **what their favourite festivals are and why**
- **what they did to celebrate them last time**
- **which festivals they will celebrate or attend next year**
- **which festival in Germany they would like to attend/celebrate and why**

Write 10 questions to ask your classmates before you start.

- Students ask about other people's favourite festivals.
- This activity encourages students to plan and carry out research, to generate and explore different ideas, to communicate their learning in order to achieve goals and to work confidently with others. It covers the Independent enquirers, Creative thinkers, Reflective learners, Team workers and Self-managers groups of skills from the framework of personal, learning and thinking skills.

4–9

PLTS

Aktive Grammatik

Seiten 86–87

Planner

➤ Objectives
- To practise using the present tense of irregular verbs
- To practise using the imperfect tense
- To practise using dative pronouns
- To practise using the future tense

➤ Resources
Students' Book, pages 86–87
Exam Skills Workbooks, page 42
Grammar Workbook, pages 46, 53, 56
Activity Sheet 33
Resources and Planning OxBox CD-ROM

➤ Grammar
- The present tense of irregular verbs
- Imperfect tense
- Dative pronouns
- The future tense

➤ PLTS
All questions: Reflective learners/Self-managers

➤ Present tense of irregular verbs

1 **Organise the verbs below into a list of regular and irregular verbs.**
- This question focuses on recognising which are the irregular verbs in German.

Answers:

regular	irregular
brauchen; kochen; machen; besuchen; benutzen; feiern; spielen; kaufen; arbeiten; singen; zeigen; zahlen; organisieren	lesen; gehen; schlafen; nehmen; fahren; sprechen; vergessen; essen; sehen; trinken; treffen; schwimmen

2 **Complete the sentences with the correct form of the verb.**
- This question focuses on conjugating verbs.

Answers:

a triffst; **b** treffen; **c** macht, kauft; **d** isst, esse; **e** benutze, spielt; **f** trägst, brauche; **g** zeigen; **h** feiern, arbeitet.

➤ Imperfect tense

3 **Change these sentences from the present into the imperfect tense.**
- Practice of the imperfect tense of regular verbs.

Answers:

a Er spielte am Samstag Fußball.
b Ihr kauftet viel nutzloses Zeug.
c Sie zeigten den Film am Donnerstag.
d Du kochtest für mich jeden Abend.
e Ich besuchte oft meine Großeltern.
f Sie machte viele gute Geschäfte bei eBay.

4 **Identify which tense is used in the following sentences.**
- Practice of recognising the imperfect tense of irregular verbs.

Answers:

a imperfect; **b** perfect; **c** present; **d** present; **e** imperfect.

5 **Translate the following sentences into English.**
- Further practice of the imperfect tense of irregular verbs.

Answers:

a We often went shopping on Saturdays.
b I met up with friends yesterday evening.
c He sang in the choir at Christmas.
d You did your homework much too late.
e They didn't tell the whole truth in the blog.

➤ Dative pronouns

6 **Replace the words in brackets with the correct dative pronouns.**
- Practice of using dative pronouns.

Answers:

a ihm; **b** ihr; **c** ihm; **d** mir; **e** dir

7 **Translate the sentences into German.**
- Further practice of dative pronouns.

Answers:

a Er zeigt mir sein neues Hemd.
b Das Kleid steht ihr gar nicht.
c Ich möchte euch/ihnen eine Geschichte erzählen.
d Ich zeigte ihnen den Film.
e Es gefällt uns nicht.

➤ Future tense

8 **Translate the following sentences into German using the future tense.**
- Students practise using the future tense.

Answers:

a Ich werde nächsten Woche bei den Stadion anrufen.
b Er wird nächstes Jahr auf das Oktoberfest gehen.
c Wir werden uns verkleiden für Fasching.
d Sie werden viele Weihnachtsgeschenke kaufen.
e Du wirst viel Geld ausgeben.

Kompetenzen

Seite 88

Planner

➤ Objectives

- Summarising what you have learnt

➤ Resources

Students' Book, page 88
CD 2, track 12
Exam Skills Workbooks, page 43
Activity Sheet 34
Resources and Planning OxBox CD-ROM

➤ Skills

- Using tone both to understand what you hear and to add variety to what you say
- Using tone to work out if something is a question or a statement
- Listening out for linking words
- Asking questions in a variety of different ways
- Adding examples to extend your answers and make what you say more interesting

➤ PLTS

Question 3, Listening: Reflective learners/Team workers/Self-managers
Question 2, Speaking: Creative thinkers/Reflective learners/Self-managers

In this unit, students have learnt how to...

➤ Beim Hören

1 **Use tone both to understand what they hear and to add variety to what they say.**

2 **Use tone to work out if something is a question or a statement.**
- Students listen to the five sentences and decide which of them are questions.

CD 2, track 12 **Seite 88, Beim Hören, Übung 2**

1 Du hast morgen keine Zeit?
2 Du liest ja gern.
3 Du willst also ins Kino gehen.
4 Du hast doch einen Computer zu Hause, oder?
5 Du verbringst Weihnachten immer bei deinen Großeltern, nicht wahr?

Answers: Sentences 1, 4 and 5 are questions.

3 **Listen out for linking words.**

PLTS

- From memory, students note down the German for the linking words listed.
- They then work in pairs. A asks questions, and B gives answers using one of the linking words.
- This encourages students to communicate their learning in order to achieve goals and to work confidently with others. It covers the Reflective learners, Team workers and Self-managers groups of skills from the framework of personal, learning and thinking skills.

Answers: jedoch, trotzdem, aber, trotz

➤ Beim Sprechen

1 **Ask questions in a variety of different ways.**
- Students list two different ways of turning a statement into a question in German.
- They list five question words in German.
- They write five sentences using the question words they listed to find out information about what is on on Friday night.

2 **Add examples to extend their answers and make what they say more interesting.**
- Students answer the questions listed, adding examples to give detail.
- This activity encourages students to generate and explore ideas and to communicate their learning in order to achieve goals. It covers the Creative thinkers, Reflective learners and Self-managers groups of skills from the framework of personal, learning and thinking skills.

3 **Use *nicht wahr* and *oder*.**
- Students ask five questions using *nicht war* or *oder*.

Szenario

Planner

➤ **Objectives**
- Responding to an e-mail from a German exchange partner
- Surveying classmates about how they use computers and presenting the results in an oral report

➤ **Resources**
Students' Book, page 89
Exam Skills Workbooks, pages 40–41
Resources and Planning OxBox CD-ROM

➤ **Skills**
- Writing practice
- Speaking practice

➤ **PLTS**
Question 2, Writing: Creative thinkers/Reflective learners/Self-managers
Question 3, Speaking: Independent enquirers/Reflective learners/Self-managers

➤ Zum Schreiben

In this section, students write an email about festivals in the UK and parties and celebrations that they have recently attended. Encourage them to use as many grammatical structures from this unit as possible, including dative pronouns and the imperfect and future tenses.

It is possible for students to obtain GCSE grades A–F depending on their ability:
Grade F students write a short plan using simple sentences and communicate some information.
Grade C students include a variety of structures which may include different tenses or time frames. They communicate information and express personal opinions.
Grade A students include a variety of vocabulary, structures and verb tenses. They convey information, narrate events and express and explain ideas and points of view.

1 **Create a spider web with some ideas about the kinds of things you might want to include in your reply in German.**
- Students read the email from their German exchange partner and think about how they might reply, using the points listed prompts.

2 **Now write your response, giving as many details as you can.**
- Students use what they have prepared in activity 1 to write a response.

PLTS
- This activity encourages students to think creatively by generating and exploring ideas, to communicate their learning to achieve goals and to organise time effectively. It covers the Creative thinkers, Reflective learners and Self-managers groups of skills from the framework of personal, learning and thinking skills.

➤ Zum Sprechen

In this section, students prepare and deliver a presentation about computer use in their class. Encourage them to rehearse their material thoroughly. Suggest recording it to help improve their accent and intonation. This could be done using the record/playback facility on the OxBox CD-ROM.

It is possible for students to obtain GCSE grades A–F and they are marked on Communication, Quality of language and Pronunciation and intonation:
Grade F students communicate a limited number of ideas, expressing simple opinions. A few phrases or short sentences are accurate enough to be recognisable. There are very few instances of clear pronunciation and intonation.
Grade C students communicate the essential elements, readily expressing points of view. They occasionally hesitate and can respond to some unpredictable questions. They use straightforward vocabulary and structures which may contain different tenses or time frames. Pronunciation and intonation is generally accurate.
Grade A students use relevant information to develop and justify individual ideas and points of view. There is no hesitation and they are able to respond to unpredictable questions. They use a wide range of clause types, vocabulary and structures accurately. The presentation is fluent and coherent with just minor errors. Pronunciation and intonation is very accurate with a few minor slips.

1 **Work in pairs to create a survey asking your classmates about how they use computers. Write at least 10 questions.**
- This activity serves as an introduction to the task. Encourage students to use the ideas presented in the unit for support.

2 **Interview other students in the class to get their answers.**

- Students use the questions they have prepared in activity 1 to collect information in preparation for the next activity.

3 **Produce a short oral report about computer use in your class. You can record this using the OxBox software.**

- Students use the work they have done in activities 1 and 2 to produce and present a presentation.
- PLTS This encourages students to plan and carry out research and evaluate information, to use what they have learnt to achieve goals and to organise time and resources effectively. It covers the Independent enquirers, Reflective learners and Self-managers groups from the framework of personal, learning and thinking skills.

Vokabeln

Seite 90

Planner

➤ **Resources**
Students' Book, page 90
Activity Sheet 35

This page provides a summary of the key language covered in each spread of this unit. It could be used as a handy reference for students as they work through the unit. Alternatively, students could use its clear German–English format when learning vocabulary.

Lesen

Seiten 179–180

Planner

➤ Objectives

- To encourage independent reading and develop reading strategies
- To provide alternative class and homework material

Pages 179–180 provide magazine-style reading texts in the context of the unit.

➤ Resources

Students' Book, pages 179–180

➤ Skills

- Reading practice

➤ PLTS

Question 2 (part 1): Independent enquirers/ Reflective learners/Team workers/Self-managers
Question 3 (part 2): Creative thinkers/Reflective learners/Self-managers

Lesen A: Hier gibt es alles!

1 Beantworte die Fragen auf Englisch.

- Students read the text and answer the questions.

Answers:

a You can sell things you don't want anymore and buy things you do want.
b mobile phones, DVDs and computer games
c they are often cheaper so he saves money
d books that she needs for her studies
e they are cheaper than in bookshops which don't always stock the books she needs
f When she has finished studying she intends to sell the books on e-Bay.
g He runs a specialist music shop.
h He can't afford his own website and reaches new customers through e-Bay.
i Some of the people who use it just want to make lots of money.
j buying tickets for 50 Euros and selling them for 300 Euros

2 Was kaufen deine Mitschüler im Internet? Welche Webseiten sind die besten? Warum? Mach eine Umfrage in der Klasse.

- Students prepare and carry out a survey to find out which websites the class likes best and why.
- This activity encourages students to carry out research, to communicate their learning to achieve goals and to work confidently with others. It covers the Independent enquirers, Reflective learners, Team workers and Self-managers groups of skills from the framework of personal, learning and thinking skills.

3 Schreib einen Artikel über eine Webseite, auf der du einkaufst. Sag, was du dort gekauft hast und warum.

- Students write an article about a website they shop from.
- They include details of what they buy and why.

Lesen B: Rock in Deutschland

1 Lies den Text und wähl die richtige Antwort.

- Students read the text and choose the correct answer each time.

Answers: **1** b; **2** a; **3** b; **4** b

2 Füll die Lücken mit einem passenden Wort aus.

- Students now complete the sentences.

Answers:

a Musikfeste; **b** Zeltplatz; **c** Welt; **d** günstig; **e** einer Gruppe von Freunden; **f** gut

3 Beschreib ein Musikfest oder ein anderes Fest, das du besucht hast.

- Students describe a music festival or any other festival that they have been to/celebrated.
- This activity encourages students to generate and explore ideas and to communicate their learning to achieve goals. It covers the Creative thinkers, Reflective learners and Self-managers groups of skills from the framework of personal, learning and thinking skills.

Unit 3B: Die Medien		Overview grid		
Spread	**Contexts and objectives**	**Skills**	**Grammar**	**Vocabulary**
pages 92–93 **Wie man seine Meinung über Lesestoff sagt**	• Discussing books and newspapers	• Giving your opinion	• Subordinate clauses	*die Handlung; der Roman; gehen um; handeln von; sich interessieren für bekannt; spannend; ich denke, dass; ich glaube, dass; ich finde; mir gefällt (+ sing)/mir gefallen (+ pl)*
pages 94–95 **Wie man die Musik vergleicht, die man früher mochte und heute mag**	• Describing music types, bands and singers	• Comparing the past with the present day	• The pluperfect • The comparative • Weak nouns	*die Gruppe; der Sänger stehen auf (gestanden); vergleichen mit früher damals*
pages 96–97 **Wie man über Fernsehen spricht**	• Discussing television programmes	• Giving an opinion about television programmes	• The superlative • Impersonal verbs	*die Folge; der Kanal; der Krimi; die Nachrichten; die Sendung; der Wettbewerb gucken; laufen blöd; wenig; mehr*
pages 98–99 **Wie man eine Filmkritik schreibt**	• Discussing films and actors	• Using a dictionary	• Adjective endings	*der Preis; der Schauspieler; der Zuschauer; zeigen*
pages 100–101 **Wie man die Persönlichkeit des Jahres wählt**	• Discussing famous people	• Describing people and things in detail	• Relative clauses • Comparatives and superlatives before nouns	*die berühmte Persönlichkeit; der Erfolg; kommen aus; berühmt; verheiratet*
pages 102–103 **Aktive Grammatik**	• Grammar		• Relative clauses • The pluperfect tense • Adjective endings	
page 104 **Kompetenzen**	• Summarizing what you have learnt	• Using knowledge of English to infer meaning • Using knowledge of single German words to guess the meaning of compound nouns • Using the context to infer meaning • Using a dictionary • Using relative clauses • Using longer sentences by combining a main clause with a subordinate clause • Comparing things • Using the pluperfect tense • Varying expression		
page 105 **Szenario**	• Preparing a review of books/films in German	• Speaking practice • Writing practice		
page 106 **Vokabeln**	• Key language			
pages 181–182 **Lesen**	• Films • To encourage independent reading and develop reading strategies • To provide alternative class and homework material for students who finish other activities quickly	• Reading practice		

3B Die Medien

Unit Objectives

Contexts and cultural focus: the media
Skills focus: using knowledge of English to infer meaning; using knowledge of German to infer meaning, inferring meaning from the context; handling a dictionary with confidence; avoiding repetition; using a variety of sentence structures
Grammar: relative clauses; the pluperfect tense; adjective endings

Controlled assessment opportunities

Writing: Students' Book, page 93 activity 10
Writing: Students' Book, page 95 activity 8
Speaking: Students' Book, page 97 activity 6
Writing: Students' Book, page 99 activity 10
Speaking: Students' Book, page 101 activity 7
Speaking: Students' Book, page 105 Zum Sprechen, activity 3
Writing: Students' Book, page 105 Zum Schreiben, activity 4

See also ***GCSE German for OCR Assessment OxBox CD-ROM.***

An introduction to the unit Seite 91

- *Aim*: To introduce the themes of the unit.
- The opening spread of each unit is styled as the contents page of a teenage magazine. Illustrations, captions and skills summaries provide a preview of what is to come:

	Students' Book
Weißt du schon, wie man seine Meinung über Lesestoff sagt?	pages 92–93
Weißt du schon, wie man die Musik vergleicht, die man früher mochte und heute mag?	pages 94–95
Weißt du schon, wie man über Fernsehen spricht?	pages 96–97
Weißt du schon, wie man eine Filmkritik schreibt?	pages 98–99
Weißt du schon, wie man die Persönlichkeit des Jahres wählt?	pages 100–101

- Allow time for students to read the questions and cross-refer to the relevant pages of the Students' Book. They could do this individually or in pairs/groups, followed by whole-class discussion.
- This spread also provides an opportunity for students to recap on familiar language. Ask them to think about language they already know that might be useful when working on the themes of the unit.
- At the end of work on Unit 3B:
  - If time permits, ask students to devise a replacement opening spread. What do they think should be on it, in terms of pictures, captions, etc.? What would they change/keep the same, and why? Ask them to imagine it is the contents page of a teenage magazine: what sort of captions and pictures do they feel would attract people to buy the magazine? This sort of activity encourages students to think about features of a text that make it suitable for a particular audience or purpose.
  - Allow time for students to return to this opening spread to answer the questions, review what they have learned and reflect on areas for improvement. What did they find difficult, interesting, etc.? What do they think are the most important things they have learned in this unit?

Wie man seine Meinung über Lesestoff sagt

Seiten 92–93

Planner

➤ Objectives
- Discussing books and newspapers

➤ Resources
Students' Book, pages 92–93
CD 2, track 17
Grammar Workbook, page 63

➤ Key language
die Handlung; der Roman
gehen um; handeln von; sich interessieren für
bekannt; spannend
ich denke, dass; ich glaube, dass; ich finde;
mir gefällt (+ sing)/mir gefallen (+ pl)

➤ Skills
- Giving your opinion

➤ Grammar
- Subordinate clauses

➤ PLTS
Question 8: Creative thinkers/Reflective learners
Question 9: Creative thinkers/Reflective learners/Team workers
Question 10: Creative thinkers/Reflective learners/Self-managers

➤ Starters
- Display a list of book titles students are likely to be familiar with (e.g. Harry Potter), in English and in German, and set a time limit for students to match them up. Ask students to keep a note of the German titles, because they may want to use some them later.
- Students work in pairs to choose a few book titles they are familiar with (these can be in English). They brainstorm adjectives and phrases to describe these books and the characters who feature in them. Collect all of the adjectives and phrases they come up with and start a list of these that can be added to as they work through the spread.
- Start by asking a confident student, *Was liest du lieber, Zeitungen oder Zeitschriften?* Once the student has answered, he/she asks another student the same question. Continue around the class.

➤ Plenaries
- Revisit the list of adjectives and phrases from starter activity 2. Give students the opportunity to add to the list. Then ask volunteers to use one of the adjectives or phrases listed in a sentence, e.g. *Ich glaube, dass Büche interessanter als Zeitungen sind.* Students should try to include subordinating clauses. Remind them to watch out for word order.
- Display a list of conjunctions (subordinating and coordinating) and give students a time limt to put each of them into a sentence. If necessary, display an example sentence of a subordinating and a coordinating conjunction for support. Remind them of the word order for each type of conjunction. When the time is up, ask students to feed back what they have written and check that the word order is correct.
- Students decide on a book they would like to take with them to a desert island. Allow them to prepare brief notes: the name of the book, author, what it is about, why they like it. Students then take turns to present their book to the class, using their notes, but not reading from a script, to try to persuade the other students that their book is the best. On the strength of the presentations, the class votes for the book they would choose as their 'desert island book'.

1a Welcher Zeitungs-Typ bist du? Mach das Quiz auf Seite 92. Was ist für dich richtig – *a* oder *b*?

4–6

- As an introduction to the spread, students read the magazine-style quiz and answer the questions to see which type of newspaper they prefer.

1b Glaubst du, dass diese Beschreibung stimmt? Warum (nicht)? Diskutiert zu zweit.

4–6

- Students read through the descriptions in the key again and decide if they think they are correct.
- They should give reasons for their answer.

2 Wie sagt man auf Deutsch…?

- Students find the German for the English phrases listed.

Answers:

a Ich denke, dass…; **b** Ich glaube, dass…; **c** Meiner Meinung nach.; **d** mir gefällt (+ sing), mir gefallen (+ pl), ich mag, ich … gern

3 Mach eine Umfrage in der Klasse.

4–6

- Students carry out a survey in the class to find out which newspapers or magazines are the most popular amongst the class and why.

- This activity provides an opportunity to practise expressing an opinion. Read the *Tipp* box as a class and encourage students to use as many phrases as possible to express their opinion.

4 *Jugendmagazin* hat Sophie zum Thema Lesen interviewt. Welche Antworten (1–6) auf Seite 92 passen zu den folgenden Fragen?

- Students read Sophie's answers on page 92 and match the answers to the questions listed.

4–6

Answers: **a** 5; **b** 1; **c** 4; **d** 6; **e** 3; **f** 2

5 Welche Buch-Wörter kannst du in den Fragen und Antworten von Übung 4 finden? Wie heißen sie auf Englisch?

- Students look at the questions and answers from activity 4 again and pick out book-related words.
- They translate these into English.

4–6

Answers:

der Autor(en) – *author*; die Lieblingsautorin(nen) – *favourite female author*; das Buch(¨er) – *book*; der Roman(e) – *novel*; der Band(¨e) – *volume*; die Trilogie(n) – *trilogy*; erscheinen (erschienen) – *to be published*; handeln von – *to deal with*; es geht um. – *it is about*; der Charakter(e) – *character*; die Handlung(en) – *plot*; das Kapitel(-) – *chapter*

A36 Activity Sheet 36 provides further practice of media-related vocabulary.

A38 A39 Further practice of listening to, and giving, opinions on books is provided on Activity Sheets 38 and 39.

6 Hör dir das Interview mit David an und lies die Sätze. Sind sie richtig (R), falsch (F) oder nicht im Text (NT)?

- Students listen to the Interview with David and read the sentences.
- Students decide if the sentences are true, false or not mentioned.

4–6

CD 2, track 17 **Seite 93, Übungen 6 und 7**

Interviewer/in: Wie oft liest du Bücher oder Zeitungen?
David: Ich glaube, dass ich ziemlich viel lese. Wir bekommen jeden Tag die Frankfurter Allgemeine, denn wir haben ein Abonnement. Beim Frühstück lese ich immer, aber ich lese nicht die ganze Zeitung – nur drei oder vier Artikel.
Interviewer/in: Warum liest du die Frankfurter Allgemeine gern?
David: Mir gefällt diese Zeitung, weil ich mich für Politik interessiere, und es gibt immer viele politische Artikel.
Interviewer/in: Liest du auch Bücher?
David: Natürlich. Ich habe auch viel gelesen, als ich jünger war. Ich hatte alle Harry-Potter-Bücher gelesen, bevor ich zwölf Jahre alt war. Heute finde ich Flugzeuge interessant und ich lese manchmal Sachbücher über Flugzeuge. Während der Ferien habe ich mehr Zeit und dann lese ich auch Romane.
Interviewer/in: Welche Romane kannst du denn empfehlen?
David: Moment, letztes Jahr habe ich einen Roman von Bernhard Schlink gelesen – *Der Vorleser* – und das Buch war echt toll. Meiner Meinung nach waren die Hauptpersonen in diesem Roman total realistisch und die Handlung war nie langweilig. Ich mag das Buch, obwohl ich normalerweise lieber Krimis lese.
Interviewer/in: Lesen deine Freunde auch viel?
David: Nicht alle. Meine Freundin Mia liest viel, besonders die englischen Klassiker. Jetzt liest sie einen Roman von Jane Austen. Nachdem sie den gelesen hat, will sie Charles Dickens lesen.
Interviewer/in: David, wir danken dir für das Gespräch.
David: Kein Problem.

Answers:

a R, **b** F, **c** NT, **d** F, **e** R, **f** NT, **g** R, **h** F

7 Im Hörtext sind folgende Konjunktionen. Wie heißen sie auf Englisch? Hör das Interview noch einmal an. Sind das beiordnende (coordinating) oder unterordnende (subordinating) Konjunktionen, die das Verb ans Ende senden? Füll die Tabelle aus.

- Students listen to the interview again and translate the conjunctions listed into English.
- They then state whether each of the conjunctions is coordinating or subordinating (sends the verb to end). Refer students to the relevant section of the grammar section, if necessary, before they attempt the activity.

4–6

Answers:

dass – that – subordinating; denn – for – coordinating; aber – but – coordinating; weil – because – subordinating; und – and – coordinating; als – when (for single event in the past) – subordinating; bevor – before – subordinating; während – during – subordinating; wenn – when/if – subordinating; obwohl – although – subordinating; nachdem – after – subordinating

8 Schreib einen Satz für jede unterordnende Konjunktion.

- Students write their own sentences for each of the subordinating conjunctions.
- This encourages students to generate and explore ideas whilst communicating previous learning. It covers the Creative thinkers and Reflective learners groups of skills from the framework of personal, learning and thinking skills.

4–6

PLTS

9 Imagine you are a journalist working for *Jugendmagazin* who has to write an article in German entitled *Welche Bücher lesen Jugendliche heute?* Interview three classmates and make notes. Use the questions from activity 4.

- This activity serves as preparation for activity 10 and brings together what students have learnt in the spread.
- It encourages students to generate and explore ideas whilst communicating previous learning and to collaborate with others to achieve results. It covers the Creative thinkers, Reflective learners and Team workers groups of skills from the framework of personal, learning and thinking skills.

4–9

PLTS

10 **Use your notes from activity 9 and write your article. Remember to include interviewees' reasons for liking their chosen books. Use the expressions from activity 2. Watch out for word order!**

- Students write their article. This is an ideal assessment opportunity.
- This encourages students to generate and explore ideas for their article whilst setting goals, communicating previous learning and managing their time and resources effectively. It covers the Creative thinkers, Reflective learners and Self-managers groups from the framework of personal, learning and thinking skills.

4–9

PLTS

Success criteria:

- information communicated
- variety of vocabulary and structures used
- personal opinions expressed

Wie man die Musik vergleicht, die man früher mochte und heute mag

Seiten 94–95

Planner

➤ Objectives

- Describing music types, bands and singers

➤ Resources

Students' Book, pages 94–95
CD 2, track 18
Grammar Workbook, page 55
Activity Sheet 38

➤ Key language

die Gruppe; der Sänger
stehen auf (gestanden); vergleichen mit
früher, damals

➤ Skills

- Comparing the past with the present day

➤ Grammar

- The pluperfect

➤ PLTS

Question 8: Creative thinkers/Reflective learners/ Self-managers

➤ Starters

- As a class, brainstorm types of music in German. Once you are happy with your list, go round the class asking each student in turn: *Welche Musik magst du?* If necessary, model example answers, e.g. *Ich mag Metal. Ich höre gern Rap. Ich finde Reggae toll.*
- In preparation for work on the pluperfect tense, practise the imperfect tense. Split the class into two teams. Call out a verb in the present tense, e.g. *Ich habe* the first team to tell you the imperfect form (*Ich hatte*) wins a point.
- Display the key language in one column and the English translations of these words and phrases jumbled up in a second column. Students work in pairs to match each term with its English translation. Compare answers as a class.

➤ Plenaries

- Repeat starter activity 1, but this time using the pluperfect tense. Using the same list of music types, go round the class asking: *Welche Musik hattest du gemocht vor zwei Jahren?*
- Display some music-related words from the spread, e.g. different music types and bands, etc. Challenge students to write sentences using these words. Compare sentences as a class.
- Have a class quiz using the reading text from page 94. Divide the class into two teams and ask questions about the text, e.g. *Mit zehn Jahren hatte Ole oft Silbermond gehört! Richtig oder Falsch?; Was hatte Anna früher gemocht?*, etc.

1 **Finde die Vergangenheitsformen dieser Meinungsausdrücke im Text.**

- As an introduction to the spread, students read the article and find the past forms of the phrases listed.

4–6

Answers:

ich mag – ich mochte – ich habe gemocht
ich finde – ich fand – ich habe gefunden
mir gefällt – mir gefiel – mir hat gefallen

2 **Welche Musik mögen sie? Füll die Tabelle aus.**

- Students read the article again and this time note down what type of music each young person likes.

4–6

Answers:

Name	Now	Before	Long ago
Ole	Rap	Reggae	*Die Toten Hosen*
Anna	MIA	*Seeed*	Metal
Saskia	*Silbermond*	*Die Fantastischen Vier*	*Rammstein*
Mehmet	*Wir sind Helden*	Hiphop	Techno
Hufi	*2raumwohnung*	*Culcha Candela*	*Die Ärzte*

3 **Ergänze die Tabelle jetzt für Mehmet, Saskia und Hufi. Unterstreiche die Verben im Imperfekt in Grün, die Verben im Perfekt in Orange und die Verben im Plusquamperfekt in Rot.**

- Read the *Grammatik* section.
- Ask students to fill in the table for Saskia, Mehmet and Hufi.

Answers:

	What happened in the past (imperfect or perfect tense)?	What happened **before** the event in the past (pluperfect tense)?
Mehmet	Mir gefiel Hiphop.	Ich hatte mir manchmal Techno-CDs gekauft.
Saskia	Ich habe die *Fantastischen Vier* gemocht.	Ich hatte manchmal *Rammstein* gehört.
Hufi	Mir hat *Culcha Candela* gefallen.	Ich war in ein *Ärzte*-Konzert gegangen.

4 **Vier junge Leute sprechen über Musik. Hör gut zu und notiere:**
a was den jungen Leuten heute gefällt.
b was sie früher mochten.
c was sie davor gut gefunden hatten.

- Students listen to the four young people speaking about music and note what they like now, what they liked in the past and what they found good about it.

4–6

CD 2, track 18 **Seite 95, Übung 4**

1
Vor zwei Jahren habe ich mir ganz viele Techno-CDs gekauft, weil wir diese Musik immer in meinem Jugendklub gehört haben. Als ich klein war, hatte ich oft mit meinen Großeltern Musik gehört, nämlich Rock'n'Roll. Die fünfziger Jahre waren cool, denke ich. Heute mag ich vor allem Rap.

2
Ich bin ein großer Punk-Fan, aber meine Freundinnen hören immer nur diese doofen Boybands. Rockmusik hatte mir schon mit sieben oder acht Jahren gefallen. Später fand ich Hip-hop ziemlich gut.

3
Also, ich höre eigentlich nicht so oft Musik, aber manchmal natürlich schon. Mein Geschmack hat sich über die Jahre geändert. Nachdem ich erst oft *Rammstein* gehört hatte, mochte ich das später nicht mehr so gern. Dann mochte ich die *Ärzte*, besonders den Schlagzeuger. Heute finde ich *Silbermond* besser.

4
Seit ich letztes Jahr bei dem Festival in der Nähe von Köln war, interessiere ich mich vor allem für Metal, weil ich da ganz fantastische Bands gehört habe. Aber früher hatte ich Indie am besten gefunden, weil mein Bruder das oft gehört hatte. Danach fand ich Reggae total cool, aber nur für kurze Zeit.

Answers:

1	Punk [a]	Rockmusik [c]	Hiphop [b]
2	Rammstein [c]	Die Ärzte [b]	Silbermond [a]
3	Metal [a]	Indie [c]	Reggae [b]

A38 Activity Sheet 38 provides a listening activity on the topic of music.

5 **Lies die Texte auf Seite 94 noch einmal. Wie sagt man auf Deutsch ...?**

Answers:

a besser als; **b** schlechter als; **c** genauso gut wie

6 **Partnerarbeit. Was denkt ihr? Vergleicht und schreibt Sätze. Benutzt unterschiedliche Meinungsausdrücke.**

- Students then practise using the comparative by discussing items a–f with a partner and then writing sentences.

4–9

7 **You are a journalist for *Jugendmagazin*. Carry out a survey in German in your class and note down the results.**

- Students carry out a survey on the class' music tastes, now and in the past.
- They record the results.

4–6

8 **Use your notes from activity 7 to write your own article for *Jugendmagazin*. Use a computer and design a magazine layout for your article.**

- Students use their notes from activity 12, and the material they have covered in this spread, to write an article for *Jugendmagazin*. This is an ideal assessment opportunity.
- This activity encourages students to generate and explore ideas whilst communicating previous learning and to organise their time and resources effectively. It covers the Creative thinkers, Reflective learners and Self-managers groups of skills from the framework of personal, learning and thinking skills.

4–9

PLTS

Success criteria:

- amount of information communicated
- variety of vocabulary and structures used
- number of personal opinions given

Wie man über Fernsehen spricht

Seiten 96–97

Planner

➤ Objectives
- Discussing television programmes

➤ Resources
Students' Book, pages 96–97
CD 2, track 19
Grammar Workbook, pages 25–27
Activity Sheets 38–39

➤ Key language
die Folge; der Kanal; der Krimi; die Nachrichten; die Sendung; der Wettbewerb
gucken; laufen
blöd; wenig; mehr

➤ Skills
- Giving an opinion about television programmes

➤ Grammar
- The superlative
- Impersonal verbs

➤ PLTS
Question 6: Creative thinkers/Reflective learners/Team workers
Question 7a: Creative thinkers/Reflective learners/Self-managers

➤ Starters
- Display the types of TV programme from the spread, together with a list of titles of English programmes that students will be familiar with. Students race against the clock to match the programme types to the titles.
- Ask all students in the class to stand up. Begin by calling out the name of a TV programme and nominating someone in the class. Without hesitating, this student says something about the programme (e.g. what type of programme it is and an opinion about it using the superlative if possible.)
- Students work in pairs to choose a few TV programmes with which they are familiar. They brainstorm adjectives to describe these programmes and the characters/actors/presenters, etc. who feature in them. Collect these ideas to use later on.

➤ Plenaries
- Display the impersonal sentences from the grammar box. Also display a list of at least five dative pronouns. Ask students to rewrite the impersonal sentences, substituting *mir* each time with a dative pronoun from the list. Compare sentences as a class.
- Give Students a couple of minutes, working in pairs, to list as many different types of TV programme as they can, giving an example of each along with their opinion of it. When the time is up, they compare their lists with another pair, scoring a point for each type of programme not mentioned by the other pair.
- Display the adjectives from starter activity 3 and ask students to write these in the superlative. Students then choose a celebrity and imagine what they like and dislike watching on TV. They write a paragraph on behalf of the celebrity, expressing their opinions of TV programmes and using the adjectives listed in the superlative form.

1 Mach eine Liste mit Fernsehwörtern. Wie heißen die Wörter auf Englisch? Schau dann im Wörterbuch nach.

4–6

- As an introduction to the spread, students read the texts and make a list of TV-related words. They then translate these into English.
- Students check in a dictionary that they have translated the words correctly.

Answers:

Kindersendung; Quizsendung; Cartoon; Krimi; Horrorfilm; Actionfilm; Serie; Reality-Show; Soap; Musiksendung; Komödie; Film; Nachrichten; Sportsendung; Dokumentarfilm; Glotze; gucken; laufen auf; Staffel; Folge; Kanal; Kinderkanal; Pro7; Viva; Arte; ARD

2 Lies die vier Texte auf Seite 96. Wer sagt das?

- Students read the four texts and note down who said each of the statements listed.

Answers:

4–6

a Hussain; **b** Katja; **c** Emma; **d** Jakob; **e** Katja; **f** Hussain

3 Lies die Texte noch einmal und füll die Tabelle aus.

- Read through the *Grammatik* section on the superlative as a class.
- Students read the texts again and fill in the table.

4–6

Answers:

Positive	**Comparative**	**Superlative**
toll	toller	am tollsten
spannend	spannender	am spannendsten
gern	lieber	am liebsten
gut	besser	am besten
viel	mehr	am meisten

4 Partnerarbeit. Schaut euch das Diagramm an. Diskutiert folgende Fragen.

4–9

- Students discuss the questions listed with a partner. Remind them to use the vocabulary they have already met in the spread and to use the superlative.

5 *JuRa*, die Radiosendung für junge Leute, hat Lisa, Tim, Lea und Finn nach ihrer Meinung über Fernsehsendungen gefragt. Hör das Gespräch an und entscheide: Was finden sie besser?

4–9

- Students listen to the radio programme and decide which of the options each person prefers.

CD 2, track 19 **Seite 97, Übung 5**

Moderator: Herzlich willkommen im *JuRa*-Studio. Heute wollen uns Lisa, Finn, Lea und Tim sagen, was sie gern im Fernsehen gucken. Es gibt ja junge Leute, die das ganze Wochenende nur vor der Glotze sitzen. Du auch, Lisa?
Lisa: Nein, normalerweise gucke ich nicht so viel fern. Meine kleine Schwester sieht immer Kindersendungen, und wir haben nur einen Fernseher. Aber ein paar Sendungen gucke ich jede Woche. Am liebsten sehe ich *Rach, der Restauranttester*. Die Sendung ist mega-cool!
Moderator: Worum geht es?
Lisa: Das ist eine Reality-Show, wo Herr Rach Restaurants testet. Das Essen schmeckt den Leuten nie und manchmal ist das Restaurant sehr schmutzig. Einmal gab es Ratten in der Küche – mir ist schlecht geworden! Ich finde die Sendung interessant, weil meine Eltern auch ein Restaurant haben, aber da gibt es keine Ratten!
Moderator: Magst du auch andere Reality-Shows?
Lisa: Andere Reality-Shows finde ich nicht so gut, da sind Quizsendungen besser. Krimis mag ich aber noch lieber, vor allem Agatha Christie-Filme. Ich finde, die Miss Marple-Filme sind besser als die Hercule Poirot-Filme, weil dieser Detektiv ziemlich unrealistisch ist.
Moderator: Danke, Lisa. Tim, wie oft siehst du fern?
Tim: Viel zu oft. Das ist nicht gut, ich weiß, aber ich finde viele Sendungen total lustig. Früher mochte ich Actionfilme sehr, zum Beispiel die alten James Bond-Filme, und Cartoons fand ich auch toll. Gute Cartoons gucke ich manchmal heute noch, aber Actionfilme interessieren mich nicht mehr. Sportsendungen finde ich klasse, besonders Bundesliga-Fußballspiele. Es wäre besser, wenn ich selbst Sport treiben würde und nicht nur Sport im Fernsehen sehen würde, aber es tut mir Leid – ich bin ziemlich faul. Reality-Shows sind fantastisch, zum Beispiel *Bauer sucht Frau*. Das handelt von Bauern. Die Bauern wollen heiraten, aber sie finden keine Frau – das ist wahnsinnig komisch. Die *Supernanny* finde ich auch toll. Reality-Shows gucke ich ziemlich oft, aber Serien finde ich am besten. Wenn ich bequem auf meinem Sofa fernsehen kann, geht es mir gut...
Moderator: Manche Soaps sind wirklich klasse. Lea, was kannst du uns zum Thema Fernsehen sagen?
Lea: Als ich zehn Jahre alt war, habe ich den ganzen Tag ferngesehen. Besonders Serien waren sehr wichtig für mich. Quizsendungen fand ich auch toll, zum Beispiel *Wer wird Millionär?* Heute gefallen mir die meisten Serien nicht und Quizsendungen finde ich auch uninteressant. Manche Filme gucke ich aber gern – keine Actionfilme, aber Komödien.
Moderator: Finn, wie ist es mit dir?
Finn: Unter der Woche sehe ich wenig fern, aber am Wochenende gucke ich manchmal mehr. Ich finde, es gibt fantastische Dokumentarfilme über Afrika und die Wüste Sahara. Sie sind sehr realistisch. Mir ist heiß, wenn ich das sehe! Ich interessiere mich auch für Musik, und am liebsten gucke ich Musiksendungen. Es gibt eine Frau, die Gülcan heißt, und die präsentiert auf Viva eine Musiksendung. Die Sendung ist klasse und die Frau auch. Seit letztem Jahr sehe ich manchmal Nachrichten. Früher fand ich das langweilig, aber jetzt nicht mehr. Filme im Fernsehen interessieren mich wenig. Da gehe ich lieber ins Kino. Reality-Shows finde ich ziemlich blöd und Serien sehe ich absolut nie.
Moderator: Nicht einmal *Gute Zeiten, schlechte Zeiten*?
Finn: Das habe ich noch nie gesehen.
Alle: Was???! Nein!!!
Moderator: Oje! Und ich dachte, ***alle*** Leute in Deutschland gucken um 19.40 Uhr abends diese Serie! Unsere Sendezeit ist um. Vielen Dank, dass ihr mit uns gesprochen habt.

Answers:

a Quizsendungen; **b** Krimis; **c** Cartoons; **d** Serien; **e** Filme; **f** Komödien; **g** Musiksendungen; **h** Nachrichten

A38 A39 Activity Sheet 38, activity 4, and Activity Sheet 39, activity 1, provide further practice of discussing television programmes.

6 Interview your partner in German. How much television does he/she watch? Which programmes does he/she like and dislike? Why?

4–9 PLTS

- Students draw together the vocabulary and grammar points covered in the spread to interview their partner. This activity also acts as preparation for activities 10a and 10b. This is an ideal assessment opportunity.
- It encourages students to generate and explore ideas whilst communicating previous learning and to collaborate successfully with others. It covers the Creative thinkers, Reflective learners and Team workers groups of skills from the framework of personal, learning and thinking skills.

Success criteria:

- ideas communicated
- pronunciation and intonation and fluency
- range of vocabulary and structures used
- tenses or time frames used

7a Write about your partner's likes and dislikes in German, but do not write your partner's name. Instead call him/her *die mysteriöse Person.*

- Students write a paragraph outlining their partner's likes and dislikes.
- This activity encourages students to generate and explore ideas whilst communicating previous learning and to organise their time and resources effectively. It covers the Creative thinkers, Reflective learners and Self-managers groups of skills from the framework of personal, learning and thinking skills.

4–9

PLTS

7b Pin up your texts on the classroom wall and read each other's texts. How many of the *mysteriöse Personen* do you recognise?

- A fun game to draw together activities 9 and 10.

4–9

Wie man eine Filmkritik schreibt

Seiten 98–99

Planner

➤ Objectives

- Discussing films and actors

➤ Resources

Students' Book, pages 98–99
CD 2, track 20
Grammar Workbook, pages 21–23
Activity Sheets 37

➤ Key language

der Preis; der Schauspieler; der Zuschauer
zeigen

➤ Skills

- Using a dictionary

➤ Grammar

- Adjective endings

➤ PLTS

Question 6: Independent enquirers/Reflective learners/Team workers
Question 10: Independent enquirers/Creative thinkers/Reflective learners/Self-managers

➤ Starters

- Display a list of films that students are likely to be familiar with (e.g. the Harry Potter films), in English and in German, and set a time limit for students to match them up. Ask students to keep a note of the German titles, because they may want to use some of them later.
- Display a list of actors/actresses and ask students to brainstorm as many adjectives as possible to describe each of them. Compile a list of adjectives and keep this to add to.
- Display a list of simple sentences in English containing words that could be either verbs or nouns, e.g. He wanted to **action** the plan. The film was full of **action**. Ask students to state each time whether the word in bold is a verb or a noun. If there is time, they could use a dictionary to translate the sentences into German.

➤ Plenaries

- Display a few of the films mentioned in the spread along with a few actors/actresses and the adjectives from starter activity 2. Ask students if they would like to add any more adjectives to the list, e.g. some to describe films as well as actors and actresses. Once students are happy with the list, challenge them to write a short paragraph about one of the films mentioned, describing the film, saying who plays the lead role and describing him/her. Confident students present their paragraph to the class.
- Display the list of adjectives from the first plenary activity. Also display the words, *wenig*, *etwas* and *viel*. Ask students to write three sentences using each of the words *wenig*, *etwas* and *viel* and one of the adjectives with the appropriate ending, e.g. *Etwas Gutes passiert.* Compare answers as a class.
- Students work in pairs. Each chooses a film that they like. They then prepare and perform a role-play. Each tries to persuade the other that their film is the best, giving reasons why they find their film good, and why their partner's film is bad.
  Student A: *Mein Lieblingsfilm ist … Ich habe den Film … gesehen, weil …*
  Student B: *Mein Lieblingsfilm ist … Der Film spielt im Jahr …*

1 **Wie viele Wörter wie „populär“ kannst du im Text finden?**

- Read the *Tipp* sections and then ask students to read the text about the film *Das Wunder von Bern*.
- Students compile a list of words that look or sound like English words.

4–6

Answers:

Film; Filmkritikerin; Sport; interessieren; Publikum; Perspektive; kommen; lang; Familie; Probleme; Konflikte; Finale; Stadion; Rolle; exzellent; fantastisch; realistisch; Preis; prestigeträchtig; Millionen

2 **Wie viele Wörter wie „Kinofans“ kannst du finden?**

- Students compile a list of longer words from the reading text that are made up of smaller parts.

Answers:

4–9

Filmkritikerin, Hauptdarsteller, zusammenleben, Fußball, Fußballverein, Fußballweltmeister, Fußballweltmeisterschaft, Filmpreis, Familiengeschichte

3 **Benutze die dritte Strategie, um diese Wörter und Phrasen im Text zu finden.**

- Students look at the context of words in order to find the German words and phrases in the text that correspond with the English words and phrases listed.

4–6

Answers:

a er läuft (im Kino); **b** das Publikum, die Zuschauer; **c** der Hauptdarsteller; **d** die Handlung; **e** der Film spielt in…; **f** zeigen; **g** der Regisseur des Films; **h** einen Film drehen

4 **Partnerarbeit. Versteht ihr den Text? Der Text ist in drei Teilen – was steht in jedem Teil? Diskutiert zu zweit und schreibt Stichwörter auf Englisch.**

- Students work with a partner to discuss what each part of the text is about. They note down key words in English.

Answers:

4–9

Possible key words:
Part 1: introduction
Part 2: summary of plot
Part 3: evaluation (quality of acting, details of director, reception of film, opinion)

5 **Lies den Text noch einmal. Finde Beispiele von Adjektivendungen ohne einen Artikel. Kannst du sie erklären?**

- Students list examples of adjective endings without an article and explain these.

6 **Interviewt eure Klassenkameraden. Was ist ihr Lieblingsfilm? Warum? Macht Notizen. Sehen Mädchen und Jungen die gleichen Filme gern oder gibt es Unterschiede? Wenn ja, welche? Warum?**

- Students interview classmates to find out what is their favourite film and why.
- They analyse the answers: do girls and boys watch the same films or do their tastes tend to differ?

4–9

They expand on this to say which films they like to watch and how their tastes differ if this is the case.

PLTS

- This activity encourages students to carry out research and analyse information whilst communicating previous learning. It also encourages them to collaborate with others to achieve results. It covers the Independent enquirers, Reflective learners and Team workers groups of skills from the framework of personal, learning and thinking skills.

7 **Schreib eine Zusammenfassung von der Handlung eines Films, den du nicht magst. Sag, warum dir der Film nicht gefällt. Vorsicht bei der Benutzung des Wörterbuchs!**

- Read the *Tipp* section on ‘how to use a dictionary’.
- Students summarise in writing the plot of a film they don’t like. They say why they don’t like it.
- Students can use dictionaries, but remind them to watch out for any traps they could fall into.

4–9

8 **Hör zu, was Adrian über seine Lieblingsschauspielerin sagt. Sind die Sätze richtig oder falsch? Korrigiere die falschen Sätze.**

- Students listen to the recording and state whether the sentences are true or false.
- They correct any false statements.

4–6

CD 2, track 20 **Seite 99, Übung 8**

Interviewer/in:	Was ist dein Lieblingsfilm?
Adrian:	Mein Lieblingsfilm ist *Lola rennt*. Ich habe den Film sechsmal gesehen, weil mir die Schauspielerin, die die Hauptrolle spielt, so total gut gefällt.
Interviewer/in:	Wer spielt denn die Hauptrolle?
Adrian:	Franka Potente.
Interviewer/in:	Wann und wo ist sie geboren?
Adrian:	Sie ist 1974 in Nordwestdeutschland geboren, das heißt, dass sie jetzt Mitte dreißig ist.
Interviewer/in:	Wie ist sie Schauspielerin geworden?
Adrian:	Sie war auf einer Schauspielschule in München und dann ein Jahr auf einer in Manhattan.
Interviewer/in:	Wo lebt sie?
Adrian:	In Berlin.
Interviewer/in:	Und ihr Privatleben?
Adrian:	Franka Potente war die Freundin von Elijah Wood, einem amerikanischen Schauspieler, und von Tom Tykwer, dem Regisseur von *Lola rennt*.
Interviewer/in:	Wie sieht sie aus?
Adrian:	Sie ist mittelgroß, schlank, sehr fit und in *Lola rennt* hat sie ganz rote Haare.
Interviewer/in:	Und was weißt du sonst noch über sie?
Adrian:	Ich habe gehört, dass sie nicht nur Deutsch und Englisch, sondern auch gut Französisch spricht – toll!
Interviewer/in:	Wie ist denn die Handlung in deinem Lieblingsfilm?
Adrian:	In dem Film arbeitet Lolas Freund Manni für einen Drogenhändler. Manni verliert eine Tasche mit viel Geld und er hat nur zwanzig Minuten Zeit, um das Geld zu finden. Lola rennt zur Bank, wo ihr Vater Direktor ist. Lolas Vater will

	aber nicht helfen und Lola und Manni stehlen Geld aus einem Supermarkt. Aber Lola stirbt, weil ein Polizist sie erschießt. Hier beginnt der Film zum zweiten Mal, aber jetzt stirbt Manni am Ende bei einem Verkehrsunfall. Dann fängt die Handlung zum dritten Mal an, und in der dritten Version gibt es ein Happyend. Der Film ist extrem schnell und spannend und es kommen darin auch Cartoonfiguren – sehr kreativ!
Interviewer/In:	Und welche anderen Filme hat sie gedreht?
Adrian:	Viele. *Der Krieger und die Kaiserin* zum Beispiel, und seit 2001 macht sie auch Filme in englischer Sprache. Sie hatte eine Rolle in *Blow*, das war mit Johnny Depp, und in *The Bourne Identity* mit Matt Damon.
Interviewer/in:	Warum ist sie deiner Meinung nach eine gute Schauspielerin?
Adrian:	Ich finde, dass Franka Potente ziemlich toll aussieht, und das gefällt mir natürlich. Ich mag auch den Charakter Lola.

Answers:

a richtig; **b** falsch: Sie war an zwei Schauspielschulen.
c falsch: In *Lola rennt* hat Franka Potente rote Haare.
d richtig; **e** richtig; **f** falsch: Der Film ist extrem spannend.
g falsch: „The Bourne Identity" ist mit Matt Damon. **h** richtig

A37 Further activities on the topic of film are provided on Activity Sheet 37.

9 With a partner, discuss in German your opinion of films that you have seen recently. Note down the aspects that you like and dislike about each film and make a list of adjectives to describe each one.

4–9

- This activity draws together what students have learnt in the spread.

10 Write a review in German of your favourite film for *Jugendmagazin*. Use the structure of the review of *Das Wunder von Bern* and your notes from activity 9.

4–9

PLTS

- A writing activity to draw together the vocabulary, ideas, and grammar points covered in the spread. This is an ideal assessment opportunity.
- This encourages students to carry out research and to generate ideas and explore possibilities to work towards goals whilst communicating previous learning. It also encourages them to manage their time and resources effectively. It covers the Independent enquirers, Creative thinkers, Reflective learners and Self-managers groups of skills from the framework of personal, learning and thinking skills.

Success criteria:

- amount of information communicated
- variety of vocabulary and structures used
- number of personal opinions given

Wie man die Persönlichkeit des Jahres wählt

Seiten 100–101

Planner

➤ Objectives
- Discussing famous people

➤ Resources
Students' Book, pages 100–101
CD 2, track 21
Grammar Workbook, pages 25–27, 65

➤ Key language
die berühmte Persönlichkeit; der Erfolg
kommen aus
berühmt; verheiratet

➤ Skills
- Describing people and things in detail

➤ Grammar
- Relative clauses
- Comparatives and superlatives before nouns

➤ PLTS
Question 6b: Creative thinkers/Reflective learners/Team workers
Question 7: Creative thinkers/Reflective learners/Self-managers/Team workers/Effective participants

➤ Starters
- Display some words from the key language of the spread with the vowels missing. Students race against each other to fill in the missing letters. Elicit the English for the words included.
- Display some German-speaking celebrities (some well known and some less well known), e.g.*Roger Federer*, *Heidi Klum*, *Nina Hagen*, *Arnold Schwarzeneger*. Also display professions e.g. *Sänger(in)*, *Schauspieler(in)*, *Model*, etc. Split the class into teams and give them a fixed amount of time to match the stars to their professions. The team that matches the most stars and professions correctly wins. If there is time, students pretend to be one of the celebrities and mime their profession. The rest of the class has to guess who they are

pretending to be, e.g. *Bist du die sängerin, Nina Hagen?*
- Practise adjective endings. Display sentences containing adjectives with the ending missing, e.g. *Ich lese das lang_ Buch.* Students fill in the appropriate endings, e.g. *Ich lese das lange Buch.* Explain that this will come in useful when using the comparative and superlative before nouns.

➤ Plenaries
- Have a quiz on the reading texts on page 100. Split the class into two teams and ask questions based on the texts, e.g. *Wer ist der Regisseur, der einen Oscar für den besten Film gewonnen hat?* Students score a point for a correct answer, e.g. *Florian Henckel von Donnersmarck* and an extra point for replying in a full sentence, e.g. *Florian Henckel von Donnersmarck ist der Regisseur, der einen Oscar für den besten Film gewonnen hat.*
- Display a few example relative clauses. Ask students to write some relative clauses of their own about films they have seen, or celebrities they like/don't like.
- Ask students to imagine that they are one of the celebrities featured in the spread. They write a paragraph saying why they deserve to be celebrity of the year. Encourage them to include relative clauses and the comparative and superlative where possible. A few confident volunteers present their paragraphs to the class in the form of a speech. The class votes for who they consider to be the most deserving winner.

1 Lies die Informationen über die berühmten Leute. Vervollständige die Sätze mit Wörtern aus dem Kasten unten.

- As an introduction to this spread, students read the information about famous people.
- Students complete the sentences with words from the box.

4–6

Answers:

a der Komiker; **b** die Sängerin; **c** das Model; **d** die Regisseure

2 Kannst du die blau, rot, grün und orange markierten Wörter aus Übung 1 erklären? Wo ist das Verb in den Relativsätzen?

- Read through the *Grammatik* section on 'relative clauses' as a class.
- Students explain what the red, green and yellow words in activity 1 are. They also identify the position of the verb in relative clauses.

Answers:

4–6

The blue word 'der' refers to a masculine noun, the red word 'die' to a feminine noun, the green word 'das' to a neuter noun and the orange word 'die' to a plural noun. The verb is at the end of the relative clause.

3 Lies die Texte auf Seite 100 noch einmal. Wie viele Komparative und wie viele Superlative vor Nomen kannst du finden?

- Read through the second *Grammatik* section on 'comparatives and superlatives in front of nouns with students.
- Students read through the texts on page 100 again and note down any comparatives or superlatives before nouns they find.

Answers:

Comparative: die erfolgreicheren Filme, vielseitigere Interessen

Superlative: das bekannteste deutsche Model, die höchste Besucherzahl, für den besten fremdsprachigen Film, ihr berühmtester Song

4 Ergänze die folgenden Sätze mit Komparativ- oder Superlativformen. Die Tabelle mit Adjektivendungen auf Seite 70 hilft dir dabei.

- Students complete the sentences with comparative or superlative forms.
- Refer students to the table of adjective endings on page 00 for support.

Answers:

a erfolgreicheren; **b** berühmtesten; **c** bekannteren; **d** meisten

5 Wird der Schauspieler Til Schweiger die Persönlichkeit des Jahres? *JuRa* hat ihn interviewt. Hör den Dialog an und vervollständige die Sätze.

- Students listen to the recording and then write the correct version of the sentences listed.

CD 2, track 21 **Seite 101, Übung 5**

JuRa: Herr Schweiger, das *Jugendmagazin* wählt nächste Woche die Persönlichkeit des Jahres. Vielleicht werden Sie gewählt. Wie wichtig ist das für Sie?

Schweiger: Es wäre fantastisch, wenn ich die Wahl gewinnen würde. Dieser Preis wäre der Höhepunkt meiner Karriere.

JuRa: Sie haben gerade einen Film gedreht. Können Sie uns etwas über den Film sagen?

Schweiger: Natürlich. Der Film heißt *Keinohrhasen* und er ist sehr erfolgreich. Der Film hat 4,2 Millionen Euro gekostet, aber in nur vier Monaten haben sechs Millionen Zuschauer in Deutschland den Film gesehen.

JuRa: Warum heißt der Film *Keinohrhasen*?

Schweiger: In dem Film gibt es ein Spielzeugkaninchen, also einen Hasen, und der Hase hat keine Ohren. *Keinohrhasen* ist eine romantische Komödie. Ich spiele die Hauptrolle, den Ludo. Ludo ist Journalist.

JuRa: Sie waren also ein Schauspieler in *Keinohrhasen…*

Schweiger: … und der Regisseur.

JuRa: Herzlichen Glückwunsch zu Ihrem großen Erfolg! Welche anderen Schauspieler haben in dem Film mitgespielt?

Schweiger: Die andere Hauptrolle spielt Nora Tschirner. Für mich war wichtig, dass alle meine Kinder eine Rolle hatten.

JuRa: Wie viele Kinder haben Sie?

Schweiger: Vier. Mein Sohn Valentin ist 1995 geboren, und meine Töchter Luna, Lilli und Emma 1997, 1999 und 2002.

JuRa: Und Ihre Frau?

Schweiger: Das ist das amerikanische Model Dana Carlson. Leider haben wir uns 2005 getrennt.

JuRa: Wie hat Ihre Karriere begonnen? Haben Sie im Theater gespielt?

Schweiger: Nein, leider nie. Seit 1989 habe ich drei Jahre lang in der Serie *Lindenstraße* mitgespielt. Danach habe ich Rollen in achtzehn Filmen gehabt, z.B. in *Traumschiff Surprise*.

JuRa: Und was werden Sie jetzt machen?

Schweiger: Für dieses Jahr habe ich vier Filmprojekte, zwei davon sind in englischer Sprache.

JuRa: Wir wünschen Ihnen weiterhin guten Erfolg und bedanken uns für das Gespräch.

Schweiger: Gern geschehen.

Answers:

a wichtig; **b** vier; **c** Journalisten; **d** auch; **e** drei; **f** Amerika; **g** Fernsehen; **h** deutscher und englischer

6a Imagine you are a radio journalist interviewing a candidate for the personality of the year award voted for by listeners. Choose a celebrity or an author and list questions in German to ask him/her.

4–9

- This activity draws together the vocabulary, ideas and grammar points covered in this spread.

6b You are the star chosen to be interviewed by your partner, the interviewer. Make notes. B ↔ A.

4–9 PLTS

- Students use the questions from activity 8a to carry out an interview. They are then interviewed by their partner.
- This activity encourages students to generate and explore ideas whilst communicating previous learning and to collaborate successfully with others to achieve a common goal. It covers the Creative thinkers, Reflective learners and Team workers groups of skills from the framework of personal, learning and thinking skills.

7 Do a PowerPoint presentation about your star in front of the class. Discuss which star you liked most, then vote for the personality of the year.

4–9 PLTS

- Students use the information they have gathered from the previous activity to prepare a PowerPoint presentation to present to the class. This is an ideal assessment opportunity.
- This activity encourages students to think creatively and explore different ideas whilst communicating previous learning. It also encourages them to organise their time and resources effectively and to work with and influence others. It covers the Creative thinkers, Reflective learners, Self-managers, Team workers and Effective participators groups of skills from the framework of personal, learning and thinking skills.

Success criteria:

- ideas communicated
- pronunciation, intonation and fluency
- range of vocabulary, adjectives and structures used
- tenses or time frames used

Aktive Grammatik

Seiten 102–103

Planner

➤ Objectives
- To practise relative clauses
- To practise the pluperfect tense

➤ Resources
Students' Book, pages 102–103
Exam Skills Workbooks, page 46
Grammar Workbook, pages 21–23, 55, 65
Activity Sheet 40
Resources and Planning OxBox CD-ROM

➤ Grammar
- Relative clauses
- The pluperfect tense
- Adjective endings

➤ PLTS
All questions: Reflective learners/Self-managers

➤ Relative clauses

1 **Complete the sentences with the correct relative pronoun.**
- This question focuses on using the correct pronoun depending on number, gender and case.

Answers:

a die; **b** die; **c** das; **d** der; **e** die; **f** das; **g** den; **h** die

2 **Write the relative clauses in German.**
- This question focuses on students producing relative clause with correct word order and with the correct relative pronoun.

Answers:

a Ich habe viele DVDs, die sehr interessant sind.
b Der Sound, der typisch für diese Band ist, gefällt mir nicht.
c Wir haben die CDs gefunden, die wir mögen.
d Die Musik, die sie hört, ist nicht schlecht.
e Ich mag die Zeitschrift, die für Jugendliche ist.
f Das Festival, das du jedes Jahr besuchst, war toll.

➤ The pluperfect tense

3 **Use the pluperfect tense to complete these sentences.**
- This question focuses on using the correct form of the auxiliary verb and past participle to form the pluperfect tense.

Answers:

a hatte, geübt; **b** hatte, gedreht; **c** gekauft, hatte; **d** gegangen, war; **e** hatten, ferngesehen; **f** gefahren, wart

4 **Write the following sentences in the imperfect and pluperfect tenses.**
- Students write the sentences listed in the imperfect and pluperfect tenses.

Answers:

a Wir hörten Rap-CDs.
Wir hatten Rap-CDs gehört.
b Sie mochte Indie sehr. Sie hatte Indie sehr gemocht.
c Simon fuhr zum *Silbermond*-Konzert.
Simon war zum *Silbermond*-Konzert gefahren.
d Fandest du Techno gut?
Hattest du Techno gut gefunden?
e Mir gefiel Punk total.
Mir hatte Punk total gefallen.
f Steffen und Natalie gingen in die Stadt und kauften ein neues Hiphop-Album.
Steffen und Natalie waren in die Stadt gegangen und hatten ein neues Hiphop-Album gekauft.
g Kamst du zum Gig mit?
Warst du zum Gig mitgekommen?

5 **Write sentences about the music, TV programmes and films…**
a you liked when you were a small child (use the pluperfect tense),
b you liked aged twelve (use the perfect or imperfect tense), and
c you like today (use the present tense).
- Question five focuses on using a variety of tenses to write sentences based on the topics covered in the spread.

➤ Adjective endings

6 **Translate the following sentences into German.**
- Read the *Grammatik* box.
- Students translate the sentences.

Answers:

a Ich will etwas Interessantes sehen.
b Der Musikfilm hatte tollen Sound.
c Das ist wirklich gutes Kino!
d Ich habe viel Langweiliges auf dem Sender/Kanal gesehen.

Kompetenzen

Seite 104

Planner

➤ Objectives
- Summarising what you have learnt

➤ Resources
Students' Book, page 104
Exam Skills Workbooks, page 47
Activity Sheet 41
Resources and Planning OxBox CD-ROM

➤ Skills
- Using knowledge of English to guess the meaning of German words
- Using knowledge of single German words to guess the meaning of compound nouns
- Using the context to guess the meaning of unknown words
- Using a dictionary correctly
- Using relative clauses
- Using longer sentences by combining a main clause with a subordinate clause
- Comparing things
- Using the pluperfect tense
- Varying expression

➤ PLTS
Question 2, Reading: Independent enquirers/Reflective learners/Self-managers
Question 2, Writing: Creative thinkers/Reflective learners

In this unit, students have learnt how to...

➤ Beim Lesen

1 Use their knowledge of English to guess the meaning of German words.
- Students work out what the words mean.

Answers:

to film; to publish; historic/historical; career

2 Use their knowledge of single German words to guess the meaning of compound nouns.

PLTS
- Students guess the meaning of the words listed. They look up the components of the words in a dictionary if necessary.
- This activity encourages students to reflect upon what they have learnt and build on this. It covers the Independent enquirers, Reflective learners and Self-managers groups of skills from the framework of personal, learning and thinking skills.

Answers:

TV actor; soap star; film plot; film script author

3 Use the context to guess the meaning of unknown words.
- Students work out what the words in bold mean.

Answers:

published; publisher's; stage; to appear (on stage)

➤ Beim Schreiben

1 Use a dictionary correctly.
- Students look up the words listed in a dictionary, paying attention to the small print. They then compare notes with their partner.

Answers:

ausschalten (*sep*); singen – sang – gesungen (*irregular*); der Fall (*in general*), der Kasus (*grammar*), der Koffer (*suitcase*); *verb*: können; *noun*: Dose

2 Use relative clauses.

PLTS
- Students write four sentences about famous people containing relative clauses.
- This activity encourages students to think creatively and explore different ideas whilst communicating previous learning. It covers the Creative thinkers and Reflective learners groups of skills from the framework of personal, learning and thinking skills.

3 Use longer sentences by combining a main clause with a subordinate clause.
- Students make a list of all the subordinating conjunctions they can remember, e.g. *obwohl.*
- They use each conjunction to write a sentence.

4 Compare things.
- Students write down how to say 'X is smaller/greater/more talented/more creative than Y.'
- They then write down how to say 'X is the smallest/greatest/most talented/most creative.'
- Finally, they compare their results with those of their partner.

Answers:

X ist kleiner/größer **oder**: toller/talentierter/kreativer als Y.

X ist am kleinsten/größten **oder**: tollsten/talentiertesten/kreativsten.

5 Use the pluperfect tense.
- Students work with a partner to discuss in which situation they would use the pluperfect tense and how to form it.
- Each student then writes one example sentence.

Answer:

The pluperfect is used to describe something which took place **before** another action in the past. It is formed using the imperfect tense of *haben* or *sein* in second position and the past participle of the verb at the end of the clause.

6 **Vary their expression.**

- Students write down four different phrases for expressing their opinion.
- As an extension activity, or homework activity, students write sentences beginning with these phrases on the themes of the unit.

Answers:

Meiner Meinung nach…; Ich denke, dass…; Ich glaube, dass…; Ich finde…; Ich mag…; Mir gefällt…, etc.

Szenario

Seite 105

Planner

➤ Objectives

- Preparing and acting out a sample interview in German
- Writing a review of books or films in German

➤ Resources

Students' Book, page 105
Exam Skills Workbooks, pages 44–45
Assessment Sheets 17–24
Resources and Planning OxBox CD-ROM

➤ Skills

- Speaking practice
- Writing practice

➤ PLTS

Question 1, Speaking: Independent enquirers/ Reflective learners/Self-managers
Question 2, Writing: Independent enquirers/ Reflective learners/Self-managers

➤ Zum Sprechen

In this section, students produce a sample interview to enter into a competition for the chance to interview a famous person of their choice. Encourage them to use the Internet for research and to rehearse their material thoroughly. Suggest recording it to help improve their accent and intonation. This could be done using the record/playback facility on the OxBox CD-ROM.

It is possible for students to obtain GCSE grades A–F depending on their ability and they are marked on Communication, Quality of language and Pronunciation and intonation:
Grade F students communicate a limited number of ideas, expressing simple opinions. A few phrases or short sentences are accurate enough to be recognisable. There are very few instances of clear pronunciation and intonation.
Grade C students communicate the essential elements, readily expressing points of view. They occasionally hesitate and can respond to some unpredictable questions. They use straightforward vocabulary and structures which may contain different tenses or time frames. Pronunciation and intonation is generally accurate.
Grade A students use relevant information to develop and justify individual ideas and points of view. There is no hesitation and they are able to respond to unpredictable questions. They use a wide range of clause types, vocabulary and structures accurately. The presentation is fluent and coherent with just minor errors. Pronunciation and intonation are very accurate with a few minor slips.

1 **Research the German actors Martina Gedeck and Daniel Brühl by going to www.martinagedeck.com and www.fan-lexikon.de/film-tv/daniel-bruehl or searching for other suitable German websites on www.google.de. Note down as much information as you can.**

PLTS

- This activity serves as an introduction to the task. Encourage students think about what they learnt in the unit in order to write useful notes.
- It encourages students to identify questions to answer and to plan and carry out research whilst reflecting upon what they have learnt and organising time and resources effectively to achieve goals. It covers the Independent enquirers, Reflective learners and Self-managers groups of skills from the framework of personal, learning and thinking skills.

2 **Write down what you would ask either Daniel Brühl or Martina Gedeck, and how you think they would answer your questions, in German.**

- This activity allows students to think in more detail about the task.

3 **Now practise the interview with a partner, each taking turns to play the celebrity, and asking additional questions based on the other person's replies.**

- Students use what they have prepared in activities 1 and 2 to act out their interview. This activity is an ideal assessment opportunity.

➤ Zum Schreiben

In this section, students write a review of two books or two films for the school magazine of their German partner school.

It is possible for students to obtain GCSE grades A–F:
Grade F students write a short review using simple sentences and communicate some information.
Grade C students include a variety of structures which may include different tenses or time frames. They communicate information and express personal opinions.
Grade A students include a variety of vocabulary, structures and verb tenses. They convey information, narrate events and express and explain ideas and points of view.

1 **Start by considering your choice of material. Which books or films have you read or seen recently that made a strong impression on you? Jot down the things that you particularly liked and disliked about them.**
- This activity serves as an introduction to the task.

2 **Now start to plan out your review. Note down information for each of the points listed.**

PLTS
- This activity allows students to think in more detail about the task. Encourage them to look back at the work they have done in this unit and to use the Internet for research.
- This activity encourages students to plan and carry out research and evaluate information, to use what they have learnt to achieve goals and to organise time and resources effectively. It covers the Independent enquirers, Reflective learners and Self-managers groups of skills from the framework of personal, learning and thinking skills.

3 **Can you think of anything else you'd like to include? Add it to the list.**
- This activity encourages students to identify any information that is missing or that would add to the review.

4 **Now write up your review. You should try to use all the grammatical features and skills you have practised in this unit. Try to write at least 300 words.**
- Students draw together their research and planning in the previous three activities and write their review.
- This activity is an ideal assessment opportunity.

Vokabeln

Seite 106

Planner

➤ Resources
Students' Book, page 106
Activity Sheet 42

This page provides a summary of the key language covered in each spread of this unit. It could be used as a handy reference for students as they work through the unit. Alternatively, students could use its clear German–English format when learning vocabulary.

Lesen

Seiten 181–182

Planner

➤ Objectives

- To encourage independent reading and develop reading strategies
- To provide alternative class and homework material for students who finish other activities quickly

Page 177 provides a reading text in the context of the unit.
Page 178 provides a newspaper-style reading text, again in the context of the unit.

➤ Resources

Students' Book, pages 181–182

➤ Skills

- Reading practice

➤ PLTS

Question 4 (part 1): Creative thinkers/Reflective learners
Question 1 (part 2): Reflective learners/Self-managers

Lesen A: Keinohrhasen

1 **Lies die Informationen über den Film und beantworte die folgenden Fragen auf Englisch.**

- Students read the film poster and information and answer the questions in English.

4–6

Answers:

a 111 minutes; **b** Til Schweiger and Nora Tschirner; **c** in 2007; **d** a romantic comedy; **e** Ludo Decker and Anna Gotzlowski; **f** from the age of 12 ; **g** in Germany; **h** Til Schweiger and Anika Decker

2 **Lies die Zusammenfassung der Handlung und übersetze den Text ins Englische. Benutze wenn nötig ein Wörterbuch.**

- Students read the summary of the plot and translate it into English.
- They can refer to a dictionary, but remind them to bear in mind what they learnt about using dictionary earlier in the unit.

4–6

Answer:

Ludo Decker works as a journalist. At his work he did something illegal. The court of law says that as a punishment he has to work for 300 hours in a nursery school. There he meets Anna Gotzlowski. As children, Anna und Ludo lived in the same town and back then Ludo was not nice to Anna. Now Anna is not nice to Ludo. But at the end of the film Ludo knows that Anna is very important to him and there is a happy ending.

3 **Wie könnte der Filmtitel auf Englisch heißen? Die zweite Strategie auf Seite 99 kann dir dabei helfen.**

- Students translate the film title into English.
- Refer them to the *Tipp* section on page 99 for support.

Answer:

No-ear-rabbit/hare (The title refers to soft toys Ludo has to sew. He is not very good at it and his rabbit or hare ends up without ears.)

4 **Würdest du den Film gern sehen? Warum (nicht)? Schreib Sätze, um deine Meinung zu begründen.**

- Students write sentences saying if they would like to see this film, giving reasons for their opinion.
- This activity encourages students to think creatively and explore different ideas whilst communicating previous learning. It covers the Creative thinkers and Reflective learners groups of skills from the framework of personal, learning and thinking skills.

4–9

PLTS

Lesen B: Das Leben der Anderen (2006)

1 **Wie heißen die mit Rot markierten Wörter auf Englisch? Benutze die Strategien auf Seite 99, um ihre Bedeutung zu erraten.**

- Students read the review of the film *Das Leben der Anderen* and note down the meaning of words highlighted in red in English.
- Refer students to the *Tipp* section on page 99 for support.
- This activity encourages students to use what they have learnt to work towards and achieve goals. It covers the Reflective learners and Self-managers groups of skills from the framework of personal, learning and thinking skills.

4–6

PLTS

Answers:

totalitär – *totalitarian*; Ostdeutschland – *East Germany*; Fall der Berliner Mauer – *fall of the Berlin Wall*; sich konzentrieren auf – *to concentrate on*; persönlich – *personal*; politisch – *political*; Geheimpolizei – *secret police*; sich identifizieren mit – *to identify with*; System – *system*; Dramatiker – *dramatist, playwright*; Mikrofon – *microphone;* installieren – *to install*; Politiker – *politician*; Minister – *minister (politics)*; attraktiv – *attractive*; beginnen – *to begin*; systemkritisch – *critical of the system*; Idee – *idea*; schmuggeln – *to smuggle*; Situation – *situation*; erscheinen – *to be published, to appear*, Suizid begehen – *to commit suicide*; Ende – *end*; Karriere – *career*, Stasi-Akten – *Stasi/secret police files*; Drehbuchautor – *screenplay writer*,

Rekorde brechen – *to break records*; Filmpreis – *film prize*; Nomination – *nomination*; englischsprachig – *English-language*; brillant – *brilliant*; historisch – *historic(al)*; psychologisch – *psychological*; realistisch – *realistic*; Situation – *situation*; exzellent – *excellent*; konstruiert – *constructed*; kommerziell – *commercial(ly)*; Kinozuschauer – *cinema goer*; produzieren – *to produce*

2 Vervollständige die folgenden Sätze.

- Students read the review again and complete the sentences.

4–6

Answers:

a politischer; **b** Geheimpolizei; **c** Mikrophone; **d** attraktive; **e** Artikel; **f** Karriere; **g** fällt; **h** exzellent konstruiert

3 Beantworte jetzt die folgenden Fragen auf Englisch.

- To check they fully understand the review, students answer the questions in English.

4–9

Answers:

a There is a greater emphasis on politics.
b He identifies with it/supports it.
c Wiesler transcribes all conversations which take place in Dreyman's flat.
d Wiesler begins to find Christa-Maria attractive and once he gets to know Dreyman's ideas, he understands them.
e It is the director's first ever film.
f The film was a box office hit owing to the brilliant actors, the historically and psychologically realistic situation it depicted and the excellently constructed plot.

Unit 4A: Urlaub und Austausch		Overview grid		
Spread	**Contexts and objectives**	**Skills**	**Grammar**	**Vocabulary**
pages 108–109 **Wie man sich ein Urlaubsziel aussucht**	• Choosing a holiday	• Making suggestions	• The conditional	*das Ausland; die Landschaft; die Unterkunft* *bieten; sich entspannen; klettern; sich sonnen; verbringen* *günstig; verschieden*
pages 110–111 **Wie man einen Urlaub bucht**	• Making reservations	• Recognising tenses	• Sentences containing two verbs	*die Anzeige; der Ausflug; die Auskunft; der Flug; der Hafen; das Verkehrsamt* *brauchen; buchen; empfehlen; erklären; schicken* *gültig; möglich*
pages 112–113 **Wie man seine Meinung über einen Urlaub sagt**	• Expressing your opinion on a holiday	• Expressing your opinion	• Sentences expressing opinions in the past tense	*der Aufzug* *reisen; schmecken; vorbereiten; zeigen; zelten* *ausgezeichnet; dreckig; einzig; furchtbar; herrlich; hübsch; lecker* *außerdem; im Freien*
pages 114–115 **Wie man einen Austausch plant**	• Planning an exchange	• Reading transcripts	• Verbs with *zu*	*der Austausch; der Berg; das Picknick* *dauern; sich entschuldigen*
pages 116–117 **Wie man einen Urlaub beschreibt**	• Describing a holiday	• Using different tenses	• Asking questions	*das Andenken; der Dom; das Fest; die Sorge; der Unterschied* *ankommen; sich verabschieden* *froh; zufrieden; gratis; umsonst*
pages 118–119 **Aktive Grammatik**	• Grammar		• The conditional tense • *wenn* • Strong and weak verbs • Verbs with and without *zu*	
page 120 **Kompetenzen**	• Summarising what you have learnt	Skills • Making suggestions • Giving your opinion • Using transcripts to develop your listening skills • Listening for different tenses • Predicting what will come next • Preparing for the exam		
page 121 **Szenario**	• Planning a stay in Germany, Austria or Switzerland • Producing a brochure for a holiday destination	• Speaking practice • Writing practice		
page 122 **Vokabeln**	• Key language from the unit			
pages 183–184 **Lesen**	• Holidays • Working holidays • To encourage independent reading and develop reading strategies • To provide alternative class and homework material for students who finish other activities quickly	• Reading practice		

4A Urlaub und Austausch

Unit Objectives

Contexts and cultural focus: holidays and exchanges
Skills focus: making suggestions using *könnte* and *sollte*; giving your opinion in a variety of different ways; complaining when something is unsatisfactory; using transcripts to develop your listening skills; listening for different tenses; predicting what will come next; preparing for the listening exam
Grammar: the conditional; using different tenses; infinitive constructions; *wenn*

Controlled assessment opportunities

Writing: Students' Book, page 109, activity 7
Writing: Students' Book, page 111, activity 9
Speaking: Students' Book, page 113, activity 8
Writing: Students' Book, page 115, activity 7
Writing: Students' Book, page 117, activity 7
Speaking: Students' Book, page 121, Zum Sprechen, activity 4
Writing: Students' Book, page 121, Zum Schreiben, activity 2

See also ***GCSE German for OCR Assessment OxBox CD-ROM.***

An introduction to the unit Seite 107

- *Aim*: To introduce the themes of the unit.
- The opening spread of each unit is styled as the contents page of a teenage magazine. Illustrations, captions and skills summaries provide a preview of what is to come:

	Students' Book
Weißt du schon, wie man sich ein Urlaubsziel aussucht?	pages 108–109
Weißt du schon, wie man einen Urlaub bucht?	pages 110–111
Weißt du schon, wie man seine Meinung über einen Urlaub sagt?	pages 112–113
Weißt du schon, wie man einen Austausch plant?	pages 114–115
Weißt du schon, wie man einen Urlaub beschreibt?	pages 116–117

- Allow time for students to read the questions and cross-refer to the relevant pages of the Students' Book. They could do this individually or in pairs/groups, followed by whole-class discussion.
- This spread also provides an opportunity for students to recap on familiar language. Ask them to think about language they already know that might be useful when working on the themes of the unit.
- At the end of work on Unit 4A:
  - If time permits, ask students to devise a replacement opening spread. What do they think should be on it, in terms of pictures, captions, etc.? What would they change/keep the same, and why? Ask them to imagine it is the contents page of a teenage magazine: what sort of captions and pictures do they feel would attract people to buy the magazine? This sort of activity encourages students to think about features of a text that make it suitable for a particular audience or purpose.
  - Allow time for students to return to this opening spread to answer the questions, review what they have learned and reflect on areas for improvement. What did they find difficult, interesting, etc.? What do they think are the most important things they have learned in this unit?

Wie man sich ein Urlaubsziel aussucht

Seiten 108–109

Planner

➤ Objectives
- Choosing a holiday

➤ Resources
Students' Book, pages 108–109
CD 2, tracks 25–26
Grammar Workbook, page 57
Activity Sheet 43

➤ Key language
das Ausland; die Landschaft; die Unterkunft
bieten; sich entspannen; klettern; sich sonnen; verbringen
günstig; verschieden

➤ Skills
- Making suggestions

➤ Grammar
- The conditional

➤ PLTS
Question 4: Creative thinkers/Reflective learners/ Team workers
Question 7: Creative thinkers/Reflective learners/ Self-managers

➤ Starters
- Students brainstorm in German activities they like to do on holiday, e.g. *Tennis spielen, schwimmen, Museen und Galerien besichtigen,* etc. Once you feel the list is long enough, challenge students to write a couple of simple sentences using this vocabulary e.g. *Ich will schwimmen.* Compare sentences as a class. Keep the list of vocabulary to use later.
- Display the some key language from the spread and give students a time limit to write the English translations.
- Display some nouns in the singular and plural. Students categorise them under the headings, *singular* and *plural*. Check answers as a group and elicit why students have categorised them as they have.

➤ Plenaries
- Challenge students to write five sentences on the theme of the spread using *könnte* or *sollte*. Compare sentences as a class.
- Display the following beginnings of sentences: *ich würde, du würdest, er/sie würde, ihr würdet, wir würden, sie/Sie würden*. Students finish the sentences, saying where each person would like to go on holiday. Compare sentences as a class.
- Students imagine that they are a celebrity and describe their ideal holiday, using vocabulary from the spread and the conditional, e.g. *Ich würde am liebsten nach Afrika fahren.* The class guesses who they are pretending to be.

1 Lies die vier Anzeigen aus einer Reisebroschüre. Wie sagt man auf Deutsch…?

4–6

- As an introduction to the spread, students read the four adverts from a travel brochure.
- They then find the German for the English words listed.

Answers:

a Entspannung; **b** Klettern; **c** Abenteuer; **d** verschiedenen; **e** Wüste; **f** höchsten … der Welt

2 Welches Reiseziel ist am besten für die folgenden Aktivitäten?

- Students read through the adverts again and decide which destination is best for each activity.

4–6

Answers:

a Berlin; **b** Lake Constance; **c** Lake Constance; **d** Namibia; **e** Namibia; **f** Zermatt; **g** Zermatt; **h** Berlin; **i** Namibia

3 Hör gut zu. Welche Person hat die folgenden Prioritäten – Jens, Maria, Thorsten oder Sonia?

- Students listen to the four people and note down who has what priorities.

4–9

CD 2, track 25 **Seite 109, Übung 3**

Jens
Wenn ich in Urlaub fahre, will ich faulenzen und nicht viel machen. Ich verbringe meine Ferien am liebsten am Strand, wo ich mich sonnen kann. Die besten Urlaubsziele für mich sind also kleine Städte an der Küste. Dort will ich lesen, Musik hören und mit Freunden plaudern. Gute Restaurants sind mir wichtig, sowie ein bequemes Hotel.

Maria
Ich will etwas anderes erleben, wenn ich in Urlaub fahre. Ich fahre am liebsten ins Ausland und weit weg. Ich brauche kein teueres Hotel. Ich bin gern in der Natur und gehe gern wandern. Wichtig ist, dass es total anders ist als der Alltag.

Thorsten
Ich mache gern Kurzurlaub in Städten. Selbst in nur ein paar Tagen kann man viel sehen. Interessante Museen, Galerien und so finde ich ganz toll. In einer Großstadt kann man viel unternehmen, und auch die Unterkunft muss nicht viel kosten. In Jugendherbergen zum Beispiel gibt es gute Zimmer zu einem günstigen Preis.

Sonia
Wenn ich in Urlaub fahre, will ich keine Sehenswürdigkeiten besichtigen – das finde ich zu stressig. Ich will aktiv und in der Natur sein. Letztes Jahr habe ich mit meinen Freunden eine Radtour gemacht und das hat wahnsinnig Spaß gemacht. Wir haben auf Campingplätzen übernachtet, und der ganze Urlaub hat nicht viel gekostet. Und im Winter fahre ich gern Ski – das ist dann aber ziemlich teuer.

Answers:

a Maria, Thorsten; **b** Jens; **c** Jens; **d** Thorsten; **e** Thorsten; **f** Sonia; **g** Maria; **h** Maria; **i** Sonia; **j** Jens

4 Partnerarbeit. Seht euch noch einmal die Anzeigen aus der Reisebroschüre an. Wohin könnten Jens oder Maria fahren? Was sollten Thorsten oder Sonia machen? Diskutiert und schreibt Sätze.

4–9

PLTS

- Read the *Tipp* section on using *könnte* or *sollte* to say what someone could or should do.
- Students read the adverts on page 108 again and discuss with a partner where the people from activity 3 could go and what they should do. If necessary, listen to the recording again.
- This activity encourages students to think creatively, whilst communicating previous learning and to work confidently with others. It covers the Creative thinkers, Reflective learners, Team workers groups of skills from the framework of personal, learning and thinking skills.

5 Hör gut zu. Wohin würden diese Personen fahren? Was würden sie dort machen? Füll die Tabelle aus.

4–9

- Read through the *Grammatik* section on the conditional as a class.
- Students practise listening out for the conditional. They listen to the recording and fill in the grid in English.

CD 2, track 26 **Seite 109, Übung 5**

Sven
Ich würde am liebsten nach Amerika fahren – ich würde gern Großstädte wie New York besuchen, um die Sehenswürdigkeiten zu besichtigen und einkaufen zu gehen.

Erika
Ich würde am liebsten nach Griechenland fahren. Das Wetter dort ist immer toll, und ich würde den ganzen Tag am Strand liegen und mich sonnen.

Dirk
Ich würde am liebsten nach China fahren – die Kultur dort ist faszinierend und ich würde das gern erleben.

Carola
Ich würde am liebsten einen Wassersporturlaub machen – vielleicht in Spanien. Ich würde dann Wasserski fahren oder windsurfen. Da ich in der Schule Spanisch lerne, würde ich auch mein Spanisch verbessern.

Answers:

	Destination	**Activity**
Sven	America	visit big towns such as New York; go sightseeing and shopping
Erika	Greece	spend all day lying on the beach, sunbathing
Dirk	China	experience the culture
Carola	Spain	do watersports (waterskiing or windsurfing); improve her Spanish

A43 Activity Sheet 43 provides further practice on the topic of holidays.

6a Write a list of questions in German to ask your partner about their holiday preferences.

4–9

- This activity draws together the vocabulary and grammar points students have practised in the spread.

6b Interview your partner and suggest where they should go. Then swap roles.

4–9

- Students use the questions they wrote in activity 6a to interview their partner.
- Remind students to use the conditional when making suggestions; the vocabulary box is there for support.

7 Write your own holiday brochure advert either for somewhere near where you live or for somewhere you have visited.

4–9

PLTS

- Students use what they have practised in activities 6a and 6b, as well as what they have practised throughout the spread to write their own holiday brochure. This is an ideal assessment opportunity.
- This activity encourages students to think creatively, generating ideas and exploring possibilities whilst communicating their learning in relevant ways and to work towards goals showing initiative and commitment. It covers the Creative thinkers, Reflective learners and Self-managers groups of skills from the framework of personal, learning and thinking skills.

Success criteria:
- ideas communicated
- range of vocabulary and structures used
- tenses or time frames used
- number of personal opinions given

Wie man einen Urlaub bucht

Seiten 110–111

Planner

➤ Objectives
- Making reservations

➤ Resources
Students' Book, pages 110–111
CD 2, tracks 27–29
Grammar Workbook, pages 58, 66

➤ Key language
die Anzeige; der Ausflug; die Auskunft; der Flug; der Hafen; das Verkehrsamt
brauchen; buchen; empfehlen; erklären; schicken
gültig; möglich

➤ Skills
- Recognising tenses

➤ Grammar
- Sentences containing two verbs

➤ PLTS
Question 8: Creative thinkers/Reflective learners/Team workers/Self-managers
Question 9: Creative thinkers/Reflective learners/Self-managers

➤ Starters
- Display some key language from the spread. Students work in teams and have a time limit to translate each word or phrase into English. When the time is up, compare answers.
- Display some sentences in the past, present and future tenses, e.g. *Ich möchte nach Lindau fahren. Ich werde nach Lindau fahren. Ich bin nach Lindau gefahren.* Also display the headings past, present and future. Ask students put the sentences into the correct column. Compare answers as a class. Elicit from students why they have categorised sentences as they have, e.g. contains the verb *werden* and an infinitive, past participles, etc.
- Display some sentences from the spread in jumbled order, e.g.
  Zeitung habe Ich Ihre gesehen Anzeige in der.
  ein reservieren Einzelzimmer Ich gern mit würde Dusche.
  Give students a time limit to unjumble the sentences. Compare answers as a class.

➤ Plenaries
- Display some words from the spread and challenge students to use them in sentences on the topic of the spread, e.g. *Sehenswürdigkeiten; besichtigen; Sportmöglichkeiten*, etc. Compare answers as a class.
- Students work with a partner to book an unusual holiday, e.g. on the moon. Volunteers read out their conversation to the class. The class votes for the most unusual holiday.
- As a class have a quick look through some of the dialogues from the spread (read through the transcripts to remind them of the listening texts). Display some of the useful phrases and vocabulary. The class then creates a dialogue along the same lines. You start, e.g.
  Teacher: *Guten Tag. Ich denke daran, im Sommer nach X zu fahren, und möchte Auskunft über die Stadt.*
  Student 1: *Das ist kein Problem.*
  Student 2: *Welche Sehenswürdigkeiten gibt es in Lindau?*
  Student 3: *Es gibt...*

1 Hör gut zu. Anna ruft beim Verkehrsamt in Lindau an. Welche Fragen und Antworten passen zusammen?

4–6

- As an introduction to the spread, students listen to the recording and match answers a–g to questions 1–7.

CD 2, track 27 — **Seite 110, Übung 1**

Anna:	Guten Tag. Ich habe vor, im Sommer nach Lindau zu fahren, und möchte Auskunft über die Stadt.
Angestellter:	Das ist kein Problem.
Anna:	Welche Sehenswürdigkeiten gibt es in Lindau?
Angestellter:	Sie können hier den Hafen und das Rathaus besichtigen und wir haben auch ein kleines Stadtmuseum.
Anna:	Und welche Sportmöglichkkeiten gibt es?
Angestellter:	Es gibt eine Wasserskischule, ein Freibad und einen Tennisplatz und natürlich können Sie auch im See baden.
Anna:	Wann ist das Freibad geöffnet?
Angestellter:	Im Sommer jeden Tag von 10 bis 19 Uhr.
Anna:	Welche Ausflüge kann man machen?
Angestellter:	Schaffhausen ist einen Besuch wert und ist nicht zu weit entfernt.
Anna:	Was kann man abends machen?
Angestellter:	Wir haben ein Kino, Diskos, Konzerte mit klassischer Musik und viele Kneipen.
Anna:	Welche anderen Aktivitäten gibt es?
Angestellter:	Sie sollten auf jeden Fall eine Schifffahrt auf dem See machen.
Anna:	Danke. Könnten Sie mir bitte einige Informationen zuschicken?
Angestellter:	Natürlich. Ich schicke Ihnen eine Broschüre.

Answers:

1 b; **2** e; **3** a; **4** g; **5** d; **6** c; **7** f

2 Anna hat eine E-Mail ans Hotel Schlink geschrieben, um ihren Urlaub in Lindau zu buchen. Wie sagt man auf Deutsch...?

- Students read Anna's e-mail and note down the German for the English expressions listed.

4–6

Answers:

a Ich hätte gern ein Zimmer mit Seeblick. **b** Wie weit ist ... entfernt? **c** Informationen über; **d** eine Schifffahrt; **e** haben Sie eine Broschüre darüber? **f** Ich interessiere mich für...

3a Partnerarbeit. Lest die folgenden Satzanfänge. Wie werden eurer Meinung nach die Sätze enden?

- Students read the sentence beginnings listed and discuss with a partner how they think they would end, e.g. with a past participle, an infinitive, etc.

3b Findet jetzt die richtige Endung für jeden Satz.

- Students now find the correct endings for the sentence beginnings in activity 3a.

Answers:

1 ... über das Hotel gelesen. **2** ... bleiben. **3** ... mit ihrer Mutter und einer Freundin. **4** ... aufregend. **5** ... über die Wassersportanlage wissen. **6** ... möchte eine Schifffahrt machen.

4 Hör dir das Telefongespräch zwischen Herrn Schlink und Anna an. Notiere auf Englisch, welche Aktivitäten in der Vergangenheit, im Präsens und in der Zukunft sind.

- Read the *Tipp* section as a class.
- Students listen to the telephone conversation and note down in English which of the activities mentioned are in the past, which are in the present, and which are in the future.

4–6

CD 2, track 28 **Seite 111, Übung 4**

Herr Schlink: Guten Tag. Hier Herr Schlink vom Hotel Schlink in Lindau.
Anna: Guten Tag, Herr Schlink.
Herr Schlink: Wir haben Ihre E-Mail bekommen, und wir haben die Reservierung für Sie vorgenommen.
Anna: Das ist prima – und ich habe auch ein paar Fragen gestellt.
Herr Schlink: Ja, Sie werden ein Zimmer mit Seeblick haben, das ist kein Problem. Ich habe Ihnen auch eine Broschüre über unsere Wassersportanlage geschickt. Im Sommer werden wir neue Wasserskikurse anbieten, und Sie können bereits jetzt reservieren.
Anna: Ich werde Sie zurückrufen, wenn ich die Broschüre bekommen habe.
Herr Schlink: Das Hotel ist 15 Minuten von der Stadtmitte entfernt und unser Hotelbus fährt alle 30 Minuten dorthin. Es gibt auch ein paar Diskos in Lindau, sowie viele Restaurants. Und der Bus fährt auch abends.
Anna: Toll! Gibt es auch regelmäßige Schifffahrten auf dem See?
Herr Schlink: Ja, ich habe Ihnen den Fahrplan geschickt.
Anna: Vielen Dank, Herr Schlink. Auf Wiederhören.

Answers:

past: received e-mail and made the reservation; asked a few questions; sent a brochure about their watersport facilities; sent boat trip timetable
present: can reserve a place on the new waterskiing courses; the hotel bus goes to the town centre every thirty minutes; the bus also runs in the evening; there are regular boat trips
future: will have a room with a sea view; will offer new waterskiing courses in the Summer; will phone back when the brochure arrives

5 Partnerarbeit. A kommt aus Deutschland und möchte Auskunft über eure Stadt. B arbeitet auf dem Verkehrsamt. Entwerft einen Dialog. Übung 1 hilft euch dabei.

- Students work with a partner to ask for and give information about a town.
- Encourage students to refer back to activity 1 for support and also to bear in mind what they have practised in the other activities on the spread and the *Grammatik* and *Tipp* sections.

4–9

6 Hör gut zu. Annas Freund Ludger ruft an, um seinen Urlaub in Namibia zu buchen. Sind die Aussagen richtig oder falsch? Verbessere die falschen Aussagen.

- Students continue to think about booking holidays. They listen to the recording and note down whether each of the statements is true or false.
- Students correct any false statements.

4–9

CD 2, track 29 **Seite 111, Übung 6**

Ludger:	Guten Tag, ich habe Ihre Anzeige für die Safaritour im Internet gesehen und ich möchte einen Platz reservieren.
Angestellte:	Aber gern. Wie heißen Sie?
Ludger:	Ludger Hauer.
Angestellte:	Und welche Tour wollen Sie?
Ludger:	Die Tour am 26. Juli, bitte.
Angestellte:	Ja, wir haben noch einen Platz in der Gruppe frei, aber der Flug am Freitag ist schon voll. Sie können aber am Donnerstag, also am 25., fliegen und einen Tag in Windhoek verbringen. Der Rest der Gruppe kommt dann am Samstag.
Ludger:	Ja, das ist kein Problem. Wann ist der Flug?
Angestellte:	Es ist ein Direktflug mit Lufthansa. Sie fliegen um 20 Uhr von Frankfurt ab und sind dann um 6 Uhr am nächsten Morgen in Windhoek.
Ludger:	Und können Sie ein Hotel in Windhoek für mich buchen?
Angestellte:	Natürlich. Was für ein Zimmer möchten Sie?
Ludger:	Ich möchte ein Zimmer mit Dusche und ich möchte auch Frühstück.
Angestellte:	Das Hotel bietet auch Vollpension.
Ludger:	Nein, ich suche mir abends lieber ein Restaurant. Hat das Hotel ein Schwimmbad?
Angestellte:	Ja, es hat einen schönen Swimmingpool.
Ludger:	Prima. Und was kostet die Tour?
Angestellte:	Die Tour kostet insgesamt 1900 Euro. Zahlen Sie mit Kreditkarte?
Ludger:	Ja, und ich habe noch ein paar Fragen. Was muss ich alles mitbringen?
Angestellte:	Sie bekommen von uns einen Bestätigungsbrief, und darin ist alles erklärt, was Sie für die Tour brauchen. Haben Sie schon einmal eine Safari gemacht?
Ludger:	Nein, das wird das erste Mal sein.
Angestellte:	Ich wünsche Ihnen viel Spaß!
Ludger:	Vielen Dank!

Answers:

a F – Ludger hat im Internet über die Safaritour gelesen. **b** F – Er will am 26. Juli fahren. **c** R; **d** R; **e** F – Es ist ein Direktflug. **f** F – Ludger bucht ein Zimmer mit Dusche. **g** R; **h** R; **i** R; **j** F – Das wird das erste Mal sein.

7 Lies die Bestätigungsmail von Namibia Tours. Füll die Lücken mit Wörtern aus dem Kasten aus. Schau neue Vokabeln im Wörterbuch nach.

4–6

- Students read the letter of confirmation.
- They use the words from the box to fill in the gaps.
- They look up any new vocabulary in a dictionary. Remind them to read through their completed text to check that it is grammatically correct and that it makes sense.

Answers:

a inbegriffen; **b** zentral; **c** klimatisiert; **d** nehmen; **e** Schlafsack; **f** bequeme; **g** Arzt

8 Using the adverts on page 108, prepare two dialogues with a partner. A calls the tourist information office in either Zermatt or Berlin to ask about booking a holiday there. Use the pictures below for some ideas for questions. B works in the tourist information office and gives the answers. B ↔ A

4–9

PLTS

- This activity draws together what students have learnt in the spread.
- It encourages students to generate and explore ideas, to communicate previous learning and to collaborate with others to work towards goals. It covers the Creative thinkers, Reflective learners, Team workers and Self-managers groups from the framework of personal, learning and thinking skills.

9 Now write an email to book your holiday in either Berlin or Zermatt. Make sure you specify your accommodation requirements and include at least three questions.

4–9

PLTS

- Students use what they have discussed in activity 8 to write an email to book their holiday. This is an ideal assessment opportunity.
- This activity encourages students to generate and explore ideas, to communicate previous learning and to work towards goals. It covers the Creative thinkers, Reflective learners and Self-managers groups of skills from the framework of personal, learning and thinking skills.

Success criteria:

- amount of information communicated
- variety of vocabulary and structures used
- number of personal opinions given

Wie man seine Meinung über einen Urlaub sagt

Seiten 112–113

Planner

➤ Objectives

- Expressing your opinion on a holiday

➤ Resources

Students' Book, pages 112–113
CD 2, tracks 30–31
Grammar Workbook, page 48
Activity Sheets 44, 46

➤ Key language

der Aufzug
reisen; schmecken; vorbereiten; zeigen; zelten
ausgezeichnet; dreckig; einzig; furchtbar; herrlich; hübsch; lecker
außerdem; im Freien

➤ Skills

- Expressing your opinion

➤ Grammar

- Sentences expressing opinions in the past tense

➤ PLTS

Question 4: Independent enquirers/Creative thinkers/Reflective learners/Team workers/Self-managers
Question 8: Creative thinkers/Reflective learners/Self-managers

➤ Starters

- The class brainstorm adjectives to describe holidays. Go round the class asking each student to give you an adjective that could be used to describe a holiday. Specify to each student whether this adjective should be positive or negative, e.g.
  Teacher: *positive;* Student: *wunderschön;*
  Teacher: *negative;* Student: *furchtbar*
  When all students have said an adjective, the class tries to recall all of the adjectives mentioned. List these in two columns, postive adjectives in one column, negative ones in the other. Keep the list to use in plenary activity 1.
- Divide the class into teams. Display some of the complaints mentioned in the spread, but jumbled up, e.g.
  den gab Es Wasser in Duschen kaltes nur.
  Give students a time limit to unjumble each sentence and to translate it into English. Compare answers as a class.
- Play a memory game around the class, *Ich bin in den Ferien gefahren und…* Begin by saying, e.g.
  Teacher: *…die Landschaft hat mir gefallen.*
  Student 1: *…die Landschaft hat mir gefallen und man konnte viel unternehmen.*
  Student 2: *…die Landschaft hat mir gefallen, man konnte viel unternehmen und…*

➤ Plenaries

- Students use some of the adjectives listed in starter activity 1, along with *da* and *weil* to create five interesting sentences on the themes of the spread. Compare sentences as a class. Elicit from students what happens to the word order with *weil.*
- Students work in pairs to make up complaints and resolutions. Encourage them to be as creative and original as possible. They then act these out in front of the class. The class votes for most original complaint and resolution.
- Students work as a class to describe an unusual holiday in the past. You begin with an introductory sentence and go round the class with students adding to this, e.g.
  Teacher: *Wohin bist du in den Ferien gefahren?*
  Student 1: *Ich bin nach Lappland gefahren.*
  Student 2: *Was hat dir gefallen?*
  Student 3: *Die Landschaft hat mir gefallen, weil sie…*
  Students should try to incorporate structures and vocabulary from the spread.

1 In den zwei Texten gibt es viele positive und negative Adjektive. Finde sie und mach zwei Listen.

- As an introduction to the spread, students read the e-mails and list the positive and negative adjectives.

4–6

Answers:

Positive: wunderschön; herrlich; bezaubernd; fantastisch; freundlich; informativ; schön; leckere; okay; hübsch; lustig
Negative: kalt; furchtbar; kaputt; ekelhaft; schrecklich

2 Beantworte die folgenden Fragen auf Englisch.

- Students read the texts again, this time in more detail, and answer the questions in English.

4–6

Answers:

a it was wonderful; **b** it was enchanting; **c** the desert; **d** it was fun, but cold at night; **e** the lift was out of order and their room was on the fifth floor; **f** the television in her room was broken, the food was disgusting, there was only occasionally hot water and in the neighbouring room, there was a baby who cried all night; **g** she liked it – pretty and a lot to do; **h** She went waterskiing for the first time and went on a few marvellous outings

3a Hör gut zu. Was sagen diese Personen über ihren Urlaub? Füll die Tabelle aus.

4–9

- Students listen to the people describing their holiday and fill in the table in German.

CD 2, track 30 **Seite 113, Übung 3**

Peter
Letztes Jahr habe ich einen Campingurlaub in der Schweiz gemacht. Die Schweiz war wunderbar – man konnte viel unternehmen, und das Wetter war herrlich. Aber der Campingplatz hat mir nicht sehr gut gefallen. Die Toiletten waren dreckig und es gab nur kaltes Wasser in den Duschen. Außerdem war der Campingplatz überfüllt und es war sehr laut.

Anja
Letztes Jahr habe ich meinen Urlaub in einem kleinen Hotel an der italienischen Küste verbracht. Ich habe Florenz besucht, und die Stadt hat mir sehr gut gefallen. Unser Hotel war ziemlich gut. Ich hatte einen schönen Blick aufs Meer, und das Essen war lecker. Aber das Zimmer war sehr klein und es gab keine Klimaanlage. Nachts war es sehr heiß.

Thorsten
Letztes Jahr haben wir Skiurlaub in Österreich gemacht. Leider waren die Pisten zu voll und es gab nicht genug Schnee. Aber die Ferienwohnung war sehr schön und hatte einen großen Balkon. Es gab auch ein Schwimmbad. Das Nachtleben im Skiort war auch prima.

Sara
Letztes Jahr habe ich eine Kreuzfahrt auf dem Rhein gemacht. Die Landschaft war sehr schön, und wir haben viele interessante Städte besichtigt. Das Schiff war sauber und das Essen hat gut geschmeckt. Das einzige Problem – meine Mutter war seekrank.

Michael
Letztes Jahr bin ich mit meiner Familie nach Ibiza gefahren. Es war furchtbar. Die Strände waren alle voll, und unser Hotel war neben der Disko. Es gab die ganze Nacht laute Musik und wir konnten nicht schlafen. Das einzig Gute war das Wetter – wir hatten jeden Tag strahlenden Sonnenschein.

Answers:

	Where?	**Positive aspects**	**Negative aspects**
Peter	Switzerland	lots to do; wonderful weather	the campsite – dirty toilets; only cold water in the showers; overcrowded and noisy
Anja	on the Italian coast	Florence; good sea view; delicious food	very small room; no air-conditioning
Thorsten	Austria	nice holiday apartment – big balcony, swimming pool; night life in ski resort was great	pistes crowded; not enough snow
Sara	cruise along the Rhein	nice landscape; visited interesting towns; ship was clean; tasty food	mother was seasick
Michael	Ibiza	sunshine everyday	beaches all crowded; hotel near the disco – loud music and couldn't sleep

3b Hör noch einmal zu. Welche anderen Adjektive kannst du dir merken? Füg sie der Liste aus Übung 1 hinzu.

4–9

- Read the *Tipp* section on giving opinions.
- Students listen to the recording again and note down any other adjectives they hear.

4 Mach eine Umfrage zum Thema Urlaub in deiner Klasse.

4–9

PLTS

- Read through the *Grammatik* section on opinions about past events as a class.
- To practise giving opinions about past events, students take part in a class survey on holidays.
- This encourages students to plan and carry out research, to generate and explore ideas, to communicate their learning in relevant ways and to collaborate with others to work towards goals. It covers the Independent enquirers, Creative thinkers, Reflective learners, Team workers and Self-managers groups of skills from the framework of personal, learning and thinking skills.

5 Schreib ein paar Sätze über die Ergebnisse der Umfrage. Vergiss nicht, *ihm* oder *ihr* zu benutzen.

4–6

- Students now write a few sentences on the results of the survey.
- Remind them to use *ihm* or *ihr* and encourage them to refer back to previous activities for useful vocabulary and structures.

6a Hör gut zu. Annas Mutter ruft beim Hotel Schlink an, um sich zu beschweren. Welche Vorschläge macht der Hoteldirektor? (2 Dinge)

4–9

- Students listen to Anna's mother complain to the hotel manager and note down what suggestions the manager makes.

CD 2, track 31 **Seite 113, Übung 6**

Hotel:	Hotel Schlink in Lindau. Guten Tag.
Annas Mutter:	Guten Tag, Frau Bremer am Apparat. Ich möchte bitte mit dem Hoteldirektor sprechen.
Hotel:	Worum geht es, bitte?
Annas Mutter:	Ich habe letzte Woche in Ihrem Hotel übernachtet, und ich war überhaupt nicht damit zufrieden. Ich möchte mich beschweren.
Hotel:	Ich verbinde Sie sofort. ...
Hoteldirektor:	Herr Förster hier. Was kann ich für Sie tun?
Annas Mutter:	Herr Förster, mein Aufenthalt in Ihrem Hotel letzte Woche war eine einzige Katastrophe. Erstens war der Aufzug außer Betrieb...
Hoteldirektor:	Oh, das tut mit Leid...
Annas Mutter:	Dabei waren unsere Zimmer im fünften Stock! Zweitens gab es kein heißes Wasser. Meine Tochter und ich mussten uns kalt duschen – und das im Urlaub!
Hoteldirektor:	Oje, ja, wir hatten ein Problem mit dem Wasserboiler...
Annas Mutter:	Das Essen war auch schrecklich – haben Sie jemals in Ihrem eigenen Restaurant gegessen, Herr Förster? Ich würde es Ihnen nicht empfehlen!
Hoteldirektor:	Frau Bremer, es tut mir so schrecklich Leid. Hören Sie, ich mache Ihnen ein Sonderangebot, extra für Sie, als Entschädigung für Ihre schlechte Erfahrung bei uns. Kommen Sie an Weihnachten für eine Woche zu uns, und Sie und Ihre Tochter bekommen zwei kostenlose Übernachtungen im Hotel. Sie bekommen auch eine Schifffahrt zur Insel Reichenau. Was sagen Sie dazu?
Annas Mutter:	Herr Direktor, ich glaube, Sie haben mich missverstanden. Ich fand Ihr Hotel furchtbar – ich möchte auf keinen Fall wieder bei Ihnen übernachten – und erst recht nicht an Weihnachten. Was für eine Schnapsidee! Weihnachten im Horrorhotel!
Hoteldirektor:	Frau Bremer, beruhigen Sie sich! Wir haben Ihnen nicht absichtlich Probleme bereitet! Wie wäre es denn mit einer Ermäßigung auf Ihre Rechnung? 10 Prozent vielleicht?
Annas Mutter:	10 Prozent?!?! Und das soll alles besser machen? Dieser Urlaub hat mich ein Vermögen gekostet! Ich denke, 50 Prozent wären angemessen.
Hoteldirektor:	50 Prozent!!! In Ordnung, Frau Bremer, in Ordnung...

Answers:

1 staying in the hotel for a week at Christmas with 2 free overnight stays and a free boat trip
2 10% reduction from bill

6b Hör noch einmal zu. Wie sagt man auf Deutsch...?

- Students listen again and note down the German phrases used for the English phrases listed.

4–9

Answers:

a Ich möchte bitte mit dem Hoteldirektor sprechen. **b** sich beschweren; **c** Worum geht es, bitte? **d** Ich verbinde Sie sofort. **e** es tut mir so schrecklich Leid; **f** ich mache Ihnen; **g** ein Sonderangebot; **h** Ermäßigung

7 Partnerarbeit. A ist der Kunde/die Kundin, und B ist der Vetreter des Reiseveranstalters (*tour rep*). Entwerft Dialoge. B ↔ A.

4–9

- Students work with a partner to practise complaining about an unsatisfactory holiday.
- Encourage students to refer back to activities 6a and 6b for useful vocabulary.

A44 Activity Sheet 44 provides activities on describing and giving an opinion on an exchange trip.

A46 Activity Sheet 46 provides activities on complaining about unsatisfactory holidays.

8 Prepare a one-minute presentation about holidays. You can record your presentation using the OxBox software.

4–9

PLTS

- This activity draws together the vocabulary and grammar students have practised in this spread. It is an ideal assessment opportunity.
- It encourages students to generate ideas and explore possibilities, to communicate their learning in relevant ways and to work towards goals. It covers the Creative thinkers, Reflective learners and Self-managers groups of skills from the framework of personal, learning and thinking skills.

Success criteria:

- ideas communicated
- pronunciation and intonation and fluency
- range of vocabulary and structures tense or time frames used
- number of personal opinions given

9 Write a letter complaining about problems with your accommodation during your holiday. Follow this model for how to start and end your letter.

4–9

- This activity draws together what students have learnt about complaining. It also provides practice of writing a formal letter.
- Remind students to follow the model letter for how to start and end their letter.

Wie man einen Austausch plant

Seiten 114–115

Planner

➤ Objectives
- Planning an exchange

➤ Resources
Students' Book, pages 114–115
CD 2, track 32
Grammar Workbook, page 58

➤ Key language
der Austausch; der Berg; das Picknick
dauern; sich entschuldigen

➤ Skills
- Reading transcripts

➤ Grammar
- Verbs with *zu*

➤ PLTS
Question 6: Independent enquirers/Creative thinkers/Reflective learners/Team workers/Self-managers
Question 7: Creative thinkers/Reflective learners/Self-managers

➤ Starters
- Display a list of activities mentioned in the spread that you might do on an exchange trip, e.g. *Schlittschuh laufen.* Next to these display the English translations jumbled up. Students have a fixed amount of time to match them up. Check the answers as a class.
- Go round the class, asking students questions from the spread, e.g. *Gibt es etwas, was du nicht isst?* Students answer in full sentences, e.g. *Ich esse nicht so gern Fisch.*
- Display the sentence beginning, *Wenn wir Zeit haben,...* and challenge students to write as many sentences as possible with this beginning, e.g. *Wenn wir Zeit haben, machen wir eine Schifffahrt auf dem Rhein.* Compare sentences as a class.

➤ Plenaries
- Display a few words and phrases from the spread and challenge students to use them all in a short paragraph based on the themes of the spread. Confident students present their paragraph to the class.
- Using Sebastian's e-mail as a model, students write their own plan for an exchange partner who is going to visit. They can make it up, or base it on their town. Volunteers present their plan to the class. The class votes for the most interesting plan.
- Students work in pairs to prepare and perform a role-play. They play two students having a conversation before an exchange. Student A is the host, Student B, the visitor. Student A makes suggestions as to what they can do each day. Student B disagrees with all of the suggestions, giving reasons why and suggesting alternatives, e.g.
  Student A: *Hier in ... gibt es eine Eisbahn. Möchstest du Schlittschuh laufen?*
  Student B: *Nein, ich kann nicht Schlittschuh laufen. Wir können vielleicht ins Kino gehen?*
  Student A: *Nein, es gibt kein Kino. Wenn das Wetter schön ist, könnten wir ein Picknick machen.*
  Student B: *Nein...*

1 Hör gut zu. Naomi fährt nächste Woche im Rahmen eines Schüleraustauschs nach Deutschland. Ihr Austauschpartner Sebastian ruft an. Bring die Gesprächsthemen in die richtige Reihenfolge.

7–9

- As an introduction to the spread, students listen to the dialogue.
- They then put the themes listed into the correct order.

CD 2, track 32 — **Seite 114, Übungen 1, 2 und 3**

Sebastian: Hallo, Naomi, wie geht's?
Naomi: Gut, danke, Sebastian. Ich freue mich auf den Austausch nächste Woche.
Sebastian: Ich mich auch. Ich habe ein paar Fragen für dich. Gibt es etwas, was du nicht isst? Bist du zum Beispiel Vegetarierin?
Naomi: Nein, aber ich esse nicht so gern Fisch.
Sebastian: Ich auch nicht, das ist also kein Problem. Ich möchte auch etwas für das Wochenende planen, aber du machst schon Ausflüge mit deiner Klasse, nicht wahr?
Naomi: Das stimmt. Hast du das Programm noch nicht bekommen?

Sebastian:	Nein, ich weiß nur, du kommst am Freitag mit mir in die Schule. Das ist mein Lieblingstag, weil ich zwei Stunden Sport habe.
Naomi:	Gut, dass ich das weiß – ich werde also meine Turnschuhe mitbringen. Ich kann dir das Programm für die Woche mailen. Ich weiß, dass wir einen Tag nach Köln fahren und ins Museum gehen und dass wir auch die Burg Eltz besichtigen.
Sebastian:	Ach, die Burg Eltz ist wunderschön. Hier in Koblenz gibt es auch eine Eisbahn. Kannst du Schlittschuh laufen?
Naomi:	Nein, aber ich möchte es lernen.
Sebastian:	Gut – vielleicht machen wir das. Schick mir das Programm und ich werde mit meinen Eltern einen Plan fürs Wochenende besprechen.
Naomi:	Toll! Bis bald, Sebastian!
Sebastian:	Ja. Bis Donnerstagabend! Tschüs.

Answers:

b, a, e, c, d

2 Hör noch einmal zu. Sind die Aussagen richtig oder falsch?

- Students listen again and note down whether the statements are true (R) or false (F).

Answers:

7–9 **a** F; **b** R; **c** R; **d** F; **e** R; **f** F; **g** F; **h** R

3 Hör dir das Gespräch zwischen Naomi und Sebastian noch einmal an und lies den Text.

- Read through the *Tipp* section on using transcripts as a class.
- Students listen to the conversation between Naomi and Sebastian again whilst reading the transcript. They list any words they now understand that they didn't when just listening. They correct any answers they got wrong.

7–9

4a In welcher Reihenfolge schlägt Sebastian die folgenden Aktivitäten vor?

- Students read Sebastian's e-mail and put the activities in the order Sebastian mentions them.

Answers:

7–9 **1** e; **2** f; **3** c; **4** g; **5** d; **6** a; **7** b

4b Lies die E-mail von Sebastian. Was passt zusammen?

- Students read Sebastian's e-mail.
- They then match the sentence halves.

Answers:

7–9 **1** c; **2** e; **3** a; **4** g; **5** d; **6** b; **7** f

5 Lies die E-Mail noch einmal und schreib Sätze über Sebastians Pläne. Das *zu* nicht vergessen!

- Read through the *Grammatik* section on verbs with *zu* as a class. Work through a few examples.
- Students read Sebastian's e-mail again and write sentences about his plans using *zu*.

6 Work with a partner to create a dialogue between two students before an exchange. Prepare a list of questions to ask. Include the points listed.

- This activity draws together the vocabulary and grammar practised in the spread.
- It encourages students to identify questions to answer and to generate ideas. It also encourages them to communicate their learning in relevant ways, and to collaborate with others to work towards goals. It covers the Independent enquirers, Creative thinkers, Reflective learners, Team workers and Self-managers groups from the framework of personal, learning and thinking skills.

4–9

PLTS

7 Write an email to your German exchange partner about your forthcoming visit. Include the points listed.

- Students use what they have learnt in the spread to write an email. This is an ideal assessment opportunity.
- This encourages students to think creatively, generating ideas and exploring possibilities, to communicate their learning in relevant ways and to work towards goals. It covers the Creative thinkers, Reflective learners, and Self-managers groups of skills from the framework of personal, learning and thinking skills.

4–9

PLTS

Success criteria:

- amount of information communicated
- variety of vocabulary and structures used
- number of personal opinions given

Wie man einen Urlaub beschreibt

Seiten 116–117

Planner

➤ Objectives
- Describing a holiday

➤ Resources
Students' Book, pages 116–117
CD 2, track 33
Grammar Workbook, pages 45–57
Activity Sheet 45

➤ Key language
das Andenken; der Dom; das Fest; die Sorge; der Unterschied
ankommen; sich verabschieden
froh; zufrieden; gratis; umsonst

➤ Grammar
- Using different tenses

➤ Skills
- Asking questions

➤ PLTS
Question 6: Creative thinkers/Reflective learners/ Team workers/Self-managers
Question 7: Creative thinkers/Reflective learners/ Self-managers

➤ Starters
- Display some words from the key language of the spread with the vowels missing. Students race against each other to fill in the missing letters. Elicit the English for these words.
- Go round the class, calling out a question word from the spread, e.g. *Wann? Warum? Was? Was für...? Welche? Wie?* or *Wie lange?* Challenge students to ask you a question on the theme of the spread using the word you have called out. Make a list of the questions to use later.
- Display sentences from the spread in a variety of tenses, e.g. *Am Donnerstagabend sind wir angekommen. Heute Abend gibt es ein großes Fest. Wir werden unsere Partner bald wiedersehen.* Ask students to identify which tense is being used each time and elicit how they know this, e.g. use of *haben* or *sein* with past participle, etc. If there is time, cover up some of the words in each sentence and ask students to replace them with their own alternatives, e.g. *Am **Montagabend** sind wir **nach Köln gefahren**.*

➤ Plenaries
- Display the list of questions from starter activity 2 and challenge students to write answers to these. Compare answers.
- Call out a word from the spread. Students respond by putting it into a sentence, e.g.
  Teacher: *deutschen Partnern*
  Student: *Wir haben eine Woche bei unseren deutschen Partnern verbracht.*
  Encourage students to use a many different tenses as possible and to use question words.
- Students write a description of an imaginary exchange that they didn't enjoy, giving reasons why it wasn't very good, e.g. didn't like exchange partner, the food, etc. They then present their description to the class. The class votes for the best description of a bad exchange visit.

1 **Naomi macht ein Interview für die Webseite der deutschen Schule, die sie für eine Woche besucht hat. Hör zu und beantworte die Fragen auf Englisch.**

4–6

- As an introduction to the spread, students listen to Naomi and answer the questions in English.

CD 2, track 33 — **Seite 116, Übung 1**

Karsten: Heute machen wir ein Interview mit Naomi Browning über ihre Woche mit uns am Thomas-Mann-Gymnasium. Ich bin Karsten Fries. Guten Tag, Naomi.
Naomi: Guten Tag, Karsten.
Karsten: Also, Naomi, hat dir die Woche bei uns gut gefallen?
Naomi: Ja, ich habe mich super mit Sebastian verstanden und wir haben hier sehr viel gesehen und gemacht. Es ist sehr schön hier in Koblenz.
Karsten: Was hat dir am besten gefallen?
Naomi: Das Wochenende war wirklich super – wir sind ins Phantasialand gefahren und haben auch einen Ausflug nach Boppard gemacht.
Karsten: Und wie findest du unsere Schule?
Naomi: Sehr gut – die Schüler und Lehrer waren alle sehr freundlich und hilfsbereit.
Karsten: Besser als die Schule in England?
Naomi: Die Schule beginnt hier ein bisschen zu früh für mich, aber es ist gut, dass ihr keine Schuluniform habt.
Karsten: Welche anderen Unterschiede gibt es zwischen Deutschland und Großbritannien?
Naomi: Also, hier isst man die Hauptmahlzeit mittags und zu Hause essen wir da meistens ein Brot oder etwas Leichtes. Und ich denke, die Deutschen sind umweltfreundlicher.

Answers:

a she enjoyed it; **b** she got on well with Sebastian, did and saw a lot and liked Koblenz; **c** the weekend – they went to Phantasialand and on a trip to Boppard; **d** The teachers and pupils were all friendly and helpful; **e** the school day begins too early; **f** In Germany, they tend to eat their main meal at lunchtime; **g** She thinks that Germans are more environmentally friendly

2 Naomis Freund Mark schreibt einen Artikel über den Austausch für die Schülerzeitung. Lies den Text. Wie sagt man auf Deutsch...?

7–9

- Students read Mark's article about the exchange.
- They pick out the German for the English phrases.

Answers:

a gleich; **b** wir haben das alle überlebt; **c** Andenken; **d** Die Woche ist wirklich schnell vorübergegangen! **e** sich verabschieden; **f** wir freuen uns darauf

A45 Activity Sheet 45 provides further activities on describing holidays.

3 Wähl für jede Frage die richtige Antwort.

- Read the *Tipp* section on answering multiple-choice questions as a class.
- Students then read Mark's article again and choose the correct answer for each question.

7–9

Answers:

1 a; **2** b; **3** c; **4** a

4 Formuliere Fragen an Mark mit den Fragewörten aus der Tipp-Box.

- Read the *Tipp* section on question words.
- To practise using question words, students use the options listed to form questions to ask Mark.

4–6

5 Partnerarbeit. A stellt die Fragen aus Übung 4, B spielt die Rolle von Mark. B ↔ A.

- Students work with a partner. Partner A asks the questions from activity 5, Partner B plays the part of Mark and answers the questions. They then swap roles.

4–9

6a Write your own list of questions to ask a partner about an exchange or a recent holiday, using your answers to activity 5 as a guide. Then conduct the interviews.

- This activity draws together what students have learnt in the spread.
- This encourages students to generate and explore different ideas, to assess themselves and others, identifying opportunities and achievements, to communicate their learning in order to achieve goals and to work confidently with others. It covers the Creative thinkers, Reflective learners, Team workers and Self-managers groups of skills from the framework of personal, learning and thinking skills.

4–9

PLTS

6b Record yourselves conducting your interviews on OxBox to assess pronunciation and listen for any mistakes.

7 Write your own account of a recent exchange visit or holiday using your own questions to give you a structure. You should aim to write around 250 words. Make sure you use at least three tenses.

- This draws together what students have prepared in previous activities. It is an ideal assessment opportunity.
- It encourages students to generate ideas and explore possibilities, to communicate their learning in order to achieve goals and to organise their time effectively. It covers the Creative thinkers, Reflective learners, and Self-managers groups of skills from the framework of personal, learning and thinking skills.

4–9

PLTS

Success criteria:

- variety of vocabulary and structures used
- different tenses or time frames used
- number of personal opinions given

Aktive Grammatik

Seiten 118–119

Planner

➤ Objectives

- Practising the conditional tense
- Using *wenn*
- Strong and weak verbs
- Using verbs with and without *zu*

➤ Resources

Students' Book, pages 118–119
Exam Skills Workbooks, page 50
Grammar Workbook, pages 45, 46, 56, 57, 58
Activity Sheet 47
Resources and Planning OxBox CD-ROM

➤ Grammar

- The conditional tense
- *wenn*
- Strong and weak verbs
- Verbs with and without *zu*

➤ PLTS

All questions: Reflective learners/Self-managers

➤ The conditional

1 **Change the sentences below from the present to the conditional.**

- This question practises forming the conditional.

Answers:

a Ich würde jeden Tag im See schwimmen. **b** Wir würden mit dem Zug fahren. **c** Wohin würdest du fahren? **d** Was würdet ihr machen? **e** Wir würden in die Schweiz fliegen. **f** Er würde 10 Tage bleiben. **g** Sie würden zwei Wochen in den Bergen verbringen. **h** Sie würde eine Ferienwohnung mieten. **i** Ich wäre seekrank. **j** Ich hätte Heimweh.

2 **Translate the following sentences into German.**

- Further practice of the conditional.

Answers:

a Ich würde jeden Tag an den Strand gehen. **b** Wir würden viel Spaß haben. **c** Du würdest dich bräunen. **d** Sie würden Deutsch viel schneller lernen. **e** Er würde mit der Straßenbahn in die Schule fahren.

➤ *Wenn*

3 **Read the texts on page 115 and identify sentences using *wenn*. Make a list of them and note whether *wenn* appears at the beginning or in the middle of the sentence.**

- Practice of *wenn*.

4a **Complete these sentences with *wenn*.**

- Students complete the sentences for themselves, remembering that *wenn* is a subordinating conjunction and sends the verb to the end of the clause.

4b **Now rewrite each of your sentences from activity 4a with *wenn* at the start of the sentence.**

- Remind students to watch out for word order, as it will change.

5 **Translate the following sentences into German using *wenn*.**

- Further practice of *Wenn*.

Answers:

a Es macht mir Spaß, wenn ich mit meinen Freunden in Urlaub fahren.
b Wenn sie an den Strand geht, kriegt sie einen Sonnenbrand.
c Du hast Angst, wenn du fliegen.
d Ich schaue im Internet, wenn ich einen Urlaub buche.
e Mein Vater ist immer froh, wenn er zurück zu Hause kommt.

6 **Fill in the table with the different verb tenses. Make sure you know which are strong and weak before you start.**

- Practice of strong and weak verbs.

Answers:

ich mache; ich werde machen; ich würde machen; ich fahre; ich bin gefahren; ich werde fahren; ich habe gespielt; ich werde spielen; ich würde spielen; er schwimmt; er ist geschwommen; er würde schwimmen; sie sind gegangen; sie werden gehen; sie würden gehen; du isst; du wirst essen; du würdest essen; Sie trinken; Sie haben getrunken; Sie werden trinken; wir kaufen; wir werden kaufen; wir würden kaufen; ihr habt gesehen; ihr werdet sehen; ihr würdet sehen; ich bin; ich werde sein, ich wäre; er hat; er hat gehabt; er hätte; ich lese; ich habe gelesen; ich werde lesen; wir haben besucht; wir werden besuchen; wir würden besuchen; sie lernt; sie wird lernen; sie würde lernen; ich kaufe ein; ich habe eingekauft; ich würde einkaufen; wir amüsieren uns; wir haben uns amüsiert; wir werden uns amüsieren; du bist geblieben; du wirst bleiben; du würdest bleiben; ich verbringe; ich habe verbracht; ich würde verbringen

➤ Verbs with and without *zu*

7 **Translate these sentences into German.**

- This question focuses on knowing when to use *zu* in a sentence with two verbs.

Answers:

a Hast du Lust, ins Kino zu gehen? **b** Ich habe vor, am Wochenende meine Großeltern zu besuchen; **c** Ich möchte eine Weltreise machen. **d** Willst du morgen einkaufen gehen? **e** Ich hoffe, nächtes Jahr mehr zu reisen.

Kompetenzen

Seite 120

Planner

➤ Objectives
- Summarising what you have learnt

➤ Resources
Students' Book, page 120
Exam Skills Workbooks, page 51
Activity Sheet 48
Resources and Planning OxBox CD-ROM

➤ Skills
- Making suggestions
- Giving your opinion
- Using transcripts to develop your listening skills
- Listening for different tenses
- Predicting what will come next
- Preparing for the exam

➤ PLTS
Question 2, Speaking: Creative thinkers/Reflective learners/Self-managers
Question 3, Listening: Creative thinkers/Reflective learners/Self-managers

In this unit, students have learnt how to...

➤ Beim Sprechen

1 **Make suggestions.**
- To practise using *könnte* or *sollte*, students write five sentences to say what tourists could or should do in their town.

2 **Give their opinion**

PLTS
- Students make a list of adjectives that could be used to express an opinion.
- They then list other words and phrases they could use to give their opinion.
- Finally they write ten sentences to give their opinion of a recent holiday. Remind them to use *weil* and *obwohl* and to watch out for word order.
- This encourages students to generate ideas and explore possibilities and to communicate their learning in order to achieve goals. It covers the Creative thinkers, Reflective learners and Self-managers groups of skills from the framework of personal, learning and thinking skills.

➤ Beim Hören

1 **Use transcripts to develop their listening skills.**
- Students listen to the dialogue between Anna's mother and the hotel manager on page 113 again.
- They look at the excerpt from the transcript and mark any parts they didn't understand when listening.
- They list words they couldn't distinguish when listening, but that they can now identify. They to look up any words they don't know.

2 **Listen for different tenses.**
- Students write down key features that will help them identify: the perfect tense; the future tense; the conditional.

Answers:

perfect tense: auxiliary verb, *haben* or *sein* + past participle
future tense: *werden* + infinitive
conditional: conditional form of *werden* + infinitive

3 **Predict what will come next.**

PLTS
- Students look at the sentences, decide what kind of word is missing and fill each gap with a sensible word.
- This encourages students to generate ideas and explore possibilities and to communicate their learning in order to achieve goals. It covers the Creative thinkers, Reflective learners and Self-managers groups of skills from the framework of personal, learning and thinking skills.

Answers:

a adjective; **b** verb; **c** verb; **d** adjective; **e** noun

4 **Prepare for the exam.**
- Students look at the listening papers in the Exam Practice section at the back of the book and list the types of questions they are likely to encounter in the exam.
- They then make a list of things they should look out for when answering each type of question.

Szenario

Planner

➤ Objectives
- Planning a stay in Germany, Austria or Switzerland
- Producing a brochure for a holiday destination

➤ Resources
Students' Book, page 121
Exam Skills Workbooks, pages 48–49
Resources and Planning Oxbox CD-ROM

➤ Skills
- Speaking practice
- Writing practice

➤ PLTS
Question 1, Speaking: Independent enquirers/Self-managers
Question 4, Speaking: Reflective learners
Question 2, Writing: Creative thinkers/Reflective learners/Self-managers

➤ Zum Sprechen

In this section, students will research and plan a stay in Germany, Austria or Switzerland. They will then present their plans to the class. Encourage them to use the Internet for research and to rehearse their material thoroughly. Suggest recording it to help improve their accent and intonation. This could be done using the record/playback facility on the OxBox CD-ROM.

It is possible for students to obtain GCSE grades A–F and they are marked on Communication, Quality of language and Pronunciation and intonation:
Grade F students communicate a limited number of ideas, expressing simple opinions. A few phrases or short sentences are accurate enough to be recognisable. There are very few instances of clear pronunciation and intonation.
Grade C students communicate the essential elements, readily expressing points of view. They occasionally hesitate and can respond to some unpredictable questions. They use straightforward vocabulary and structures which may contain different tenses or time frames. Pronunciation and intonation is generally accurate.
Grade A students use relevant information to develop and justify individual ideas and points of view. There is no hesitation and they are able to respond to unpredictable questions. They use a wide range of clause types, vocabulary and structures accurately. The presentation is fluent and coherent with just minor errors. Pronunciation and intonation is very accurate with a few minor slips.

1 Research a tourist area in a German-speaking country on the Internet or at a travel agent's, investigating what there is to see and do there. You might want to choose an area near your partner school, a major city like Berlin, Zurich or Vienna, or a popular holiday destination such as the Rhineland or the Swiss Alps.

- Students use the Internet or brochures to find out about a German-speaking destination.

PLTS
- They make notes on what there is to do and see.
- This encourages students to plan and carry out research, organising time and resources and prioritising actions to work towards goals. It covers the Independent enquirers and Self-managers groups of skills from the framework of personal, learning and thinking skills.

2 You are planning a four-day trip to your chosen destination. Prepare a presentation about your planned trip. You should mention the points listed.

- Students use their notes to plan their trip and to start to prepare a presentation about it.

3 Go over the vocabulary and expressions from this unit you will need to use, e.g. *ich habe vor, ich plane,* etc.

- Students look through the unit to ensure that they have included useful vocabulary and expressions.
- They then read through their presentation again to check that it flows well.

4 Present your plans in German using visual aids, ICT, handouts, etc. Be prepared to answer any questions from other members of the class.

- Students present their plans to the class. Remind them to rehearse well and to check their pronunciation and intonation is correct. They should try to predict what questions other class members might ask.

PLTS
- This activity encourages students to invite feedback and deal positively with praise, setbacks and criticism. It covers the Reflective learners group of skills from the framework of personal, learning and thinking skills.

➤ Zum Schreiben

In this section, students produce a brochure about a holiday resort using their research from the *Zum Sprechen* section.

It is possible for students to obtain GCSE grades A–F:
Grade F students write a short plan using simple sentences and communicate some information.
Grade C students include a variety of structures that may include different tenses or time frames. They communicate information and express personal opinions.
Grade A students include a variety of vocabulary, structures and verb tenses. They convey information, narrate events and express and explain ideas and points of view.

1 **Prepare a tourist brochure in German about your chosen destination using your research. Decide what sections to include in the brochure, e.g. *Museen*, *Unterkunft*, *Nachtleben*, and how you will structure it.**
- This activity serves as an introduction to the task. Encourage students to think about how holiday brochures at the travel agent's are presented.

2 **Write each section, giving recommendations for what visitors should do. Remember to use modals to give advice.**
- Students use the structure they have produced in activity 1 to write the brochure in full.

PLTS
- This encourages students to generate ideas and explore possibilities, to communicate their learning in relevant ways in order to work towards goals. It covers the Creative thinkers, Reflective learners and Self-managers groups of skills from the framework of personal, learning and thinking skills.

Vokabeln

Seite 122

Planner

➤ Resources
Students' Book, page 122
Activity Sheet 49

This page provides a summary of the key language covered in each spread of this unit. It could be used as a handy reference for students as they work through the unit. Alternatively, students could use its clear German–English format when learning vocabulary.

Lesen

Seiten 183–184

Planner

Objectives
- To encourage independent reading and develop reading strategies
- To provide alternative class and homework material for students who finish other activities quickly

Pages 183–184 provide magazine-style reading texts in the context of the unit.

Resources
Students' Book, pages 183–184

Skills
- Reading practice

PLTS
Question 3 (part 1): Creative thinkers/Reflective learners/Self-managers
Question 3 (part 2): Creative thinkers/Reflective learners/Team workers/Self-managers/Effective participators

Lesen A: Urlaub ohne Eltern

1 Wie sagt man auf Deutsch...?
- Students read the text and find the German for the English phrases listed.

4–6

Answers:

a Betreuer; **b** Zelten; **c** Kajaktouren; **d** neue Freunde gewinnen; **e** zusammen machen

2 Beantworte die Fragen auf Englisch.
- Students read the text again and answer the questions.

7–9

Answers:

a Weil sie oft andere Interessen als Mutti und Vati haben.
b *Du!* organisiert Reisen ohne Eltern für Jugendliche zwischen 12 und 18.
c Basteln, Fotografie, Feten und Feiern, Segeln, Zelten, Kajaktouren
d Weil seine Eltern gern kulturelle Sachen im Urlaub machen oder sie wollen einfach nur am Strand liegen und er wollte was anderes machen.
e in einem Jugendhotel
f Es hat Spaß gemacht.
g Er hat viele neue Aktivitäten wie Kajakfahren ausprobiert, und er hat auch neue Freunde gewonnen.
h Er will wieder eine Jugendreise machen.

3 Was findest du besser – Urlaub mit oder ohne Eltern? Mach eine Liste der Vor- und Nachteile.
- Students use the ideas in the text, what they have practised in the unit and their own expreience to write a list of advantages and disadvantages of holidays with and without parents.
- This activity encourages students to generate and explore ideas and to communicate their learning to achieve goals. It covers the Creative thinkers, Reflective learners and Self-managers groups of skills from the framework of personal, learning and thinking skills.

4–9

PLTS

Lesen B: Im Urlaub: Lernen und was Gutes tun!

1 Wie sagt man auf Deutsch...?
- Students read the text and find the German for the English phrases listed.

4–6

Answers:

a freiwillige Mitarbeiterin; **b** Erlebnis; **c** Naturschutzgebiet; **d** schützen; **e** wohnen

2 Beantworte die Fragen auf Englisch.
- Students read the text again and answer the questions in English.

7–9

Answers:

a She wanted to do something other than sit on the beach all day during her holidays.
b at a nature reserve in Costa Rica
c She had a Spanish lesson everyday.
d she tended footpaths, sold entrance tickets to visitors, helped to protect turtles
e with a family; thought it was great as she got to see how the people there really live
f After her studies, she would like to do environment-related work and would also like to visit Costa Rica again.

3 Arbeitet mit einem Partner oder einer Partnerin und entwerft ein Interview mit Ute über ihren Aufenthalt in Costa Rica.
- Students work with a partner and draw upon the work from activities 1 and 2 to make up an interview with Ute about her stay in Costa Rica.
- This encourages students to generate and explore ideas, to communicate their learning and to collaborate and negotiate effectively with others to achieve goals. It covers the Creative thinkers, Reflective learners, Team workers, Self-managers and Effective participators groups of skills from the framework of personal, learning and thinking skills.

4–9

PLTS

Unit 4B: Die Welt und die Umwelt		Overview grid		
Spread	**Contexts and objectives**	**Skills**	**Grammar**	**Vocabulary**
pages 124–125 **Wie man über die Umwelt redet**	• Discussing the environment	• Reading for gist and detail	• The gender of compound nouns	*die Hauptstadt; der Schutz; die Umwelt; die Verschmutzung* *bauen* *arm; trocken* *ohne; während*
pages 126–127 **Wie man über Bedrohungen für die Umwelt diskutiert**	• Discussing environmental problems	• Asking questions while reading	• Prepositions that take the genitive	*der Müll* *vergiften; wegwerfen* *dank; trotz*
pages 128–129 **Wie man ökologisch Urlaub macht**	• Discussing eco-tourism	• Checking your answers	• The imperfect subjunctive	*der Bauernhof; das Feuer; die Halbpension; das Holz; der Schaden; der Strom* *retten; schützen* *gemütlich*
pages 130–131 **Wie man die Umwelt schützt**	• Discussing environmental activities	• Making notes while listening	• *wenn* with the imperfect subjunctive	*der Automat; die Reparaturwerkstatt; der Stand; die Werkstatt* *ausmachen; sammeln; sparen*
pages 132–133 **Wie man verschiedene Länder und Kulturen zu schätzen lernt**	• Discussing national characteristics and cultures	• Practising using new words	N/A	*der Abfall; die Eigenschaft* *Schlange stehen* *höflich; sauber*
pages 134–135 **Aktive Grammatik**	• Grammar		• Compound words in German • Prepositions that take the genitive • The imperfect subjunctive • 'If' clauses and the imperfect subjunctive	
page 136 **Kompetenzen**	• Summarising what you have learnt	• Determining the topic from the context and from scanning key words • Reading with questions about the topic in mind • Reading a second time for specific details • Taking effective notes while listening • Listening once for gist and again for details • Checking that your answers make sense • Practising new words		
page 137 **Szenario**	• Designing an eco-outing or holiday • Making proposals for and discussing the development of a green area	• Speaking practice • Writing practice		
page 138 **Vokabeln**	• Key language			
pages 185–186 **Lesen**	• Eco-tourism • To encourage independent reading and develop reading strategies • To provide alternative class and homework material for students who finish other activities quickly	• Reading practice		

4B Die Welt und die Umwelt

Unit Objectives

Contexts and cultural focus: the environment
Skills focus: determining the topic from the context and from scanning key words; reading with questions about the topic in mind; reading again for details; checking that your answers make sense; taking effective notes while listening; listening for gist and then again for details
Grammar: gender of compound nouns; prepositions that take the genitive case; the imperfect subjunctive; *wenn* and the imperfect subjunctive

Controlled assessment opportunities

Writing: Students' Book, page 125, activity 9
Speaking: Students' Book, page 127, activity 7
Writing: Students' Book, page 129, activity 6
Writing: Students' Book, page 131, activity 5
Writing: Students' Book, page 133, activity 6
Writing: Students' Book, page 137, Zum Schreiben, activity 4
Speaking: Students' Book, page 137, Zum Sprechen, activity 4
See also ***GCSE German for OCR Assessment OxBox CD-ROM.***

An introduction to the unit Seite 123

- *Aim*: To introduce the themes of the unit.
- The opening spread of each unit is styled as the contents page of a teenage magazine. Illustrations, captions and skills summaries provide a preview of what is to come:

	Students' Book
Weißt du schon, wie man über die Umwelt redet?	pages 124–125
Weißt du schon, wie man über Bedrohungen für die Umwelt diskutiert?	pages 126–127
Weißt du schon, wie man ökologisch Urlaub macht?	pages 128–129
Weißt du schon, wie man die Umwelt schützt?	pages 130–131
Weißt du schon, wie man verschiedene Länder und Kulturen zu schätzen lernt?	pages 132–133

- Allow time for students to read the questions and cross-refer to the relevant pages of the Students' Book. They could do this individually or in pairs/groups, followed by whole-class discussion.
- This spread also provides an opportunity for students to recap on familiar language. Ask them to think about language they already know that might be useful when working on the themes of the unit.
- At the end of work on Unit 4B:
  - If time permits, ask students to devise a replacement opening spread. What do they think should be on it, in terms of pictures, captions, etc.? What would they change/keep the same, and why? Ask them to imagine it is the contents page of a teenage magazine: what sort of captions and pictures do they feel would attract people to buy the magazine? This sort of activity encourages students to think about features of a text that make it suitable for a particular audience or purpose.
  - Allow time for students to return to this opening spread to answer the questions, review what they have learned and reflect on areas for improvement. What did they find difficult, interesting, etc.? What do they think are the most important things they have learned in this unit?

Wie man über die Umwelt redet

Seiten 124–125

Planner

➤ Objectives
- Discussing the environment

➤ Resources
Students' Book, pages 124–125
CD 2, track 37
Grammar Workbook, page 8
Activity Sheets 50, 53

➤ Key language
die Hauptstadt; der Schutz; die Umwelt; die Verschmutzung
bauen
arm; trocken
ohne; während

➤ Skills
- Reading for gist and detail

➤ Grammar
- The gender of compound nouns

➤ PLTS
Question 8: Reflective learners/Self-managers
Question 9: Independent enquirers/Creative thinkers/Reflective learners/Self-managers

➤ Starters
- Display some key language from the spread and give students a time limit to write the English translations. Compare answers as a class.
- Students brainstorm compound words in German, on the theme of the spread if possible. Make a list of these. With the help of a dictionary, students determine the gender of each of the compound words. If necessary, add a few more compound words to the list. Compare answers as a class and elicit from students how you determine the gender of a compound word in German. Keep the final list to use later.
- Display some words containing the sounds *ü* and *u*. As a class, practise pronouncing these. Remind students of the importance of pronouncing these words correctly: an umlaut can change the meaning of a word.

➤ Plenaries
- Split the class into two teams and have a class quiz in German about Namibia. Base questions on the texts on page 124, e.g. *Namibia war eine Kolonie von Deutschland, richtig oder falsch?* The team with the most correct answers wins.
- Display the list of compound words from starter activity 2. Challenge students to write five sentences on the theme of the spread, each containing a compound word. Compare sentences as a class.
- Students choose a country they have visited, or know about and, using the dialogue in the spread as a model, write as much as they can about the weather and geography of the country. Point out that it doesn't matter if what they write it isn't entirely true, but that they should try to make their German as creative, accurate and interesting as possible. Volunteers read out their work to the rest of the class.

1 Lies den Text A auf Seite 124 und wähl jeweils das richtige englische Wort.

4–6

- As an introduction to the spread, students read text A on page 124.
- They then choose the correct English word each time to complete the English text.

Answers:

history; Namibia; 19th; colony; give up; victors

2 Lies den Text B auf Seite 124. Welche Kontraste gibt es in Namibia? Vervollständige die Sätze auf Englisch.

-6

- Students read text B on page 124 and complete the English sentences.

Answers:

a …residential blocks, shopping centres and streets with lots of cars.
b …many poor people who live in primitive huts without electricity or water.
c …desert and a coast line.

3 Lies den Dialog C auf Seite 124 und hör gut zu. Wie heißt das auf Deutsch? Finde diese Umweltausdrücke im Text.

- Students read text C on page 124 and also listen to the recording.
- They then find the German for the English phrases listed.

7–9

CD 2, track 37 **Seite 125, Übung 3**

Fritz: Im Unterricht habe ich an meinen Onkel gedacht. Er arbeitet in Namibia. Deutsch ist dort eine offizielle Nationalsprache.
Therese: Wie gefällt ihm das Leben dort?
Fritz: Sehr gut. Das Wetter ist toll – 300 Tage Sonne im Jahr!
Therese: So viel Sonne hätte *ich* gern! Hier ist es kalt – es schneit gleich. Brrr!
Fritz: Aber ohne Regen hat Namibia Wasserprobleme. Die Wüste ist groß und es gibt manchmal Wasserverschmutzung.
Karl: Wasserverschmutzung haben wir auch in Deutschland! Gibt es in Namibia Probleme mit Touristen?
Fritz: Es gibt viel Tourismus, aber Namibia ist gegen Massentourismus.
Karl: Gibt es Öko-Tourismus, so mit Safaris?
Fritz: Ja, Namibia ist pro-Umwelt. Es ist das erste Land auf der Welt, in dem Naturschutz in der Verfassung steht!
Therese: Ich wünschte, wir hätten *hier* mehr Umweltschutz! Die neue Autobahn durch den Wald ist furchtbar!
Karl: Und CO_2 verursacht globale Erwärmung!

Answers:

a Nationalsprache; **b** Wasserprobleme; **c** Wasserverschmutzung; **d** Massentourismus; **e** Naturschutz; **f** Umweltschutz

4 Lies den Dialog noch einmal und mach eine Liste von den Wetter-Ausdrücken und den geografischen Wörtern im Text. Kennst du auch andere Wörter? Schau im Wörterbuch nach.

4–9

- Students study the dialogue in more detail and make a list of weather-related expressions and geographical words.
- They then think of any other similar words. They can look in the dictionary.

A50 Activity Sheet 50 provides further activities on environment-related vocabulary.

5 Partnerarbeit. Vergleicht das Wetter und die Geografie von eurer Gegend mit Namibia.

4–9

- Students work with a partner to compare the weather and geography of their region with that in Namibia.

A53 Activity Sheet 53 provides further activities on the topic of local environment.

6 Kennst du auch andere Umweltwörter? Bilde Wörter mit Hilfe eines Wörterbuchs.

- Read through the *Grammatik* section on compound words in German as a class.
- Students use a dictionary to build environment-related words from words they already know.

7 Gruppen- oder Partnerarbeit. Lest zusammen den Dialog auf Seite 124 vor. Wechselt die Rollen.

4–6

- In pairs or groups, students read the dialogue from page 124 together.
- Remind them to focus on pronunciation, especially of the *ü* and *u* sounds.

8 Was hast du über Namibia gelernt? Ergänze den Text auf Englisch.

4–9

PLTS

- Students complete the text in English to see how much they have learnt about Namibia.
- This encourages students to review progress, acting on the outcomes to work towards goals. It covers the Reflective learners and Self-managers groups of skills from the framework of personal, learning and thinking skills.

Answers:

Namibia is known as a country that is keen on environmental **protection**. They promote eco-**tourism** and Namibia is the first country in the world to have included the **protection of nature** in their national constitution. A serious environmental problem in Namibia is the lack of **water**, mostly due to natural causes.

9 Write an information brochure for young German tourists about the geography, natural features and weather in your area.

4–9

PLTS

- This activity draws together what students have practised in the spread. It is an ideal assessment opportunity.
- Remind students to try and be as creative as possible. They may find it useful to carry out some research about their area on the Internet or at the library.
- This activity encourages students to plan and carry out research, to think creatively, generating ideas, and to communicate their learning in relevant ways to work towards goals. It covers the Independent enquirers, Creative thinkers, Reflective learners and Self-managers groups of skills from the framework of personal, learning and thinking skills.

Success criteria:

- amount of information communicated
- variety of vocabulary and structures used
- variety of tenses or time frames used

10 With a partner prepare a short discussion in German for a podcast to send to a Namibian school about environmental problems in today's world from a UK perspective. Practise and then record your discussion using OxBox software.

4–9

- Students use what they have practised in the spread to prepare their own discussion about environmental problems.
- Remind students to rehearse well, especially pronunciation and intonation.

Wie man über Bedrohungen für die Umwelt diskutiert

Seiten 126–127

Planner

Objectives
- Discussing environmental problems

Resources
Students' Book, pages 126–127
CD 2, track 38
Grammar Workbook, page 18
Activity Sheet 52

Key language
der Müll
vergiften; wegwerfen
dank; trotz

Skills
- Asking questions while reading

Grammar
- Prepositions that take the genitive

PLTS
Question 5: Creative thinkers/Reflective learners/Team workers/Self-managers
Question 8: Independent enquirers/Creative thinkers/Reflective learners/Self-managers

Starters
- Display some language from the spread, e.g. *der Müll, wegwerfen,* etc. Students work in teams and have a time limit to translate each word into English. Compare answers as a class.
- Ask students if they can remember the useful prepositions mentioned in the spread that take the genitive: *wegen, während, dank, trotz*. Ask them to give you the English for each of these. Display the definite articles *der, die, das* and *die* and ask students to note down what these would be in the genitive, *des, der, des, der*. Can they also tell you what happens to adjectives and nouns in the genitive?
- Display some sentences from the spread in jumbled order, e.g.
  auch Sie unsere könnten Zukunft bedrohen. (*Sie könnten auch unsere Zukunft bedrohen.*)
  Wir werfen viel Wir zu weg und kaufen viel zu. (*Wir kaufen zu viel und wir werfen zu viel weg.*)
  kennen noch alle wir Die Konzequenzen nicht. (*Die Konzequenzen kennen wir noch nicht alle.*)
  Give students a time limit to unjumble the sentences. Compare answers as a class.

Plenaries
- Display some words from the spread and challenge students to use them in sentences on the topic of the spread. Compare answers as a class.
- Display the prepositions that take the genitive from the spread. Challenge students to use each of them in a sentence. They should also include an adjective in front of the noun in their sentence. Compare sentences as a class and elicit from students what the definite articles, adjective and noun endings should be in the genitive.
- Students discuss the question from activity 5, *Wird die Umwelt in deiner Gegend bedroht?* as a class. Display some useful vocabulary from the spread for support. Encourage debate and remind students to try to incorporate sentences in the genitive.

1a Partnerarbeit. Lest den ersten Artikel auf dieser Seite 126 und übersetzt ihn ins Englische.

- As an introduction to the spread, students work with a partner to read the first article on page 126 and translate it into English.

7–9

Answers:

Problems that threaten our environment

There are many enviromental problems that have a bad effect on our life today. They could also threaten our future. We buy too much and throw too much away which causes problems with rubbish. Industry, pesticides, cars and rubbish pollute the environment. We consume too much water and too much energy. We don't yet know what are all of the consequences, but we could have difficulties in the future in finding clean water and in producing healthy food.

1b Lest den Artikel noch einmal. Was passt zusammen?

- Students read the article again.
- They then match the sentence halves.

7–9

Answers:

1 c; **2** d; **3** e; **4** a; **5** b

1c Schreib ganze Sätze aus Übung 1b in dein Heft.

4–6

- To practise writing sentences about the environment, students write the complete sentences from activity 1b in their exercise books.

2a Partnerarbeit. Gibt es andere Bedrohungen, die nicht im Text erwähnt sind? Macht eine Liste auf Englisch und auf Deutsch mit Hilfe eines Wörterbuchs.

- Students think of any more threats to the environment that aren't mentioned in the text. They list them in English.
- They then use a dictionary to list these in German.

4–9

2b Vergleicht eure Liste mit den Listen eurer Klassenkameraden.

4–6

- Students compare lists as a class and add any threats they didn't think of to their list.

3 Sind die Probleme in Namibia von der Natur oder von Menschen verursacht worden? Ordne die Probleme in die Tabelle ein.

- Read through the *Tipp* section on reading with questions in mind as a class.
- Students read the second text on page 126 and fill in the grid.

7–9

Answers:

Natural problems: Problems with water due to too little rain
Problems caused by people: Without protection the soil becomes poor; water problems due to pollution from chemicals produced by industry.

4a Hör gut zu. Was sind die zwei Hauptthemen des Gesprächs? Kreuz die richtigen Antworten an.

- Students listen to the recording.
- They then tick the two main themes.

7–9

CD 2, track 38 **Seite 127, Übung 4**

Boy: Hast du gehört? Der kleine Fluss hinter unserem Haus ist vergiftet!
Girl: Was? Wie ist das passiert?
Boy: Wir glauben, Pestizide sind ins Wasser gelangt.
Girl: Pestizide!
Boy: Jetzt sind die Fische alle tot.
Girl: Wegen der Pestizide! Schrecklich!
Boy: Sie wollen auch in unserer Gegend 500 neue Häuser bauen.
Girl: Das ist viel! Werden die Häuser umweltfreundlich sein?
Boy: Nein, keine Solaranlagen, nichts. Auch keine neue Schule, keine Geschäfte, aber viele neue Straßen.
Girl: Dank der neue Straßen werden wir viel mehr Autoverkehr haben.
Boy: So ist es!

Answers:

1 b; **2** c (which will lead to a)

4b Hör noch einmal zu. Sind die folgenden Sätze richtig oder falsch? Korrigiere die falschen Sätze und schreib alle Sätze vollständig in dein Heft.

- Students listen again and note down whether each sentence is true or false. They then correct any false sentences.
- They write all sentences out in full in their exercise book.

7–9

Answers:

a F – Die Katastrophe im Fluss ist durch **Pestizide** verursacht worden.
b F – Heute kann man dort **nicht** schwimmen, weil den Fluss vergiftet ist.
c F – Die neuen Häuser sind **umweltfeindlich**.
d R
e R

5 Wird die Umwelt in deiner Gegend bedroht? Diskutiert mit einem Partner/einer Partnerin.

- Students work in pairs to discuss whether the environment in their region is under threat.
- This encourages students to connect their own and others' ideas and experiences in inventive ways, to communicate their learning in relevant ways and to collaborate with others to work towards goals. It covers the Creative thinkers, Reflective learners, Team workers and Self-managers groups of skills from the framework of personal, learning and thinking skills.

4–9

PLTS

A52 Activity Sheet 52 provides further activities on environmental problems.

6 Vervollständige die folgenden Sätze.

- Read through the *Grammatik* section on prepositions that take the genitive as a class.
- Students complete the sentences.

Answers:

a **des**, Sommer**s**; **b** **des**, schön**en**, Wetter**s**; **c** **der**, heiß**en**; **d** **der**, lang**en**

7 In a small group make notes to describe a man-made or a natural threat to your local environment. Then make an oral presentation in German to the class, which you could record using OxBox software, to send to a school in Namibia or to another German-speaking country.

- This activity draws together what students have learnt in the spread. It is an ideal assessment opportunity.

4–9

Success criteria:

- ideas communicated
- pronunciation and intonation and fluency
- range of vocabulary and structures tense or time frames used
- number of personal opinions given

8 Write a short article in German about Namibia for your German partner school's newspaper. Use expressions from this and the preceding spread. www.namibia-facts.de will give you further information about Namibia. Or search for 'Namibia' on www.google.de. Include the points listed.

- Students use what they have learnt about Namibia to write a short article.
- This activity encourages students to plan and carry out research, analysing and evaluating information and judging its relevance and value.

4–9

PLTS

It also encourages them to generate and explore ideas, to communicate their learning in relevant ways and to organise time and resources. It covers the Independent enquirers, Creative thinkers, Reflective learners and Self-managers groups of skills from the framework of personal, learning and thinking skills.

Wie man ökologisch Urlaub macht

Seiten 128–129

Planner

➤ Objectives

- Discussing eco-tourism

➤ Resources

Students' Book, pages 128–129
CD 2, track 39
Grammar Workbook, page 57

➤ Key language

der Bauernhof; das Feuer; die Halbpension; das Holz; der Schaden; der Strom
retten; schützen
gemütlich

➤ Skills

- Checking your answers

➤ Grammar

- The imperfect subjunctive

➤ PLTS

Question 5: Independent enquirers/Creative thinkers/Reflective learners/Team workers/Self-managers/Effective participators

➤ Starters

- The class brainstorm expressions to describe an eco-holiday. Go round the class asking each student to give you a word or expression, e.g.
  Student A: *Gesundes Leben*
  Student B: *Spa*
  List all of the words mentioned and keep the list to use later.
- Ask students if anyone can explain when the imperfect subjunctive should be used. Once a student has given a correct explanation, ask who can tell you how it is formed. Once you have an answer, display the infinitives: *haben, sein, werden, können, sollen* and *mögen*. Explain to students that you will call out a subject, e.g. *Ich* and one of the infinitives, e.g. *können* and that they should write down the correct form in the imperfect subjunctive, e.g. *Ich könnte*. At the end, compare answers as a class.
- Have a class quiz. Divide the class into teams and ask questions based on the texts on page 128, e.g. *Was kann man auf dem Bauernhof essen?* How much can students remember about the texts? The team with the most correct answers wins.

➤ Plenaries

- Challenge students to write five sentences on the theme of the spread, using the imperfect subjunctive. Compare sentences as a class.
- Divide the class into two groups. Group A thinks that eco-holidays are great, Group B doesn't. Both groups note down reasons to justify their opinion. The two groups then have a debate.
- Students describe an imaginary eco-holiday they have been on. Display the list from starter activity 1 for support. Volunteers present their description to the class.

1a Partnerarbeit. Lest und diskutiert Reklame C vom Bauernhof auf dieser Seite. Welche Aspekte findet ihr umweltfreundlich? Warum? Macht eine Liste.

- As an introduction to the spread, students work with a partner to read text C from page 128.
- They then discuss it, listing aspects they find environmentally friendly and giving reasons why.

1b Hör gut zu. Ist das Öko-Tourismus? Drei Schüler sprechen über den Öko-Urlaub in Österreich. Ordne die Ausdrücke unten in die Tabelle ein.

- Students listen to three school pupils speak about eco-holidays in Austria.
- They then put the expressions from the box into the appropriate column of the grid.

CD 2, track 39 — **Seite 129, Übung 1b**

Ist das Öko-Tourismus oder nicht?

Franz: So einen Urlaub möchte ich gerne machen. Reiten, Mountain-Biking und im See schwimmen!

Dieter: Na, so ökologisch ist dieser Urlaub nicht! Denk an die Flugmeilen nach Innsbruck!

Sieglinde: Ich denke, dass dies Öko-Tourismus ist. Das ist ein Biobauer, er benutzt keine Chemikalien für seine Produkte. Und die Aktivitäten stören die Natur nicht. Wenn man reitet, kann man ganz nahe an wilde Tiere herankommen, ohne sie zu stören.

Franz: Du hast Recht. Das ist Öko-Tourismus. Der Bauernhof hat vielleicht eine Solaranlage, um Strom zu erzeugen.

Dieter:	Das glaube ich nicht. Dieser Bauernhof liegt in der Nähe der Stadt Innsbruck. Er kriegt bestimmt Strom vom Stadtnetz.
Sieglinde:	Aber die Stromerzeugung für Innsbruck ist erneuerbar – dank Wasserturbinen. Mit dem Wald in der Nähe hat der Bauer Holz für die Heizung.
Franz:	Ein gutes Argument. Ich würde gern im Wald beim Holzhacken helfen!
Dieter:	Aber durch Holzfeuer entsteht CO_2 und das verursacht globale Erwärmung!

Answers:

Environmentally-friendly	**Not environmentally-friendly**
Bio-Obstanbau	Flugmeilen
erneuerbare Stromerzeugung	Natur stören
Solaranlage	CO_2
Wasserturbinen	Holzfeuer

1c Wie heißen die Ausdrücke aus Übung 1b auf Englisch?

- Read the *Tipp* section on checking answers.
- Students note down the English for the expressions in activity 1b in order to check that their answers make sense.

4–6

Answers:

Bio-Obstanbau – *organic fruit-growing*; Flugmeilen – *air miles*; erneuerbare Stromerzeugung – *renewable energy sources*; Natur stören – *disturbing nature*; Solaranlage – *solar power plant*; CO_2 – *carbon dioxide*; Wasserturbinen – *water turbines*; Holzfeuer – *wood fire*

1d Wie heißen deiner Meinung nach die folgenden Ausdrücke auf Deutsch? Rate!

- Students write what they think that German expressions mean in English.

Answers:

4–6

a Bio-Gemüseanbau; **b** Automeilen; **c** Gasfeuer

2 Füll die Lücken mit Verben im Konjunktiv II aus.

- Read through the *Grammatik* section on the imperfect subjunctive as a class.
- Students complete the sentences.

Answers:

a sollte; **b** könntest; **c** wäre; **d** würde

3 Beantworte die Fragen in ganzen Sätzen.

- Students answer the questions in full sentences using verbs in the imperfect subjunctive.

4a Partnerarbeit. Lest die Reklamen A, B und D für Öko-Reisen. Was könnte bei jeder Reise ökologisch sein?

- Students read texts A, B and D on page 128.
- In pairs they then discuss what could be considered ecological about each trip.
- Remind them to use the imperfect subjunctive in their discussion.

4–9

4b Welche Umweltprobleme könnte jede Reise verursachen? Schreib ganze Sätze.

- Students write sentences saying what environmental problems each trip could cause.

4–9

5 Groupwork. Brainstorm and discuss the details of an eco-tourism venture for German tourists in Namibia. Use 'eco-tourism' and 'Namibia' as key words to search the Internet. Do a group presentation of the venture in German to the class.

- This activity draws together the vocabulary, ideas and grammar covered in this spread.
- Students could benefit from using the OxBox CD-Rom to record and playback their presentation in order to practise pronunciation.

4–9

PLTS

- This encourages students to analyse and evaluate information, judging its relevance and value. It also encourages them to generate ideas and explore possibilities, to review progress, acting on the outcomes, and to collaborate and negotiate with others to work towards goals. It covers the Independent enquirers, Creative thinkers, Reflective learners, Team workers, Self-managers and Effective participators groups of skills from the framework of personal, learning and thinking skills.

6 Design an eco-tourism holiday brochure for German tourists to your area. Use as many expressions from this spread as possible, putting an emphasis on activities for environmental protection or improvement. Be inventive!

- This activity draws together what students have learnt in this spread. It is an ideal assessment opportunity.

4–9

Success criteria:

- amount of information communicated
- variety of vocabulary and structures used
- variety of tenses or time frames used

Wie man die Umwelt schützt

Seiten 130–131

Planner

➤ Objectives

- Discussing environmental activities

➤ Resources

Students' Book, pages 130–131
CD 2, tracks 40–42
Grammar Workbook, page 57
Activity Sheet 51

➤ Key language

der Automat; die Reparaturwerkstatt; der Stand; die Werkstatt
ausmachen; sammeln; sparen

➤ Skills

- Making notes while listening

➤ Grammar

- *wenn* with the imperfect subjunctive

➤ PLTS

Question 5: Creative thinkers/Reflective learners/Self-managers
Question 6: Creative thinkers/Reflective learners/Self-managers

➤ Starters

- Display a list of activities an environmentally friendly person might do, e.g. *zu Fuß gehen*, etc. Give students a time limit to note down the English for these activities. When the time is up, go through the answers.
- Play a memory game. Go round the class asking students, *Was machst du, um umweltfreundlich zu sein?* The first student gives an activity, the next student continues by repeating what the first student said and adding an activity of their own e.g.
  Student A: *Ich komme zu Fuß zur Schule.*
  Student B: *Ich komme zu Fuß zur Schule und ich trenne den Müll.*
  Student C: *Ich komme zu Fuß zur Schule, ich trenne den Müll und . . .*
- Call out a word from the spread and challenge students to use it in a sentence, e.g.
  Teacher: *trennen*
  Student: *Wir **trennen** unseren Müll.*

➤ Plenaries

- Display a few words and phrases from the spread and challenge students to use them all in a short paragraph based on the themes of the spread. Confident students present their paragraph to the class.
- Display the sentence beginning: *Wenn ihr die Umwelt schützen wollt,. . .* and challenge students to think of at least three ways to end the sentence. Compare answers as a class. Elicit from the class what happens with word order when a sentence begins with *wenn*.
- Students write a paragraph about an imaginary very environmentally **un**friendly person. What does he/she do that makes him/her so environmentally unfriendly and what **should** he/she do to become more environmentally friendly, e.g. *Er fährt immer mit dem Auto. Wenn er zu fuß gehen würde, könnte er die Umwelt schützen.* Compare paragraphs as a class.

1a Partnerarbeit. Was tut die Schule in Namibia für die Umwelt? Schaut euch das Plakat an und diskutiert.

4–9

- As an introduction to the spread, students study the first poster on page 130.
- In pairs, they then discuss what the school in Namibia does for the environment.

1b Eine Schülerin aus Namibia spricht über ihre Schule und die Umwelt. Hör gut zu und ergänze die Sätze.

- Students listen to a student from Namibia speak about her school and the environment.
- They complete the sentences.

7–9

CD 2, track 40 **Seite 131, Übung 1b**

Hier in der Windhoeker Oberschule versuchen wir, umweltfreundlich zu sein. Wir sammeln zum Beispiel Regenwasser vom Dach in Wassertonnen und benutzen es für die Toiletten in der Schule. Die meisten Schüler gehen zu Fuß zur Schule; einige fahren mit dem Bus. Unser Schulkoch kauft nur lokale Produkte vom Markt, natürlich ohne Plastikverpackung! Vor der Schule haben wir einen Stand, wo die Schüler ihre alten Uniformen, die nicht mehr passen, verkaufen können.

Answers:

a Regenwasser, Dach in Wassertonnen, Toiletten in der Schule; **b** gehen zu Fuß, fahren, Bus; **c** lokale; **d** Verpackung; **e** verkaufen

2a Partnerarbeit. Was tut die Schule in Deutschland für die Umwelt? Schaut euch das Plakat an und diskutiert.

4–9

- Students study the second poster on page 130.
- In pairs, they then discuss what the German school does for the environment.

2b Drei deutsche Schüler sprechen über ihre Schule und die Umwelt. Hör gut zu und ergänze die Sätze.

7–9

- Students listen to the German school students.
- They then complete the sentences.

CD 2, track 41 **Seite 131, Übung 2b**

Boy 1: Hey! Euer Plakat sieht schon gut aus. Habt ihr alles drauf?
Girl: Ich denke schon. Wir haben hier die vier verschiedenen Mülltonnen, um den Müll zu trennen – Plastik, Glas, Papier, Biomüll. Ich habe hier versucht zu zeigen, dass wir immer das Licht ausmachen, wenn ein Klassenzimmer leer ist.
Boy 2: Das Thermometer zeigt, dass wir die Heizung nicht zu warm haben. Die Schüler sollen ihre Jacken oder Pullover anziehen, wenn es zu kühl wird.
Girl: Wir haben keine Automaten mehr, wo man Schokolade und Süßigkeiten kaufen kann.
Boy 2: Ja, hier sind die neuen Wassertonnen für das Regenwasser für die Toiletten.
Boy 1: Toll!

Answers:

a Müll; **b** Licht; **c** Heizung, Jacken oder Pullover; **d** Automaten; **e** Regenwasser

2c Was könnte man für die Umwelt noch machen? Hör gut zu und mach Notizen. Hat dein Partner/deine Partnerin ähnliche Ideen?

7–9

- Read the *Tipp* section on making notes when listening.
- Students listen to the recording and make notes on what could still be done for the environment.
- They compare their notes with those of a partner.

CD 2, track 42 **Seite 131, Übung 2c**

Was könnte man noch für die Umwelt machen?

Boy 1: Was meint ihr? Was könnten wir in der Schule noch tun, um umweltfreundlicher zu sein?
Girl: Ich meine, dass weniger Autos hierherfahren sollten.
Boy 1: Ja, du hast Recht. Wenn mehr Schüler mit dem Fahrrad oder zu Fuß zur Schule kommen würden, würde es weniger Abgase geben.
Boy 2: Wir könnten eine Fahrradreparatur-Werkstatt in der Schule aufmachen. Die könnte am Nachmittag geöffnet sein.
Boy 1: Das ist eine tolle Idee! Ich würde mein Fahrrad dorthin bringen.
Girl: Ich finde auch, wir sollten alle lernen, unsere eigenen Klamotten zu reparieren, Knöpfe anzunähen und so weiter. Das könnten auch die Jungs lernen.
Boy 2: Das finde ich gar nicht schlecht. Meine Mutter arbeitet und hat keine Zeit, meine zerrissenen Sachen zu nähen. Das könnte ich selber machen.
Girl: Wir sollten auch herausfinden, wo man die Lebensmittel für das Essen in der Kantine kauft. Ich meine, sind sie aus dem Ausland oder ist alles aus unserer Gegend?
Boy 1: Was haltet ihr von einer Solaranlage auf dem Dach, um warmes Wasser zu erzeugen?
Boy 2: Eine gute Idee, aber leider sehr teuer.
Girl: Du hast Recht! Heh! Warum nicht Geld dafür sammeln? Wir könnten zum Beispiel ein Schulfest machen und Geld für eine Solaranlage sammeln.

3a Partnerarbeit. Was macht ihr, um umweltfreundlich zu sein? Diskutiert und macht Notizen. Schreibt ganze Sätze in eure Hefte.

4–9

- Students work with a partner to discuss what they do to be environmentally friendly.
- They make notes and then write these as full sentences in their exercise books.

3b Vergebt Punkte für jede Umweltaktion – wer ist am umweltfreundlichsten in der Klasse?

4–9

- Students discuss their answers from activity 3a as a class and allocate points for each environmentally friendly action.
- The student with the most points is the most environmentally friendly.

A51 Activity Sheet 51 provides an activity on environmental activities.

4 Setz die passenden Verbformen ein.

- Read through the *Grammatik* section on 'if' clauses with the imperfect subjunctive as a class. Work through the examples, drawing students' attention to word order in particular.
- Students write the verbs in their correct form.

Answers:

a hätten, würden; **b** hätte, könnte; **c** wäre; **d** würde, würde; **e** würdest, könntest; **f** solltet

5 Make a poster of your school like those on page 130, showing and labelling its eco-friendly aspects. Then add other things that would make it even more sustainable, each with a short German text explaining why. Use sentences with *wenn*.

4–9

PLTS

- This activity draws together the vocabulary and grammar practised in the spread. It is an ideal assessment opportunity.
- This encourages students to generate ideas and explore possibilities. It also encourages them to communicate their learning in relevant ways, to work towards goals, showing initiative, commitment and perseverence. It covers the Creative thinkers, Reflective learners and Self-managers groups of skills from the framework of personal, learning and thinking skills.

Success criteria:

- amount of information communicated
- variety of vocabulary, structures, tenses or time frames used
- number of personal opinions given

6 **Design a brochure for your German partner school giving advice in full sentences on how to be more eco-friendly.**

4–9

PLTS

- Students use what they have learnt in the spread to design a poster.
- This encourages students to think creatively, generating ideas and exploring possibilities, to communicate their learning in relevant ways and to work towards goals, organising their time and resources. It covers the Creative thinkers, Reflective learners, and Self-managers groups of skills from the framework of personal, learning and thinking skills.

Wie man verschiedene Länder und Kulturen zu schätzen lernt

Seiten 132–133

Planner

➤ Objectives
- Discussing national characteristics

➤ Resources
Students' Book, pages 132–133
CD 2, track 43

➤ Key language
der Abfall; die Eigenschaft
Schlange stehen
höflich; sauber

➤ Skills
- Practising using new words

➤ PLTS
Question 4b: Independent enquirers/Self-managers
Question 7: Reflective learners/Self-managers

➤ Starters
- Display some words from the key language of the spread with the vowels missing. Students race against each other to fill in the missing letters. Elicit the English for the words included.
- Go round the class, and ask students to call out an adjective or expression that they think describes German people today, e.g. *freundlich*, etc. Make a list of these. Do the same for British people. Keep the lists to use later.
- Choose a famous German-speaking person covered in the course, e.g. Michael Schumacher, Roger Federer, etc. Go round the class asking each student to give an adjective, noun or expression to describe this person's characteristics. Does the class consider him/her to be typically German/Swiss/Austrian? You could play this as a memory game, e.g.
  Student 1: *Er ist stolz Deutscher zu sein.*
  Student 2: *Er ist stolz Deutscher zu sein und er lacht gern.*

➤ Plenaries
- Call out words from the spread and challenge students to use them in a sentence on the theme of the spread, e.g.
  Teacher: *hilfsbereit*
  Student: *Meiner Meinung nach, sind die Deutsche meistens **hilfsbereit**.*
- Students note down what they think are the characteristics of a different nationality, other than German or British, e.g. French, Spanish, Italian, etc. Volunteers read out their descriptions to the class. The class tries to guess which nationality they are describing.
- Students choose a famous person who they think most represents what it is to be British. They then write a description of him/her to explain why. Display the list from starter activity 2 for support. Compare answers as a class.

1 **Hör gut zu. Deutsche Schüler sprechen über einen Schüleraustausch nach England. Verbinde die Bilder auf Seite 132 mit den passenden deutschen und englischen Wörtern.**

4–6

- As an introduction to the spread, students listen to German students speak about a school exchange to England.
- They then match the pictures on page 132 with the appropriate German and English words.

CD 2, track 43 **Seite 133, Übungen 1 und 2a**

Thomas: Hallo, alle miteinander! Ihr seid jetzt zurück vom Schüleraustausch. Wie war es in England?

Girl 1: Grüß dich, Thomas. Es war toll, ganz toll! Es ist schade, dass du nicht mitkommen konntest. Die Engländer sind sehr freundlich und höflich, viel höflicher als wir Deutschen während des Unterrichts in der Schule!

Girl 2: Das Essen ist ganz anders in England, besonders in der Schule. Sie haben Automaten, wo sie Essen und Getränke kaufen können, allerdings kein gesundes Essen – Schokolade, Cola und so weiter!
Boy 1: Viele Eltern bringen ihre Kinder mit dem Auto zur Schule.
Boy 2: Ich muss sagen, sie sind viel weniger öko als wir in Deutschland. Es gibt überall Plastikbeutel und Abfall. Ich glaube, sie trennen den Müll nicht.
Boy 1: Sie sind auch nicht besonders an Europa interessiert.
Girl 1: Auf der anderen Seite sind sie an ihren eigenen Gesellschaftsproblemen und weltweiten Sozialproblemen interessiert. Wir haben „Red Nose Day" erlebt, wo sie viel Geld für Wohlfahrtsorganisationen gesammelt haben. Das Geld geht an arme Menschen in Afrika, an bedürftige Kinder, an viele!
Thomas: Das ist interessant. Hier in Deutschland werden Wohlfahrtsaktivitäten von der Kirche organisiert. Hast du Schlangestehen gesehen?
Boy 2: Oh, „queueing up". Ja, das haben wir viel gesehen. Das gehört zur englischen Höflichkeit.

Answers:

1 d, iv; **2** c, v; **3** e, i; **4** a, iii; **5** b, ii

2a Partnerarbeit. Hört das Gespräch noch einmal zu. Ist das, was die Schüler über England sagen, richtig oder falsch? Was meint ihr? Macht Listen.

4–9

- Students listen to the recording again and work with a partner to decide whether they think what the students are saying about England is true or false.

2b Lest eure Listen aus Übung 2a einander vor.

4–6

- Students read their lists from activity 2a to one another.

2c Schreib noch andere Eigenschaften auf, die typisch für Jugendliche in Großbritannien sind.

4–9

- Students write down more characteristics that they consider to be typical of young British people.

3a Lies den Text und mach Notizen. Welche Eigenschaften findet man heutzutage unter den Deutschen? Mach eine Liste. Wenn du nicht alles verstehst, schau im Wörterbuch nach.

7–9

- Students read the text on page 132.
- They then list the characteristics typical of German people today.
- If there is anything they don't understand, they should look it up in a dictionary.

Answers:

Dichter und Denker, Philosophen, Künstler, Musiker, stellen tolle Autos her, freundlich, hilfsbereit, meistens gute Arbeiter, Städte sind sauber, die Menschen warten immer auf das grüne Männlein, mögen Spaß und lachen gern, multikulturelles Volk, an die Meinungsfreiheit glauben

3b Übersetze deine Liste aus Übung 3a ins Englische. Vergleiche deine Liste mit einem Partner/einer Partnerin.

4–6

- Students translate their list from activity 3a into English.
- They then compare it with that of a partner.

Answer:

poets and thinkers, philosophers, artists, musicians, make great cars, friendly, helpful, mostly good workers, towns are clean, people always wait for the green man before crossing the road, like to have fun and to laugh, multicultural people, believe in freedom of opinion

4a Die berühmten Leute im Kasten unten sprachen alle Deutsch. Ordne sie in die Tabelle ein.

- Students use their knowledge of German culture to put the famous German-speakers into the correct column of the grid.

Musiker	Dichter	Künstler	Philosoph
Bach	Schiller	Klimt	Nietzsche
Beethoven	Goethe		Schiller
Wagner			
Mozart			

4b Kennst du noch andere berühmte Deutsche/Österreicher/ Schweizer? Such im Internet nach und schreib die Namen hinzu. Sehe auch Einheit 2a.

PLTS

- Students use the Internet to find other famous German-speakers to add to the list.
- This encourages students to plan and carry out research to work towards goals and manage their time and resources effectively to achieve these goals. It covers the Independent enquirers and Self-managers groups of skills from the framework of personal, learning and thinking skills.

5a Worauf können junge Leute in Großbritannien heute stolz sein? Macht eine Liste mit einem Partner/einer Partnerin.

4–6

- Students work with a partner to make a list of things young people in Britain can be proud of.

5b Welche berühmten Personen sollten auf deiner Liste in Übung 5a stehen? Was haben diese Personen in ihrem Leben gemacht? Schreib mindestens einen Satz für jede Person.

4–9

- Students decide which famous people should be in the list from activity 5a and write a sentence for each person saying what he/she has done.

6 What does it mean to be British? Write a response to the magazine article in German. Remember to include the points listed.

4–9

- This activity draws together what students have learnt in the spread and is an ideal assessment opportunity.

Success criteria:

- amount of information given
- variety of vocabulary and structures used
- number of personal opinions given

7 **Discuss with a partner the differences, if any, you think there are between young people in Germany and young people in Great Britain today. List them and then list what similarities you think there are. Do you think young people in different countries are more similar now than they were in the past? Write down why or why not. Compare your lists with those of other students.**

4–9

PLTS

- This activity provides students with the opportunity to draw together what they have prepared in previous activities.
- This encourages students to communicate their learning in relevant ways and to collaborate and negotiate with others in order to achieve goals. It covers the Reflective learners, and Self-managers groups of skills from the framework of personal, learning and thinking skills.

Aktive Grammatik

Seiten 134–135

Planner

➤ Objectives

- Practising forming compound words in German
- Using prepositions that take the genitive
- Practising the imperfect subjunctive
- Practising 'if' clauses and the imperfect subjunctive

➤ Resources

Students' Book, pages 134–135
Exam Skills Workbooks, page 54
Grammar Workbook, pages 18, 65
Activity sheet 54
Resources and Planning OxBox CD-ROM

➤ Grammar

- Compound words in German
- Prepositions that take the genitive
- The imperfect subjuntive
- 'If clauses and the imperfect subjunctive

➤ PLTS

- All questions: Reflective learners/Self-managers

➤ Compound words in German

1 **Form compound words in German and then translate them into English. How many more compound words can you make?**

- This question focuses on understanding how to form and use compound words in German.

Answers:

a die Hauptstadt – *capital city*; **b** die Wassertemperatur – *water temperature*; **c** der Energieverbrauch – *energy consumption*; **d** der Umweltschutz – *conservation of the environment*; **e** die Klimaerwärmung – *global warming*

2 **Combine the words in the box below to form one of the most famous compound words in German. (Enter *das längste deutsche Wort* on www.google.de to find others.)**

- Students continue to think about compound words in German.

Answer:

der Donaudampfschiffahrtsgesellschaftkapitän

➤ Prepositions that take the genitive

3 **Complete these sentences, remembering to keep the verb as the second element of the sentence. Translate your sentences into English.**

- Students complete the sentences for themselves, remembering that the verb should remain the second element of the sentence. They then translate them into English.

4 **Revision: 'the preposition test'. Complete this story with the correct adjective endings, remembering to use the correct case (accusative, dative or genitive) that follows each preposition.**

- This questions focuses on adjective endings and cases following prepositions.

Answers:

ein**em**, alt**en**, i**m**, d**em**, d**er**, d**as**, a**m**, nächst**en**, ein**er**, unser**em**, dies**er**, toll**en**, d**en**, alt**en**, i**m**, d**em**

➤ The imperfect subjunctive

5 **Fill in the imperfect subjunctive form of the verb, complete the sentence and then translate it into English.**

- This question practises forming the imperfect subjunctive.

Answers:

a sollte – *In order to be environmentally friendly, the school should (students' own ending)*; **b** könnten – *We could, for example (students'own ending)*; **c** würde – *Personally, I would prefer (students' own ending)*; **d** wäre – *It would be good,* *(students' own ending)*; **e** hätten – *Without electricity we would have (students' own ending)*; **f** möchten – *Would we like (students' own ending)*

➤ 'If' clauses and the imperfect subjunctive

6 **Translate these sentences into English**
- This question practises translating the imperfect subjunctive correctly.

Answers:

a If we would like to collect money for solar panels, we should have a school open day.
b Should the school open day be in the afternoon after school, or at the weekend?
c More people would come at the weekend and we could collect more money.

7 **Translate these sentences into German.**
- This question checks students' understanding of *wenn*.

Answers:

a Wenn wir Geld hätten, würden wir Solaranlagen kaufen.
b Wenn wir Regenwasser sammeln könnten, sollten wir es für die Toilette benutzen?
c Es wäre besser, wenn wir unseren Müll in der Schule trennen könnten.
d Wenn wir Strom sparen würden, könnten wir das Geld für wohltätige Zwecke spenden.

8 **Revision. Use *wenn* and the present tense to express simple conditional (if/when... then) sentences.**
- Practice of the *wenn* and the present tense.

Answers:

a habe, kann; **b** habe, muss; **c** bleibe, findet; **d** mache, hoffe, kreigen werde; **e** gibt, kann

9 **Translate these sentences into English.**
- This question checks students' understanding of *wenn* and *als*.

Answers:

a When you have homework, at what time do you do it?
b If you had homework, would you do it now?
c Whenever I had homework, I did it in the evening after the evening meal.
d When you had homework on Monday, did you do it after school or in the evening?

Kompetenzen

Seite 136

Planner

➤ Objectives
- Summarising what you have learnt

➤ Resources
Students' Book, page 136
Exam Skills Workbooks, page 55
Activity Sheet 55
Resources and Planning OxBox CD-ROM

➤ Skills
- Determining the topic from the context and from scanning key words
- Reading with questions about the topic in mind
- Reading a second time for specific details
- Taking effective notes while listening
- Listening once for gist and again for details
- Checking that your answers make sense
- Practising new words

➤ PLTS
Question 4, Beim Lernen: Self-managers

In this unit, students have learnt how to...

➤ Beim Lesen

1 **Determine the topic from the context and from scanning key words.**
- Students check the context, any pictures and the layout of a reading text for clues about its meaning.
- They also quickly scan key words to confirm what they think the topic is.

2 **Read with questions about the topic in mind**
- Once students think they know what the topic of the text is, they ask themselves what words and phrases they might come across.

3 **Read a second time for specific details.**
- When doing a reading activity, students try to allow themselves time to go back over a text to note details which will help them answer specific questions.

➤ Beim Hören

1 **Take effective notes while listening.**
- Students check the task to organise in their head how they will take notes during the listening.

2 **Listen once for gist and again for details.**
- During the first listening, students determine the topic and gist of the passage, using context, task and tone of voice. They listen for details during the second listening, focussing on answers they are not sure about.

3 **Check that their answers make sense.**
- At the end of the listening passage, students check that their answers make sense for the topic and the speakers.

➤ Beim Lernen

1 **Practise new words.**
- Students repeat words and phrases as soon as possible after they have first heard or read them.

2 **Develop a list of idioms.**
- Students write down a list of idioms to refer to when writing German or preparing a speech.

3 **Remember new vocabulary.**
- Students read through their list of idioms, phrases or vocabulary before going to sleep to help them to remember.

4 **Use English to remember some German verb tenses.**

PLTS
- Students make their own list of key verbs and their tenses along the lines of the examples given.
- This activity encourages students to work towards goals, showing initiative, commitment and perseverence. It covers the Self-managers group of skills from the framework of personal, learning and thinking skills.

Szenario

Seite 137

Planner

➤ Objectives
- To design the perfect eco-outing or eco-holiday
- To make proposals for and discuss the development of a green area

➤ Resources
Students' Book, page 137
Exam Skills Workbooks, pages 52–53
Assessment Sheets 25–32
Resources and Planning OxBox CD-ROM

➤ Skills
- Writing practice
- Speaking practice

➤ PLTS
Question 1, Writing: Independent enquirers/ Reflective learners/Team workers/Self-managers/ Effective participators
Question 2, Speaking: Reflective learners/Team workers/Self-managers/Effective participators

➤ Zum Schreiben

In this section, students design the perfect eco-outing or eco-holiday using what they have practised in this unit.

It is possible for students to obtain GCSE grades A–F:
Grade F students write a short plan using simple sentences and communicate some information.
Grade C students include a variety of structures which may include different tenses or time frames. They communicate information and express personal opinions.
Grade A students include a variety of vocabulary, structures and verb tenses. They convey information, narrate events and express and explain ideas and points of view.

1 **In a small group, decide on where to go and then brainstorm in German the things which you will need to consider when planning the trip, including travel, overnight accommodation, food (from shopping to serving), activities that are for leisure, for learning and to support the community or locality. Divide the topics among pairs in the group.**
- This activity serves as an introduction to the task. Students work in groups to begin to think about planning their eco-outing or eco-holiday.

PLTS
- This encourages students to explore issues, events or problems from different perspectives, to set goals with clear success criteria and to collaborate and negotiate with others, organising time and resources effectively to achieve these goals. It covers the Independent enquirers, Reflective learners, Team workers, Self-managers and Effective participators groups of skills from the framework of personal, learning and thinking skills.

2 **In pairs, discuss all aspects of your particular topic and how best to make them sustainable.**
- Students work with a partner to discuss the topic that they have been allocated.
- Encourage them to draw upon the vocabulary and ideas presented in this unit for support.

3 **After your discussion, write down a plan, explaining each aspect and why it would be ecologically acceptable, and if not, what compensation you propose.**

- Students use what they have discussed in activities 1 and 2 to write a plan.

4 **Bring your texts together as a group and present the complete plan/proposal to the class. Take a vote on which projects are the most eco-friendly. Finish by creating a poster of your project.**

- Students bring together their individual texts to write a complete plan. Remind them to check through their work carefully to ensure that it is accurate and that word order is correct.
- They then present their plan to the class.
- Finally, they create a poster of their project. Encourage them to make the poster as interesting as possible. They shouldn't neglect the quality of their German and should write in full sentences and check that their writing is correct.

➤ Zum Sprechen

In this section, students will make proposals for and discuss the development of a green area. Encourage them to rehearse their material thoroughly. Suggest recording it to help improve their accent and intonation. This could be done using the record/playback facility on the OxBox CD-ROM.

It is possible for students to obtain GCSE grades A–F and they are marked on Communication, Quality of language and Pronunciation and intonation:
Grade F students communicate a limited number of ideas, expressing simple opinions. A few phrases or short sentences are accurate enough to be recognisable. There are very few instances of clear pronunciation and intonation.
Grade C students communicate the essential elements, readily expressing points of view. They occasionally hesitate and can respond to some unpredictable questions. They use straightforward vocabulary and structures which may contain different tenses or time frames. Pronunciation and intonation is generally accurate.
Grade A students use relevant information to develop and justify individual ideas and points of view. There is no hesitation and they are able to respond to unpredictable questions. They use a wide range of clause types, vocabulary and structures accurately. The presentation is fluent and coherent with just minor errors. Pronunciation and intonation is very accurate with a few minor slips.

1 **In groups of four, decide the basic outlines of the development – what? for whom? where? time frame? Discuss and take notes in German.**

- This acts as an introduction to the task.
- Encourage students to draw upon the ideas and vocabulary presented in the unit as well as their own experience for support.

2 **Then divide up into sides: 2 students for and 2 students against the development.**

- Students begin to think of arguments for and against the development.
- PLTS This activity encourages students to communicate their learning in relevant ways and to collaborate and negotiate with others to work towards goals. It covers the Reflective learners, Team workers, Self-managers and Effective participators groups of skills from the framework of personal, learning and thinking skills.

3 **In pairs, both sides bring together arguments, either for or against the development with a focus on the environment, social aspects and what you consider to be sustainable.**

- Students bring together what they have discussed in activity 2.
- Remind them to rehearse their material thoroughly – they must make sure they can put their arguments forward in just one minute.

4 **Each side presents their arguments to other students or the whole class. Each speaker has 1 minute to present his/her case.**

- Students present their arguments to the class.

5 **Everyone votes on who should win the debate.**

- The class listens and decides which side has put forward the most convincing arguments.

Vokabeln

Seite 138

Planner

➤ **Resources**
Students' Book, page 138
Activity Sheet 56

This page provides a summary of the key language covered in each spread of this unit. It could be used as a handy reference for students as they work through the unit. Alternatively, students could use its clear German–English format when learning vocabulary.

Lesen

Seiten 185–186

Planner

➤ **Objectives**
- To encourage independent reading and develop reading strategies
- To provide alternative class and homework material for students who finish other activities quickly

Page 185 provides a letter in the context of the unit.
Page 186 provides a magazine-style reading text in the context of the unit.

➤ **Resources**
Students' Book, pages 185–186

➤ **Skills**
- Reading practice

➤ **PLTS**
Question 3 (part 1): Creative thinkers/Reflective learners/Self-managers
Question 3 (part 2): Reflective learners/Self-managers

Lesen A: Lieber Fritz

1 **Lies den Brief. Wie sieht der Alltag von Max aus? Mach Notizen.**

7–9
- Students read the letter and make notes to describe Max's daily routine.

2 **Vergleiche deinen Alltag mit dem von Max. Schreib Sätze.**

4–9
- Students read the text again and compare their daily routine with that of Max.

3 **Wie könnte eine Wohlfahrtsaktion oder Hilfsprogramm in Namibia aussehen? Mit einem Partner/einer Partnerin schaut unter „Namibia helfen" im Internet für Ideen und schreibt einen kurzen Bericht auf Deutsch über das, was ihr gefunden habt. Teilt euren Bericht in Themen, wie zum Beispiel „Häuser", „Kinder" und so weiter.**

PLTS 7–9
- Students research on the Internet in order to write a short report on what a relief programme in Namibia would comprise.
- Encourage students to refer back to previous activities for useful vocabulary and structures.
- This activity encourages students to plan and carry out research, setting goals with clear success criteria, to collaborate with others and to organise their time and resources effectively to achieve these goals. It covers the Creative thinkers, Reflective learners and Self-managers groups of skills from the framework of personal, learning and thinking skills.

Lesen B: Vor- und Nachteile des Öko-Tourismus

1 **Wie heißen die folgenden Ausdrücke auf Englisch? Kannst du sie erraten? Wenn nicht, schau im Wörterbuch nach.**

4–6
- Students read the text.
- They then try to guess what the German phrases listed are in English.
- If they can't, they look in a dictionary.

Answers:

a jobs; **b** customs; **c** destroyed; **d** spread; **e** to cause damage; **f** to clear your conscience; **g** ecological

2 **Trenne die Vorteile und Nachteile von Öko-Tourismus und schreib sie in zwei Listen auf. Übersetze die Listen ins Englische.**

4–6

- Students read the text again and list the advantages and disadvantages of eco-tourism.
- They translate their lists into English.

Answers:

Advantages: brings money and jobs; causes little damage; eco-hotels are ecological with water and electricity consumption; you can take part in local projects

Disadvantages: the culture and customs are spoilt or destroyed; illnesses are often spread through tourism; air miles which originate with long flights

3 **Beantworte die folgenden Fragen auf Englisch.**

7–9

PLTS

- Students use what they have read in this text and what they have practised in the unit to answer the questions in English.
- This activity encourages students to communicate their learning in relevant ways to achieve goals. It covers the Reflective learners and Self-managers groups of skills from the framework of personal, learning and thinking skills.

4 **Beschreib einen Tag einer Öko-Safari in Namibia. Wo übernachtest du? Was isst du? Was machst du während des Tages? Wenn du reist, womit fährst du?**

- Students use what they have read in this text and what they have prepared in activity 3 to describe a day of an eco-safari in Namibia.

Unit 5A: Schulleben	Overview grid			
Spread	**Contexts and objectives**	**Skills**	**Grammar**	**Vocabulary**
pages 140–141 **Wie man über Schule und Geld spricht**	• Discussing school subjects and part-time jobs	• Preparing for a listening activity	• Revising word order with *weil*	*Biologie; Chemie; Deutsch; Englisch; das Fach; Erdkunde; Geografie, Geschichte; Informatik; der Jugendliche; Kochen; Kunst; das Labor; Latein; der Lehrer/-in; das Lieblingsfach; Mathematik, Mathe; Musik; Naturwissenschaften; Physik; Religion; Spanisch; Sport; das Taschengeld; ausgeben; austragen; sich erinnern; verdienen*
pages 142–143 **Wie man sagt, was in der Schule los ist**	• Discussing school subjects, the school day and opinions	• Asking questions using tone	N/A	*der Ingenieur/-in; die Note; die Pause; der Sekretär/-in; der Schultag; der Stundenplan; der Unterricht*
pages 144–145 **Wie man das Schulleben in verschiedenen Ländern vergleicht**	• Discussing school and marks	• Discussing pros and cons	• Nouns from adjectives and adverbs	*das Abitur; die Berufsschule; die Fachhochschule; die Fremdsprache; die Ganztagsschule; die Gesamtschule; die Grundschule; das Gymnasium; die Halbtagsschule; die Hauptschule; die Hochschule; die Prüfung; die Mittlere Reife; die Realschule; die SMV; das Zeugnis ausgezeichnet; befriedigend; mangelhaft*
pages 146–147 **Wie man über Geldverdienen redet**	• Discussing pocket money and part-time jobs	• Embellishing the truth to show your German to its best advantage	• Revision of *um...zu*	*ausgehen*
pages 148–149 **Wie man Schule und Nebenjob kombinieren kann**	• Discussing part-time jobs for school pupils	• Using a question to form an answer	• Reflexive verbs with the dative	*sich entscheiden; sich etwas vorstellen; sich leisten*
pages 150–151 **Aktive Grammatik**	• Grammar		• Reflexive verbs and the dative • Weak nouns • Weak adjectival nouns	
page 152 **Kompetenzen**	• Summarising what you have learnt	• Listening and reading • Using the visuals that accompany a listening task to preview what you are likely to hear • Reviewing what key words might come up • Checking that your guesses make sense • Using intonation to turn a sentence into a question • Using words in a question to formulate the answer • Saying more in your speaking exam		
page 153 **Szenario**	• Preparing an agenda for a discussion with staff • Preparing and acting out a presentation about a job	• Writing practice • Speaking practice		
page 154 **Vokabeln**	• Key language			
pages 187–188 **Lesen**	• Student council • Tutoring • To encourage independent reading and develop reading strategies • To provide alternative class and homework material for students who finish other activities quickly	• Reading practice		

5A Schulleben

Unit Objectives

Contexts and cultural focus: school, pocket money and part-time jobs
Skills focus: anticipating questions by context and preparing answers; creating questions from statements; embellishing the truth to give a fuller answer; knowing what to listen out for in a conversation or audio clip; evaluating guesses; practising listening by reading aloud
Grammar: adjectival nouns; weak noun endings; reflexive verbs that take a dative pronoun

Controlled assessment opportunities

Writing: Students' Book, page 141 activity 8
Writing: Students' Book, page 143 activity 6
Writing: Students' Book, page 145 activity 6
Speaking: Students' Book, page 147 activity 9
Speaking: Students' Book, page 149 activity 8
Writing: Students' Book, page 153 Zum Schreiben, activity 3
Speaking: Students' Book, page 153 Zum Sprechen, activity 3

See also ***GCSE German for OCR Assessment OxBox CD-ROM.***

An introduction to the unit Seite 139

- *Aim*: To introduce the themes of the unit.
- The opening spread of each unit is styled as the contents page of a teenage magazine. Illustrations, captions and skills summaries provide a preview of what is to come:

	Students' Book
Weißt du schon, wie man über Schule und Geld spricht?	pages 140–141
Weißt du schon, wie man sagt, was in der Schule los ist?	pages 142–143
Weißt du schon, wie man das Schulleben in verschiedenen Ländern vergleicht?	pages 144–145
Weißt du schon, wie man über Geldverdienen redet?	pages 146–147
Weißt du schon, wie man Schule und Nebenjob kombinieren kann?	pages 148–149

- Allow time for students to read the questions and cross-refer to the relevant pages of the Students' Book. They could do this individually or in pairs/groups, followed by whole-class discussion.
- This spread also provides an opportunity for students to recap on familiar language. Ask them to think about language they already know that might be useful when working on the themes of the unit.
- At the end of work on Unit 5A:
  - If time permits, ask students to devise a replacement opening spread. What do they think should be on it, in terms of pictures, captions, etc.? What would they change/keep the same, and why? Ask them to imagine it is the contents page of a teenage magazine: what sort of captions and pictures do they feel would attract people to buy the magazine? This sort of activity encourages students to think about features of a text that make it suitable for a particular audience or purpose.
  - Allow time for students to return to this opening spread to answer the questions, review what they have learned and reflect on areas for improvement. What did they find difficult, interesting, etc.? What do they think are the most important things they have learned in this unit?

Wie man über Schule und Geld spricht

Seiten 140–141

Planner

➤ Objectives

- Discussing school subjects, favourite subjects and part-time jobs

➤ Resources

Students' Book, pages 140–141
CD 3, track 1
Grammar Workbook, page 63
Activity Sheet 57

➤ Key language

Biologie; Chemie; Deutsch; Englisch; das Fach; Erdkunde; Geografie, Geschichte; Informatik; der Jugendliche; Kochen; Kunst; das Labor; Latein; der Lehrer/-in; das Lieblingsfach; Mathematik, Mathe; Musik; Naturwissenschaften; Physik; Religion; Spanisch; Sport; das Taschengeld; ausgeben; sich erinnern; verdienen

➤ Skills

- Preparing for a listening activity

➤ Grammar

- Revising word order with *weil*

➤ Starters

- Play 'Hangman' with school subjects. Divide the class into two teams. The teams take turns to call out a letter. The first team to guess the word scores a point. Teams lose a point for an incorrect guess. The team with the most points at the end wins. Make a list of all the subjects guessed to use later.
- Go round the class asking each student, *Hast du ein Lieblingsfach? Warum?* Students reply, e.g. *Mein Lieblingsfach ist Geschichte, weil ich gern über die Vergangenheit lese.* If necessary model an answer before you begin and display the list of school subjects from starter activity 1 for support.
- Mime a part-time job, e.g. delivering newspapers. Students try to guess what you are doing by watching the mime and asking questions e.g. *Bekommen Sie dafür etwas Geld? Arbeiten Sie im Supermarkt? etc.*

➤ Plenaries

- Challenge students to write five sentences, each with *weil* on the themes of the spread. Compare sentences as a class and elicit from the class what happens to the word order of a sentence when *weil* is used.
- Call out a word from the spread. Students put it into a sentence, e.g.
  Teacher: *Hunde!*
  Student: *Meine Schwester und ich führen Hunde aus.*
- Students work in pairs to decide what they think is the best and worst part-time job mentioned in the spread and why. Volunteers act out their discussion in front of the class. Does the rest of the class agree with them?

1 Sieh dir die Bilder oben an. Wie heißen diese Fächer auf Deutsch? Welche anderen Fächer gibt es in deiner Schule? Mach eine Liste.

4–6

- Students write complete the list of school subjects and add to it with any other subjects that aren't mentioned.

Answers:

Englisch; Erdkunde; Mathe; Chemie; Deutsch; Physik; Informatik; Sport; Französisch; Spanisch; Geschichte; Biologie; Kochen; Kunst; Latein; Musik; Religion

2a Thomas fragt Schüler über ihre Lieblingsfächer. Hör gut zu und füll die Tabelle aus. Die Tipp-Box hilft dir dabei.

7–9

- Read through the *Tipp* section on listening.
- Students listen to the recording and fill in the table.

CD 3, track 1 — **Seite 141, Übung 2a**

Thomas:	Hallo! Darf ich mich vorstellen? Ich heiße Thomas und ich bin gekommen, um herauszufinden, was in der Schule eigentlich los ist. Fangen wir mal mit den Schulfächern an, und zwar mit Lieblingsfächern. Mein Lieblingsfach ist Journalismus. Ich bin Journalist! Und du, Brigitte, was ist dein Lieblingsfach?
Brigitte:	Hallo, Thomas. Mein Lieblingsfach ist Geografie.
Thomas:	Geografie? Und warum ist das dein Lieblingsfach?
Brigitte:	Ich liebe Geografie, weil es interessant ist!
Thomas:	Klaus, was ist dein Lieblingsfach und warum?
Klaus:	Mein Lieblingsfach ist Geschichte, weil ich gern über die Vergangenheit lese.
Thomas:	Ach, so alte Geschichten! Und du, Maria? Ich erinnere mich, dass du Englisch magst.
Maria:	Aber mein Lieblingsfach ist Spanisch, weil ich gern Flamenco tanze, und der Lehrer ist toll.
Thomas:	Olé!
Maria:	Ach, du!

Thomas: Udo. Magst du Spanisch?
Udo: Nein, überhaupt nicht. Mein Lieblingsfach ist Chemie, weil ich später in einem Labor arbeiten möchte.
Thomas: Vielen Dank!

Answers:

Name	**Lieblingsfach**	**Warum?**
Thomas	Journalismus	Er ist Journalist
Brigitte	Geografie	sie ist interessant
Klaus	Geschichte	liest gern über die vergangenheit
Maria	Spanisch	tanze gern Flamenco, und der Lehrer ist toll
Udo	Chemie	will später im Labor arbeiten

2b Welche Fächer gefallen euch? Warum? Diskutiert zu zweit.

- Students discuss their subject preferences.

A57 Activity Sheet 57 provides further activities on school subjects.

3a Hast du ein Lieblingsfach? Ergänze die Sätze und schreib dann die ganzen Sätze auf.

- Read the *Grammatik* section on word order with *weil* to recap what happens to the verb when *weil* is used.
- Students complete the sentences for themselves and then write out the whole sentence.

3b Oder hast du vielleicht kein Lieblingsfach?

- Students complete the sentences about subjects they don't like.

4 Welche sind die positiven Gründen und welche die negativen Gründe?

- Students read the list of reasons and decide if each is positive or negative.
- Encourage students to remember some of these reasons, as they may come in useful in their own writing.

4–6

Answers:

a negative; **b** positive; **c** negative; **d** negative; **e** negative; **f** positive or negative

5a Thomas hat die elfte Klasse auch über Geld interviewt. Schau dir das Kreisdiagramm an und schreib für jeden Abschnitt einen Satz.

- Students look at the pie-chart on page 140 and write a sentence for each segment.

7–9

5b Frag einen Partner/einer Partnerin über sein taschengeld. Benutz die Fragen auf Seite 140.

- Students discuss pocket money.

6a Partnerarbeit. Hat er/sie einen Nebenjob? Lest die Sätze einem Partner/einer Partnerin vor. Welcher Satz passt zu welchem Bild?

- Students look at young people's statements on page and read them out loud to a partner.
- They then match the statements with the appropriate picture.

4–6

Answers:

1 d; **2** f; **3** c; **4** e; **5** g; **6** a; **7** b

6b Was bedeuten die roten Wörter? Schau wenn nötig im Wörterbuch nach.

- Student note the meaning of the words in red.

Answers:

deliver newspapers; is not enough; stables; free of charge;

7 Write a short paragraph in German about your own school subjects and your opinion of them. Why do/don't you like them?

- This actvity draws together what students have learnt in the spread on the topic of school subjects.

4–9

8 Have a group debate: how much pocket money should a young person get? What do young people spend money on? Is too much money a bad thing? Record your discussion on the OxBox.

- This actvity draws together what students have learnt in the spread on the topic of pocket money. It is an ideal assessment opportunity.
- Encourage students to use the vocabulary, ideas and structures they have met in the spread and to include their own views. Remind them to incorporate *weil* remembering to watch out for word order.

4–9

Success criteria:

- information communicated
- variety of vocabulary and structures used
- personal opinions expressed

Wie man sagt, was in der Schule los ist

Seiten 142–143

Planner

➤ Objectives

- Discussing school subjects, the school day and opinions

➤ Resources

Students' Book, pages 142–143
CD 3, tracks 2–3
Grammar Workbook, pages 25, 27, 29
Activity Sheet 59

➤ Key language

der Ingenieur/-in; die Note; die Pause; der Sekretär/-in; der Schultag; der Stundenplan; der Unterricht

➤ Skills

- Asking questions using tone

➤ PLTS

Question 3c: Reflective learners/Team workers

➤ Starters

- Three quick warm-up activities to revise school subjects, clock times and days of the week:
  - Display the names of school subjects with all the vowels missing. Challenge students to write them out in full within a time limit.
  - Display anagrams of days of the week. Students race to solve the anagrams and list the days in order.
  - Revise times using a clock face with movable hands (either a real clock or an OHP or interactive whiteboard clock). Call out some times and invite students to set the clock accordingly, or set the clock yourself and ask students to give the times.
- Go round the class asking questions about the timetable, e.g. *Was hast du am Montag in der zweiten Stunde? Wann hast du Deutsch?* etc.
- Display a list of school subjects from the spread. As a class brainstorm possible reasons for studying these subjects, e.g. *toll, macht spaß, gute Noten kreigen, nützlich (für die Zukunft)*, etc. Once the list is long enough, ask a few volunteers which reasons they would put with which subject. Keep the list to use later.

➤ Plenaries

- Practise asking questions. Go round the class. Each student asks the student next to them a question based on the theme of the spread. Each student answers the question they are asked and then asks the student next to them a question. Students can either use question words, or intonation, e.g. *Wie lange dauert eine Stunde? Dein Lieblingsfach ist?*
- Display the list from starter activity 3 and challenge students to write sentences using the subjects and reasons, e.g. *Musik macht mir Spaß. Ich kriege gute Noten. Geografie ist einfach toll, aber ich weiß nicht, ob sie für meine Zukunft nützlich ist.*
  Compare the sentences as a class.
- Students describe their ideal school day. You could do this as a written activity and ask students to write a paragraph in German describing their ideal timetable, e.g. *Die Schule beginnt um 10 Uhr. Eine Klassenstunde dauert zehn Minuten und wir haben wir eine lange Pause um elf Uhr.* etc. Alternatively, go round the class asking each student to contribute a sentence, e.g.
  Student A: *Die Schule beginnt um 10 Uhr.*
  Student B: *Eine Klassenstunde dauert zehn Minuten.* etc.

1 Schau dir den Stundenplan auf Seite 142 an und ergänze die Sätze. Hör dann zu, um deine Antworten zu prüfen.

4–6

- As an introduction to the spread, students look at the timetable on page 142 and complete the sentences. They then listen to check.

CD 3, track 2 **Seite 143, Übung 1**

1 Heikes Schultag beginnt um acht Uhr fünfzehn.
2 In der Woche hat Heike vier Stunden Mathe.
3 Sie hat Deutsch am Montag in der zweiten Stunde und am Freitag in der dritten Stunde.
4 Die Pause beginnt um zehn Uhr fünfundfünfzig und dauert zwanzig Minuten.
5 Am Samstag hat sie eine Doppelstunde Geschichte.
6 Die Schule ist um zwei Uhr zu Ende.
7 Heikes Wahlfächer sind Geografie, Kunst und Spanisch.

Answers:

a acht Uhr fünfzehn; **b** vier; **c** Deutsch, Montag, zweiten, Freitag, der, dritten; **d** zehn Uhr fünfundfünfzig, zwanzig; **e** Doppelstunde; **f** zwei Uhr; **g** Geografie, Kunst, Spanisch

2 Ergänze die folgenden Fragen.

4–6

- Students complete the questions.

Answers:

a Klasse, gehst; **b** Schule, Wann; **c** Lieblingsfach; **d** dein; **e** Tag, Tage, Uhr, (ein Fach)

3a Füll die Tabelle aus. Beginne mit deinem eigenen Namen. Stell Fragen an drei Klassenkameraden/ Klassenkameradinnen.

4–9

- Read through the *Tipp* section on asking questions.
- Students fill in the table for themselves.
- They then interview three classmates and fill in the table for them.

3b Benutze die Informationen aus Tabelle 3a und schreib Sätze über dich selbst und eine andere Person.

4–9

- Students use the information from the table in activity 3a to write sentences about themselves and one other person.

3c Lies deine Sätze aus Übung 3b einem Partner/einer Partnerin vor, um deine Aussprache zu üben.

PLTS

- Students read their sentences from activity 3b out loud to a partner in order to practise their pronunciation.
- This encourages students to evaluate their strengths and limitations and to monitor their own performance and progress, inviting feedback from others. It also encourges them to work confidently with others. It covers the Reflective learners and Team workers groups of skills from the framework of personal, learning and thinking skills.

4a Thomas fragt Schüler: Welches Fach hast du als Wahlfach gewählt und warum? Lies die Aussagen auf Seite 142, hör zu, und füll die Tabelle aus.

7–9

- Students read the extracts on page 142 and fill in the table.

CD 3, track 3 **Seite 143, Übung 4a**

Thomas: Hallo! Heute möchte ich wissen, welche Wahlfächer ihr habt und warum ihr dieses Wahlfach gewählt habt. Ich fange mit Natalie an. Welches Wahlfach hast du, Natalie?
Natalie: Ich habe zwei: Informatik und Buchhaltung.
Thomas: Und warum hast du sie gewählt?
Natalie: Ich habe sie gewählt, weil ich hoffe, Sekretärin zu werden.
Thomas: Danke dir! Und du, Karl, hast du ein Wahlfach?
Karl: Oh ja, das ist Geografie.
Thomas: Warum hast du Geografie gewählt?
Karl: Weil Geografie einfach toll ist.
Thomas: Und für deine Zukunft?
Karl: Ach, ich weiß es noch nicht.
Thomas: So. Jochen, du hast Musik als Wahlfach, nicht wahr?
Jochen: Jawohl, weil mir Musik Spaß macht und ich gute Noten in Musik kriege. Der Georg hat Chemie als Wahlfach gewählt. Wahnsinn!
Georg: Aber Chemie ist wichtig für mich. Ich studiere Chemie, weil ich sie für meine Zukunft im Labor brauche.
Thomas: Vielen Dank, Georg. Karen, welches Wahlfach hast du gewählt?
Karen: Ich habe Physik gewählt.
Thomas: Warum?
Karen: Weil ich später Ingenieurin werden möchte.
Thomas: Und du, Heidi? Dein Wahlfach ist Französisch, oder?
Heidi: Ja.
Thomas: Warum?
Heidi: Weil ich den Lehrer mag.
Heidi: Und ich will nach Paris fahren!
Thomas: Vielen Dank euch allen.

Answers:

Name	**Wahlfach**	**Warum?**
Natalie	Informatik; Buchhalten	Sekretärin werden
Karl	Geografie	weiß nicht
Jochen	Musik	macht Spaß; gute Noten
Georg	Chemie	im Labor arbeiten
Karen	Physik	Ingenieurin werden
Heidi	Französisch	nach Paris fahren

4b Partnerarbeit. Benutzt die Informationen aus Übung 4a, um ganze Sätze zu schreiben.

4–9

- Students work with a partner. They use the information from activity 4a to write full sentences.

A59 Further activities on school subjects and the school day are provided on Activity Sheet 59.

5 Prepare an interview in German with a partner about a school day. Compare a school day in Great Britain with Heike's school day. The final question should be: where is being a student better, in Germany or in Britain?

4–9

- This activity draws together what students have learnt in the spread.
- Students can record their interview using OxBox software.

6 **Your parents want you to spend a term in Germany to improve your German. Write a letter in German to your new school, the Heinrich-Schütz-Gymnasium. Explain why you want to study there and ask which subjects you will have and what the school day is like. Describe yourself and your interests at school.**

4–9

- This activity provides students with the opportunity to use what they have learnt in the spread to produce a letter. It is an ideal assessment opportunity.

Success criteria:

- information communicated
- variety of vocabulary and structures used
- personal opinions expressed

Wie man das Schulleben in verschiedenen Ländern vergleicht

Seiten 144–145

Planner

➤ Objectives

- Discussing schools and marks

➤ Resources

Students' Book, pages 144–145
CD 3, tracks 4–5
Grammar Workbook, page 10
Activity Sheet 58

➤ Key language

das Abitur; die Berufsschule; die Fachhochschule; die Fremdsprache; die Ganztagsschule; die Gesamtschule; die Grundschule; das Gymnasium; die Halbtagsschule; die Hauptschule; die Hochschule; die Prüfung; die Mittlere Reife; die Realschule; das Zeugnis
ausgezeichnet; befriedigend; mangelhaft

➤ Skills

- Discussing pros and cons

➤ Grammar

- Nouns from adjectives and adverbs

➤ PLTS

Question 4b: Independent enquirers/Creative thinkers/Team workers/Effective participators

➤ Starters

- Display the key language with vowels missing. Divide students into small groups and give them a time limit to complete the words. Check answers as a class.
- Divide the class into two teams. Using the list of key language as support, the teams take it in turns to produce a simple sentence describing a difference between German and British schools, e.g. *In Deutschland muss man das Schuljahr wiederholen, wenn man schlechte Noten bekommt.*
- Call out each of the different types of school in Germany, *die Ganztagsschule, die Gesamtschule, die Grundschule, das Gymnasium, die Halbtagsschule, die Hauptschule, die Hochschule* and *die Realschule*. Students note down an advantage and a disadvantage of each. Compare answers as a class.

➤ Plenaries

- Display some nouns from adjectives or adverbs from the spread, e.g. *das Beste, das Schlechteste, das Längste* and challenge students to use these in sentences. Compare sentences as a class.
- After looking at the diagram showing different types of German schools on page 144, display a list of the German school-types and ask students to write as much as they can about each of them in note form in German. Compare answers as a class.
- Students use what they have learnt in the spread to write a paragraph describing their ideal school. This could be a mixture of all of the different types of German school, e.g. *Es ist eine Halbtagsschule und hat eine Schülermitvertretung.* etc.

Liesl zieht nach Deutschland um. Lies die Texte und mach Notizen auf Englisch.

- As an introduction to the spread, students read the text about Liesl and make notes.

4–6

1 Es gibt in Deutschland viele Schularten. Sieh das Diagramm auf Seite 144 an und verbinde den Schultyp mit der Beschreibung unten.

7–9

- This activity introduces students to the many types of German school.
- Students study the diagram on page 144 and then match the school types and descriptions.

Answers:

1 a; **2** d; **3** c; **4** b; **5** f; **6** g

2 Auf was für eine Schule gehen diese Jugendlichen und was gefällt ihnen besonders daran? Hör gut zu und füll die Tabelle aus.

7–9

- Students listen to the young people speak about their school.
- They then fill in the table.

CD 3, track 4 **Seite 145, Übung 2**

Thomas: Ich bin's, der Thomas. Heute bin ich auf der Prager Straße in Dresden und ich spreche mit einigen Jugendlichen über ihre Schulen. Guten Tag! Darf ich fragen: Was für eine Schule besuchst du?
Boy 1: Ich gehe aufs Gymnasium.
Thomas: Was gefällt dir daran?
Boy 1: Das ist eine Halbtagsschule. Am Nachmittag habe ich keine Schule.
Thomas: Und du? Gehst du auch aufs Gymnasium?
Boy 2: Ach nein! Ich gehe auf die Gesamtschule. Sie ist toll. Es gibt die unterschiedlichsten Studenten dort, und in meiner Schule gibt's kein Sitzenbleiben, wenn du schlechte Noten hast.
Thomas: Und du?
Girl: Ich gehe auf eine Berufsschule. Das ist ganz prima. Ich möchte Köchin werden und in meiner Schule kochen wir viel!
Thomas: Vielen Dank!

Answers:

type of school	positive aspects
Gymnasium	half-day school
Gesamtschule	variety of students; don't repeat a year if you get bad marks
Berufsschule	wants to be a chef and cooks a lot at school

3 Partnerarbeit. Macht Substantive mit diesen Adjektiven. Erfindet noch andere!

- Read through the *Grammatik* section on 'nouns from adjectives and adverbs'.
- Students make nouns from the adjectives listed.
- They add any other nouns from adjectives that they can think of.

Answers:

a das Schöne; **b** das Schlechte; **c** das Dumme; **d** das Langsame

4a Partnerarbeit. Lest Christians Zeugnis auf Seite 144 und beschreibt seine Noten.

4–9

- Students work in pairs. They read Christians school report and then describe his marks.
- Remind them that they can add personal opinions where possible to make it more interesting.

4b Partnerarbeit. Ihr seid der Schülerrat und müsst euch entscheiden: soll Christian sitzenbleiben? Macht eine Liste von Gründen für beide Argumente.

4–9

PLTS

- Students work in groups to discuss whether or not Christian should repeat the year.
- They make a list of reasons for both arguments.
- This activity encourages students to explore issues from different perspectives, to ask questions to extend their thinking and to collaborate and negotiate with others to reach common goals. It covers the Independent enquirers, Creative thinkers, Team workers and Effective participators groups of skills from the framework of personal, learning and thinking skills.

A58 Activity Sheet 58 provides further activities on different types of German school.

5a Listen to the recording about German school routine, read the text and then discuss it with a partner.

4–9

- This activity draws together the ideas, vocabulary and skills covered in the spread. It also acts as preparation for the next activities.
- Encourage students to read the *Tipp* section again.

CD 3, track 5 **Seite 145, Jetzt seid ihr dran! Übung 5a**

Die Schule beginnt in Deutschland früh am Morgen, so um 8 Uhr. Der Schultag in einer normalen Schule endet ungefähr um 13 Uhr. Dann gehen die Schüler zum Mittagessen, und am Nachmittag haben sie keinen Unterricht. Nachmittags unter der Woche kann man in den Sportklub gehen, seinem eigenen Hobby nachgehen, freiwillige Arbeit oder einen Freizeitjob machen. Aber es gibt immer viele Hausaufgaben, und der Vormittag in der Schule ist lang und hart. Dazu kommt noch, dass in vielen Schulen auch am Samstagvormittag Unterricht ist.

Heutzutage gibt es immer mehr Ganztagsschulen, wo die Schüler so wie in England auch am Nachmittag Unterricht, also nicht frei haben. Sie haben aber nicht so viele Hausaufgaben auf.

5b Would you rather attend a half-day school or a whole-day school? Why? First make lists in German of reasons for and against each type of school. Then discuss your lists in German with a partner. Will you make any changes?

4–9

- Students use what they have heard and discussed in actvity 7a as a basis for this activity.

6 **Write a report about everything that you think is good about your school – facilities, subjects, teachers, student council, the students. Can you think of anything else?**

- Students use what they have learnt to write about their own school.
- Encourage them to incorporate the vocabulary, ideas and grammar they have met in the spread into their writing and to think creatively. Remind them that what they write doesn't have to be true.

4–9

Success criteria:

- information communicated
- variety of vocabulary and structures used
- personal opinions expressed

Wie man über Geldverdienen redet

Seiten 146–147

Planner

➤ Objectives

- Discussing pocket money and part-time jobs

➤ Resources

Students' Book, pages 146–147
CD 3, tracks 6–7
Grammar Workbook, page 58
Activity Sheet 60

➤ Key language

die Jugend
ausgehen

➤ Skills

- Embellishing to show your German to its best advantage

➤ Grammar

- Revision of *um … zu*

➤ PLTS

Question 6: Independent enquirers/Reflective learners/Team workers/Self-managers
Question 9: Reflective learners/Team workers/Self-managers

➤ Starters

- Give students a time limit to write down in German as many things as possible that young people may buy/do with pocket money. Go round the class asking each student to call out an item or activity until they can't think of any more. Compile a list and keep this to use later.
- As a class, brainstorm things you can do to earn money, either at home, or part-time jobs. Display the list. Go round the class asking students, *Was machst du um Geld zu verdienen?* Students answer using the list for support.
- Go round the class with each student asking the student next to them a question about pocket money or part-time jobs, e.g. *Bekommst du Taschengeld?*

➤ Plenaries

- Students play a memory game in small groups to practise saying what they need pocket money for and to practise the *um…zu* structure, e.g. Student A: *Ich brauche Geld, um mit meinen Freunden auszugehen.* Display the list from starter activity 1 for support, if necessary.
- Call out a word or phrase from the spread and challenge students to put it into a sentence. Explain that if the word is a verb, they can use it in any form they like, e.g. Teacher: *sparen!* Student: *Ich spare soviel Geld, wie ich kann.*
- Students write a paragraph saying how much pocket money they get, what they spend it on, if they have a job, etc. Explain that they must pretend to be somebody else, e.g. the child of a millionaire. They should try to make their paragraph as interesting as possible, e.g. *Ich kriege jeden Monat von meinen Eltern 1000 Euro Taschengeld.* Volunteers read their paragraph to the class which votes for the most interesting one.

1a Partnerarbeit. Was kann man zu Hause machen, um Taschengeld zu verdienen? Schaut euch die Bilder oben an und macht eine Liste.

- As an introduction to the spread, students work with a partner to list things you can do at home to earn pocket money.

1b Vergleicht eure Liste mit der Liste eines anderen Paars. Lest eure Listen vor, um die Aussprache zu üben.

- Students compare their list from activity 1a with that of another pair.
- They read their list out loud in order to practise pronouncing the words.

2a Umfrage. Frag deine Klassenkameraden, ob sie zu Hause helfen und ob sie Taschengeld bekommen. Die Tipp-Box hilft dir dabei.

- Students conduct a survey. They ask classmates if they help around the house and if they get pocket money for this.
- Before they start, read through the *Tipp* section on speaking. It isn't important to be completely truthful; students should use the German they know or can remember to make what they say as interesting, fluent and grammatically correct as possible.

2b Schreib auf, wie viel Taschengeld deine Klassenkameraden bekommen. Lies deine Ergebnisse einem Partner/einer Partnerin vor.

- Students write up the results of their survey from activity 2a.
- They then read these results out loud to a partner.

3a Hör gut zu und lies „Wenn das Taschengeld nicht ausreicht?". Beantworte die Fragen auf Englisch.

- Students listen to the recording and read the sentences on page 146.
- They then answer the questions in English.

CD 3, track 6 **Seite 147, Übung 3**

Hans Müller kriegt jeden Monat von seinen Eltern 15 Euro Taschengeld. Einmal ins Kino gehen kostet schon 8 Euro. Das Taschengeld reicht nicht aus! Hans braucht mehr Geld, um mit seinen Freunden auszugehen und sich Kleidung und CDs zu kaufen.

Hans ist 15 Jahre alt und darf einen Ferienjob oder Nebenjob haben, wenn er schulfrei hat. Er hat also eine Arbeit gefunden. Er arbeitet nach der Schule mittwochnachmittags und samstagnachmittags beim Tierarzt. Er verdient 6 Euro die Stunde, was gar nicht schlecht ist.

Warum hat er diesen Nebenjob angenommen? Er liebt Tiere, kriegt in der Schule gute Noten in den Naturwissenschaften und möchte vielleicht eines Tages Tierarzt werden. Er findet jetzt heraus, ob dieser Job für ihn interessant und möglich ist.

Weil er diesen Nebenjob hat, hat Hans wenig Freizeit. Seine Eltern machen sich Sorgen, dass seine Noten in der Schule schlecht werden, aber Hans passt auf, dass er jeden Tag seine Hausaufgaben macht und dass er in der Schule gut arbeitet. Im Moment ist er sehr glücklich über seinen Nebenjob und das Geld und eines Tages kann er diesen Job auch in seinem Lebenslauf mit aufnehmen!

Answers:

a 15 Euros a month; **b** No – a cinema ticket alone is 8 Euros **c** to go out with his friends and to buy clothes and CDs; **d** after school on Wednesday and Saturday afternoons; **e** at the vet's; **f** he loves animals and gets good marks in Biology at school; **g** 6 Euros an hour; **h** he can find out if he finds the job interesting and if he will be able to do it; **i** he doesn't have much spare time and his school work may suffer

3b Ergänze die Sätze. Wofür braucht Hans Geld?

- Students complete the sentences.
- This provides revision of the *um* ... *zu* structure.

Answers:

sein**en** Freunden; Kino; Kleidung; CDs

4 Partnerarbeit. Schaut euch zusammen das Kreisdiagramm an. Wofür brauchen junge Österreicher Geld? Benutzt *um* ... *zu* ... in eurem Gespräch.

- Students work with a partner and study the pie-chart on page 146.
- They discuss the information given in the pie-chart.

5 Wofür gibt man Geld aus? Hör gut zu und schreib so viel wie möglich auf.

- Students listen to the recording and write down as much information as possible.
- Remind them to try to predict what they might expect to hear by thinking about the context.

CD 3, track 7 **Seite 147, Übung 5**

Thomas:	Hallo! Hier bin ich wieder. Heute habe ich einige Schüler in der elften Klasse gefragt, wofür sie Geld brauchen. Hier sind ihre Antworten.
Boy 1:	Ich brauche Geld, um Zubehör für meine Gitarre und Musiknoten zu kaufen.
Girl 1:	Ich kaufe mir neue Sachen, besonders Schuhe. Ich liebe Schuhe!
Boy 2:	Ich gebe mein Geld für Sport aus.
Girl 2:	Mit meinem Geld kaufe ich mir CDs und DVDs.
Girl 3:	Ich spare so viel Geld, wie ich kann, damit ich nach Spanien reisen kann.
Boy 3:	Ich kaufe oft Zeitschriften. Ich gehe auch gern angeln.
Girl 4:	Ja, mein Geld gebe ich für Getränke und Bonbons und Schokolade aus.
Thomas:	Na, was meint ihr? Reicht das Geld immer aus?

6 **Umfrage. Wofür brauchen deine Klassenkameraden und -kameradinnen Geld? Frag sie und mach eine Grafik (z.B. ein Kreisdiagramm). Schreib dann einen Absatz über die Ergebnisse.**

4–9

PLTS

- Students conduct a survey amongst the class. They ask their classmates what they need money for and use the information to prepare a pie-chart.
- They write a paragraph about the results of their survey.
- This encourages students to use their learning to carry out research and to colloborate confidently with others to work towards goals. It also encourages them to manage their time and resources effectively. It covers the Independent enquirers, Reflective learners, Team workers and Self-managers groups of skills from the framework of personal, learning and thinking skills.

7 **Lies den folgenden Text und finde die deutschen Ausdrücke.**

- Students read the text and write the German for English words and phrases listed.

4–6

Answers:

a wichtig; **b** Jugendexperten; **c** regelmäßig; **d** ausgeben; **e** vorsichtig; **f** sparen

A60 Activity Sheet 60 provides further activities on pocket money and part-time jobs.

8 **Groupwork. Discuss what young people can do to earn money. There are a few ideas on page 140. List other possible ideas in German.**

4–9

- Encourage students to draw upon previous activities and texts for ideas and vocabulary.

9 **Discuss in German with a partner whether you get pocket money. Describe the role of money in your life. Do you have enough for what you want or need to buy? Do you have a job? If so, what is it? What do you spend your money on?**

4–9

PLTS

- A speaking activity to draw together the vocabulary, ideas, and grammar points covered in the spread. This is an ideal assessment opportunity.
- Remind students that they don't need to be completely truthful, but should use words they know. The point is to show off their knowledge of German!
- This activity encourages students to communicate their learning and to work confidently with others to work towards goals. It covers the Reflective learners, Team workers and Self-managers groups of skills from the framework of personal, learning and thinking skills.

Success criteria:

- ideas communicated
- pronunciation, intonation and fluency
- range of vocabulary and structures used
- tenses or time frames used

Wie man Schule und Nebenjob kombinieren kann

Seiten 148–149

Planner

➤ Objectives
- Discussing part-time jobs for school pupils

➤ Resources
Students' Book, pages 148–149
CD 3, track 8
Grammar Workbook, page 43

➤ Key language
die Reitstunde
sich entscheiden; sich etwas vorstellen; sich leisten

➤ Skills
- Using a question to form an answer

➤ Grammar
- Reflexive verbs with the dative

➤ PLTS
Question 2: Creative thinkers/Reflective learners/Team workers
Question 8: Independent enquirers/Creative thinkers/Reflective learners/Team workers/Effective participators

➤ Starters
- Go round the class asking various questions on the themes of the spread. Explain to students that they must answer using the words in the question to begin their answer, e.g.
  Teacher: *Verdienst du Geld?*
  Student: *Ich verdiene.*
- Display some subordinating conjunctions and go round the class asking each student to use one of them in a sentence on the theme of the spread. Remind them to watch out for word order.
- Brainstorm reflexive verbs with the dative, e.g. *sich Sorgen machen, sich etwas leisten, sich etwas kaufen*. Make a list of these and ask students to copy this and keep it as these are useful to use in their writing.

➤ Plenaries
- As a class, brainstorm advantages and disadvantages of a part-time job. Make a list of these. Ask students to write sentences using the advantages and disadvantages listed and a subordinating conjunction. Compare sentences as a class.
- Students work with a partner and they take turns to interview each other about their part-time job. If they don't have one, ask them to invent an imaginary one and to make up the details. Volunteers perform their interviews in front of the class. The class decides who has the best part-time job.
- Display words and phrases from the spread and challenge students to use them in sentences.

1 Lies den Text über Jörg und beantworte die Fragen auf Englisch.
- Students read the text about Jörg on page 148 and answer the questions in English.

4–6

Answers:

a midnight; **b** working in the supermarket; **c** his homework; **d** He doesn't understand his maths homework; **e** what he will say to his maths teacher

2 Schau dir das Bild an. Die elfte Klasse möchte einen Ausflug zum Vergnügungspark machen. Susanne und ihre Freunde überlegen sich, wie sie für den Ausflug Geld verdienen können. Was für Ideen haben sie? Was schlägst du vor? Mach eine Liste.
- Students study the picture on page 148.
- They state what ideas the students have to earn money in order to go on an outing and then think of other ideas and list these.
- This activity encourages students to generate and explore ideas whilst communicating previous learning and to collaborate successfully with others to achieve a common goal. It covers the Creative thinkers, Reflective learners and Team workers groups of skills from the framework of personal, learning and thinking skills.

4–9

PLTS

3a Vervollständige die Antworten.
- An activity to practise using questions to form answers. Read the *Tipp* section as a class before students start.
- Students answer the questions for themselves.

4–9

3b Partnerarbeit. Stellt euch gegenseitig die Fragen aus Übung 3a. Versucht eure Antworten z.B. mit *weil* zu erweitern. Die Tipp-Box hilft Ihnen dabei.
- Students work with a partner. They take it in turns to ask and answer the questions listed in activity 3a.

7–9

4a Interviews mit Jugendlichen über ihre Nebenjobs. Hör gut zu und füll die Tabelle aus.

- Students listen to young people speak about their part-time jobs.
- They then fill in the table.

7–9

CD 3, track 8 **Seite 149, Übung 4a**

Thomas:	Guten Tag! Ich freue mich, euch alle hier zu sehen. Heute besprechen wir das Thema „Nebenjob". Jochen, hast du einen Nebenjob?
Jochen:	Nein, aber freitags helfe ich manchmal meinem Bruder bei seinem Gig. Das kann sehr spät werden und ich bin am Samstagmorgen dann sehr müde.
Thomas:	Und du hast am Samstag Schule, nicht wahr?
Jochen:	Ja, das ist schlecht!
Thomas:	Und du, Heike? Hast du einen Nebenjob?
Heike:	Ja, ich arbeite in einem Buchladen. Das ist ganz toll. Ich liebe Bücher und kann sie zum halben Preis kaufen. Ich verdiene gut. Ich kann es mir leisten, tolle Klamotten zu kaufen.
Barbara:	Ich habe im Reitstall einen Nebenjob, aber ich verdiene nicht viel Geld. Aber das Gute daran ist, dass ich freie Reitstunden kriege.
Thomas:	Jörg, du arbeitest im Supermarkt, richtig?
Jörg:	Ja, und ich bekomme gutes Geld. Ich arbeite jeden Tag nach der Schule, und manchmal muss ich bis spätabends im Supermarkt arbeiten, und kann meine Hausaufgaben nicht machen.
Thomas:	Ja, das kann ich mir vorstellen.
Jochen:	Ich habe am Freitagabend manchmal das gleiche Problem, und wenn ich meine Schularbeiten nicht mache, kriege ich schlechte Noten.
Thomas:	Hmmm. Das ist ein echtes Problem! Es gibt also Gutes und Schlechtes an einem Nebenjob.

Possible *Answers:*

For: good money; free riding lessons; X at half price

Against: tired; don't earn much money; bad marks

4b Diskutiert mit einem Partner/einer Partnerin das Pro und das Kontra eines Nebenjobs. Benutzt die Tabelle aus Übung 4a und fügt neue Ideen hinzu.

- Students work with a partner to discuss the pros and cons of a part-time job.
- They refer back to the table in activity 4a for ideas.

4–9

5 Schule plus Nebenjob: Kann das zum Konflikt führen? Schreib ganze Sätze.

- Students use the prompts given to write six sentences on this topic.

Answers:

a Jörg hat seine Hausafugaben nicht gemacht, weil er im Supermarkt gearbeitet hat.
b Barbara hat kein Taschengeld bekommen, weil sie ihr Zimmer nicht aufgeräumt hat.
c Jochen ist samstagmorgens sehr müde, wenn er seinem Bruder beim Gig hilft.
d Seine Eltern machen sich Sorgen, weil Jörg bis spätabends arbeitet.
e Heike hat schlechte Noten bekommen, weil sie jeden Tag nach der Schule arbeitet.

6a Lies den folgenden Dialog und füll die Lücken aus. Sieh dir Seite 150 an, wenn du Hilfe brauchst.

- Students complete the dialogue.

Answers:

mir; dir; sich; mir

6b Übersetze den Dialog aus Übung 6a auf Englisch.

- Students translate the sentences from activity 6a.

Answers:

I'm considering going to a half-day school.

Then you could have a part-time job. With the money you can afford to buy more CDs.

Yes, but my parents would worry that I won't finish my homework.

Oh, I can't imagine that!

7 Do you have a part-time job? If not, imagine that you do have one. Describe the job, including the hours, pay and tasks. What is good about the job? What is not so good about it? Write as much as possible in German using full sentences and paragraphs.

- This activity draws together the vocabulary, ideas and grammar points covered in this spread.

4–9

8 In a group of 4–5 people, think up a fantastic idea for earning money as a group in your free time. Prepare a 'Dragon's Den' presentation in German for the rest of the class, with each member of your group presenting a section. Try to convince the class to give you financial support for your idea.

PLTS

- This activity provides students with the opportunity to show what they have learnt on the topic of part-time jobs and earning money. This is an ideal assessment opportunity.
- This activity encourages students to explore issues, events or problems from different perspectives, to generate and explore ideas, connecting their own and others' ideas in inventive ways, to communicate previous learning and to collaborate and negotiate successfully with others to work towards a goal. It covers the Independent enquirers, Creative thinkers, Reflective learners, Team workers and Effective participators groups of skills from the framework of personal, learning and thinking skills.

Success criteria:

- ideas communicated
- pronunciation, intonation and fluency
- range of vocabulary and structures used
- tenses or time frames used

Aktive Grammatik

Seiten 150–151

Planner

➤ Objectives
- To practise reflexive verbs and the dative
- To practise weak nouns
- To practise adjectival nouns

➤ Resources
Students' Book, pages 150–151
Exam Skills Workbooks, page 58
Grammar Workbook, pages 10, 43
Activity Sheet 61
Resources and Planning Oxbox CD-ROM

➤ Grammar
- Reflexive verbs and the dative
- Weak nouns
- Adjectival nouns

➤ PLTS
All questions: Reflective learners/Self-managers

➤ Reflexive verbs and the dative

1 **Conjugate the following reflexive verbs with dative pronouns in the *ich, du* and *wir* forms.**
- This question focuses on using the correct pronoun and verb ending depending on the form.

Answers:

a ich vorstelle mir, du vorstellst dir, wir vorstellen uns
b ich gebe mir Mühe, du gibst dir Mühe, wir geben uns Mühe
c ich mache mich Sorgen, du machst dich Sorgen, wir machen uns Sorgen

2 **Complete these sentences with the correct dative reflexive pronouns.**
- Further practise of reflexive verbs and the dative.

Answers:

a mir; **b** sich; **c** sich; **d** dir **e** mir **f** dir

3 **Use the verbs in activity 1 to complete this text. Then translate it into English.**
- This question focuses on using the correct pronoun and verb ending depending on the form.

Answers:

gibt sich; sich; sich

Today, Jörg worked until late in the evening at his part-time job at the supermarket. It is now midnight and he is tired, but he must do his homework. He makes a good effort, but he doesn't understand his maths homework. He can't imagine how he will finish it and worries a lot about what he will say to his maths teacher the next day.

4 **Write sentences with these reflexive verbs that take the dative.**
- This question focuses on students producing their own sentences using reflexive verbs that take the dative.

➤ Weak nouns

5 **Complete the sentences with the correct endings for the weak nouns, then read your answers to your partner to practise saying and hearing the endings.**
- This question focuses on using the correct endings for weak nouns.

Answers:

a Der Jung**e** hat sein**en** Nam**en** nicht gehört.
b Von allen Student**en** in der Klasse ist Jochen der Faulst**e**.
c Von den vielen Pullis, die im Ausverkauf waren, habe ich den Billigst**en** gekauft.
d Das Best**e** ist, du sparst dein Geld für die Zukunft.

6 **Add the correct endings and translate the text into English.**
- Question six provides more practice of using weak nouns.

Answers:

best**e**; best**e**; schlechtest**e**; stärkst**e**; best**en**

There are lots of good sportswomen in our class, but Heike is the best. Dieter is the best sportsman and Hans is the worst. Our football team is quite good, but not the strongest in the league. We must train a lot more in order to become the best.

Kompetenzen

Seite 152

Planner

➤ Objectives

- Summarising what you have learnt

➤ Resources

Students' Book, page 152
Exam Skills Workbooks, page 59
Activity Sheet 62
Resources and Planning OxBox CD-ROM

➤ Skills

- Listening to German while reading the text at the same time
- Using visuals that accompany a listening task to preview what you are likely to hear
- Reviewing what you know about a topic and what key words might come up
- Checking that your guesses make sense
- Using intonation to turn a sentence or phrase into a question
- Listening carefully to the words in a question and using them to formulate the answer
- Getting better marks in your speaking exam by saying more.

➤ PLTS

Question 3, Listening: Independent enquirers/ Reflective learners/Self-managers
Question 3, Speaking: Creative thinkers/Reflective learners/Self-managers

In this unit, students have learnt how to...

➤ Beim Hören

1 **Listen to German while reading the text at the same time.**
- Students listen to the sounds of the words and phrases, concentrating on remembering how they sound and what they mean.
- Students read German aloud to themselves in order to listen to the German they are seeing and saying, as well to practise speaking in German.
- They read a page of their exercise book aloud to themselves or to a partner.
- They then open their textbook randomly and read the German aloud to themselves or to a partner.

2 **Study the visuals that accompany a listening task, including the layout of the task, and use them to preview what they are likely to hear.**
- Students go through the pictures, naming them.

Answers:

Hut; Regenschirm; Aktentasche

3 **Review what they know about a topic and what key words might come up.**

PLTS
- Students imagine that the topic of a listening exercise is *Taschengeld* and think about the words and phrases that might come up. They make a quick list.
- This encourages students to reflect upon what they have learnt and build on this. It covers the Independent enquirers, Reflective learners and Self-managers groups of skills from the framework of personal, learning and thinking skills.

4 **Check that their guesses make sense.**
- Students decide which of the following might not fit the topic *Taschengeld*?

Answer:

Stundenplan

➤ Beim Sprechen

1 **Use intonation to turn a sentence or phrase into a question.**
- Students look at the sentences listed and decide what questions they could make from these without using question words?
- Remind them to use *du* if appropriate.

Possible Answers:

Eine Stunde dauert?
Hast du einen Nebenjob?
Du findest die Arbeit interessant?

2 **Listen carefully to the words in a question and use them to formulate the answer.**
- Students use the questions listed to formulate answers.

Answers:

Ich arbeite ...
Ich finde die Schule langweilig/toll, weil...
Mein Taschengeld reicht (nicht) aus.

3 **Get better marks in your speaking exam by saying more.**

PLTS
- Students answer the questions listed with more information than is strictly applicable to them.
- This encourages students to think creatively, and to communicate previous learning in order to work towards goals. It covers the Creative thinkers, Reflective learners and Self-managers groups of skills from the framework of personal, learning and thinking skills.

Szenario

Seite 153

Planner

➤ Objectives
- Preparing an agenda for a discussion with senior staff at school
- Preparing and acting out a presentation about a job that would be perfect for teenagers who are still at school and so need time for homework and school-based activities

➤ Resources
Students' Book, page 153
CD3, track 9
Exam Skills Workbooks, pages 56–57
Resources and Planning OxBox CD-ROM

➤ Skills
- Writing practice
- Speaking practice

➤ PLTS
Question 2, Writing: Creative thinkers/Reflective learners/Team workers/Self-managers/Effective participators
Question 3, Speaking: Reflective learners/Team workers/Self-managers/Effective participators

➤ Zum Schreiben

In this section, students produce their own agenda for a discussion with senior staff at school.

It is possible for students to obtain GCSE grades A–F:
Grade F students write a short review using simple sentences and communicate some information.
Grade C students include a variety of structures which may include different tenses or time frames. They communicate information and express personal opinions.
Grade A students include a variety of vocabulary, structures and verb tenses. They convey information, narrate events and express and explain ideas and points of view.

1 **Listen to a group of student representatives as they draw up a list of discussion points they wish to take up with senior staff. Here is their final list.**
- This activity serves as an introduction to the task. Encourage students to bear in mind any listening tips from the unit and to listen carefully to the vocabulary and structures used.

CD 3, track 9 **Seite 153, Übung 1**

Boy 1: So… sind wir uns einig? Auf meiner Liste steht jetzt, dass wir gerne eine neue Bank vor der Schule haben möchten, weil man dort auf den Bus warten muss. Wir machen uns Sorgen um Jochens Noten, hoffen aber, dass er nicht sitzen bleibt. Dann wollten wir auch nach Holland fahren, oder?
Girl 1: Nein, nein. Wir wollen eine Reise mit unserer Französischlehrerin nach Paris machen, um unser Französisch zu verbessern.
Boy 1: Ja, O.K. Paris. Coole Idee.
Girl 2: Und wir müssen unbedingt fragen, ob die Schule die Toilette im zweiten Stock ersetzen kann. Die Toilette ist viel zu alt und stinkt furchtbar!
Boy 1: In Ordnung!

2 **In a group, discuss in German what changes you would like to see taking place in your own school and why you want those changes.**
- Students use what they have heard in activity 1 to begin to think about changes they would like to see in their school.
- This activity encourages students to generate ideas and explore possibilities and to ask questions to extend their thinking, to communicate previous learning, and to colloborate and negotiate effectively with others to achieve goals. It covers the Creative thinkers, Reflective learners, Team workers, Self-managers and Effective participators groups of skills from the framework of personal, learning and thinking skills.

PLTS

3 **Now write up your final agenda, listing your priorities and explaining why they are important, using *weil.***
- Students use what they have heard and discussed in activities 1 and 2 to write a final agenda.

➤ Zum Sprechen

In this section, students prepare a presentation in German about a job, perfect for teenagers who are still at school and so need time for homework and school-based activities, to convince potential students to apply. They should emphasise all the advantages and try to be as persuasive as possible.

It is possible for students to obtain GCSE grades A–F and they are marked on Communication, Quality of language and Pronunciation and intonation:
Grade F students communicate a limited number of ideas, expressing simple opinions. A few phrases or short sentences are accurate enough to be recognisable. There are very few instances of clear pronunciation and intonation.
Grade C students communicate the essential elements, readily expressing points of view. They occasionally hesitate

and can respond to some unpredictable questions. They use straightforward vocabulary and structures which may contain different tenses or time frames. Pronunciation and intonation is generally accurate.

Grade A students use relevant information to develop and justify individual ideas and points of view. There is no hesitation and they are able to respond to unpredictable questions. They use a wide range of clause types, vocabulary and structures accurately. The presentation is fluent and coherent with just minor errors. Pronunciation and intonation are very accurate with a few minor slips.

1 **Working in a group of 4–5, write job descriptions in German for jobs that would be perfect for teenagers who are still at school and so need time for homework and school-based activities.**

- This activity serves as an introduction to the task and draws together what students have learnt in the unit.

2 **Prepare a presentation in German about one of the jobs to convince potential students to apply. Emphasise all the advantages and try to be as persuasive as possible.**

- This activity allows students to think in more detail about the task.

3 **Do a formal presentation for the job to another group and be prepared to answer any questions they might have.**

- This activity draws together what students have prepared in activities 1 and 2.
- It encourages students to invite feedback and deal positively with praise setbacks and criticism, to work effectively with and try to influence others, and to organise time and resources effectively. It covers the Reflective learners, Team workers, Self-managers and Effective participators groups of skills from the framework of personal, learning and thinking skills.

PLTS

Vokabeln

Seite 154

Planner

➤ **Resources**
Students' Book, page 154
Activity Sheet 63

This page provides a summary of the key language covered in each spread of this unit. It could be used as a handy reference for students as they work through the unit. Alternatively, students could use its clear German–English format when learning vocabulary.

Lesen

Seiten 187–188

Planner

➤ Objectives

- To encourage independent reading and develop reading strategies
- To provide alternative class and homework material for students who finish other activities quickly

Page 187 provides a reading text in the context of the unit.
Page 188 provides a reading text, again in the context of the unit.

➤ Resources

Students' Book, pages 187–188

➤ Skills

- Reading practice

➤ PLTS

Question 2 (part 1): Creative thinkers/Reflective learners/Team workers
Question 2 (part 2): Reflective learners/Self-managers

Lesen A: Brauchst du Hilfe bei deiner Schularbeit?

1 Lies die Werbung und beantworte die Fragen auf Englisch.

- Students read the advert and answer the questions in English.

Answers:

a 12–16-year-old school pupils; **b** help with homework, preparing for exams, individual learning strategies; **c** you get an individual learning programme; **d** better marks, help with problems, e.g. with teachers or specific subjects; **e** 12–16 years old; **f** as arranged – mainly afternoons after school; **g** by phone

2 Was sind deiner Meinung nach nützliche Lernstrategien? Mach eine Liste und diskutiere sie mit einem Partner/einer Partnerin.

- Students work with a partner to discuss useful learning strategies. They list these.
- This encourages students to generate ideas and explore possibilities, connecting their own and others' ideas, to communicate previous learning to achieve goals and to collaborate effectively with others. It covers the Creative thinkers, Reflective learners and Team workers groups of skills from the framework of personal, learning and thinking skills.

3 Für welche Fächer brauchst du Nachhilfe? Wie soll die Nachhilfe aussehen? Warum? Schreib einen kurzen Absatz.

- Students think about subjects or homework they would like help with.
- They write a short paragraph saying the type of help they would like and why.

Lesen B: Deine Schülermitverwaltung braucht dich!

1 Beschreib auf Englisch, wer in dem Schülerrat ist.

- Students read the school webpage.
- They then describe in English who makes up the team of student representatives.

Answer:

2 class spokespeople (the spokesperson and the substitute) are elected from each class. From the spokespeople, 2 students representatives are elected for classes 7–10.

2 Beschreib auf Englisch, was der Schülerrat macht und was sie dieses Jahr machen will.

- Students read the webpage again and this time describe in English what the student represetatives do and what they want to do this year.
- This encourages students to use previous learning to achieve goals. It covers the Reflective learners and Self-managers groups of skills from the framework of personal, learning and thinking skills.

Answer:

They represent the interests of the pupils, make proposals to improve school equipment and buying new items, organise school events, support pupils experiencing conflict at school (either with other pupils or teachers), publish the school newspaper on a regular basis, represent the school outside of school.
This year, they want:
to have a say in the shaping the new computer course
all school benches to be renovated
their complaints to be listened to by teachers and the headteacher

3 Schreib über das Problem, das der Schülerrat hat, und wie es gelöst werden könnte und von wem.

- Students now write a paragraph about the problem the school representatives have and how it can be solved and by whom.

Unit 5B: Arbeit und Zukunftspläne		**Overview grid**		
Spread	**Contexts and objectives**	**Skills**	**Grammar**	**Vocabulary**
pages 156–157 **Wie man ein Praktikum wählt**	• Discussing interests and work experience	• Using context and your knowledge to understand a text	• The future with *werden* + infinitive	*der Chor; die Feuerwehr; der/die Kunde/Kundin; das Mitglied; das Praktikum; planen; sich interessieren für etwas; verbessern; vorhaben; werden*
pages 158–159 **Wie man eine interessante Arbeit findet**	• Discussing job advertisements, looking for a job, job particulars	• Guessing the meaning of compound words	• Word order with *wenn*	*das Alter; die Anzeige; die Vorstellung; verboten*
pages 160–161 **Wie man einen Lebenslauf schreibt**	• Discussing how to write a curriculum vitae	• Checking spelling	• Formal and informal address	*der Arbeitgeber; das Bergsteigen; der Lebenslauf; die Stelle; pünktlich*
pages 162–163 **Wie man ein Vorstellungsgespräch überlebt**	• Discussing being interviewed on the telephone	• Using conjunctions and word order to understand a sentence	• Revising conjunctions	*die Erfahrung; der Erfolg; der Käfig; der Traum; füttern; träumen; dann; gefährlich*
pages 164–165 **Wie man über Ausbildung und Berufe spricht**	• Discussing work experience and future plans	• Writing longer sentences to get better marks	• Inverted word order	*der Alptraum; die Ausbildung; der Friseur, die Friseuse; der Beruf; die Lehre; der Lehrling; eine Lehrstelle; ärgerlich*
pages 166–167 **Aktive Grammatik**	• Grammar		• Inverted word order • Word order with subordinating conjunctions • Future tense • Formal and informal forms of address	
page 168 **Kompetenzen**	• Summarising what you have learnt	• Using formula phrases to tell a story in sequence • Checking word order in a sentence affected by inverted word order or subordinating conjunctions • Choosing whether to use formal or informal writing styles • Checking for errors as you write • Working out the gist from the context • Inferring word meanings • Recognising sound-spelling links • Avoiding making wild guesses		
page 169 **Szenario**	• Preparing arguments for, and having a debate on one of the themes of the spread • Writing an interesting story about work experience	• Writing practice • Speaking practice		
page 170 **Vokabeln**	• Key language			
pages 189–190 **Lesen**	• Work experience • Dream careers • To encourage independent reading and develop reading strategies • To provide alternative class and homework material for students who finish other activities quickly	• Reading practice		

5B Arbeit und Zukunftspläne

Unit Objectives

Contexts and cultural focus: work experience, work and future plans
Skills focus: using formula phrases; checking word order; choosing whether to use formal or informal writing styles; checking for errors as you write; using context for getting the gist of a passage; recognising sound-spelling links; avoiding making wild guesses
Grammar: the future tense; 'if' sentences; formal/informal forms of address; conjunctions

Controlled assessment opportunities

Writing: Students' Book, page 157 activity 5
Writing: Students' Book, page 159 activity 5b
Writing: Students' Book, page 161 activity 6
Writing: Students' Book, page 163 activity 5
Writing: Students' Book, page 165 activity 7
Speaking: Students' Book, page 169 Zum Sprechen, activity 3
Writing: Students' Book, page 169 Zum Schreiben, activity 5

See also ***GCSE German for OCR Assessment OxBox CD-ROM.***

An introduction to the unit Seite 155

- *Aim*: To introduce the themes of the unit.
- The opening spread of each unit is styled as the contents page of a teenage magazine. Illustrations, captions and skills summaries provide a preview of what is to come:

	Students' Book
Weißt du schon, wie man ein Praktikum wählt?	pages 156–157
Weißt du schon, wie man eine interessante Arbeit findet?	pages 158–159
Weißt du schon, wie man einen Lebenslauf schreibt?	pages 160–161
Weißt du schon, wie man ein Vorstellungsgespräch überlebt?	pages 162–163
Weißt du schon, wie man über Ausbildung und Berufe spricht?	pages 164–165

- Allow time for students to read the questions and cross-refer to the relevant pages of the Students' Book. They could do this individually or in pairs/groups, followed by whole-class discussion.
- This spread also provides an opportunity for students to recap on familiar language. Ask them to think about language they already know that might be useful when working on the themes of the unit.
- At the end of work on Unit 5B:
  – If time permits, ask students to devise a replacement opening spread. What do they think should be on it, in terms of pictures, captions, etc.? What would they change/keep the same, and why? Ask them to imagine it is the contents page of a teenage magazine: what sort of captions and pictures do they feel would attract people to buy the magazine? This sort of activity encourages students to think about features of a text that make it suitable for a particular audience or purpose.
  – Allow time for students to return to this opening spread to answer the questions, review what they have learned and reflect on areas for improvement. What did they find difficult, interesting, etc.? What do they think are the most important things they have learned in this unit?

Wie man ein Praktikum wählt

Seiten 156–157

Planner

➤ Objectives
- Discussing interests and work experience

➤ Resources
Students' Book, pages 156–157
CD 3, track 12
Grammar Workbook, page 56
Activity Sheet 64

➤ Key language
der Chor; die Feuerwehr; der/die Kunde/Kundin; das Mitglied; das Praktikum
planen; sich interessieren für etwas; verbessern; vorhaben; werden

➤ Skills
- Using context and your knowledge to understand a text

➤ Grammar
- The future with *werden* + infinitive

➤ PLTS
Question 4: Creative thinkers/Reflective learners/Team workers
Question 5: Creative thinkers/Reflective learners/Self-managers

➤ Starters
- Before reading and listening to the dialogue, *Das Praktikum*, list some interests in German in one column, e.g. *singen*, *Sport* and possible jobs in a second column, e.g. *Chordirektorin, im Sportgeschäft arbeiten*, etc. Give students a time limit to match the interests to the jobs. Compare answers as a class.
- Divide the class into small groups. Display some of the types of work experience from the spread with letters missing. Give the groups a set time to fill in the missing letters. Compare answers as a class.

➤ Plenaries
- Go round the class asking each student, *Wo wirst du arbeiten? Warum?* Students reply, e.g. *Ich werde bei einem Architekten arbeiten, weil ich mich sehr dafür, Häuser zu entwerfen interessiere.* If necessary model an answer before you begin for support.
- To practise intonation, display the dialogue from activity 1a and choose some volunteers to play the parts of Johann, Annie, Thomas, Silvia and Karl. They act out the dialogue paying particular attention to intonation. Continue with new volunteers.
- Students work in pairs and interview each other about their interests. Each of them then decides what type of work experience would be ideal for the other. Each pair presents their conclusions to the class, e.g. *Er interessiert sich für Fußball. Er fotografiert gern und macht gern Videos. Er könnte als Sportfotograf arbeiten*. etc.

1a Hör gut zu und lies den Dialog auf Seite 156. Beantworte die folgenden Fragen auf Englisch.
- As an introduction to the spread, students listen to and read the dialogue on page 156.
- They then answer the questions in English.

CD 3, track 12 **Seite 157, Übung 1a**

Johann: So, habt ihr alle eure Praktikumsstellen organisiert?
Annie: Ja, ich werde bei einem Architekten in der Stadt arbeiten. Ich möchte später an der Uni Architektur studieren. Ich interessiere mich sehr für Haus-Design!
Thomas: Ich werde mein Praktikum bei der Feuerwehr machen. Dort bietet man ein tolles Praktikumsprogramm an, wo man viel lernt! Schade, dass ich nicht viel Geld verdienen werde.
Silvia: Ich werde ein freiwilliges Arbeitspraktikum beim Gesangsverein machen, da ich Chorleiterin werden möchte, so wie ich es im Fernsehen gesehen habe. Ich werde meinen Lebenslauf auch an die Chorleiter verschiedener Kirchen schicken um mich dort auch zu bewerben. Und du, Johann?
Johann: Ich werde im Sportgeschäft arbeiten. Dort werde ich beim Verkauf und bei der Inventur helfen. Ich werde die neuesten Sportartikel sehen und ich werde gutes Geld kriegen! Ich möchte später an der Berufsschule Sport studieren. Und du, Karl, was wirst du machen?
Karl: Keine Ahnung! Ich habe noch nicht so richtig gesucht. Ich weiß nicht, was ich machen könnte!
Thomas: Was? Mach was, das dich wirklich interessiert! Du fährst doch gern Rad! Mach etwas mit Fahrrädern!
Karl: Na, ein Fahrradgeschäft gibt es in unserer Stadt ja schon, aber verkaufen, das möchte ich nicht. Das ist der große Nachteil vom Fahrradgeschäft. Ich will keine Kunden bedienen. Ich bin eine große Null im Verkaufen!
Thomas: Du brauchst nicht zu verkaufen. Du kannst Reparaturen machen. Und warum nicht in Frankreich? Irgendwo auf der Route der Tour de France! Du kannst dein Französisch verbessern und die fantastischen Radfahrer bei der Tour sehen. *Quelle chance!*

Karl: Du hast Recht! Radfahren ist meine Leidenschaft! Ich werde etwas mit Fahrrädern machen! Am besten suche ich gleich im Internet.

Answers:

a where they are going to do their work experience; **b** She would like to study architecture at university and become an architect. **c** they offer a great training programme where you learn a lot; **d** the church choir; **e** he will see the latest sports equipment and will earn good money; **f** he doesn't know what he can do; **g** making repairs to bikes; working in France on the *Tour de France* route; searching for bike-related work experience on the Internet

1b Gruppenarbeit. Lest in Gruppen von 2–5 Personen das Gespräch auf Seite 156 vor.

- Read the *Tipp* section on intonation as a class.
- Students read the dialogue aloud in small groups.

2 Vervollständige die folgenden Sätze.

4–6

- Students read the dialogue again.
- They then practise word order with *weil* by completing the sentences.

Answers:

a …sie später an der Uni Architektur studieren möchte und sie interessiert sich sehr für Haus-Design!
b …sie ein tolles Praktikumsprogramm anbietet, wo man viel lernt.
c …er die neuesten Sportartikel sehen wird und er wird gutes Geld kriegen! Er möchte auch später an der Berufsschule Sport studieren.
d …sie Chordirektorin werden möchte.
e …Radfahren seine Leidenschaft ist.

3 Lies den Text über Georg und mach Notizen. Gibt es Wörter, die ihr nicht versteht? Diskutiert.

4–9

A64

- Students read the text about Georg and make notes.
- They discuss any words they don't understand with a partner.

Activity Sheet 64 provides further activities on the subject of work experience.

4 With a partner, discuss in German the advantages and disadvantages of doing work experience. Decide whether each of the following points is an advantage or a disadvantage.

4–9

PLTS

- Students work with a partner to discuss advantages and disadvantages of work experience. They decide whether the sentences listed are positive or negative.
- Encourage debate and remind students to draw on the vocabulary and structures they have met in this spread so far.
- This activity encourages students to generate and explore ideas, making original connections, to communicate previous learning, to work collaboratively with others to reach agreements, managing discussions to achieve results. It covers the Creative thinkers, Reflective learners and Team workers groups of skills from the framework of personal, learning and thinking skills.

5 Imagine a work experience you have chosen to go on that relates to your interests or hobbies. Write a short paragraph in German in the future tense about it. Include as much information as you can. Be creative!

4–9

PLTS

- This activity draws together the vocabulary, grammar points and skills covered in this spread. It an ideal assessment opportunity.
- Encourage students to think back to previous activities and to use the vocabulary, ideas and structures they have met in the spread. Remind them what they write doesn't have to be completely true; they can embellish to make it more interesting.
- This activity encourages students to generate and explore ideas, to communicate previous learning and to show creativity to work towards goals . It covers the Creative thinkers, Reflective learners and Self-managers groups of skills from the framework of personal, learning and thinking skills.

Success criteria:

- information communicated
- variety of vocabulary and structures used
- personal opinions expressed

Wie man eine interessante Arbeit findet

Seiten 158–159

Planner

➤ Objectives

- Discussing job advertisements, looking for a job, job particulars

➤ Resources

Students' Book, pages 158–159
CD 3, track 13
Grammar Workbook, page 63

➤ Key language

das Alter; die Anzeige; die Vorstellung; verboten; wenn

➤ Skills

- Guessing the meaning of compound words

➤ Grammar

- Word order with *wenn*

➤ PLTS

Question 3c: Reflective learners/Team workers/Self-managers
Question 5a: Creative thinkers/Reflective learners/Team workers

➤ Starters

- A quick warm-up activity. Go round the class asking each student to say a part-time job in German, e.g. *Zeitungen austragen*. Make a list of these. Keep the list to use later.
- Display some sentences from the beginning of the spread in jumbled order, e.g. *Deutschland ist in Kinderarbeit verboten.* (*Kinderarbeit ist in Deutschland verboten.*) and give students a time limit to unjumble them. Compare answers as a class. Then ask students to tell you what the sentences mean in English.
- Display the list of part-time jobs from Starter activity 1. As a class brainstorm possible reasons for taking these jobs, e.g. *gern am Computer arbeiten,* etc.

➤ Plenaries

- Display anagrams of some of the jobs/places of work mentioned in the spread and give students a time limit to unjumble them, e.g. *mfriabua* (Baufirma). To make this easier, display the keep the initial letter as uppercase, e.g. *mfriaBua*. Go through the answers as a class.
- Ask students to look at the job adverts on page 158 again and to write a short paragraph saying which one they would most like to apply for and why. Volunteers read out their paragraph to the class.
- Give students a time limit to write three sentences on the theme of the spread using *wenn*. When the time is up go round the class asking students to read out their sentences. Display some of the sentences to reinforce what the word order should be with *wenn*.

Lies den Blog und beantworte die Fragen auf Englisch.

4–6

- Students read the blog and answer the questions.

Answers:

1 is 13 and wants a part-time job in office; **2** he can't as he is too young; **3** only when you are 15 or 16 can you start working a few hours a day in an office, but only as an assistant. **4** at 14 can deliver newspapers, magazines or brochures; **5** *Jugend, Arbeits, Schutz, Gesetz* = protection of health and safety standards for young people at work

1a Partnerarbeit. Lest die Stellenanzeigen auf Seite 158 und schreibt Notizen auf Englisch. Die Tipp-Box hilft euch dabei.

4–6

- Students work with a partner and read the adverts on page 158.
- They make notes in English.

Answers:

Job	Age range	Days and times	Duties	Requirements	Pay
Private tutor	*(not stated)*	*twice a week, 2 hours in afternoons*	*tutor children in maths and science*	*good in maths and science; maybe show school report?*	*€12 per hour*
Cinema assistant	16+	afternoon and evening performances	selling popcorn/drinks; taking tickets	(not stated)	€5 per hour
Courier	18+	at least 4 hours a day	taking (mostly business) packages from A to B	driving licence and own car; must often get up early and must work	Up to €10 per hour
Office assistant	(not stated)	(not stated)	telephone duties; typing on computer	must like working with computers	(not stated)

1b Partnerarbeit. Wie sagt man auf Deutsch …?

- Students work in pairs. They read through the adverts on page 158 again and find the German for the English phrases listed.

Answers:

a *die Stunde*; **b** Führerschein; **c** Päckchen; **d** von A nach B; **e** eigenes Auto haben; **f** Eintrittskarten

2a Wie war das Praktikum oder der Job? Hör gut zu und schreib Notizen auf Englisch.

- Students listen to the recording and make notes in English.

CD 3, track 13 **Seite 159, Übung 2**

1
Mein Praktikum habe ich im Geschäft meines Vaters gemacht. Dort habe ich im Büro gearbeitet und habe Dateien am Computer kontrolliert. Ich habe um neun Uhr morgens angefangen und hatte ab vier Uhr nachmittags frei. Ich habe drei Wochen dort gearbeitet und ich fand es ziemlich interessant, weil ich gern am Computer arbeite.

2
Ich habe lange gesucht, um eine Praktikantenstelle zu finden, habe dann aber endlich etwas im Internet gesehen. Es war eine Stelle als Animateurin in einem Kinderheim. Ich habe zwei Wochen lang im Kinderheim gearbeitet, nur zwei Stunden am Tag. Die Arbeit hat mir gefallen, weil ich gerne mit Kindern arbeite.

3
Meine Arbeit habe ich in der Zeitung gefunden. Ich habe eine Anzeige für Stellen in einer Autofabrik gefunden. Das waren zehn Arbeitstage von 11 Uhr bis 3 Uhr nachmittags. Es war eine Art Lehrstelle, wo man ein bisschen von allem, was zum Autobau gehört, lernen konnte. Das war toll! Mir gefallen die Motoren am meisten.

4
Durch meinen besten Freund habe ich eine Stelle bei einer Baufirma gefunden. Die Firma gehört seinem Onkel. Ich habe zwei Wochen dort gearbeitet, meistens im Büro. Ich habe gelernt, wie die Firma organisiert ist. Ich war aber nicht besonders glücklich, weil ich lieber im Freien arbeite.

Answers:

	How was it found?	Where?	Kind of work?	Hours	Opinion	Why?
1	*father*	*father's office*	*checking data on computer*	*9–4 for 3 weeks*	*interesting*	*likes computer work*
2	on the Internet	children's home	working with children	2 hours a day	suited her	likes working with children
3	in the newspaper	car factory	a sort of apprenticeship to learn a bit about all aspects of car building	11–3 for 10 working days	great	likes engines best
4	through best friend	building firm	mostly in office; learnt about the running of the firm	2 weeks	not very happy	prefers working outdoors

2b Partnerarbeit. Hört noch einmal zu. Wie sagt man auf Englisch…?

- Students listen again and, in pairs, use the context to note down what the words listed are in English.

Answers:

a on the Internet; **b** in the newspaper; **c** helper in a children's home; **d** apprentice; **e** car factory; **f** building firm

3a Schreib ganze Sätze.

- Read through the *Grammatik* section on word order with *wenn* as a class.
- Students complete the sentences with their own words. Remind them to watch out for word order.

3b Schreib sechs Sätze mit *wenn*. Benutze die Anzeigen auf Seite 158.

- Students display their knowledge of word order with *wenn* and show how much vocabulary they have learnt so far from the unit by writing six sentences of their own using *wenn*.
- They refer back to the announcements on page 158 for support.

3c Partnerarbeit. Lest eure Sätze aus Übung 3b vor. Überprüft euren Tonfall und die Rechtschreibung.

- Students work with a partner. They each read the sentences they wrote in activity 3b.
- They check that their intonation is accurate and also check the spelling in their sentences.
- This encourages students to review progress, acting on the outcomes and to collaborate with others to work towards goals. It covers the Reflective learners, Team workers and Self-managers groups of skills from the framework of personal, learning and thinking skills.

4 Partnerarbeit. Findet mindestens sechs zusammengesetzte Wörter auf Seite 158–159. Wie heißen die Einzelwörter auf Englisch?

- Students find at least six compound words from the spread. Explain that a compound word is one word made up or two or more smaller words.
- Students note down what each of the smaller words means in order to try and guess what the compound word means.

5a **Work in groups of 4–5. Play the 'if' story chain game about where to find a job or work experience placement and about the hours, work, pay, etc. Each person starts a sentence with *wenn*, picking up from what the previous person said.**

PLTS 4–9

- This activity draws together the vocabulary, themes and grammar that students have learnt in the spread and acts as preparation for activity 4b.
- This activity encourages students to think creatively, to communicate their learning and to work confidently with others. It covers the Creative thinkers, Reflective learners and Team workers groups of skills from the framework of personal, learning and thinking skills.

5b **Write a short *wenn* story about finding a job, as in the groupwork activity in activity 5a.**

4–9

- Students use what they have discussed in activity 4a to write their own *wenn* story. This is an ideal assessment opportunity.

Success criteria:

- information communicated
- variety of vocabulary, time frames and verb tenses used
- correct word order

Wie man einen Lebenslauf schreibt

Seiten 160–161

Planner

➤ Objectives
- Discussing how to write a curriculum vitae

➤ Resources
Students' Book, pages 160–161
Grammar Workbook, page 37
Activity Sheet 65

➤ Key language
der Arbeitgeber; das Bergsteigen; der Lebenslauf; die Stelle; pünktlich

➤ Skills
- Checking spelling

➤ Grammar
- Formal and informal address

➤ PLTS
Question 4: Reflective learners/Team workers/Self-managers
Question 6: Creative thinkers/Reflective learners/Self-managers

➤ Starters
- Display the key language with vowels missing. Divide students into small groups and give them a time limit to complete the words. Check answers as a class. Each group scores a point for each word they have written correctly.
- Display some common infinitives and ask students to note down the *du* and *Sie* forms of these, e.g. *haben, sein, arbeiten, machen, geben,* etc. Go through the answers as a class. Ask students to explain when you would use the *du* form and when you would use the *Sie* form. If there is time, call out some scenarios and students reply with *du* or *Sie*, e.g.
  Teacher: *a job application*
  Students: *Sie*
  Teacher: *an email to a friend*
  Students: *du*
- Divide the class into two teams. Call out some of the compound words from the spread ask students to guess what they mean, e.g. *der Arbeitgeber*. The first team to answer correctly, i.e. *employer* wins a point. Teams loose a point if they answer incorrectly. The team with the most points at the end wins.

➤ Plenaries
- Display some words from the spread, e.g. *Beruf, Mühe, anfangen, Firma*, etc. and challenge students to use these in sentences. Compare sentences as a class.
- Students write a job application, but include five deliberate mistakes (these could be wrong form of address, spelling mistakes, wrong verb endings, etc.). They then pass their application to a partner who finds and corrects the mistakes.
- Students work in pairs. Each partner reads their corrected job application from plenary activity 2 out loud to practise pronunciation and intonation. Confident volunteers read their applications out to the class.

1a Lies den Lebenslauf von Johannes oben und beantworte die Fragen auf Englisch.

- Students read Johannes' curriculum vitae and answer the questions in English.

Answers:

a Salzburg in Austria; **b** 10th December; **c** *Untersberger Grundschule* and *Hauptschule Andreas Hofer*; **d** the area code; **e** skiing, climbing mountains, rambling; **f** he has the *Schulabschluss* (German equivalent of GCSEs); **g** *Bergtourleiter* = mountain tour leader; *Skifabrikant* = ski maker

1b Der Vater von Johannes übt mit seinem Sohn die Fragen, die ihm ein Arbeitgeber stellen wird. Füll die Lücken aus und schreib dann ganze Sätze.

- Students complete the sentences.
- This activity introduces them to the *Sie* form.

Answers:

a Wie; **b** Wann; **c** gebor**en**; **d** Wo; **e** Schule; **f** Schulabschluss; **g** Was; **h** Was

1c Partnerarbeit. Rollenspiel. Stellt einander Fragen aus Übung 1b und Antworten für Johannes.

- Students work with a partner. They ask each other the questions from activity 1b and answer as Johannes.

2a Partnerarbeit. Verwandle *du*-Sätze in *Sie*-Sätze und umgekehrt.

- Read through the *Grammatik* section on formal and informal address as a class.
- Students change the *du* sentences into *Sie* sentences and vice versa.

Answers:

a Wie heißen Sie?
b Um wie viel Uhr kannst du anfangen?
c Gefällt es dir, hier zu arbeiten?
d Sie haben Ihnen mit dieser Arbeit viel Mühe gegeben.
e Interessiert du dich für eine Stelle in unserer Firma?

2b Schreib die Sätze aus Übung 2a in dein Heft. Überprüfe, ob alles richtig ist. Die Tipp-Box hilft dir dabei.

- Students now write the sentences from activity 2a in their exercise books.
- They then check for errors. Read the *Tipp* section on checking for errors before they start this.

3a Schreib deinen eigenen Lebenslauf. Benutze das Format Johannes' Lebenslauf.

- Students write their own curriculum vitae.
- They use the titles from Johannes' curriculum vitae as a guide.

3b Partnerarbeit. Stellt und beantwortet die Fragen aus Übung 1b für euch. Gibt es auch andere Fragen, die ein Arbeitgeber stellen könnte?

- Students work in pairs to ask and answer the questions from activity 1b. Encourage them to answer as fully as possible.
- Students then add any additional questions they can think of that employers might ask.

3c Schreib das Rollenspiel aus Übung 3b in dein Heft.

- Students write out the role-play from activity 3b in their exercise book.
- Remind them to think back to the *Tipp* section and to check their work for errors as they go.

4 Partnerarbeit. Johannes hat eine Jobanzeige im Internet gefunden. Er hat eine Vorstellungs-E-Mail geschrieben, aber sein Vater findet diese E-Mail schrecklich. Sie ist viel zu informell. Lest die E-mail auf Seite 160 und macht eine Liste von Problemen auf Englisch.

- Students work with a partner. They read Johannes' email and list the errors.
- This activity encourages students to communicate what they have learnt and to collaborate effectively with other to work towards goals. It covers the Reflective learners, Team workers and Self-managers groups of skills from the framework of personal, learning and thinking skills.

Answers:

1 'Hallo' is a very informal way to start a formal email introducing yourself.
2 'Hansi' is his nickname, which shouldn't be used in a formal email.
3 A prospecitve employer should be addressed as *Sie* not *du*; he should have used *Ihre*.
4 *Ich will…* is very direct; it would be better to use *Ich möchte*.
5 He should use the formal *Ihrer*.
6 The job is ski-related not football-related, so that he can play football well is not relevant.
7 Saying that he works hard is not specific enough; he needs to give examples that are relevant to the job.
8 He should use the formal *Sie*, not *dich*.
9 Using *ja* in this way is far too informal and would be used in an email to a friend.
10 *Alles Gute* is an informal way to sign off; he should use the formal, *Ihre Antwort erwarte ich mit Interesse.* or *Mit freundlichen Grüßen*.

A65 Activity Sheet 65 provides further activities on writing job applications.

5 Here is a more formal introductory email by Johannes. With a partner, read it aloud to each other in German, and then translate it into English.

- This activity draws together what students have learnt in the spread.

Answer:

Dear Mr. Schmidt,

My name is Johannes Klett. I am 16 years old. I took my GCSEs this year. I am interested in the post of stocktaking assistant with your company. I am an enthusiastic sportsman and would like to work for a sports equipment firm in the future. I am punctual and friendly, and I put an effort into my work. I hope to receive a postive response from you.

Yours sincerely,

Johannes Klett

6 **Read the email in activity 5 and then write your own formal email in German to a business or company where you would like to work, or in response to one of the job adverts on page 158.**

- Students use what they have learnt in the spread to write their own job application. This is an ideal assessment opportunity.
- This encourages students to generate and explore ideas and to connect their own and others' ideas. It also encourages them to communicate previous learning to work towards goals. It covers the Creative thinkers, Reflective learners and Self-managers groups of skills from the framework of personal, learning and thinking skills.

4–9

PLTS

Success criteria:

- information communicated
- variety of vocabulary and structures used
- personal opinions expressed

Wie man ein Vorstellungsgespräch überlebt

Seiten 162–163

Planner

➤ Objectives

- Discussing being interviewed, face to face or on the telephone

➤ Resources

Students' Book, pages 162–163
CD 3, track 14
Grammar Workbook, page 63

➤ Key language

die Erfahrung; der Erfolg; der Käfig
der Traum
füttern; träumen
dann; gefährlich

➤ Skills

- Using conjunctions and word order to understand a sentence

➤ Grammar

- Revising conjunctions

➤ PLTS

Question 2b: Reflective learners/Team workers/ Self-managers

➤ Starters

- Display the key language from the spread in one column with the English translations jumbled up in a second column. Give students a time limit to match the English and the German.
- Students brainstorm as many positive personal characteristics you could include in a job application as possible, e.g. *Geduld haben, pünktlich sein,* etc.
- Display a list of vocabulary including conjunctions, verbs and nouns from the spread, e.g. *weil, und, arbeiten, kann, Anzeige*, etc. Students have a time limit to categorise these under the headings 'Conjunctions', 'Verbs', 'Nouns'. Now ask students if they can explain what happens to the word order after each of the conjunctions.

➤ Plenaries

- Test students. Divide the class into two teams. How many of the *10 Tipps zum Erfolg!* from page 162 can they remember? Give them a time limit to note down as many as possible in German. Compare answers. The team that has remembered the most wins.
- Challenge students to write sentences on the themes of the spread, using as many different conjunctions as possible, e.g. *Man sollte flexibel sein, weil man alles Mögliche machen muss.* Compare answers as a class and display the sentences. Ask students to explain the word order.
- Ask students to write a list of points in German describing a job or career they really wouldn't like. They should include details of: where, doing what, what hours and days, pay, etc. Volunteers read their list out to the class. The class decides who has described the worst job.

1a **Partnerarbeit. Lest und übersetzt die Stellenanzeige oben ins Englische.**

- Students work with a partner to read the job advertisement.
- They then translate it into English.

7–9

Answer:

Dream job

Do you dream about working at a zoo? Here, you can try it out every day after school for two weeks working as a student trainee. Ring us on: 87 886.

1b Partnerarbeit. Lest und übersetzt die zehn Tipps oben ins Englische. Habt ihr andere Tipps? Schreibt sie auf Deutsch und auf Englisch in eure Hefte.

- Students work in pairs again, this time to translate the ten tips from page 162 into English.
- They think of additional tips and write these in German and English in their exercise books.

4–9

Answers:

1 When you first contact your future employer, you will want to be self-confident and communicative.
2 You will need to have prepared a short text to introduce yourself formally. In the text include:
3 your name and age
4 the title or a description of the post in which you are interested
5 where you saw the job advertisement or how you heard about it.
6 why you are interested in this type of work.
7 Next, list your qualifications and characteristics.
8 Write a list of questions that you would like to ask the employer.
9 Read your text through to check that there are no mistakes.
10 Finally, read your text aloud a few times until you sound self-confident and communicative!

2a Gisela möchte im Zoo arbeiten und schreibt ihren Vorstellungstext für ein Telefongespräch mit dem Zoodirektor. Füll die Lücken aus.

- Students use what they have learnt so far to complete Gisela's text.

7–9

Answers:

interessiere; Anzeige; Haustieren; students' own answer; students' own answer; students' own answer; students' own answer; Schule; arbeiten

2b Partnerarbeit. Lest Giselas Vorstellungstext vor. Überprüft euren Tonfall.

- Students read Gisela's text out loud to practise their intonation.
- This encourages students to review progress, acting on the outcomes and to work confidently with others to work towards goals. It covers the Reflective learners, Team workers and Self-managers groups of skills from the framework of personal, learning and thinking skills.

PLTS

3a Finde Beispiele von Konjunktionen in Übung 2a.

- Read through the *Grammatik* section on conjunctions as a class.
- Students find examples of conjunctions in activity 2a.

Answers:

und, weil, und, und, aber, obwohl, und

3b Partnerarbeit. Verbindet die Sätze mit den Konjunktionen in Klammern. Überprüft jeden Satz.

- Students link the sentences with the conjunctions in brackets. They then check each sentence for any errors.

Answers:

a Wenn du einen Vorstellungsbrief schreibst, musst du immer ‚Sie' benutzen.
b Obwohl du Geld hast, kannst du trotzdem Arbeit suchen.
c Während du noch zur Schule gehst, kannst du einige Stunden in der Woche arbeiten.
d Du hast die Zeitung gelesen und du hast deinen Traumjob gefunden.
e Du schreibst und übst einen Vorstellungstext, damit du selbstsicher sprechen kannst.

4 Hör gut zu, sieh dir die Bilder auf Seite 162 an und füll die Lücken mit den Wörtern im Kasten aus.

- Students listen and look at the pictures on page 162.
- They fill in the gaps with the words from the box.

7–9

CD 3, track 14 **Seite 163, Übung 4**

Gisela beschreibt ihr Praktikum

Ich habe mein Praktikum im Zoo gemacht. Jeden Tag nach der Schule habe ich dort von vier bis sechs Uhr gearbeitet. Obwohl ich nur zwei Stunden am Tag gearbeitet habe, war die Arbeit hart. Als Erstes habe ich die Elefanten gefüttert, dann die Kamele. Bei den Affen konnte es gefährlich sein! Anschließend habe ich die Käfige der Vögel sauber gemacht – das war hart, eine richtige Drecksarbeit! Als Letztes musste ich die Daten über die Tiere im Computer speichern. Mein Praktikum war toll, und ich habe viel gelernt.

Answers:

Schule; sechs; Stunden; war; Elefanten; gefährlich; habe; Letztes; Computer; toll

5 Write a telephone interview text in German to introduce yourself, based on the tips on page 162, to apply for a job or work experience placement you would like.

- Students use the tips on page 162 along with what they have listed in activity 6 to write an interview text. This is an ideal assessment opportunity.

4–9

Success criteria:

- information communicated
- variety of vocabulary and structures used
- accuracy

6 Roleplay. Carry out a job interview in German. Find out as much as possible from each other about the job and the candidate.

- Students draw upon what they have learnt in the spread to interview one another for a job.

4–9

Wie man über Ausbildung und Berufe spricht

Seiten 164–165

Planner

➤ Objectives

- Discussing work experience and future plans

➤ Resources

Students' Book, pages 164–165
CD 3, tracks 15–16
Grammar Workbook, page 61
Activity Sheets 66–67

➤ Key language

der Alptraum; die Ausbildung; der Beruf; der Friseur, die Friseuse; die Lehre; der Lehrling; eine Lehrstelle; ärgerlich

➤ Skills

- Writing longer sentences to get better marks

➤ Grammar

- Inverted word order

➤ PLTS

Question 4b: Creative thinkers/Reflective learners/Self-managers
Question 6: Creative thinkers/Reflective learners/Team workers/Self-managers

➤ Starters

- Display the following words in one column and their English translations jumbled up in a second column: *Abitur; Schulabschluss; Oberstufe; Lehrstelle; Berufsschule; Fachschule; Studienplatz; Universität; Technische Hochschule; Fachhochschule; Arbeit.* Set students a time limit to match up the German and the English. Compare answers as a class.
- Students brainstorm conjunctions and formula phrases that could be used to make a basic sentence more interesting. List these as they say them. Keep the list to use in plenary activity 1.
- Call out words containing either the u or ü sound, e.g. *ich musste, ich müsste, ich würde, ich wurde* (see the pronunciation section on the OxBox for more words containing these sounds). Explain to students that when they hear the *u* sound they should remain seated, but when they hear the *ü* sound, they should stand up. You could turn this into a game with students being eliminated if they stand or remain seated at the wrong time.

➤ Plenaries

- Display some short, basic sentences in German, e.g. *Ich habe mein Praktikum gemacht.* Ask students to improve these sentences, making them longer by adding conjunctions, formula phrases, etc. e.g. *Ich habe mein Praktikum bei BMW gemacht, und das ging ganz gut.* Display the list of conjunctions and formula phrases from starter activity 2 for support.
- Display some words from the spread, e.g. *als Erstes, müde, toll, Praktikum, Zoo,* etc. and challenge students to use these to describe a work experience placement. Volunteers read their description out to the class.
- Students prepare a short paragraph about their plans for the future, using the vocabulary and structures from the spread. Refer them back to activity 5b for useful vocabulary. Volunteers then read their paragraph out to the class.

1a Partnerarbeit. Lest zusammen die Seite aus Heinrichs Tagebuch über den ersten Tag seines Praktikums im Schuhgeschäft auf Seite 165. Macht Notizen auf Englisch.

-9

- As an introduction to the spread, students read Heinrich's diary entry on page 165.
- They then make notes in English.

1b Übersetze die folgenden Ausdrücke ins Englische.

-9

- Students now translate the phrases into English.
- Encourage them to look at the context for support.

Answers:

a first of all; **b** the next thing I do; **c** then; **d** afterwards; **e** finally

2 Schreib die Sätze über Heinrichs Probleme zu Ende.

- Read the *Grammatik* section as a class.
- Students practise this by completing the sentences about Heinrich's problems.

Answers:

a **Als Erstes** waren alle Schuhe zu groß für die Kundin.
b **Als Nächstes** hat Heinrich Schuhe in die falschen Kartons getan.
c **Dann** hat er schon wieder Schuhe in den falschen Karton getan.
d **Anschließend** musste er den ganzen Nachmittag Inventur machen.
e **Zum Schluss** ging er ärgerlich nach Hause.

3a Gisela hat ein Interview. Hör gut zu und schreib Notizen auf Englisch.

7–9

- Students listen to Gisela's interview and make notes in English.

CD 3, track 15 **Seite 165, Übung 3a**

Giselas Praktikum

Interviewer: Hallo, Gisela! Erzähl mir etwas von deinem Praktikum. Du hast im Zoo gearbeitet. Um wieviel Uhr hast du jeden Tag angefangen?

Gisela: Ich habe jeden Tag um vier Uhr nachmittags angefangen, und ich war schon um sechs Uhr fertig. Ich habe zwei Stunden am Tag gearbeitet.

Interviewer: Wieviel Geld hast du verdient?

Gisela: Ich war Praktikantin und habe kein Geld bekommen.

Interviewer: Wie viele Wochen hast du diese Arbeit gemacht?

Gisela: Ich habe leider nur zwei Wochen dort gearbeitet. Die Arbeit im Zoo hat mir gut gefallen.

Interviewer: Das war also eine schöne Arbeit?

Gisela: Oh, nein, die Arbeit war hart und manchmal auch ein bisschen gefährlich. Aber die Tiere sind wunderbar.

Interviewer: Und die Leute? Wie waren deine Kollegen?

Gisela: Ja, sie waren auch toll. Die Mitarbeiter waren sehr hilfreich und freundlich. Der Zoodirektor hat mir einen Sommerjob angeboten. Ich habe natürlich ja gesagt. Arbeiten im Zoo ist mein Traumberuf!

Answers:

Start of the work day	Pay	Length of time worked there	Work conditions	Co-workers	Opinion of the job	Consequences of working there
4 o'clock	no pay	2 weeks	hard and sometimes dangerous work	great: helpful and friendly	her dream job	has been offered a summer holiday job there

3b Partnerarbeit. Wie heißt das auf Deutsch? Schreibt die Fragen und Antworten aus Übung 3a in eure Hefte.

- Students work with a partner to write the questions and answers from activity 3a in German in their exercise books.

4–9

Answers:

- Um wieviel Uhr hast du jeden Tag angefangen?
- Ich habe jeden Tag um vier Uhr nachmittags angefangen.

- Wieviel Geld hast du verdient?
- Ich war Praktikantin und habe kein Geld bekommen.

- Wie viele Wochen hast du diese Arbeit gemacht?
- Ich habe leider nur zwei Wochen dort gearbeitet.

- Das war also eine schöne Arbeit?
- Oh, nein, die Arbeit war hart und manchmal auch ein bisschen gefährlich.

- Wie waren deine Kollegen?
- Ja, sie waren auch toll. Die Mitarbeiter waren sehr hilfreich und freundlich. Der Direktor hat mir eine Stelle für einen Sommerjob angeboten. Ich habe natürlich ja gesagt. Arbeiten im Zoo ist mein Traumberuf!

4a Partnerarbeit. Lest die Sätze über die möglichen Vor- und Nachteile eines Praktikums und ordnet sie in die Tabelle ein.

- Students work with a partner to read the possible advantages and disadvantages of work experience and put them where they think they should be in the table.

7–9

Possible answers:

Vorteile: a, d, f
Nachteile: b, c, e

4b Schreib fünf weitere Vor- und Nachteile in dein Heft.

- Students now write five more advantages and disadvantages in their exercise books, using those in activity 4a as models.
- This encourages students to generate and explore ideas whilst communicating previous learning to work towards goals. It covers the Creative thinkers, Reflective learners and Self-managers groups of skills from the framework of personal, learning and thinking skills.

4–9

PLTS

5 Was sind die Zukunftspläne dieser Jugendlichen? Hör gut zu und finde die richtigen Ausdrücke auf Seite 164 für jede Person.

- Students listen to the young people's future plans and note down the relevant expressions for each of them.

7–9

CD 3, track 16 **Seite 165, Übung 5**

Die Zukunft

Max
Ich habe mein Praktikum bei BMW gemacht und das ging ganz gut. Ich werde nach meinem Schulabschluss eine Lehrstelle bei BMW suchen. Ich werde zur gleichen Zeit auf die Fachschule gehen.

Adam
Ich möchte Frisör werden. Drei Tage in der Woche werde ich auf die Berufsschule gehen, und an den anderen zwei Tagen werde ich als Lehrling im Frisörsalon arbeiten. Das werde ich drei Jahre lang machen.

Lena
Ich habe vor, Tierarztassistentin zu werden. Nach der Gesamtschule und meinem Abitur hoffe ich, einen Studienplatz an einer Technischen Hochschule zu finden.

Steffen
Ich möchte einen Beruf in der Politik. Nach dem Schulabschluss werde ich in die Oberstufe gehen und nach drei Jahren mein Abitur machen. Dann werde ich auf die Universität gehen, wo ich Politik und Geschichte studieren werde.

Sascha
Nach meinem Schulabschluss werde ich ein Jahr freiwillige Arbeit auf dem Abenteuerspielplatz in der Bergerstraße machen. Ich werde dort ein Jahr lang ein Arbeitspraktikum machen. Danach werde ich die Oberstufe besuchen und mein Abitur machen.

Answers:

Max: Schulabschluss, Lehrstelle und Fachschule
Adam: Berufsschule und Lehrling im Frisörsalon
Lena: Gesamtschule, Abitur und Technischen Hochschule
Steffen: Schulabschluss, Oberstufe, Abitur und Universität
Sascha: Schulabschluss, Arbeitspraktikum, Oberstufe und Abitur

A66 A67 Activity Sheets 66 and 67 provide further activities on work experience and future plans.

6 **With a partner write down the advantages and disadvantages of each of the possible directions taken after leaving school listed below. Then think of other possibilities, along with their advantages and disadvantages.**

4–9 PLTS

- This activity draws together what students have learnt in the spread.
- This activity encourages students to generate and explore ideas, connecting their own and others' ideas, to communicate previous learning, to collaborate with others to work towards goals. It covers the Creative thinkers, Reflective learners, Team workers and Self-managers groups of skills from the framework of personal, learning and thinking skills.

7 **Read the diary extract of Heinrich's first day of work experience on page 164 again. Then write an account in German of his entire work experience, beginning with the first disastrous day and followed by the next four days he worked in the shoe shop. Be as creative as possible and remember to write some longer sentences.**

4–9

- This activity draws together the vocabulary, grammar and skills from the spread. It is an ideal assessment opportunity.

Success criteria:

- information communicated
- variety of vocabulary and structures used
- accuracy

Aktive Grammatik

Seiten 166–167

Planner

➤ Objectives

- To practise inverted word order
- To practise word order with subordinating conjunctions
- To practise the future tense
- To practise formal and informal forms of address

➤ Resources

Students' Book, pages 166–167
Exam Skills Workbooks, page 62
Grammar Workbook, pages 37, 56, 61
Activity Sheet 68
Resources and Planning OxBox CD-ROM

➤ Grammar

- Inverted word order
- Word order with subordinating conjunctions
- The future tense
- Formal and informal forms of address

➤ PLTS

All questions: Reflective learners/Self-managers

➤ Inverted word order

1 **Identify the subject and the verb of the main sentence in the following examples.**

- This question focuses on understanding word order.

Answers:

a subject = *es*, verb = *kann*; **b** subject = *Herr Bruckner*, verb = kann; **c** subject = *Gisela*, verb = *arbeitet*; **d** subject = *er*, verb = *macht*

2 **Add a phrase from the box to the beginning of each of these sentences and change the word order to fit.**

- Further practise of inverted word order.

Answers:

a Letzte Woche hat Frido seinen Lebenslauf geschrieben.
b Am Dienstag hat er ein Vorstellungsgespräch gehabt.
c Normalerweise hört man innerhalb von ein paar Tagen, ob man den Job bekommen hat.
d Weil er noch nichts gehört hat, hat Frido vor, die Firma anzurufen.

➤ Word order: subordinating conjunctions

3 **Make longer, more interesting sentences using the conjunctions in brackets to combine short sentences. Don't forget the comma.**

- Practice of conjunctions.

Answers:

a Wenn du im Internet schaust, findest du Jobanzeigen.
b Du sollst einen Vorstellungstext schreiben, bevor du mit dem Arbeitgeber sprichst.

c Während du mit dem Arbeitgeber redest, kannst du Fragen stellen.
d Weil du kommunikativ und selbstsicher bist, kriegst du den Job!

4 **Complete these sentences. Note! Not all are subordinating conjunctions. (See page 163.)**
- Further practice of using conjunctions. Students complete the sentences.

5 **Create at least five complex sentences of your own using various coordinating and subordinating conjunctions. Read your sentences aloud with a classmate to practise saying and hearing complex sentences.**
- Students continue to practise using conjunctions.

➤ Future tense

6 **Complete the sentences with the correct form of *werden*.**
- Students form the future tense with *werden*.

Answers:

a werde; **b** wird; **c** wirst; **d** werden

7 **Put the correct forms of the verbs in brackets in the sentences where they belong.**
- Further practise of the future tense with *werden*.

Answers:

a Was wirst du als Praktikum machen?
b Im Friseursalon wirst du alles übers Haarschneiden lernen.
c Wenn Steffen gute Noten kriegt, wird er zur Universität gehen.
e Thomas ist glücklich, dass er sein Arbeitspraktikum bei der Polizei machen wird.
f Herr Paul wird ein guter Arbeitgeber sein.

➤ Formal and informal forms of address

8 **Write out the conjugations for the verbs below with *du*, *ihr* and *Sie*.**
- This question focuses on conjugating verbs in the *du*, *ihr* and *Sie* forms.

Answers:

a du gehst, ihr geht, Sie gehen; **b** du siehst, ihr sieht, Sie sehen; **c** du trinkst, ihr trinkt, Sie trinken; **d** du bleibst, ihr bleibt, Sie bleiben; **e** du beschreibst dich, ihr beschreibt euch, Sie beschreiben sich; **f** es gefällt dir, es gefällt euch, es gefällt sich; **g** du vorhast, ihr vorhabt, Sie vorhaben; **h** du arbeitest, ihr arbeitet, Sie arbeiten

9 **Write sentences with the verbs below using *du, ihr* and *Sie*.**
- Students continue to practise writing formal and informal forms of address.

Kompetenzen

Seite 168

Planner

➤ Objectives
- Summarising what you have learnt

➤ Resources
Students' Book, page 168
Exam Skills Workbooks, page 63
Activity Sheet 69
Resources and Planning OxBox CD-ROM

➤ Skills
- Using formula phrases to tell a story in sequence
- Using conjunctions
- Choosing whether to use formal or informal writing styles
- Checking for errors as you write
- Working out the gist from the context
- Inferring word meanings
- Recognising sound-spelling links
- Avoiding making wild guesses

➤ PLTS
Questions 1 and 2, writing: Creative thinkers/ Reflective learners/Team workers/Self-managers
Question 2, reading: Creative thinkers/Self-managers

In this unit, students have learnt how to…

➤ Beim Schreiben

1 **Use formula phrases to tell a story in sequence.**

PLTS
- Students make a list of German words to indicate sequence. How many others can they find?
- Students work with a partner to create a funny story, using formula phrases and being aware of inverted word order.
- This encourages students to think creatively, generating and exploring ideas. It also encourages them to communicate previous learning and to collaborate effectively with others in order to work towards goals. It covers the Creative thinkers, Reflective learners, Team workers and Self-managers groups of skills from the framework of personal, learning and thinking skills.

2 **Use conjunctions.**

PLTS
- Students make their own list of conjunctions that do not change word order.

- They then make their own list of subordinating conjunctions that do change word order.
- Finally, they practise word order with a partner.
- This encourages students to think creatively, to invite feedback, dealing positively with praise, setbacks and criticism and to collaborate effectively with others in order to work towards goals. It covers the Creative thinkers, Reflective learners, Team workers and Self-managers groups of skills from the framework of personal, learning and thinking skills.

3 **Choose whether to use formal or informal writing styles.**
- Students work with a partner to decide whether to use *du* or *ihr* or *Sie* with the people listed.
- Point out to students that there are different customs for the use of *du* and *Sie* in different areas of Germany and other German-speaking countries.

4 **Check for errors as you write.**
- Students decide which of the common mistakes they tend to make when writing.
- They then work with a partner to practise identifying and correcting errors.

➤ Beim Lesen

1 **Work out the gist from the context.**

2 **Infer word meanings.**

PLTS
- Students make a list of all the ways and methods they can use to infer the meaning of a German word or several words in a sentence or text.
- This activity encourages students to think creatively, trying different ways to tackle a problem in order to work towards goals. It covers the Creative thinkers, and Self-managers groups of skills from the framework of personal, learning and thinking skills.

3 **Recognise sound-spelling links.**
- Students work with a partner and they take it in turns to give each other spelling tests in German.
- Students use OxBox pronunciation presentations to check their hearing.

4 **Check yourself: avoid making wild guesses.**
- Remind students to double-check any guesses they make regarding meaning against everything else they understand – does it really make sense?

Szenario

Seite 169

Planner

➤ Objectives
- Preparing arguments for, and having a debate on one of the themes of the spread
- Writing an interesting story about work experience

➤ Resources
Students' Book, page 169
Exam Skills Workbooks, pages 60–61
Assessment Sheets 33–40
Resources and Planning OxBox CD-ROM

➤ Skills
- Speaking practice
- Writing practice

➤ PLTS
Question 2, Zum Sprechen: Independent enquirers/Creative thinkers/Reflective learners/Self-managers:
Question 3, Zum Schreiben: Creative thinkers/Reflective learners/Team workers/Self-managers/Effective participators

➤ Zum Sprechen

In this section, students prepare arguments for or against one of the motions for debate listed and present these arguments to the class. Encourage them to use some of the vocabulary and structures from the spread in their debate.

It is possible for students to obtain GCSE grades A–F and they are marked on Communication, Quality of language and Pronunciation and intonation:
Grade F students communicate a limited number of ideas, expressing simple opinions. A few phrases or short sentences are accurate enough to be recognisable. There are very few instances of clear pronunciation and intonation.
Grade C students communicate the essential elements, readily expressing points of view. They occasionally hesitate and can respond to some unpredictable questions. They use straightforward vocabulary and structures which may contain different tenses or time frames. Pronunciation and intonation is generally accurate.
Grade A students use relevant information to develop and justify individual ideas and points of view. There is no hesitation and they are able to respond to unpredictable questions. They use a wide range of clause types, vocabulary and structures accurately. The presentation is fluent and coherent with just minor errors. Pronunciation and intonation are very accurate with a few minor slips.

1 **In a group of four, choose one of the motions for debate in German or invent one of your own.**
- This activity serves as an introduction to the task.
- Encourage students to choose the topic they think they will be able to say most about.

2 **Two students prepare their arguments for the motion and two students prepare their arguments against it.**

PLTS
- Students make notes for or against the motion.
- Remind students that they don't necessarily have to agree with what they are saying; the important thing is to put forward a strong argument.
- This encourages students to explore issues, events or problems from different perspectives, to generate and explore ideas and to communicate their learning in relevant ways to work towards goals. It covers the Independent enquirers, Creative thinkers, Reflective learners and Self-managers groups of skills from the framework of personal, learning and thinking skills.

3 **Students present their arguments alternatively: one for, one against, the other for, the other against. Each speaker has 1 minute to present his/her case.**
- Students use their notes from activity 2 to present their arguments.
- Remind them to pay particular attention to pronunciation and intonation and to make their presentation interesting by using conjunctions and formula phrases where possible.

4 **Other students or the whole class can be the judges of which side wins. Anyone can ask challenging questions once all four debaters have spoken. The debaters should try to answer the questions quickly. Debaters should also think about what the other side might say, so that they are prepared to argue against it.**
- This activity allows the class to give feedback and encourages more debate.

➤ Zum Schreiben

In this section, alone or in smalls group of 2–3, students invent a fabulous work experience story in German using the past tense.

It is possible for students to obtain GCSE grades A–F:
Grade F students write a short passage using simple sentences and communicate some information.
Grade C students include a variety of structures which may include different tenses or time frames. They communicate information and express personal opinions.
Grade A students include a variety of vocabulary, structures and verb tenses. They convey information, narrate events and express and explain ideas and points of view.

1 **Alone or in a small group of 2–3, students write a fabulous work experience story in German using the past tense. Give your story a title which will grab the audience's attention.**
- This activity serves as an introduction to the task.
- Encourage students to think about what they are likely to include in their story in order to come up with a catchy title.

2 **Create long and interesting sentences. Include details of: where, when, with whom, doing what, for how long, what happened, etc.**

PLTS
- Students think in more detail about the task.
- This activity encourages students to think creatively, connecting their own and others' ideas and experiences in inventive ways. It also encourages them to communicate previous learning and to collaborate and negotiate with others to work towards goals. It covers the Creative thinkers, Reflective learners, Team workers, Self-managers and Effective participators groups of skills from the framework of personal, learning and thinking skills.

3 **Possibly include some dialogue that you can act out, or create a narrator's role. Check your writing as you go along.**
- This activity encourages students to make their story as interesting as possible.

4 **When you have finished writing the story, present it to the class as a competition to see who has written the best *Praktikumsgeschichte*.**
- Students tell their story to the class, acting it out where possible.
- Encourage them to make it as lively as possible.

Vokabeln

Seite 170

Planner

➤ **Resources**
Students' Book, page 170
Activity Sheet 70

This page provides a summary of the key language covered in each spread of this unit. It could be used as a handy reference for students as they work through the unit. Alternatively, students could use its clear German–English format when learning vocabulary.

Lesen

Seiten 189–190

Planner

➤ **Objectives**
- To encourage independent reading and develop reading strategies
- To provide alternative class and homework material for students who finish other activities quickly

Page 189 provides a reading text in the context of the unit.
Page 190 provides a newspaper-style reading text, again in the context of the unit.

➤ **Resources**
Students' Book, pages 189–190

➤ **Skills**
- Reading practice

➤ **PLTS**
Question 3a (part 1): Reflective learners/Self-managers
Question 3 (part 2): Team workers/Self-managers

Lesen A: Thomas und Uschi

1 Lies den Dialog und beantworte die Fragen auf Englisch.
- Students read the dialogue and answer the questions.

7–9

Answers:

a young fire brigade; **b** twelve (including Thomas and Usichi); **c** a fire fighter/instructor; **d** chemistry and physics; **e** riding on the fire engine; **f** two years; **g** swimming, barbecues, parties; **h** in the fire brigage

2 Lies den Dialog und schreib in die Tabelle, was man bei der Jugend-Feuerwehr lernt und macht.
- Students read the dialogue and fill in the table with details of what Thomas and Uschi learnt and did during their work experience programme at the fire station.

7–9

Answers:

Theoretisches Programm	Praktisches Programm	Gesellschaftliches Programm
was man bei brennenden Plastiksachen machen muss	Arbeiten mit Schläuchen, Pumpen und Feuerlöschern	Schwimmen am See
viel über Chemie und Physik lernen	mit dem Feuerwehrauto fahren	einen Grillabend oder eine Party machen

3a Rate, wie die folgenden Ausdrücke auf Englisch heißen.
- Students use previous experience and knowledge and the context to try to guess what the phrases mean in English.
- This encourages students to use previous learning to achieve goals. It covers the Reflective learners and Self-managers groups of skills from the framework of personal, learning and thinking skills.

7–9
PLTS

Answers:

a burning plastic; **b** deadly gases; **c** a practical exercise; **d** hoses, pumps, fire extinguishers

3b Wie hast du die Bedeutung erraten? Ordne a–d zu.

- Students think about how they guessed the meaning of each of the phrases in activity 2a.
- They then match strategies (1–4) with the phrases, (a–d)

Lesen B: Die heutigen Traumberufe der Jugend

1 Lies den Artikel und beantworte die Fragen auf Englisch.

- Students read the article and answer the questions in English.

7–9

Answers:

a an institute that conducts opinion polls; *Meinung* = opinion, *Forschung* = research, *Institut* = institute; **b** *Trendence*; **c** 8400 school pupils/classes 7 to 13/from *Gymnasiums*/ and *Gesamt-*/and *Realschulen*/throughout Germany; **d** How to you see your future after your school leaving certificate? What is your career preference? Which job would you like? **e** Audi, The foreign Office, Adidas, Hilton Hotels, Armed Forces, Porsche, BMW, Lufthansa, ZDF (Second German Television Channel), Politzei **f** train driver, astronaut, vet, MTV presenter, adventurer, racing driver, sports star

7–9

2a Finde die deutschen Ausdrücke im Text.

- Students read the article again and find the German phrases.

7–9

Answers:

a Umfrage; **b** Berufswunsch; **c** Traumberuf; **d** Arbeitgeber; **e** Lokführer; **f** Tierärztin; **g** Heutzutage; **h** Schulabschluss

2b Finde andere zusammengetzte Wörtern im Text, die aus zwei oder mehreren Wörtern bestehen. Wie heißen sie auf Englisch?

- Students now find other compound words in the text and translate them into English.

4–6

Possible *Answers:*

Meinungsumfrage = opinion poll; Rennfahrer = racing driver; Spitzensportler = top sports person; Ausgleich = balance; Fernsehen = television

3 Diskutiert mit einem Partner/einer Partnerin. Welches Foto passt zu welchem Arbeitgeber? Welchen Beruf kann man bei jedem Arbeitgeber ausüben? Schreib Sätze.

4–9

PLTS

- Students work with a partner to discuss which photograph matches which employer.
- They then discuss what careers each of the employers offers.
- This activity encourages students to collaborate with others to work towards goals. It covers the Team workers and Self-managers groups of skills from the framework of personal, learning and thinking skills.

Exam Practice

Planner

➤ Objectives

- Practising answering exam-style questions

➤ Resources

Students' Book, pages 191–200
CD3, tracks 19-26
Resources and Planning OxBox CD-ROM: Record and Playback activities and Pronunciation Guide

Listening

Pages 191–194

Foundation level

1 Gabi talks about her family and her home. Read the questions and look at the possible answers. Listen to the recording. You will hear it twice. Then choose the correct answer by writing down the letter for the correct picture.

CD3, track 19 **Seite 191, Exercise 1**

Ich heiße Gabi. Ich bin 15 Jahre alt. Ich habe zwei Brüder und eine Schwester. Wir wohnen in einem Reihenhaus in der Stadmitte.Unser Haus hat drei Schlafzimmer. Das Haus hat eine Garage und einen kleinen Garten. Ich habe ein Kaninchen. Meine Mutter ist Mechanikerin. Sie arbeitet in einer Werkstatt. Abends kommt sie um 18 Uhr nach Hause.

Answers:

1 b; **2** c; **3** a; **4** c; **5** b; **6** c; **7** b; **8** a

2 Christian and Bernd are on holiday. Read the questions. Answer the questions in English.

CD 3, track 20 **Seite 192, Exercise 2**

Christian: Die Sonne scheint! Möchtest du zum Strand kommen?
Bernd: Nein, danke. Es gibt immer sehr viele Leute am Strand. Ich mag das nicht.
Christian: Okay. Möchtest du also ins Freibad? Da ist es ruhiger.
Bernd: Ja, gute Idee.
Christian: Wann fahren wir dann ab?
Bernd: Gleich nach dem Frühstück?
Christian: Toll! Wir können mit dem Bus fahren.
Bernd: Ja, die Buslinie 5 fährt direct zum Freibad hin.
Christian: Vergiss nicht das Geld für die Fahrkarte!

Answers:

9 because there are too many people there; **10** going to the open-air swimming pool; **11** yes; **12** what time they should leave; **13** straight after breakfast; **14** by bus; **15** no; **16** money for the bus ticket.

3 Andreas talks about health and fitness. Read the questions. Listen to Andreas and, for each question, choose the correct answer.

CD3, track 21 **Seite 192, Exercise 3**

Hallo, ich bin der Andreas und ich bin sehr sportlich. Ich spiele gern Tennis und Fußball. Ich trainiere dreimal in der Woche für Tennis und zweimal in der Woche für Fußball. Insgesamt trainiere ich also fünfmal pro Woche. Nach dem Training bin ich immer sehr müde und brauche viel Schlaf. Ich gehe früh ins Bett – besonders wenn ich am nächsten Tag ein großes Spiel habe. Ich muss gesund essen, weil ich fit bleiben muss. Ich esse viel Brot, Gemüse und Obst. Ich muss aber aufpassen, weil ich gegen Nüsse allergisch bin. Ich darf sie nicht essen.

Answers:

17 b; **18** c; **19** c; **20** a; **21** b; **22** a; **23** c; **24** b

4 Maria and Stefan are discussing their leisure activities. Read the questions, listen to the conversation and then answer in English. You do not need to answer in full sentences.

CD3, track 22 **Seite 192, Exercise 4**

Maria: Das Fernsehen ist heute Abend so langweilig, Stefan. Was sollen wir machen?
Stefan: Ich wollte zu Hause bleiben und Musik hören.
Maria: Deine Musik finde ich aber langweilig! Außerdem ist es noch sehr früh. Warum gehen wir nicht aus?
Stefan: Ich muss noch meine Hausaufgaben machen.
Maria: Dafür brauchst du nicht den ganzen Abend!
Stefan: Was schlägst du dann vor?
Maria: Ich möchte ins Kino gehen, weil der neue Film mit Moritz Bleibtreu heute kommt.
Stefan: Moritz Bleibtreu? Wer ist das?
Maria: Er ist ein sehr berühmter Schauspieler. Er hat in *Lola rennt* und *Munich* gespielt.
Stefan: Und was für ein Film ist das?
Maria: Das ist ein Kriegsfilm. Es spielt in England im Zweiten Weltkrieg.
Stefan: Ich weiß nicht. ich kenne diesen Schauspieler nicht. obwohl mich normalerweise Kriegsfilme interessieren.
Maria: Komm, Stefan, sei nicht langweilig. Lass uns doch gehen.

Stefan:	Okay okay. Wann fängt der Film an?
Maria:	Im Odeon spielt er um 20 Uhr; im Filmpalast um 20.30 Uhr.
Stefan:	Gut. Dann fahren wir um 19.45 Uhr ins Filmpalast. Ich mache vorher meine Hausaufgaben zu Ende.
Maria:	Toll!

Answers:

25 stay at home and listen to music; **26** his homework; **27** going to the cinema; **28** who Moritz Bleibtreu is; **29** an actor; **30** England; **31** 8.30 pm; **32** his homework.

5 **Jens talks about his hobby. Read the questions. Listen to the interview and choose the correct answers.**

CD3, track 23 **Seite 193, Exercise 5**

Interviewer:	Wir sprechen über Musik. Spielst du ein Instrument, Jens?
Jens:	Ich spiele Saxophon, kann aber auch ein bisschen Klavier und Klarinette.
Interviewer:	Und seit wann spielst du?
Jens:	Ich habe mit 10 angefangen, also ich spiele insegesamt seit 6 Jahren.
Interviewer:	Hast du die ganze Zeit einen Lehrer gehabt?
Jens:	Nein, am Anfang habe ich alleine gelernt, aber das war ziemlich schwierig, weil ich die Methode nicht wusste.
Interviewer:	Und spielst du heute in einem Orchester?
Jens:	Nein, das Saxophon ist nicht wirklich das richtige Instrument dafür.
Interviewer:	Du spielst also meistens solo?
Jens:	Nein. Ich habe vor ein paar Jahren eine Jazz-Band gegründet und nun spielen wir regelmäßig zusammen.
Interviewer:	Das ist ja schön! Und gebt ihr manchmal auch Konzerte?
Jens:	Ja, ab und zu spielen wir im Jugendklub oder auf einem Fest. Meistens werden wir von Freunden eingeladen.
Interviewer:	Und kriegt ihr auch Geld dafür?
Jens:	Nein, aber manchmal bekommen wir kostenlose Getränke oder etwas zum Essen.
Interviewer:	Du hast also keine Angst, wenn du vor anderen Leuten spielst?
Jens:	Nein, überhaupt nicht. Ich finde es schön, wenn andere mithören und meine Musik genießen. Nur eines gefällt mir nicht dabei.
Interviewer:	Was ist das denn?
Jens:	Wenn ich etwas sagen muss. Spielen finde ich einfach, aber reden vor anderen Leuten ist mir sehr peinlich!

Answers:

33 b; **34** c; **35** b; **36** a; **37** b; **38** c; **39** a; **40** c

Higher level

Exercises 1 and 2 as for Foundation-level Exercises 4 and 5.

3 **Christina is telling you about her work experience. Read the questions. Listen and, for each question, choose one answer.**

CD 3, track 24 **Seite 193, Exercise 3**

Hallo! Ich heiße Christina. Ich habe letzten Monat ein Arbeitspraktikum gemacht.
Das Praktikum war sehr interessant, aber auch ein bisschen anstrengend. Meine Mutter hat mir geholfen, mein Praktikum in einer Grundschule zu finden, da sie dort als Sekretärin arbeitet.
Ich musste mit Frau Michaelson arbeiten, und sie war sehr nett, aber auch ein bisschen streng. Die Kinder haben vor ihr Angst gehabt.
Die Kinder waren sechs und sieben Jahre alt und auch ziemlich laut. Ich musste ihnen beim Lesen und Schreiben helfen.
Nachmittags haben wir Kunst gehabt, und die Kinder haben alle schöne Bilder gemalt. Ich war jeden Tag nach dem Unterricht sehr müde, aber glücklich.

Answers:

17 b; **18** c; **19** b; **20** a; **21** c; **22** b; **23** a; **24** a

4 **Frau Schmidt is discussing holidays with her class. Read the questions, listen to the recording and complete the chart in English.**

CD 3, track 25 **Seite 193, Exercise 4**

Frau Schmidt:	Unser heutiges Thema: Ferien. Also, Jutta, wo warst du diesen Sommer im Urlaub?
Jutta:	Ich bin mit meiner Schwester nach Griechenland gefahren.
Frau Schmidt:	Und wie war das, Jutta?
Jutta:	Es war klasse. Wir haben den ganzen Tag geschlafen und die ganze Nacht getanzt.
Frau Schmidt:	Danke, Jutta, und du, Susanne, wo warst du?
Susanne:	Ich bin mit meinen Eltern nach Italien geflogen.
Frau Schmidt:	Und wie war das?
Susanne:	Das war schrecklich. Meine Eltern wollten die ganze Zeit Schlösser und Museen ansehen und ich musste mit. Ich wollte aber lieber am Strand liegen.
Frau Schmidt:	Wie schade, Susanne! Und du, Paul, wo warst du?
Paul:	Ich bit mit meinem Vater nach Australien gefahren.
Frau Schmidt:	Und wie hast du Australien gefunden?
Paul:	Ich fand es wunderbar. Es war sehr heiß und trocken. Die Leute waren sehr freundlich, und es gab viel zu sehen.
Frau Schmidt:	Sehr gut, Paul, danke. Und jetzt zu dir, Marc, wo warst du in den Ferien?
Marc:	Ich bin allein zu Hause geblieben. Ich habe viel ferngesehen und Eis gegessen. Das Wetter hier war auch sehr schön. Ich fand das fantastisch.

Answers:

	Destination	Opinion
Jutta	**25** Greece	**26** great
Suzanne	**27** Italy	**28** dreadful
Paul	**29** Australia	**30** wonderful
Marc	**31** home	**32** fantastic

5 A project for the future. Read the questions. Listen and, for each question, choose one answer.

CD 3, track 26 **Seite 194, Exercise 5**

Wir haben in der Schule vor einem Monat ein neues Projekt angefangen, das helfen sollte, unsere Schule ökologischer zu machen.
Das Projekt war die Idee der Schülermitverwaltung. Während unserer letzten Sitzung haben wir darüber diskutiert, wie wir den CO_2-Fußabdruck von der Schule reduzieren könnten. Alle waren der Meinung, dass wir etwas unternehmen sollten, weil dieses Thema für unsere Zukunft so wichtig ist, obwohl es von vielen Leuten einfach ignoriert wird.
Einige der Klassenvertreter wollten Geld für eine neue Solaranlage sammeln, aber andere dachten, es wäre wichtiger, kleinere Gesten zu machen, bei denen jeder Schüler und jede Schülerin mitmachen könnte.
Paul, der Vertreter der Klasse 10E, hat vorgeschlagen, eine Umfrage zu machen, um herauszufinden, was die Schüler selbst für die wichstigsten Themen hielten. Wir haben die Umfrage eine Woche lang in der Mittagspause durchgeführt. Am Ende hatten wir insgesamt 80% der Schüler befragt.
Es stellte sich heraus, dass sich die Schüler mehr fürs Recycling und für die Quellen der Lebensmittel in der Kantine interessierten, als für die Energieversorgung.
Folglich haben wir sicher gestellt, dass jedes Klassenzimmer verschiedene Mülltonnen für die verschiedenen Kategorien von Abfall hat. Wir habe den Schuldirektor auch überredet, nur Recyclingpapier in der Schule zu verwenden. Als Nächstes werden wir mit der Küchenpersonal sprechen, um herauszufinden, ob in der Zukunft Bio-Produkte in der Kantine verwendet werden könnten.

Answers:

33 a; **34** b; **35** a; **36** c; **37** b; **38** c; **39** a; **40** b

Reading

Pages 196–199

Foundation level

1 What do these people want to do on holiday? Read the chart and write the correct name by each picture.

Answers:

1 Meike; **2** Sonia; **3** Uwe; **4** Maria

2 Read the email from Paul about his busy week. Read the sentences which follow and choose a word or phrase from the box to fill in the gaps.

Answers:

5 two hours; **6** happy; **7** scored a goal; **8** Friday

3 Read these students' plans for next year and enter in the box below what subject each will do and where.

Answers:

	School	College
9 Hannah	French	
10 Michaela		History
11 Richard		Geography
12 Heiko	Art	

4 Read Katharina's email about films. Answer the questions in English.

Answers:

13 because they are both romantic and funny
14 She likes them because she always wants to know who did it.
15 because they are scary
16 because they are too bloody and noisy

5 Read Annelore's description of her family. Read the statements which follow and choose the correct ending for each by writing down the correct letter, a, b or c.

Answers:

17 b; **18** c; **19** b; **20** b

Higher level

3 What is your attitude towards the environment? Read this blog from teenagers in Germany and Austria and find out how they feel. Who is it? Write the correct name.

Answers:

9 Jörg; **10** Franziska; **11** Katja; **12** Paul

4 Read Thomas's article for his partner school in Germany about his exchange trip. Answer the questions in English.

Answers:

13 everything went wrong; **14** nobody was there to meet him; **15** he was afraid; **16** to telephone his exchange partner's house; **17** his use of the 12-hour clock; **18** they went back home and went back to bed; **19** sorry; **20** he took a taxi.

5 Read this article about a new ecology project in Cologne from a local newspaper. Complete the sentence by choosing the appropriate letter, A, B or C.

Answers:

19 c; **20** c; **21** c; **22** c; **23** a; **24** b; **25** b; **26** c

Grammar Bank

Planner

➤ Objectives

- Practising grammar

➤ Resources

Students' Book, pages 201–210
Resources and Planning OxBox CD-ROM: Grammar presentations

1 Cases — Page 201

1.1 Identify the case (N, A, G or D) of the underlined words.

Answers:

1 N, D; **2** N, D, A; **3** N, G; **4** N, D, D; **5** N, A; **6** N, D

2 Nouns — Page 201

2.1 What gender are these nouns? What do they mean? Check in a dictionary.

Answers:

1 Politik (f) politics; **2** Bauer (m) farmer; **3** Bedienung (f) service; **4** Kaninchen (n) rabbit; **5** Schale (f) bowl/skin; **6** Schnitzel (n) cutlet; **7** Zeichnen (n) drawing; **8** Portion (f) portion; **9** Museum (n) museum; **10** Lehrerin (f) teacher; **11** Zeitung (f) newspaper; **12** Großvater (m) grandfather

2.2 Write nouns 1–6 in the plural and 7–12 in the singular. Check in a dictionary.

Answers:

1 Mädchen; **2** Lampen; **3** Bücher; **4** Gärten; **5** Hotels; **6** Tage; **7** Haus; **8** Direktorin; **9** Apfel; **10** Schwester; **11** Lehrer; **12** Bein

3 Determiners — Pages 201-202

3.1 Complete the sentences with the correct form of *der* (etc.), *ein* and *kein*. The case is given in brackets.

Answers:

1 Die; **2** der; **3** einen **4** den; **5** Ein, die; **6** kein, keine

3.2 Complete the sentences with the correct form of the possessive, demonstrative or interrogative adjective.

Answers:

1 Mein, dieses; **2** Jeder, seine; **3** Welches, eurer; **4** unserer, mein; **5** welchen, deine; **6** Meine, ihr, jede

4 Prepositions — Pages 202-203

4.1 Translate these phrases into German.

Answers:

1 durch ein Fenster; **2** für seinen Bruder; **3** die Straße entlang; **4** um die Ecke; **5** gegen die Wand/Mauer; **6** ohne meine Eltern

4.2 Complete the sentences with the correct preposition and the dative case.

Answers:

1 bei meinem; **2** Nach einer, aus dem; **3** gegenüber einem; **4** von meiner; **5** von meinem; **6** zu unseren

4.3 Choose the correct word in brackets.

Answers:

1 das; **2** den; **3** meiner; **4** den, dem; **5** mir; **6** die, die

4.4 Translate the sentences into English.

Answers:

1 Because of the cold weather we're staying near the radiator/heater.
2 She (has) invited us to the party in/at the youth club.
3 During/In the day(time) we went skiing in the mountains.
4 I'm going to the window and sitting on a chair.
5 Her/Your photo is hanging on the wall above the television.
6 In spite of his illness he cycled into town.

5 Adjectives — Pages 203-204

5.1 Complete the following sentences with the correct adjective ending.

Answers:

1 faszinierende; **2** moderne; **3** freundlichen; **4** wichtiger; **5** große, lebendigen **6** besseren, beliebte

5.2 Change the adjectives to the comparative form.

Answers:

1 höher; **2** bessere; **3** längeren; **4** älterer; **5** jüngeres; **6** freundlicheren

5.3 Choose the sentences that include a superlative and translate them into English.

Answers:

2: I watched the most interesting film about the Baader-Meinhoff group.
3: Germans are not always the most famous actors in the world.
5: It is one of the best German films.

6 Adverbs

Page 205

6.1 Translate the following sentences into German.

Answers:

1 Sie hat sehr gut gespielt.
2 Tee schmeckt besser mit Milch.
3 Du isst/Sie essen Kekse am schnellsten!
4 Ich esse gern Bananen.
5 Ich trinke lieber Tee.
6 Am liebsten essen sie Schokolade.

6.2 Make these statements into questions.

Answers:

1 Hat sie heute Geburtstag?
2 Hast du dieses Buch gelesen?
3 Kommen wir um 10 Uhr an?
4 Kostet das T-Shirt zu viel Geld?
5 Ist mein Bruder zum Stadion gegangen?
6 Hat er sich nach dem Spiel geduscht?

7 Pronouns

Pages 206–207

7.1 Complete the sentences with the correct pronoun.

Answers:

1 dich; **2** Er; **3** ihn; **4** euch; **5** mir; **6** uns

7.2 Complete the sentences with the correct reflexive pronouns.

Answers:

1 dich; **2** mir; **3** sich; **4** dir; **5** euch; **6** uns

7.3 Complete the sentences with the correct relative pronoun.

Answers:

1 die; **2** der; **3** der; **4** denen; **5** die; **6** denen

8 Verbs

Pages 207–209

8.1 Write the correct form of the verb (and pronoun) using *du*, *ihr* or *Sie*.

Answers:

1 kommt ihr; **2** gehen Sie; **3** hast du; **4** bekommt ihr; **5** fühlst du dich; **6** wollen Sie

8.2 Identify the negative sentences, and then translate them into English.

Answers:

1: I'm not at all well.
4: He's not doing any sport today.
5: The concert hasn't begun yet.
6: I'm sorry, you can't come (with us).

8.3 Translate these sentences into German.

Answers:

1 Ich kann Rugby spielen.
2 Sie will in die Stadt (gehen/fahren).
3 Ich darf keinen Tennis spielen.
4 Er soll heute arbeiten.
5 Sie müssen fernsehen.
6 Wir müssen nicht studieren, aber wir wollen lernen.

8.4 Read the sentences and say whether the verbs are separable (S) or inseparable (I).

Answers:

1 I; **2** S; **3** I, I; **4** S; **5** S; **6** I

8.5 Write out the present tense of each verb in these four forms: *ich; du; er/sie/es; wir.*

Answers:

1 ich antworte; du antwortest; er/sie/es antwortet; wir antworten
2 ich bekomme; du bekommst; er/sie/es bekommt; wir bekommen
3 ich halte; du hältst; er/sie/es hält; wir halten
4 ich lasse; du lässt; er/sie/es lässt; wir lassen
5 ich schlafe; du schläfst; er/sie/es schläft; wir schlafen
6 ich tue; du tust; er/sie/es tut; wir tun

8.6 Rewrite these sentences in the perfect tense.

Answers:

1 Wir haaben jeden Mittwoch Handball gespielt.
2 Ich habe am Wochenende für meine Mutter gearbeitet.
3 Wann hast du Leon gesehen?
4 Zu Weihnachten hat meine Familie Gans gegessen.
5 Wir sind im Februar nach Österreich gefahren.
6 Meine Großeltern sind zu Hause geblieben.

8.7 Identify the sentences that are in the past tense.

Answers:

past tense: 2, 3, 5, 6

8.8 Complete the sentences in the pluperfect tense.

Answers:

1. Er arbeitete damals in Duisburg, aber vorher **hatte** er in München **gearbeitet**.
2. Bevor ich nach Berlin kam, **war** ich nach Moskau **gefahren**.
3. Die Mannschaft **hatte** jeden Tag **trainiert**.
4. Nachdem sie nach Hause **gegangen war**, haben sie ein bisschen ferngesehen.
5. Er hatte Hunger, weil er sein Pausenbrot schon **gegessen hatte**.
6. Als Schülerin **war** sie nicht fleißig **gewesen**, aber als Studentin hat sie gute Noten bekommen.

8.9 Identify which of these sentences are in the future tense (F) and which are conditional (C).

Answers:

1 F; **2** C; **3** C; **4** F; **5** F; **6** C

9 Word order

Page 210

9.1 Rewrite these sentences with the phrase in brackets at the beginning.

Answers:

1. Jeden Abend machen wir Fitness-Training.
2. Am Wochenende fahre ich sehr gern Rad.
3. Für Sportler ist gesundes Essen sehr wichtig.
4. Im Sommer kann man im Freibad schwimmen.
5. Als Teenager hat meine Mutter viel Tennis gespielt.
6. Zweimal in der Woche sehen mein Vater und ich Sport im Fernsehen.

9.2 Rewrite these jumbled-up sentences.

Answers:

1. Ich bin freitags sehr müde in der Schule.
2. Wir sind gestern mit dem Zug nach Berlin gefahren.
3. Meine Mutter studiert seit drei Jahren für ein Diplom in der Hochschule.
4. Viele Touristen kommen im Sommer mit Reisebussen nach Salzburg.
5. Meine Schwester arbeitet jeden Abend sehr schwer im Restaurant.
6. Deutsche Sportler gewannen 2008 16 Goldmedaillen in China.

9.3 Join the sentences using the coordinating conjunction in brackets.

Answers:

1. Ich will Klempner werden, und ich suche ein gutes Praktikum.
2. Nach der Schule arbeite ich im Supermarkt, aber ich will das nicht als Beruf machen.
3. Du bleibst zwei Stunden hier, oder du gehst sofort nach Hause.
4. Bodo möchte Rennfahrer werden, denn er kann schon sehr gut fahren.
5. Steffi hat kein Geld, und/aber sie will einen Hamburger essen.
6. Wir können etwas Gesundes essen, oder/aber es gibt Pommes mit Würstchen.

9.4 Join the sentences using the subordinating conjunction in brackets.

Answers:

1. Ich fühle mich gut, obwohl ich zu viel Schokolade gegessen habe.
2. Ich will nicht Volleyball spielen, wenn ich Bauchschmerzen habe.
3. Asif sieht ziemlich nervös aus, weil er ein Vorstellungsgespräch gehabt hat.
4. Es ist mir klar, dass er heute zum Training kommen muss.
5. Damit ich gesund bleibe, esse ich viel Obst.
6. Wenn es an einem Schultag regnet, nehme ich immer den Bus.